LAW AS A MEANS TO AN END

MODERN LEGAL PHILOSOPHY SERIES: VOL. V

LAW AS A MEANS TO AN END

By

RUDOLF VON IHERING

Late Professor of Law in the University of Gottingen

TRANSLATED FROM THE GERMAN BY

ISAAC HUSIK

Lecturer on Philosophy in the University of Pennsylvania

WITH AN EDITORIAL PREFACE BY

JOSEPH H. DRAKE

Professor of Law in the University of Michigan

AND WITH INTRODUCTIONS BY

HENRY LAMM

Justice of the Supreme Court of Missouri

AND

W. M. GELDART

Vinerian Professor of English Law in the University of Oxford

GYAN

Published by

Gyan Publishing House
5, Ansari Road
Daryaganj, New Delhi-110002
Phone: 011-47034999, 9811692060
E-mail: books@gyanbooks.com

Distribution Network
gyanbooks.com
India, USA, Canada, UK, Australia, France

ISBN : 978-81-212-6346-7 (PB)
First Published, 1913

2nd Impression 2022

Printed at: Gyan Press, Delhi.

LAW AS A MEANS TO AN END
Author: RUDOLF VON IHERING

Modern Legal Philosophy Series: Vol. V

LAW

AS A MEANS TO AN END

BY

RUDOLF VON IHERING

Late Professor of Law in the University of Göttingen

TRANSLATED FROM THE GERMAN BY

ISAAC HUSIK

Lecturer on Philosophy in the University of Pennsylvania

WITH AN EDITORIAL PREFACE BY

JOSEPH H. DRAKE

Professor of Law in the University of Michigan

AND WITH INTRODUCTIONS BY

HENRY LAMM

Justice of the Supreme Court of Missouri

AND

W. M. GELDART

Vinerian Professor of English Law in the University of Oxford

1913

EDITORIAL COMMITTEE OF THE ASSOCIATION OF AMERICAN LAW SCHOOLS

LIST OF TRANSLATORS

ADALBERT ALBRECHT, North Easton, Mass. (Associate Editor of the Journal of Criminal Law and Criminology).

JOSEPH P. CHAMBERLAIN, Columbia University, New York, N. Y.

WILLIAM G. HASTINGS, Lincoln, Neb. (Dean of the Faculty of Law, State University.)

ROBERT L. HENRY, JR., Grand Forks, N. D. (Professor of Law in the State University).

ISAAC HUSIK, Philadelphia, Pa. (Lecturer on Philosophy in the University of Pennsylvania).

MRS. RACHEL SZOLD JASTROW, Madison, Wis.

ALBERT KOCOUREK, Chicago, Ill. (of the Editorial Committee).

JOHN LISLE, Philadelphia, Pa. (of the Philadelphia Bar).

MRS. ETHEL FORBES SCOTT, State University, Urbana, Ill.

FREDERIC S. SPIEGEL, Cincinnati, Ohio (Judge of the Superior Court).

GENERAL INTRODUCTION TO THE SERIES

By the Editorial Committee

"Until either philosophers become kings," said Socrates, "or kings philosophers, States will never succeed in remedying their shortcomings." And if he was loath to give forth this view, because, as he admitted, it might "sink him beneath the waters of laughter and ridicule," so to-day among us it would doubtless resound in folly if we sought to apply it again in our own field of State life, and to assert that philosophers must become lawyers or lawyers philosophers, if our law is ever to be advanced into its perfect working.

And yet there is hope, as there is need, among us to-day, of some such transformation. Of course, history shows that there always have been cycles of legal progress, and that they have often been heralded and guided by philosophies. But particularly there is hope that our own people may be the generation now about to exemplify this.

There are several reasons for thinking our people apt thereto. But, without delaying over the grounds for such speculations, let us recall that as shrewd and good-natured an observer as DeTocqueville saw this in us. He admits that "in most of the operations of the mind, each American appeals to the individual exercise of his own understanding alone; therefore in no country in the civilized world is less attention paid to philosophy than in the United States." But, he adds, "the Americans are much more addicted to the use of general ideas than the English, and entertain a much greater relish for them." And since philosophy is, after all, only the science of general ideas — analyzing, restating, and reconstructing concrete experience — we may well trust that (if ever we do go at it with a will) we shall discover in ourselves a taste and high capacity for it, and shall direct our powers as fruitfully upon law as we have done upon other fields.

Hitherto, to be sure, our own outlook on juristic learning has been insular. The value of the study of comparative law has only in recent years come to be recognized by us. Our juristic methods are still primitive, in that we seek to know only by our own experience, and pay no heed to the experience of others. Our historic bond with English law alone, and our consequent lack of recognition of the universal character of law as a generic institution, have prevented any wide contact with foreign literatures. While heedless of external help in the practical matter of legislation, we have been oblivious to the abstract nature of law. Philosophy of law has been to us almost a meaningless and alien phrase. "All philosophers are reducible in the end to two classes only: utilitarians and futilitarians," is the cynical epigram of a great wit of modern fiction.[1] And no doubt the philistines of our profession would echo this sarcasm.

And yet no country and no age have ever been free (whether conscious of the fact or not) from some drift of philosophic thought. "In each epoch of time," says M. Leroy, in a brilliant book of recent years, "there is current a certain type of philosophic doctrine — a philosophy deep-seated in each one of us, and observable clearly and consciously in the utterances of the day — alike in novels, newspapers, and speeches, and equally

[1] M. Dumaresq, in Mr. Paterson's "The Old Dance Master."

in town and country, workshop and counting-house." Without some fundamental basis of action, or theory of ends, all legislation and judicial interpretation are reduced to an anarchy of uncertainty. It is like mathematics without fundamental definitions and axioms. Amidst such conditions, no legal demonstration can be fixed, even for a moment. Social institutions, instead of being governed by the guidance of an intelligent free will, are thrown back to the blind determinism of the forces manifested in the natural sciences. Even the phenomenon of experimental legislation, which is peculiar to Anglo-American countries, cannot successfully ignore the necessity of having social ends.

The time is ripe for action in this field. To quote the statement of reasons given in the memorial presented at the annual meeting of the Association of American Law Schools in August, 1910: —

> The need of the series now proposed is so obvious as hardly to need advocacy. We are on the threshold of a long period of constructive readjustment and restatement of our law in almost every department. We come to the task, as a profession, almost wholly untrained in the technic of legal analysis and legal science in general. Neither we, nor any community, could expect anything but crude results without thorough preparation. Many teachers, and scores of students and practitioners, must first have become thoroughly familiar with the world's methods of juristic thought. As a first preparation for the coming years of that kind of activity, it is the part of wisdom first to familiarize ourselves with what has been done by the great modern thinkers abroad — to catch up with the general state of learning on the subject. After a season of this, we shall breed a family of well-equipped and original thinkers of our own. Our own law must, of course, be worked out ultimately by our own thinkers; but they must first be equipped with the state of learning in the world to date.
>
> How far from "unpractical" this field of thought and research really is has been illustrated very recently in the Federal Supreme Court, where the opposing opinions in a great case (*Kuhn* v. *Fair-*

mont Coal Co.) turned upon the respective conceptions of "law" in the abstract, and where Professor Gray's recent work on "The Nature and Sources of the Law" was quoted, and supplied direct material for judicial decision.

Acting upon this memorial, the following resolution was passed at that meeting: —

That a committee of five be appointed by the president, to arrange for the translation and publication of a series of continental masterworks on jurisprudence and philosophy of law.

The committee spent a year in collecting the material. Advice was sought from a score of masters in the leading universities of France, Germany, Italy, Spain, and elsewhere. The present series is the result of these labors.

In the selection of this series, the committee's purpose has been, not so much to cover the whole field of modern philosophy of law, as to exhibit faithfully and fairly all the modern viewpoints of any present importance. The older foundation-works of two generations ago are, with some exceptions, already accessible in English translation. But they have been long supplanted by the products of newer schools of thought which are offered in this series in their latest and most representative form. It is believed that the complete series will represent in compact form a collection of materials whose equal cannot be found at this time in any single foreign literature.

The committee has not sought to offer the final solution of any philosophical or juristic problems; nor to follow any preference for any particular theory or school of thought. Its chief purpose has been to present to English readers the most representative views of the most modern writers in jurisprudence and philosophy of law. The series shows a wide geographical representation; but the selection has not been centered on the notion of giving equal recognition to all countries. Primarily, the desire has been to represent the various schools of thought; and, consistently with this, then to represent the different chief countries. This aim, however, has involved little difficulty; for Continental thought has lines of cleavage which make it easy to represent the leading schools and the leading nations at the same time. Germany, for example, is represented in modern thought by a preponderant metaphysical influence. Italy is primarily positivist, with subordinate German and English influences. France in its modern standpoint is largely sociological, while making an effort to assimilate English ideas and customs in its theories of legislation and the administration of justice. Spain, Austria, Switzerland, Hungary, are represented in the Introductions and the shorter essays; but no country other than Germany, Italy, and France is typical of any important theory requiring additions to the scope of the series.

To offer here an historical introduction, surveying the various schools of thought and the progress from past to present, was regarded by the committee as unnecessary. The volumes of Dr. Berolzheimer and Professor Miraglia amply serve this purpose; and the introductory chapter of the latter volume provides a short summary of the history of general philosophy, rapidly placing the reader in touch with the various schools and their standpoints. The series has been so arranged (in the numbered list fronting the title page) as to indicate that order of perusal which will be most suitable for those who desire to master the field progressively and fruitfully.

The committee takes great pleasure in acknowledging the important part rendered in the consummation of this project, by the publisher, the authors, and the translators. Without them this series manifestly would have been impossible.

To the publisher we are grateful for the hearty sponsorship of a kind of literature which is so important to the advancement of American legal science. And here the Committee desires also to express its indebtedness to Elbert H. Gary, Esq., of New York City, for his ample provision of materials for legal science in the Gary Library of Continental Law (in Northwestern University). In the researches of preparation for this Series, those materials were found indispensable.

The authors (or their representatives) have cordially granted the right of English translation, and have shown a friendly interest in promoting our aims. The committee would be assuming too much to thank these learned writers on its own behalf, since the debt is one that we all owe.

The severe labor of this undertaking fell upon the translators. It required not only a none too common linguistic skill, but also a wide range of varied learning in fields little travelled. Whatever success may attend and whatever good may follow will in a peculiar way be attributable to the scholarly labors of the several translators.

The committee finds special satisfaction in having been able to assemble in a common purpose such an array of talent and learning; and it will feel that its own small contribution to this unified effort has been amply recompensed if this series will measurably help to improve and to refine our institutions for the administration of justice.

CONTENTS

EDITORIAL PREFACE TO THIS VOLUME

BY JOSEPH H. DRAKE

I. THE AUTHOR AND THE TRANSLATOR. Rudolf J. von Ihering was born at Aurich, in East Friesland, on August 22, 1818. He was descended from a long line of lawyers and administrators. Following the family tradition he studied law, hearing lectures at Heidelberg, Munich, Göttingen and Berlin. He received his doctor degree from the University of Berlin in 1842, with a dissertation entitled "De Hereditate Possidente." In the following year he began work as an instructor in law. He became professor of law at Basel in 1845, was called to Rostock in 1846, to Kiel in 1849, to Giessen in 1852, and to Vienna in 1868. In 1871 he was recalled from Austria to the newly established German university at Strassburg. After one year's residence here he received a call to Göttingen, where he continued to teach until his death, on September 17, 1892, declining calls to Leipsic and Heidelberg. During his stay at Vienna he received his title of nobility from the Emperor of Austria.

The first volume of "Der Zweck im Recht" was published in 1877; the second volume, not until 1883. The English work here presented is a translation of the first volume of the 4th German edition, published by Breitkopf and Härtel (Leipsic, 1903). The other published works of the author are: "Abhandlungen aus dem römischen Rechts" (Leipsic, 1844); "Zivilrechtsfälle ohne Entscheidung" (Leipsic, 1847; 11th edition, Jena, 1909); "Der Geist des römischen Rechts auf den verschiedenen Stufen seiner Entwickelung" (4 vols., Leipsic, 1852–1865; 5th and 6th editions, Leipsic, 1906–

07); "Ueber den Grund des Besitzschutzes" (Jena, 1868; 2nd edition, Jena, 1869); "Die Jurisprudenz des täglichen Lebens" (Jena, 1870; 13th edition, Jena, 1908); "Der Kampf ums Recht" (Regensburg, 1872; 17th edition, Vienna, 1910); "Vermischten Schriften juristischen Inhalts" (1879); "Gesammelte Aufsätze" (3 vols., 1881); "Das Trinkgeld" (Brunswick, 1882; 3rd edition, 1889); "Scherz und Ernst in der Jurisprudence" (Leipsic, 1885; 10th edition, Leipsic, 1909); "Der Besitzwille; Zugleich eine Kritik der herrschenden juristischen Methode" (Jena, 1889). After his death there appeared "Die Vorgeschichte der Indo-Europäer" (Leipsic, 1894) and "Die Entwickelungsgeschichte des römischen Rechts" (Leipsic, 1894). In 1852, he established along with Gerber the "Jahrbücher für die Dogmatik," which immediately became one of the most important legal periodicals of Germany, a position due in great part to Ihering's contributions to it.

A sketch of his life by Mitteis may be found in "Allgemeine Deutsche Biographie," Vol. L. A very interesting and sympathetic account of him as a scholar, teacher and man was published by Munroe Smith in the articles entitled, "Four German Jurists" ("Political Science Quarterly," Vol. 10, pp. 664–692 and Vol. 11, pp. 278–309). A critical appreciation of him by his pupil and life-long friend, Adolf Merkel, appeared in the "Jahrbücher für die Dogmatik" shortly after his death. This has been translated and published in this volume in Appendix I.

"Der Kampf ums Recht" has been translated into English, under the title of "The Struggle for Law," by John J. Lalor of the Chicago Bar. Chicago: Callaghan and Company, 1879. "Die Jurisprudenz des täglichen Lebens" has been translated by Henry Goudy, D. C. L., Regius Professor of Civil Law in the University of Oxford, under the title of "Law in Daily Life." Oxford: Clarendon Press, 1904.

The translator of the present volume, Dr. Isaac Husik, is a Ph.D. of the University of Pennsylvania. He is Instructor in Hebrew, Gratz College, Philadelphia and a Lecturer on Philosophy in the University of Pennsylvania, a member of the American Philosophical Association, of the American Association for the Advancement of Science and of the Third International Congress of Philosophy, held at Heidelberg, September, 1908. He has written articles on the Aristotelian philosophy and other topics, and is well known as an authority in mediæval philosophy.

II. BENTHAM AND IHERING. To American lawyers Ihering is known as the German Bentham. The similarities between them are due rather to the facts that they thought along the same lines, that each belonged to a transition period in the legal thinking of his own country, and that each suggested similar correctives for the legal fallacies of his time and his environment, than to any direct imitation of the English Utilitarian by the German jurist. In the first volume of "Der Zweck im Recht" it will be noted that Ihering makes but little use of Bentham's ideas. In the second volume, published six years after the first, when he comes to a presentation of his own ethical theory, he cites Bentham as a commendable type of the earlier Utilitarians. He credits Bentham (Vol. II, p. 133) with a very important contribution to ethical theory. "Those concepts which appear but dimly in Leibnitz ('omne honestum publice utile, omne turpe publice damnosum'), which Kant, too, had before him in his 'supremely good' ('Weltbesten'), Bentham first recognized with perfect clearness, and, under the very appropriate name of Utilitarianism developed into an independent ethical system." But it is evident that Ihering uses Bentham's fundamental concept merely as a starting point for his own philosophy. Taken as a point of departure, however, it is, as Ihering himself says, of the greatest importance.

Bentham's basic maxim was that the test of right and wrong is the greatest happiness of the greatest number. He thought that in this he had discovered a principle of ethical and legal calculus by the use of which ethical norms and legal rules could be worked out which would have absolute validity. "Nature," says Bentham, "has placed mankind under the governance of two sovereign masters, *pain* and *pleasure.* The principle of utility recognizes this subjection and assumes it as the foundation of that system. By the principle of utility is meant that principle which approves or disapproves of every action whatsoever, according to the tendency which it appears to have to augment or diminish the happiness of the party whose interest is in question." This doctrine is of course not new, but in Bentham's hands it was turned from a philosophic doctrine into a political device for the legislative reform of an effete legal system. It commends itself for its simplicity. Find out what rules are adapted to bring about the greatest happiness for the greatest number, adopt these rules as laws by the sovereign power of the state, and a political and legal millennium is assured.

Though Ihering cites Bentham's basic concept with approval, he also gives in his criticism of him the distinction between his own social utilitarianism and Bentham's purely subjective view. Utility was with Bentham that which was useful to the individual, and this "subjectively useful is wrongly exalted as the measure and criterion of the objectively and socially useful." The good of the individual is never an end in itself but only a means for accomplishing a social purpose. An individual may act for his own happiness, but this is to be done not in his own interest but in the interest of society, and this relation of the individual to society cannot be determined by "any abstract theoretical formula, but by practical considerations." Bentham's theory of law is a purely individualistic one. The law is to be invoked as a means of securing and protecting the welfare of the individual. This theory is more fully elaborated by Mill and the later English Utilitarians. With Ihering, on the other hand, law is a social force, created by society, and to be used for the benefit of the individual interest only in so far as the interest of the individual coincides with the interest of society.

Bentham and Ihering are alike in espousing an imperative theory of law, and both are brought to this not only by natural bent, but also even more by their reaction against the juristic thinking of their times. The earliest incentive to Bentham's juristic efforts came by way of repulsion to Blackstone. The doctrine of the original contract had been appealed to by Blackstone to explain the origin of society and law, and, although he disavowed definite belief in it, he had not shown just how much he really retained. He also speaks vaguely of a "natural society" that apparently grows out of the expanded family, but closes this paragraph by saying that the "original contract . . . in nature and reason must always be understood and implied in the very act of associating together." Bentham pounced on this unfortunate wabble and, after rending in tatters Blackstone's verbose contradictions, substitutes for them the simple principle of utility, which furnishes the only clew to guide one through this maze. Blackstone's definition of law was equally faulty. He puts in close juxtaposition a traditional and an imperative theory of law. Bentham boldly threw aside the traditional element in law, poured out the vials of his wrath on the Blackstonian political optimism that lauded the system of common law as the most perfect conceivable one, and brought our whole system of jurisprudence to the test of expediency, insisting that all its provisions should be brought by legislation to conform to the wants of men and to the promotion of the greatest happiness.

As Blackstone is Bentham's *bête noire*, so is Puchta that of Ihering. Savigny, the greatest German jurist of the first half of the nineteenth century, reacting against the natural law concepts of the preceding generation, had set forth with wonderful scholarly acumen and broad historical grasp the idea that law is, like language, an historical product of the life of a people. This seems to carry with it by implication a sort of legal fatalism. The jurist can have but little influence in determining how the law is to develop. His activity as an historian is limited to a study of what is and has been in legal phenomena and his juristic philosophy to a generalization of the principles which explain these facts. Savigny, as a practical jurist and historian of the law, was never carried off his feet into the whirlpool of juristic metaphysical speculation; but Puchta, his contemporary, who was more philosopher than jurist, indulged to the full the Teutonic tendency toward abstract generalization. Ihering's expressions of disgust with these philosophic vagaries, as uttered by himself in the latter part of his "Scherz und Ernst" and in the preface to "Der Besitzwille," remind one of the opening paragraphs of Bentham's "Fragment on Government," with his like condemnation of Blackstone. Ihering brought "the jurisprudence in the air" down to "a jurisprudence of realities." Denying that law was only a growth which men could simply observe and from the observation work out the principles which they saw developed, he asserted that law was also, and predominantly, the realization of a purpose, and that this purpose had been and could be attained only by struggle. Furthermore, this purpose was a social purpose and had for its aim the securing of the interests of the individual only so far as society recognized them.

Neither Bentham nor Ihering was a practical lawyer. To neither will the thoroughgoing metaphysician allow the title of philosopher, but to each is unanimously conceded the name of a great legal genius. Bentham brings all legal facts to a focus about his central idea that legislation must be shaped with reference to the greatest good for the greatest number. Ihering makes much of the proposition that the sense of right and justice must constantly affect the social purpose of law, and that our legal system must constantly be reshaped to allow the exercise of this purpose. The end and aim of Bentham's life work was codification and, although he did not live to see the Reform Bill of 1832, it is generally admitted that his life-long insistence on the simplicity, possibility and supreme desirability of law reform was one of the principal instrumentalities in starting the making over of law by legislative enactment, which has been the most characteristic feature of legal history of England during the century that has elapsed since his death. The codifying activity of Ihering was hardly more than an episode in his very active career. As a conclusion of his "Possessory Intention," he gives us some criticism of the first draft of the German Civil Code, and in the final draft of that wonderful instrument a few provisions are conceded to have been affected by his doctrines, but his actual part in shaping the form of the great German codification is not to be compared with that exerted by many of his contemporaries.

III. IHERING'S MESSAGE. Ihering's criticism of Puchta, of Savigny and of the Roman jurist, Paulus, —

whom he laughingly insults by calling him the Puchta of the classical world — is indicative of his revolt against the juristic tendencies in Germany in the middle of the nineteenth century, tendencies which are apparently still operative in America in this first quarter of the twentieth century. The jurist Paulus, in his endeavor to systematize the law of possession, had assigned as the reason for the fact of possession, the intention of the holder to possess. He gave this as the logical reason for the existence of certain anomalous rules of possession existing in the Roman law of the classical period. Ihering boldly announced that these rules had no logical explanation, but had arisen simply because of accidents in the historical development of the doctrine of possession in Roman law. Savigny had devoted his life to the careful working out of certain legal principles which in the course of history had been developed in the Roman law. Puchta had attempted to fashion these principles into a philosophic system and to crystallize them in a body of dogmatic juristic doctrine possessing a philosophic validity.

In our Anglo-American system of jurisprudence, Coke, in the earlier period, and Blackstone, in the later, have played the part of a Paulus in their giving of naïve and superficial reasons for the legal anomalies of our system. The careful investigation of the historical sources of our law and the presentation of the results in case-books and treatises, which have absorbed the energies of our best English and American legal scholars during the life of the past generation, have performed for our law a service comparable to that rendered to Roman law by the great Savigny; but we find among our own historical scholars a tendency similar to that found among the followers of Savigny, to rest content with this historical achievement and to ignore or even to ridicule the possibilities of directing by philosophic prevision the development of law in the future. As an example of this somewhat contemptuous attitude toward law as it ought to be, note the disparaging reference to the "philosophic jargon of the German" made by one of our most distinguished representatives of the English historical school of jurists. On the other hand, we find many a Puchta among our American jurists, both on and off the bench, who apply the principles that have been worked out in the development of our Common Law as though they were "à priori" mathematical axioms and not "à posteriori" working formulæ, which have to be constantly reshaped to adapt them to the ever changing requirements of a developing society.

American juristic thinking at the present time needs a von Ihering. Our jurists, our legislators and our courts, both bench and bar, are still holding fast to an historical "Naturrecht" built up on the precedents of the Common Law, which has many analogies to the type of juristic thinking in vogue in Germany during the first half of the nineteenth century. All of our lawyers, judges and legislators who are trained in the traditions of the Common Law hold with characteristic and commendable professional conservatism to the good that is and has been in our legal system, insisting, too, upon the prime virtue of a system of law that is certain, but apparently forgetting that law is not an end in itself and as such to be brought to a state of formal and static perfection, but that the end is the good of society. The public is crying out against our crystallized and inelastic theory and practice of law. The proper application of the idea of law as purpose would, in many cases, loosen our legal shackles and open the way out of our legal difficulties.

This idea of Ihering may not be the last word on the philosophy of law. Possibly the criticism made by some of his German successors that it is not a philosophy at all may be well founded. But it certainly is an uplifting and inspiring idea and is not too far ahead of our own prevalent juristic thinking to make the adoption of it a practical impossibility for us. In those very difficult cases where our judges are confronted with the task of extending a principle of law to meet a new set of facts which call loudly for a remedy, if the courts had the idea that the purpose of law was to satisfy properly our changing social demands, we should have fewer reactionary decisions that have caused so much popular discontent with the law — decisions which are justified by the courts handing them down, by the arguments that there are "no precedents" in the Common Law for them, or that to extend the principle will "open the flood-gates of litigation." The days of "laissez faire" in legal matters have gone by in America as well as in Germany. We, too, must recognize that our historical Common Law is not sufficient for the demands of present day life unless, by our struggles with a purpose, we can add to the law as it is and has been, some of the principles of the law as it ought to be, in order to satisfy our growing social needs.

INTRODUCTION TO THIS VOLUME

BY HENRY LAMM[1]

The Chairman of the Committee (may his tribe increase!) because I happen to like him, persuaded me into writing an "Introduction" to LAW AS A MEANS TO AN END. What a judge on the bench, hard beset by his tasks and busy with *Doe* v. *Roe* and *Smith* v. *Jones*, feeling for justice if perchance he can find it, has to do with introducing to critical readers a book on the philosophy of the law, is an untold story all to itself. That he is likely to make a *faux pas* of so elegant a function in politeness as an Introduction, will appear doubtless in good time and due course, if you have patience, O gentle (but quizzical) reader.

Those who amuse themselves analyzing things, who know what's what (which is said by one shrewd observer to be "as high as metaphysic wit can fly"), will be able without my help to divide this introduction into: firstly, a word about von Ihering, the author; secondly, a word or two about his book (and herein of philosophy in general); and, thirdly, into sundry and divers other heads and subheads at will.

A word more in your ear, reader. This book, taken up by me with diffidence and hesitation, was read under a glow of fascination (as it will by you), and laid down with regret, because the man had evidently something more worth while to say. A book dealing with man (which includes what Iago called the immortal part of him, *viz.*, his mind) as seen through his laws, must deal in speculative probabilities. Hence you need not believe all you read. You may have doubts yourself; but you

[1] Chief Justice of the Supreme Court of Missouri.

require that the writer believes all he writes and makes you believe that he does, or you will have none of it. You wag your head and shoot out your tongue at any other kind of a book on so serious a theme. Now, von Ihering believes in himself and his theories with all his might and main, and you will like that. He says himself: "The gift of a cold hand is compatible with an ice cold heart. . . . Only the gift of a warm hand feels warm." Von Ihering's hand was warm for mankind.

Rudolph von Ihering, the son of a practising lawyer and thus born into the law (a chip off the old block), was college bred at Heidelberg, Göttingen and Berlin, graduating a *doctor juris.* Living up to the title of "doctor," teaching became his life work. He lectured on Roman law at Berlin, Basel, Rostock, Kiel, Giessen, Vienna, and then at Göttingen, dying there in 1892, full of years (the rise of three score and ten) and of honors many. When he became old, he could "read his history" in the eyes of those who knew him.

"In appearance he was of middle stature, his face clean-shaven and of classical mould" (as became a Roman scholar), "lit up with vivacity and beaming with good nature." As those who knew him testify, so those who read after him must admit, that he had read deeply with a keen and appreciative eye as a student and lover of humanity; that his thinking, always clean and original, was sometimes daring; that his theories, formulated with precision and lucidity, were asserted with boldness and defended with a charm of wholesome and homely wit, a chaste and animated vigor of style and an uncommon brilliancy of reasoning. If he is not a god, he is at least a half-god (and a very good one at that) in philosophy.

To bring those of us who read (and think) only in the English tongue in contact with this elegant translation is permanently to widen one's horizon and open a new window through which the mind's eye, now and onward, may look down an interesting vista. If he who makes two ears of corn or two blades of grass to grow where only one grew before deserves well of mankind, as we are told, surely he who gives us two ideas where only one existed before is in the same class. So much is clear, I think, and can be said with safety of von Ihering's book.

But whether von Ihering ranks in mental stature as a philosopher with Aristotle, Plato, Socrates, Seneca, Paul, Paley, Butler, Hobbes, Locke, Bentham, Bacon, Spencer, Darwin, Kant, Hegel, Montesquieu, Mill, Hamilton, may be left to the intelligent judgment of mankind — it being true in speculative philosophies as in puddings or clothes, *viz.*, the proof of the one lies in tasting and of the other in wearing them. Verily, the reader of all philosophies must be reminded that the theories of today are sometimes exploded tomorrow; that the road man has traveled is marked by the gravestone of this or that philosophy; that what is meat to one age is poison to another; that (as Marcus Tullius Cicero tells us) "there is nothing so absurd as not to have been said by some philosopher." And does not Paul say (who was a sound philosopher and lawyer — a fine combination): "Beware lest any man spoil you through philosophy and vain deceit after the traditions of men, etc." So, the drama puts it: "There are more things in heaven and earth, Horatio, than are dreamt of in your philosophy."

To know anything well, one must know it by its cause and by its reason. True philosophy consists in looking with a piercing and discriminating eye beneath mere surfaces and appearances, the shell of things, to the real heart, the kernel, of the matter. Religion has its philosophy, nature has its philosophy, the mind has its philosophy, morality has its philosophy, history has its philosophy. Philosophy surrounds man as water does an island. As Sir John Culpepper said of monopoly in the Long Parliament, it sups in our cup, it dips in our dish, it sits by our fire. It would be strange indeed, then, if Law did not have its philosophy. It emphatically has. And it levies tribute on all other philosophies,— on ethics, logic, metaphysics, morals, nature, history, as well as on experience — which latter is a school of philosophy all to itself, withal having a bitter teacher. The philosophy of the law overlaps them all, even as Aaron's rod swallowed the magicians' rods. Peradventure, knowledge is not wisdom. "Knowledge comes, but wisdom lingers." To be a philosopher means to be a lover of wisdom, and, by virtue of the very term (all sensible men being inclined to philosophy), it follows that when we are invited, as we are in this book, to go back to the very beginning of things to get at the object and uses of law, the why and the wherefore of its existence, its cause, the invitation is alluring to all normal persons, however long and strange the journey — doubly so to the lawyer and jurist, whose concepts, profession and occupations are directly involved. Even the old man has the divine itch to inquire, to know, to see, to find out. Take Ulysses: The poet sent him on his last voyage (whereon, maybe, he would "touch the Happy Isles and see the great Achilles, whom we knew") because of

> "This great spirit, yearning in desire
> To follow knowledge like a sinking star
> Beyond the utmost bound of human thought."

Von Ihering's theory, in outline, is shadowed forth in these generalizations: "The entire scheme of the law is: I exist for myself, the world exists for me, I exist for the world"; "Law is not the highest thing in the world, not an end in itself, but it is merely a means to an end, the final end being the existence of society"; "Our objective point is the State and the Law, our starting point is the individual himself"; "Law is the sum of the conditions of social life in the widest sense of the term, as secured by the power of the State through the means of external compulsion"; "The fundamental idea of the present work consists in the thought that *purpose*" (human purpose?) "is the creator of the entire law, that there is no rule which does not owe its origin to a purpose, *i.e.*, to a practical motive."

Beginning, as do all philosophers, at the beginning (even the humorous ones, like our old imaginary friend Diedrich Knickerbocker in his *History of New York*), von Ihering takes *egoism*, self-interest, as his beginning point. "Absent egoism, there is no spring or motive power, and the machine refuses to work." Egoism is the egg from which all the phenomena of the law and social life have been hatched — by evolution, as it were. Barter, contract, property, commerce, inheritance, self-denial, self-control, duty, right, justice, the law, the State,—one and all sprang from egoism. So partnerships, competition, culture, schools, hospitals, public spirit, patriotism, right as against might, self-defense, and the splendid inventions of money, the alphabet, exchange, credit, etc., — all came by the law of cause and effect from egoism. The laws of men do not touch thoughts as thoughts. However, the laws of men have to do with the mind, the will, of men. They deal with the will of man when the purpose is once formed and comes into open view through some act or thing affecting another. Do your minds meet? Behold the contract! What does the contract, the document, the law, mean? Look for the intent! Is some form of wrong (*malum in se*) held in judgment, the inquiry is: What was the intent? For, as Justice Holmes has pointed out, even a dog knows the difference between being kicked and being stumbled over, between purpose and accident. Even *obedience* comes from egoism in von Ihering's philosophy (the will of man first having been broken and tamed by the iron fist of force). But he has some trouble with affection and friendship. What is to become of conscience he does not tell us. Under the glow of his ingenious evolution of the solitary, primal man (say, Ab, who lived in a cave and tackled the saber-toothed tiger with a club, up to a Humboldt or a Gladstone and the modern State), he indulges the daring speculation that as "an object is at first taken up by the individual, grown larger it is taken over by associated interests, at full size it falls to the lot of the State," so, "if inference from the past to the future be justified, the State will in final purpose take up within itself all social purpose."

As said, von Ihering's philosophy begins with man as a savage, and solves from thence, plus egoism, the riddles of law, civilization, government and social conditions by the rule of causality, natural evolution, in which results spring from their antecedents inevitably in an endless chain of causation. Darwin took von Ihering's primal man and traced him back to a monkey. (Thereby hangs a tale over the loss of one.) Is it all so? Maybe — and maybe not. We need not believe implicitly; but we are forced without stint to admire von Ihering's bold and inquiring spirit, which, digging through the dust of ages and casting doubt to the wind, undertakes to read the everlasting riddle of things and tell us the story in words we can understand and with an air of certainty and verisimilitude. "If the play of the world's history was renewed a thousand times," says Doctor von Ihering, "humanity would always come to the same point where it finds itself at the present, *viz.*, the law."

Was man originally a savage, or did he retrograde into savagery now and then? Is the "fall" of man an unthinkable hypothesis? Are the concepts of justice, right, truthfulness, conscience, mercy, charity, friendship, duty, religion, and all the noble precepts of natural law and natural equity, and moral law, the result of a slow evolution through the ages, the result of mere cause and effect? Or, are they of divine origin, implanted by his Maker in the breast of the just man, as some of us old-fashioned folks were taught to believe? If one were to say there had not been much, if any, advance in our conceptions of those fundamentals since Job discoursed with his three friends at the door of his tent on the plains of Uz, or since the Sermon on the Mount, would that saying be quite outside the pale of fact, or beyond the realm of philosophy?

Suppose some law-giver expelled from his laws, as with a club, the great primal, natural, God-given (as some of us believe) injunctions or concepts anent murder, theft, fraud by lying, perjury, adultery, etc., would they long stay out? What says the philosophical precept? Though you expel Nature as with a club, be sure she will return. Is there not some philosophical basis for the theory that God, Providence, has a finger both in man and in his affairs? Is it not the instinctive deference to and reliance on those natural equities, as implanted by Heaven in the human breast, that causes constitutional limitations to be put on the power of the legislature to abrogate them by law? May not jurisprudence be the knowledge of things divine and human; the science of the just and unjust? May not the law of laws be to love your neighbor as yourself? — to live honestly, not to injure another, to give to each one his due? So Ulpian put it and Justinian borrowed from him.

But this is not a disquisition. It is an "Introduction," hence an intimation of two sides to the propositions maintained by our author is enough.

In groping through the past and present, as with a candle, to find the philosophy of law, what is the philosophical basis or point of view, if any, for the opposition to much *written* law? The proverbs of the fireside as well as the observations of philosophers show that such exist. For instance: Plutarch tells us that one of the wise men of Greece told Solon when he was compiling his code of written laws that he was wasting his time. Written laws, said the doubting wiseman (even at that early day), were mere cobwebs through which big flies break and in which little ones are caught. "When the State," says Tacitus, "is most corrupt, then laws are most multiplied." So, Doctor Johnson: "A corrupt society has many laws." So the proverbs: As fast as laws are devised, their evasion is contrived; God keep me from the Judge and Doctor; He that goes to law does as the sheep that in a storm runs to a briar; There is nothing certain about law but the expense; In a thousand pounds of law there is not one ounce of love; The laws are not made for the good; The law has a nose of wax, one can twist it as he will; The more laws, the least justice; The more laws, the more offenders; There is no law without a hole in it if one can find it out. In fact, I recall that one, ambitious for power (even as Archimedes longed for a certain lever and fulcrum), declared: "Give me the making of the songs of the people and I care not who makes their laws."

But it is not allowed to a man to know everything, and, peradventure, there may be no philosophical basis at all for such views. In either view of it, Doctor von Ihering was justified in omitting them. It may be the austere and dry style of most of them, or the forbidding bulk of law books may cause many to be frightened into not reading them. Certainly the wind sits in that quarter. Books, says one who knew them and loved them, that you may carry to the fire and hold readily in your hand, are the most useful after all. A man will often look at them and be tempted to go on, when he would be frightened at books of a larger size and more erudite appearance. Von Ihering's law book fills the bill of Johnson's description. Another philosopher has said: "Some books are to be tasted, others swallowed, and some few to be chewed and digested." LAW AS A MEANS TO AN END is one of those Bacon had in mind to be chewed and digested.

INTRODUCTION

By W. M. Geldart[1]

"Der Zweck im Recht," "Law as a Means to an End," or, to translate the German words more literally, "Purpose in Law," — such is the title which Jhering gave to his last great work. In this title he proclaimed a principle, which, if it has never been inoperative — for indeed its constant working is of the essence of his thesis — has yet never, save perhaps by Bentham, been so clearly enunciated, and has been too often forgotten by lawyers, alike in the countries of the Common Law and in those which to a greater or less extent received the law of Rome. Every art and science must needs have its proper principles with which to do its work, and is fairly entitled to protest against unwarranted interference from outside, whether it be the interference of the plain man, or of an alien department of thought. But the workers in each special department are too apt to forget that their branch is but a branch of the tree of life and of knowledge. Sooner or later the complete separation of any human activity from other human activities will mean withering and death. Or, in other words, the separation of different departments is a division of labor, and division of labor is a form of social co-operation. Sooner or later every group of workers must render an account of its stewardship, and must seek fresh authority from humanity at large. The isolation in which law even now finds itself has its counterpart in the separation of our Faculties of Law from the departments which bear or bore such names as Arts, Humanity, or Literæ Humaniores.

[1] M.A., B.C.L.; Fellow of All Souls College, and Vinerian Professor of English Law in the University of Oxford.

Whether Jhering's work which is now presented to the English speaking world is a work of legal philosophy, or whether he is entitled to the name of a legal philosopher, is a question which may be left to the judgment of those who have framed a definition, satisfactory to themselves and others, of legal philosophy. Of such definitions an abundance may be found in an earlier volume of this series.[2] Jhering himself regretted his want of early training in general philosophy, and a recent school, which affects to belittle him, has taken him at his word. But if the best thought, which is not purely technical, on any subject may be called its philosophy, then undoubtedly Jhering is a legal philosopher of the first rank, the greatest thinker on law whom Germany has produced since Savigny.

And Jhering is something more than a philosopher of law. Far more clearly than the majority of his countrymen he grasped the essential difference between law and other modes of social regulation, but he saw at the same time the impossibility of a fruitful study of law in isolation from other social factors. His insistence on the positive character of law is in substantial agreement with the attitude of Austin, but his concern is with questions of function rather than of formal definition; and while he never loses touch with the historical method and spirit, his ultimate objective is what we are accustomed to call censorial jurisprudence, or the theory of legislation. And even this is for him only a part of a larger theory of social functions. Thus in his second volume he was led to turn aside from law and to enter on a consideration of the workings of morality and social habits and customs, and to descend even to a detailed discussion of the significance of the forms of intercourse and language.

[2] *Berolzheimer*, "The World's Legal Philosophies.'

Jhering's theory has a value for legal and social thought in the English speaking countries no less than among his countrymen and upon the Continent of Europe. But the form in which it is cast is largely conditioned by his intellectual environment, and the conditions of his own upbringing, from which throughout his life he was emancipating himself. Often the English reader will be inclined to feel that he is unnecessarily laboring a point, or dealing at disproportionate length with matters which might be taken for granted. This is partly due to a thoroughness which is never content to build until the foundations have been completely tested; partly to a vivid interest in details which he indulges at the expense of form and system; but very often also to the fact that he is making a protest against doctrines from which he has only by great efforts freed himself, and of which we have never felt the hold and pressure.

Therefore it may be worth while to say something by way of contrasting the very different course which legal development has taken in Germany as compared with the countries of the Common Law.

In England the law of the King's Courts was not a subject of University study. We may trace here and there the influence of a mediæval logic on the formation of legal conceptions, we may find here and there that a reference to the law of nature will serve to help an argument on its way, but for the most part our law remained, in the ordinary sense of the word, frankly unacademic. In this there was enormous gain. If we lost the advantages of method which a study of the civil law gave, we were saved the dangers of putting new wine into old bottles, we were saved from the importation of doctrines which had little to do with facts. The King's Courts and the Moots and Readings of the Inns were the Common Lawyer's University,—a narrow school it may be, if we think of general culture, but a school at every moment in touch with practice and with life. Formalism and fiction and artificiality there might be; but through these and by means of these the needs of men were realized. Over and over again Jhering's thesis might be illustrated from our own law. In many a development, where much else is obscure, the purpose is as clear as daylight. The formal reasons which are given for the effect of a common recovery in barring an estate tail are unsatisfying enough; about the purpose which was at work there can be no doubt. How the doctrine of consideration came to be adopted is a matter still of discussion and research, but the enforceability of informal agreements was a concession to practical needs, and one may suspect that practical requirements had as much as anything to do with the refusal to extend enforceability in the absence of consideration. And if we ask why our Courts drove a coach and four through the Statute of Uses, the true answer is not that a use cannot be engendered of a use (which even formally is not the whole truth), but that Englishmen could not live without uses and trusts.

Still, as time went on, all was not well with the Common Law. It could break new ground; it could still in the eighteenth century embody large parts of the Law Merchant; but it could not reject what was once accepted.[4] The worst parts of the Criminal Law, of the law of evidence, of real property, of the law of husband and wife, were irrevocably fixed. The more the law

[4] The movement from precedent to precedent is not always broadening; it may lead into the narrowest of blind alleys. It is one thing to see the immediate needs of the particular case; another to find a principle which will serve for the future. Many a time the good sense of our judges has enabled them to keep the wider end in view; but not always. Often the dead past barred the way.

showed itself at variance with the needs of modern life, the more inclined were its defenders to treat it as the perfection of reason. The debt which the seventeenth century owed to the formalism which had saved the liberties of England was repaid with usurious interest by the complacency of the eighteenth. It needed the genius of Bentham to make men see once more that law was made for man and not man for law. Since his time legislation has been active enough, and most of the abuses against which he protested have been removed or mitigated. But much of the evil of a divorce between law and the life of the community remains. Rules and distinctions survive which have ceased to have any practical value, if they ever had. Law remains a very esoteric science. Legislative reform has made it more serviceable but not more intelligible to the layman, and lawyers and judges constantly immersed in the details of a particular case rarely have time to think of the wider purposes for which law exists. Public policy has rightly been described as an unruly steed: but sometimes there is no other; and woe to the untrained rider.

Very different has been the course of legal development in Germany. Without any but the most shadowy political unity, with no common legislature, no common judicial system, it was saved from a complete diversity in the development of its local laws only by the reception of the Roman Law. Thus a learned law, a law taught and learned in Universities, became the Common Law of Germany, largely superseding the native and local law, ready to step in, at any rate, where the local law was silent.

It followed that the field upon which law could make new growth was the University rather than the Courts: the men "learned in the law" were professors or writers rather than judges and advocates, and the former class exercised an influence over its development which it is hard for us, brought up in the traditions of judge-made law, to understand. These conditions had the advantage of preserving for law a place among other liberal studies and fertilizing it by contact with them; but they weakened its hold upon immediate practical needs, and hindered the drawing of any sharp line between law and the principles of moral and political science. The Roman Law texts were largely inapplicable to modern conditions; but it was assumed that a right interpretation could find in them underlying principles of universal applicability. And while on the one hand the eighteenth century system of "natural law" or "natural rights" was largely a generalized statement of principles ultimately derived from Roman Law as viewed in the light of modern usage, violence was often done to the texts in the desire to make them fit in with the results of *a priori* theory. The philosophical upheaval at the end of the eighteenth and the beginning of the nineteenth century shattered the basis of the doctrine of natural rights, and the spirit of scholarship and historical investigation, of which Savigny was the foremost representative in the field of law, insisted on a truthful interpretation of the texts, which in the long run was bound to be incompatible with their adaptation to the needs of modern life.

The characteristic doctrine of the German historical school that law is a growth determined by a somewhat mystically conceived national will, had the immediate effect of checking schemes for codification and legislation. The production of law was regarded as something analogous to a natural process, with which the legislator could not and ought not to interfere; the most that might be permitted to him was to give a clearer expression to the national will as manifested in existing practice and custom, or to apply correctives in matters of detail. The civilized world owes an enormous debt to the historical school for the services of brilliant and patient investigation which it has rendered, and which have been continued in Germany and elsewhere long after its favorite doctrines had fallen to the ground: and Germany has good cause to be grateful to it for preventing a premature codification. But its conception of law was bound to be sterile of practical results, above all in a country where popular participation in the making and application of the law was at a minimum. For all practical purposes the popular will had to be regarded as residing in the legislator, the judge and the scientific lawyer (above all the latter), in whom alone it could find any conscious expression. No doubt by the stress which it laid on national individuality, the historical school stimulated the investigation of German legal antiquities, and favored the dream of a reconstruction and revival of the native law; and this tendency has had important practical results in the modern Imperial Code. But for immediate purposes recourse was had again to the texts of the Roman Law. They were subjected to a critical examination, assisted by all the resources of modern scholarship: leading conceptions were discovered in them, and from these conceptions the consequences must be deduced with rigorous logic. The conceptions must be reasonable, if not in regard to practical needs, at any rate in regard to the requirements of the philosophy of law; they must also be consistent with the texts. Extraordinary acuteness, ingenuity and labor were brought to bear upon the task, and with the most fruitful results; it is not too much to say that without the work of Savigny and his followers the Imperial Code of modern Germany would have been an impossibility.

But it is equally true that it would have been impossible without Jhering. For the method against which he revolted was fundamentally unsound. It could only work by something like a pious fraud. Though natural rights were discarded, there was bound to be a reversion to something like the procedure of the natural rights school. The fundamental conceptions must carry conviction as in themselves necessary, and they must be present, or at least implied in, or consistent with the texts. An unconscious juggling was inevitable; you must put into your legal concept the results which you wish to get out of it; you must put a non-natural sense upon the text to make it square with the concept. Worst of all, in the desire to satisfy the requirements of philosophy and scholarship practical considerations were forgotten or deliberately neglected. "Law," says Bethmann-Hollweg, a favorite pupil of Savigny, "is an object of pure science, and pure science is in no way concerned with the question of application or applicability."[5] In the present work Jhering has occasion to reprobate the teaching of Puchta that the legislator may deprive customary law of its enforcement in the Courts and yet cannot deprive it of its character as law. An English lawyer will have no difficulty in understanding the sarcasm which Jhering elsewhere pours out on the "Begriff-jurisprudenz" of Puchta, when he learns that the latter asserted as matters of principle the absolute inconceivability of a partial intestacy and of a genuine representation of the principal by the agent.[6]

Yet Jhering was himself brought up in this very school, and dedicated the first part of his "Geist des römischen Rechts" ("Spirit of the Roman Law") to Puchta's

[5] Quoted by *Landsberg*, "Geschichte der deutschen Rechtswissenschaft," III, 2, notes, 110.

[6] *Landsberg*, III, 2–453.

memory. Even here one can see the beginnings of the breach with his teacher. It is one thing (as he sees) to have to deal with Roman Law as existing law, another to understand it in its historical development; its method and its history are of value for all time, but the rules of Roman Law have no universal validity. "Through Roman Law but beyond it" is the motto which sums up in his eyes the significance of the Roman Law for the modern world. Thus his outlook was directed ever more towards the present and the future. The "Spirit of the Roman Law" was never finished. More and more as the work proceeded he felt the trammels which his program imposed on his utterance of the thoughts which he now had most at heart. In the last portion which appeared of the "Spirit" (the first division of the third part) his repudiation of the treatment of law as if it were a system of logical categories and his conceptions of purpose as the determining factor in law, of "protected interest" as the essence of legal right, came to the front. But he could no longer be content to expound fundamental doctrines under the guise of criticism of ancient law.

It was thus that the "Zweck im Recht" came to be written, a work of which it may fairly be said that it freed German legal thought from the shackles of the Digest and the usurpations of philosophic systems. Not but what much, incalculably much of permanent value had been accomplished under those hard task-masters: Jhering's work itself could not have been done but for them. But the time had come for a return to the realities of the present, and for raising the embargo which Savigny had laid on legislation.

Of the significance of Jhering's teaching for the student of the social sciences and for those who are concerned, whether as thinkers or as practical men, with social and legislative problems, a few words may be said. His repudiation of a "jurisprudence of concepts" and of the "written reason" of the Roman Law as the last word in legal and legislative theory led him to reject the individualism of the early and middle nineteenth century, and the stress which he laid on social utility gave an impulse and a justification to the "collectivism" (to use the word in the wide sense with which Professor Dicey[7] has used it) which has been the most characteristic tendency of our own time and the force of which is not yet spent. That is on the face of it the most striking and immediate consequence of Jhering's doctrine. It is at any rate the practical conclusion which he drew for our own time, and whether we approve of it or not, it is at least to his credit that he foresaw the urgency of claims, which, when he wrote, were barely beginning to make themselves heard. For my own part, I believe that for present needs this "collectivist" tendency is justified, and its dangers often unnecessarily feared and exaggerated. But a comparison of Jhering's doctrine with that of Bentham seems to me to show that the principle of social utility as conceived by Jhering is not inconsistent with, and indeed requires, a due appreciation of the claims of the individual, while Bentham's teaching is capable of conversion to the uses of the completest absolutism.

But before I turn to this comparison, I should like to call attention to some practical considerations of a more general kind which follow from Jhering's main position.

On the one hand the conception of law as determined by purpose will strengthen our respect for and confidence in law. We shall believe that for the most part it is

[7] "Law and Opinion," Lecture IV, *et passim*.

the outcome of human experience and has received and retained its force because it gives effect to the greatest common measure of human needs. We shall be prepared to meet the demands for innovation or revolution on a common ground. We shall not present our law as a closed system of unalterable principles in which no breach may be made; we shall not put it forward as the perfect work of reason. On the contrary we shall admit the claim that human institutions must satisfy human needs. But we shall assert with some confidence that this claim has never been wholly disregarded in the making of law. We shall rely on a strong presumption that, at least in its main outlines, our law serves and has served those needs. Where a crying evil is pointed out as calling for immediate reform of the law, we shall ask whether it is certain that the law has not already taken account of it, refused to interfere for the good reason that to do so would be to prejudice higher and wider needs. It is only in this fashion that the existing legal order can be defended against rash claims, whether founded on self-interest or sympathy.

On the other hand, we shall oppose no deaf ears to such claims. If we give up, as I believe we are bound to do, the notion of natural rights in the sense of particular institutions to which every system of positive law ought without regard to consequences to give effect, we shall not be able to set up any rule of law as sacred and exempt from criticism and attack. For if the belief in the purposive character of law is a justification for optimism, this is no uncritical optimism; and it is no part of Jhering's doctrine that law has at any time succeeded fully in giving effect to the purposes which it serves, and it is no answer to that doctrine to point to the fallibility of lawyers and legislators. Again, it is true that law would have been impossible if at every moment it was required to have regard to purpose. The purposes of law are embodied in legal conceptions which must develop in independence and cannot at every step be called upon to conform to particular needs. Otherwise system and certainty would be unattainable. But this autonomy of law, if it were only because of excess or defects of logic, will lead to a divergence between law and the needs of life, which from time to time calls for correction. Further, the preponderance now of this, now of that class in the community has led to the advancement of purposes which are at variance with the interests of other classes which attain or seek political power. Lastly, changes whether in economic conditions or in opinions and ideals bring to light new purposes which the law, formed under other conditions, material or moral, is incapable of adequately serving. Law cannot therefore refuse at any time to submit to criticism any, even its most fundamental principles, if they are challenged on the ground that they do not serve or have ceased to serve the needs of mankind; it can only insist that the challenge shall be made good by proof. How far if at all the needful changes can or ought to be carried out by judicial decisions or the development of legal theory, and how far the intervention of the legislator will be called for, is a matter that will vary from one legal territory to another according to the accepted traditions as to the binding force of precedents, the character of the enacted law, and the wider or narrower liberty of judicial interpretation.

Jhering stands alone, or almost alone, among German writers in his admiration for Bentham's work; there is much in common in the qualities of their genius, in their deep but not uncritical optimism, in their repugnance to doctrines of natural right, in their determination to keep in touch with the facts of life. Both show a curious trait of what looks like pedantry, Bentham in his elaborate classifications and love of coining words for the purpose of marking distinctions, Jhering in his rather naïve faith in the possibility of discovering the inner meaning of a word by a reference to its derivation. But these are mere surface mannerisms. Both are fundamentally at one in their conceptions of the functions of law.

But Jhering has two great advantages. In the first place Bentham's unhistorical mind often made him see in the past and present nothing but a record of folly and injustice, and led him to believe that a new heaven and a new earth could be established by the recognition and application of the principle of utility. Jhering, though alive to the one-sidedness of the historical school, was full of the historical spirit, and could see that the principle of utility had always been at work, however unconsciously, in human affairs. In the second place, Bentham had embarrassed his doctrine by a particular and untenable theory of the nature of utility, the theory that the only purposes of human action are in the last resort the pursuit of pleasure and the avoidance of pain, and had professed to establish a calculus by means of the summation of pleasures and pains, which should afford a criterion of ethics and legislation.

It was this, above all, that stood in the way of Bentham's recognition in philosophic Germany. What made him the force that he was in England and in the English speaking world was not his hedonism, but his acute perception of the purposes which intelligent men would desire to see carried out, and of the reforms which were necessary in order to carry them out. It did not need a theory of the greatest happiness of the greatest number to convince men that humanity in the criminal law, reasonable rules of evidence, freedom from antiquated restrictions on contract, would further desirable purposes. The calculus of pains and pleasures was a superstructure which men might accept or reject, but which made no difference in the value of the reforms, when once men had grasped the idea that the law was their servant and not their master. Jhering rejects hedonism and eudæmonism; as he sees that human nature rejects them; and he finds no short cut, like Bentham's calculus, to the determination of the priorities among competing purposes.

We must remember that his book is a fragment, and that he never lived to carry out his intention (stated at the end of Chapter IV) of answering the question, "What is purpose?" But if he had done so, it seems probable that the answer to this question would have been a determination rather of the form of the conception of purpose than of its content. The truth is that to set out an order of priority among purposes as universally valid would be to fall back on something very like "natural right"; as indeed Bentham's greatest happiness principle was unconsciously a reversion to that doctrine. We cannot measure the value of ends by reference to some other standard, and therefore the search for such a standard is illusory. All that we can demand is such a conception of their relations to each other as will be consistent with men's moral consciousness. That this consciousness differs from man to man may afford a problem for ethical theory; but for the practical life of the individual, and even more for the task of the legislator, the agreement far outweighs the differences.

In one sense Bentham is an individualist, while Jhering's conception is one of social utility. For Bentham all ends are the pleasures and pains of individuals: society is nothing but a sum of individuals, and utility depends on nothing but the sum of their pleasures and pains. It is true that Jhering's work as far as we have it is so much concerned with the exposition of the use which society makes of the egoistic motives, and in the showing that the balance of accounts between the individual and society shows a balance of individual satisfaction in his favor, that one may get the impression that at bottom his social utility would turn out to be nothing but a sum of individual utilities. It is true that he nowhere clearly works out the conception, but his criticism of Bentham in his second volume makes it clear to my mind that he would have rejected such a conclusion. What he says there of patriotism seems inconsistent with the notion that he would have treated patriotism as nothing more than an interest in the welfare of a number of present or future individuals.

Further, it is notorious than in a very practical sense Bentham was an individualist, because he believed that the removal of restrictions would tend to a very great increase in human happiness including a high degree of equality in the distribution of wealth. Jhering has no such confidence. It is true that he rightly appreciates the value of contract and property as levers in the social mechanism, but he refuses to approve as a matter of course of the enforcement of every contract merely because it is a contract not subject to some specific vice: he approves of guild regulations and the suppression of the interloper; he is clear that the right of property is founded upon, and may have to give way to considerations of social utility. This is a difference in the application of principles rather than in the principles themselves, and Bentham's views on the relief of poverty and the limitation of the rights of succession to property show that he was no unbending individualist. Nevertheless for practical purposes Bentham's direct influence was all on the side of the individualism of the early nineteenth century, while Jhering may fairly be reckoned as a herald of the collectivism which marked its close.

But from another point of view the positions are reversed. Once satisfy the Benthamite that the economic assumptions on which his individualism is based are unsound, and for purposes of practical politics that individualism collapses. If unlimited freedom of contract does not make for the greatest happiness of the greatest number (and in practice material well being will be the main consideration), if it seems likely that such well-being can be increased by regulation and interference, then Bentham's utilitarianism not only permits, but requires that individualism shall give way to the greatest practicable collectivism. Professor Dicey has rightly called attention to the debt of collectivism to Bentham.[8] Now it is certain that Jhering would have sympathized with the general trend of modern legislation in this direction and would probably have approved of it largely in detail.

It is clear that he looked with approval on the movement which transferred large departments of action first from individuals to voluntary societies and then from societies to the state. He was not prepared to set any limits to the increase of state activity. Further, it is clear, from his criticism of von Humboldt and John Stuart Mill in the eighth chapter, that he sees no way to define a sphere of individual liberty within which the interference of the State is illegitimate. But what is equally clear is that he did not draw the easy conclusion that all rights of the individual must disappear in the last resort in the face of the claims of social utility. On the contrary he recognizes the question of the limits of

[8] Law and Opinion, Lecture IX.

the power of the state and the law over against the sphere of individual liberty as a real problem, and one which bars his way and which he cannot solve. He cannot solve it, that is, in the sense in which the upholders of natural right claim to find a solution, a formula which shall be good for all time and under all conditions. And he seems right in holding that in this sense the question is an insoluble one, that it is as he says an "ever fluid" question, one which will receive a different answer at different times and under varying conditions. But the admission that there is a problem is a concession of all that is worth preserving in the doctrine of natural rights, namely its insistence on the reality and value of the individual. And while he rejects its attempt to treat law and society as merely derivative, at the same time he steers clear of the tendency of some at least of its critics to treat society as the only reality. Bentham's doctrine, while it on the one hand repudiates natural rights and on the other looks upon the institutions of society as nothing more than a machinery for increasing the sum total of pleasurable sensations, puts no value upon the individual save as the receptacle of such sensations; it has no answer, for instance, to the claim of a majority to oppress a minority, if once the majority is satisfied that the increase of its pleasure will outweigh in quantity the pain of the oppressed.

It has been said of Jhering that with all his theoretical utilitarianism he remained a practical idealist. This estimate correctly emphasizes the two sides of his social philosophy; but it should not mislead us into thinking that there is any inconsistency between them. Plato too was a utilitarian, as well as an idealist, and his example should warn us against the confusion of utilitarianism and hedonism. In its true sense utilitarianism is nothing but a refusal to isolate any part of human action and to consider it apart from its consequences, a refusal to believe that in the last resort ideals can be unrelated or hostile to one another. It is by his insistence on this truth that Jhering's work has done and will continue to do the greatest service in furthering the advancement of law and legal science, and bringing them into a right relation to other departments of human activity and knowledge.

All Souls College, Oxford.
October, 1913.

AUTHOR'S PREFACE

The book, of which I herewith present the first half to the public, is an offshoot of my work on the Spirit of Roman Law ("Geist des römischen Rechts"). The last volume of that treatise (Part III, division 1), which appeared in 1865 in its first edition, concluded with the establishment of a theory of "rights in the subjective sense." In it I gave a definition differing from the prevailing one, by putting Interest instead of Will at the basis of law. The further justification and illustration of this point of view was reserved for the succeeding volume. In the course of its development, however, I soon went beyond this point of view. The concept of Interest made it necessary for me to consider Purpose, and "right in the subjective sense" led me to "right in the objective sense." Thus the original object of my investigations was transformed into one of much greater extent, into the object of the present book, *viz.*, Law as a means to an end. Once this question came before me, I was no longer able to avoid it; it always emerged again in one form or another. It was the sphinx which imposed its question upon me, and I must solve its riddle if I would regain my scientific peace of mind.

I think it necessary to make this explanation because it tells the reason which prevented me from continuing the above work. I cannot return to it until the present work is finished. For me, personally, the latter has become my paramount interest, and it has relegated the above work, which I had formerly considered my life work, to a secondary place. It is possible that the judgment of the world will determine the relative value of the two works differently from the way I do. But to me, personally, no choice was left between the two.

The fundamental idea of the present work consists in the thought that Purpose is the creator of the entire law; that there is no legal rule which does not owe its origin to a purpose, *i.e.*, to a practical motive. The second part of the book is devoted to the establishment of this principle, and to the detailed exposition and illustration of it in connection with the most important phenomena of law. The first part was originally outside of my calculation, it was wrested from me against my will. I had to say to myself that a book which intends to make purpose the foundation of the entire system of law must give an account of the concept of purpose. I should have been glad to borrow it from others and build upon the results gained by them, but I was convinced that they did not give me what I was looking for. The best thing I met in my search is, according to my opinion, the discussions of *Trendelenburg* in his "Logische Untersuchungen," (Vol. 2, 3d ed. Leipzig, 1870, pp. 14 ff.), masterly in form and content. But the height and the breadth in which the problem is there conceived, *viz.*, purpose as a world-forming principle, yielded nothing for the limited point of view from which I had to consider purpose, *viz.*, its significance for the human will. Nor did I find anything in other writers, whether philosophers or jurists, which satisfied me in this direction.

I found myself obliged therefore to attack the problem myself. The first part of the work (The Concept of Purpose) is devoted to an attempt at its solution. I had originally counted on a volume of moderate size for the two parts together. But in the course of working it out, the first part alone assumed such proportions that I had to think of a separate volume of good size for it, and I was not even able to keep within these extended limits, for I found it necessary, from external considerations, in order, namely, not to let the first volume swell out of all proportion to the second, to assign the concluding chapters of the first part to the second volume, in order to bring about an external equilibrium of the two volumes.

The problem of the first part placed me in a domain where I am a dilettante. If I ever deplored the fact that the period of my development came at a time when philosophy was in discredit, it was in connection with the present work. What the young man missed at that time by reason of the unfavorable disposition toward philosophy that then prevailed, could no longer be made up by the man of mature age. If, nevertheless, I was not frightened away from treating a philosophical theme, it was because I hoped that the knowledge of the positive juristic material, in which I have the advantage over the professional philosopher, would at least furnish him with data which may be useful for his purposes. The spell under which philosophy lay at the time of Hegel, the anathema placed on anyone who, without being trained in the subject, presumed to give his opinion on philosophical questions, the sovereign contempt with which the philosopher of the Hegelian school looked down upon the man of positive science, has fortunately given way to a different disposition. Surely not to the detriment of philosophy. Philosophy may reject or rectify what the philosophical naturalist brings to light, but his attempt to philosophize in his domain, *i.e.*, to search out universal ideas, is hardly altogether devoid of benefit to philosophy, provided only the man brings to his task the necessary knowledge of his subject, scientific earnestness and an eye for the universal. And I hope that this will prove to be true also in my case.

I have taken care not to economize in the use of illustrative material, for the sake of the philosopher as well as of the jurist. I made use of every opportunity which presented itself to me of placing the particular in the service of general ideas. For the sake of the philosopher, in order to bring before him the material; for the sake of the jurist, in order to present to him the general idea in the material, and the connection of the particular with the whole. I have endeavored at the same time to present the purely juristic material in such a manner as to make it intelligible to the educated layman.

I must be prepared for readers who will judge the value of the work only by the particular views contained in it. It is the usual standard of the jurist in judging works of his profession. In a work which, like the present, pursues no practical or dogmatic purpose, but takes for its task the presentation of the whole connection of law, such judgment would show the lack of all understanding for the meaning of the problem. Its difficulty lay for me, after I had made up my mind regarding my fundamental idea, just in the building up of the whole, *viz.*, in the discovery of the right connection, how one thing is joined to the other, in the logical articulation of the individual parts, in the development of the concept unbroken by any leaps, advancing step by step from the simplest to the higher. Upon this systematic or dialectic element I expended the utmost care, and I have for this purpose touched upon a mass of points and questions in strict logical progression solely in order to denote the point where they enter into the general framework of the law.

This endeavor after strict logical articulation is responsible for the arrangement of the chapters. Every chapter treats a topic complete in itself. This explains the very unequal length of the chapters, which may seem very strange to one who sees in a chapter ending nothing more than a resting point to take breath. Such a reader may lose his wind in my seventh and eighth chapters. But he will find his chapters there also in another form, namely in the numbered subdivisions into which these chapters are divided. They denote the articulations, or individual branches of the fundamental idea to which these two chapters (Reward and Coercion) are devoted, and what I have just said about the strictly progressive development of the concept which I have proposed to myself as a standard, applies here with special force.

For the rest I refer the reader to the book itself. There is only *one* more point on which I must add a few words. It is the opposition between the 'law of causality' and the 'law of purpose' in the first chapter. No philosopher of the present day will admit such opposition, and very properly so. Only one of two things is possible. Either cause is the moving force of the world, or purpose. In my opinion it is purpose. Purpose can give forth the law of causality, the law of causality cannot give forth purpose. Or, to speak more plainly, the assumption of a purpose in the world, which, since I am simple enough not to be able to think of purpose without a conscious will, is synonymous in my mind with the assumption of a God, — the assumption, I say, of a purpose in the world posited by God, or of a divine idea of purpose, is quite compatible, in my opinion, with the affirmation of the strictest law of causality. Granted that the latter works just as the extreme Darwinists teach, crushing inexorably what cannot maintain itself in the struggle of existence, beginning with the Moneron and without any further creative act bringing forth everything out of itself, progressing from one step to the other up to man — still, when I set a boulder in motion on the top of the mountain in order that it may drop into the valley, was it not purpose which first set the law of causality in motion in the stone? If cause has been so formed by purpose from the very beginning that in its continuous motion it produces one thing out of the other, and finally arrives at the point which purpose has foreseen and willed, is it purpose or cause which governs the entire motion? When the statue which he wants to create stands before the mind of the sculptor, and years glide by until the hand completes it according to the laws of mechanics, *i. e.*, according to the law of causality, is it a work of the hand or of the mind? I do think it is a work of the hand in the service of the mind. I, for my part, do not presume any judgment on the correctness of the Darwinian theory, although the very results at which I personally have arrived in reference to the historical development of law confirm it to the fullest extent in my sphere. But even if the truth of the theory were as firm in my mind as a rock, I do not see how it would in the least disturb my belief in a divine idea of purpose. In the Moneron, which according to Haeckel leads with necessity to man, God foresaw man, as the sculptor forsees the Apollo in the marble, or, as Leibnitz has already said, "In Adam God pre-formed and willed the entire human race."

The assumption of a two-fold law in the world of phenomena, of the law of causality for inanimate creation and the law of purpose for animate, is not in the least opposed to this conception. Both find their unity in the law of purpose as the highest world-forming principle. Matter may obey the one, and the will the other; both of them, each in its own manner and sphere, simply carry out the works which were imposed upon them from the beginning by purpose. One legal purpose is produced out of the other with the same necessity with which, according to the Darwinian theory, one animal species is developed from the other. And if the world should be created a thousand times as it was once created, — after milliards of years the world of law would still bear the same form; for purpose has the same irresistible force for the creations of the will in law as cause has for the formation of matter. Thousands of years may elapse before this compelling force of purpose becomes visible in a particular point in law — what are a thousand years in comparison with milliards? Law obeys this compulsion willingly or unwillingly. But the compulsion proceeds step by step. Law knows no leaps any more than nature, the antecedent must be there first before the higher can follow. But when it is once there, the higher is unavoidable — every antecedent purpose produces the following one, and from the sum of all particulars is produced later, through conscious or unconscious abstraction, the universal — the legal ideas, legal intuition, the sense of justice. It is not the sense of right that has produced law, but it is law that has produced the sense of right. Law knows only one source, and that is the practical one of purpose.

But I must stop, in order not to anticipate the discussions which must be reserved for the second part of my work. What has already been said will suffice to meet the attacks to which my distinction between the law of causality and the law of purpose may be exposed.

DR. RUDOLPH VON JHERING.

GÖTTINGEN, Dec. 6, 1877.

Law as a Means to an End

LAW AS A MEANS TO AN END

PART I

THE CONCEPT OF PURPOSE

CHAPTER I

THE LAW OF PURPOSE

§ 1. CAUSE AND PURPOSE. — § 2. PROBLEM OF THE WILL IN THE LIVING BEING. — § 3. THE ANIMAL; PSYCHOLOGICAL LEVER OF ITS WILL; INFLUENCE OF EXPERIENCE. — § 4. THE CONCEPT OF LIFE. — § 5. THE VOLUNTARY PROCESS IN MAN: I. INNER STAGE. — 1. PURPOSE; 2. RELATION OF PURPOSE TO ACTION; 3. THE LAW OF PURPOSE; 4. PURPOSE IN THE FORM OF REASON; HABITUAL ACTION. — II. EXTERNAL STAGE IN THE VOLUNTARY PROCESS; THE LAW OF CAUSALITY.

According to the "Principle of Sufficient Reason" nothing ever happens of itself ("causa sui"), for everything that happens, every change in the world of sense, is the consequence of another antecedent change, without which the former would not have taken place. This fact, postulated by our thinking, and confirmed by experience, we designate, as is well known, by the phrase, the *Law of Causality.*

§ 1. *Cause and Purpose.* This law holds also for the will. Without sufficient reason a movement of the will is as unthinkable as a movement of matter. Freedom of the will, in the sense that the will can set itself in motion spontaneously without a compelling reason, is the Münchhausen of philosophy, who can pull himself out of a swamp by his own hair.

There is just as much need, therefore, of sufficient reason for the will as in the processes of material nature. But in the latter it is *mechanical*, and is called *cause* ("causa efficiens"); in the will it is *psychological*, and we call it *purpose* ("causa finalis"). Thus, the stone does not fall in order to fall, but because it must fall, because its support is taken away; whilst the man who acts does so, not *because* of anything, but *in order* to attain to something. This purpose is as indispensable for the will as cause is for the stone. As there can be no motion of the stone without a cause, so can there be no movement of the will without a purpose. In the former case we speak of the *mechanical* law of causality, in the latter of the *psychological*. I shall designate the latter henceforth as the *Law of Purpose;* partly for the sake of brevity, partly to indicate in the very name that purpose forms the only psychological reason of the will. The mechanical law of causality, therefore, will need no additional description, and I shall henceforth designate it simply as the Law of Causality.

The law of causality may now be restated: There can be no process in the external world of sense without another antecedent process which has effected it, or in the words of the well-known formula: *No effect without a cause.* The law of purpose is: *no volition*, or, which is the same thing, *no action*, *without purpose*. . . .

In "*Cause*" the object upon which the effect is produced is passive. The object appears simply as a single point in the universe at which the law of causality is carried out in that moment. In "*Purpose*," on the other hand, the thing which is set in motion by it appears as self-active; it acts. Cause belongs to the past, purpose to the future. External nature, when questioned regarding the reason of its processes, directs the questioner to look back; whilst the will directs him forward. The answer of the one is "quia," of the other, "ut." To be sure this does not mean that in Purpose the process of nature is reversed, which requires the determining cause to precede the thing determined by it. The determining reason belongs here also to the present; the determining cause here too precedes the thing determined by it; this is the idea (or purpose), which existing in the agent induces him to act. But the content of this idea is constituted by something in the future (that which the agent wishes to attain), and in this sense we may say that in volition the practical motive lies in the future.

§ 2. *Problem of the Will in the Living Being.* Where life in nature develops itself into soul, there too begins that provision for one's own life, that self-determination and self-preservation which we know as will and purpose. Every living being is so constituted as to be its own keeper, the guardian and preserver of itself, and nature further has provided that this fact shall not remain hidden from it, and that the living being shall not lack the necessary means to solve his own problems of existence.

Life in this sense begins in nature with the lower animal, and at the same point also begins the problem of the will. Here, low in the scale of life, where with the will appears also for the first time the indispensable motive — purpose, let us try to get our first view of volition.

The dry sponge fills itself with water; the thirsty animal drinks. Is it the same process? Externally, yes; internally, no. For the sponge does not fill itself in order to do so, but the animal does drink in order to quench its thirst. Who tells us this is so? The animal itself. A well trained dog will not drink when his master forbids him. How is this? Because over against the idea of the water which he knows can quench his thirst, there presents itself to him the idea of the beating which he receives when he drinks against his master's orders, — an idea evoked by no present sensible impression, but coming rather as a result of memory. The idea of the blows does not remove for the dog the dryness of his palate and that sensible condition of his thirst which is called forth thereby. A fact cannot be removed by an idea; but an idea may and does attack that which is similar to it, *viz.*, another idea, and will subdue it when it is stronger. But if the overcoming of the incitement to drink be in this case (since it rests upon the co-operation of the memory) a psychological process, and not a mechanical one, the incitement itself, whether the animal resists or yields, is a psychological act.

§ 3. *The Animal; Psychological Lever of its Will; Influence of Experience.* The physical condition of the dryness of the palate does not therefore as such bring about the drinking, it does this solely by changing the physical and mechanical pressure into a psychological. This process therefore does not come under the law of causality, but under that of purpose. The animal drinks in order to quench its thirst; it forbears in order not to receive blows. In both cases it is the idea of something in the future which impels the animal to its conduct.

In another way also we may convince ourselves of the correctness of our position. For whether we dip the sponge in water or in sulphuric acid or in anything else, it always fills itself, even though the fluid destroy it. Whereas the animal, though taking the water, will reject the sulphuric acid. Why? Because it feels that the sulphuric acid is fatal to it. The animal therefore, distinguishes between that which is beneficial to its existence and that which is injurious; it discriminates before it decides and makes use of former experiences. Right action for the animal is by no means indicated in instinct alone; for there is hereditary experience to guide him; the animal is directed by the experience of the species as well as by that of his individual self. The understanding of height and depth and the estimate of distance by the eye, his judgment of the degrees of heat of food and drink which is beneficial or injurious and so on, must be learned by the young dog and cat by way of falling down some step and burning his muzzle; the animal too must gain sense through pain. A stick may fall a thousand times, and it always falls again; because for the stick, there is no experience. But a dog which has once been deceived by a trap in the shape of a loaf of bread or a stone is thereafter made the wiser. For the animal, therefore, experience is a factor; the memory of what was pleasant or unpleasant, beneficial or injurious exists for it, and the practical ability to turn to account such impressions for future use; hence the realization of purpose.

§ 4. *The Concept of Life.* With this is most closely connected the concept of animal life. Consciousness alone is not yet life. If the faculty of thought were granted the stone, it would remain a stone; the figures of the external world would merely be reflected in it as the moon is reflected in the water. Even the richest knowledge is not life; a book in which the secret of the whole world were revealed, though it became conscious of itself, would still remain a book. Neither is sensation life any more than is knowledge. If the plant felt an injury done it as painfully as the animal, it would not yet thereby be like the latter. Animal life, as nature has actually thought and formed it, is the *maintenance of existence with one's own power* ("volo," not "cogito, ergo sum"); *life is the practical application, by way of purpose, of the external world to one's own existence.* The entire equipment of the living being: sensation, understanding, memory, has meaning only as a protection thereof. Understanding and sensation alone would not be able to effect this if it were not for the addition of memory. It is memory that gathers together and secures in experience the fruit of these two, in order to apply such experience to the purposes of existence.

The will is no more dependent upon self-consciousness than is life; and he who has the sense of the inner connection existing between the two will justly regard as superficial and prejudiced that view of the animal which would deny its purposing power the name of will because of a defective self-consciousness which is less complete than man's own. This low view of animal volition is by no means the profound thing it professes to be.

The essential characteristics of the human will (with the exception of self-consciousness, which in man also may be wanting or pass out of function permanently or temporarily), are found, as we shall see later, also in the animal. And even the animal's faculty of thinking, which is presupposed in its power to will, is incomparably higher than at first sight it has the appearance of being. It is so easy to say, the idea of a future event impels the animal to action. And yet how much is involved in this! The idea of the future means an idea subsumed under the category of possibility. The animal, therefore, in comparing this idea with that of the present state, proves its ability practically to employ the two categories of the actual and the possible. Similarly it makes use of the categories of purpose and of means. It would not at all be thinkable that it should will if its understanding did not control them. I, for my part, am so farfrom looking down contemptuously upon the will of the animal, that on the contrary I regard it as worthy of the highest respect, and in the following chapter I shall make the attempt to derive from it the scheme of purpose in general.

§ 5. *The Voluntary Process in Man.* Our discussion hitherto has shown us that purpose is the idea of a future event which the will essays to realize. This concept of purpose, which by no means exhausts the essence of the latter, must suffice for the present until the progress of our investigation has put us in a position to replace it by one that is completely adequate. We shall operate with it in what follows, as the mathematician operates with x, in dealing with an unknown quantity.

Turning now to the human will, let us confine our task in this chapter merely to the proof of the law of purpose, or the principle: ***no volition without purpose.*** The negative form of this expression is: volition, the inner process of the formation of the will, does not come under the law of causality; its efficient reason is not cause but purpose. But the realization of the will, its emergence into the world of sense, does come under the law of causality. The former is the internal stage of the will, the latter the external.

I. *Internal Stage:* 1. *Purpose.* The internal stage begins with an act of the faculty of ideation (representation). There emerges in the soul a picture, an idea (representation) of a future possible state, which promises the subject a greater satisfaction than the state in which he finds himself at the moment. The reason why the idea emerges lies partly in the subject himself, in his individuality, his character, his principles, his view of life; partly in external influences. That in the soul of the criminal there emerges the thought of a wicked deed — this presupposes the man himself with his criminal nature; in the soul of the good man such a thought does not arise. The same holds of the idea of a good deed which arises in the soul of the latter; it would not have been possible in the former. Thus, the possibility of the first impulse to a deed is conditioned by the given individuality of the subject, in whom lies the ultimate reason for the impulse. The external influences, on the other hand, give only the impulse to the deed, the occasion for its performance. They indicate to us the point at which the law of causality is able to exercise an influence on the formation of the will, but they indicate at the same time also the limit of this influence. For as was shown above (p. 4) in our discussion of the voluntary process in the animal, these external influences have no direct power over the will; they acquire such only by being converted into psychological motives, and not until they are thus converted. Whether they can do this depends upon the measure of resistance which they find within the subject.

The idea of the future state is distinguished from other ideas in being practical in its nature. It contains within itself a challenge to action, it is a prefiguring of the deed, presented before the will by the faculties of ideation and desire. The acceptance of the presentation depends upon the preponderance of the reasons for the deed over the reasons against it. Without such a preponderance the will can no more be set in motion than the balance can move when there is an equal weight in both scales — it is like the case of the well-known ass of Buridan between the two bundles of hay. The decision shows that in the judgment of the agent the preponderance was there; every decision ("Entschluss") is preceded by an antecedent balancing ("Schliessen"), *i. e.*, a trying, which is brought to an end by the decision ("Entschluss").

2. *Relation of Purpose to Action.* The satisfaction

which the person who wills promises himself from the act forms the purpose of his volition. The act itself is never the purpose, but only a means to the purpose. Whoever drinks wants indeed to drink, but he wants it only for the sake of the consequence which it has for him; in other words, in every act, it is never the act itself we want, but only its effect upon us. This means in other words: in our action we want only the purpose. It might be objected that my statement in the above example is true only when one drinks because he is thirsty. In that case, to be sure, he is not concerned about drinking but only about quenching his thirst. But the statement is not true, it will be said, when he drinks for the sake of enjoyment, for then drinking is a purpose, not a means. When the latter affords him no enjoyment, for example if the wine be spoiled or is tasteless, he leaves off drinking. The illusion that the act itself might be the purpose has its explanation only in the circumstance that the latter may be connected with it in a two-fold manner. The purpose may be directed either upon the effect which the action produces *during* the act of its undertaking, or upon the effect which it produces *after* the termination of the act. Whoever drinks water because he is thirsty, or takes a business trip, is concerned with that which lies beyond the drinking or beyond the trip. But if a person drinks wine for the sake of the enjoyment, or takes a pleasure trip, he intends that which lies in the action. That the purpose may extend equally to both needs not to be mentioned.

3. *The Law of Purpose.* But however the purpose may be combined with the act, and whatever the nature of the purpose may be, without a purpose action is unthinkable. *Acting, and acting with a purpose, are synonymous.* An act without a purpose is just as much an impossibility as is an effect without a cause.

We have now arrived at the point which we laid down above to be proved, *viz.*, the existence of the law of purpose. It deserves the name of a law only if its realization is absolutely necessary, and the possibility of a deviation or exception unthinkable; otherwise it is a rule, not a law. Has it really a claim to that name? So far as I see, this can be denied only on two grounds. The first is that we act not only with a purpose, but also for a reason, for example, because we are compelled, because duty or the law of the State demands it. The second is that there is also completely unconscious and purposeless action, for example, the action of the insane, or action which has become habitual to such a degree that we no longer think anything in the doing of it.

4. *Purpose in the Form of Reason.* The first objection *seems* to be unanswerable. For if it were groundless, we should have to make use of the particles, *in order to, that, in order that* ("ut"), which express purpose, in assigning the motive of an action, and not of the particle, *because* ("quia"), which expresses reason. The linguistic usage, however, of all nations employs both particles equally.

Let us try to see what the actual truth is about the particle "because." If one says, "I drink because I am thirsty," his statement is quite intelligible to everyone. If he were to say, "because it rained yesterday," no one would understand him. Why not? Because there is no visible connection between the reason assigned and the drinking. Such a connection, however, is established through the particle "because," only where the phrase "in order to" is concealed behind it. The *reason* in action is only another form of expressing *purpose;* where this is not the case there is no action, but an event. "He leaped from the tower because he wanted to commit suicide" — here the term "because" signifies "in order to." "He lost his life because he fell from the tower" — here the particle really does signify "because." In the former case there was an act, here an event.

But why do we use the term "because" instead of "in order to"? We do it preferably in those cases where the agent did not possess full freedom of resolution, but where there was some sort of a constraint, whether physical, legal, moral, or social. Where this is not the case, we either simply communicate the fact, if there can be no doubt about the purpose; or where more than one purpose may be thought of, we also indicate the purpose in order to assign a motive for the fact. A person is not apt to say that he has given his children Christmas presents in order to afford them joy, or that he has bought a house in order to live in it. But if a person has bought a house to tear it down, to let it, or to sell it again, he will, if he wants to assign a motive, add the purpose.

Let us see now whether the above statement will stand the test. Let us first take the case of *physical compulsion*. Where the robber deprives his victim violently of his watch and his purse, there is no action at all on the part of the victim, but only on the part of the robber. But the threats of the robber determine the person threatened to give up his watch and his purse. The latter acts, even though under the influence of (psychological) compulsion. Does he act here for a reason or with a purpose? Doubtless the latter. He gives his watch and his purse in order to save his life. His life is worth more to him than his watch, and he sacrifices the less valuable in order to retain the more valuable. He may possibly believe that submission were a disgrace to his honor and so undertake a fight with the robber. Here too it is a purpose which is held in view. That in this case there is an actual act of the will, and not merely the outward appearance of such, the Roman jurists with their keen understanding have rightly recognized,[1] and it is hard to comprehend that there still are those among our jurists of today for whom this truth has been discovered in vain. For if any one should have an open eye for this truth, it is the jurist, to whom, if he deserve this name, a practical understanding should tell where it would lead to if we should deny in case of coercion the presence of will. In that case every one would be unfree who yielded to external influences in making his decision. The jailer who, softened by the tears and entreaties of relatives, allows the criminal, condemned to death, to escape, is unfree. The cashier laying hands on the safe in order to furnish bread to his hungry children, is unfree. Where would be the limit? If the drowning person who promises his fortune for the rope that is thrown to him can repudiate his promise on the ground that it was forced from him only through the condition of constraint in which he found himself, why not also the traveller, who is forced on the journey to submit to higher prices than the native, or than he himself would have paid at home? Casuistry can easily put together an entire chain of such cases with gradually rising or diminishing constraint, and bid us tell at what particular link of the chain constraint ceases and freedom begins. The law may in many such cases deny the juristic validity of an action, as the Roman law has done where coercion exceeds the measure of the ordinary resisting power of man ("metus non vani hominis, sed qui merito et in hominem constantissimum cadat," 4.2. 6). But this is without significance for the question as to whether we are to assume an act of will, for this question does not at all come before the forum of the

[1] In two words *Paulus*, in Dig. 4. 2. 21, § 5, hits the nail on the head: "coactus *volui*" — I willed because I was compelled.

law,[2] it belongs to psychology. The law also declares immoral contracts void, but it has not yet occurred to any one to deny them for that reason the character of voluntary acts. The State also coerces us by its laws — are our actions then not free because we follow the laws?

The question leads us to another instance in which cause seems to exclude purpose. The debtor pays his debt. Why? Who would not be inclined to answer, because he owes it? But here, too, a disguised "in order to" lurks behind the term "because." The debtor pays in order to free himself from his debt. If this can be done in another way, or if the circumstances are such that the external act of payment is juristically inadequate to the purpose, he does not pay. He who sees the determining reason of the payment in the pressure of the debt, might just as well, in the case of the prisoner who throws off his chains, call the chains the reason of the act. If the prisoner had not felt the desire for freedom, he would not at all have taken advantage of the opportunity to get rid of his chains. The same is true of the debt. He who is not pressed by it does not pay, and he who pays does not do it because of the debt, *i.e.*, because of a fact in the past, but on account of the future, namely, a purpose, in order to remain an honest man, in order not to endanger his credit or reputation, in order not to expose himself to a legal action. If we are not always conscious of these special purposes in our payments, this is a matter to be referred to the chapter on purpose in habitual action (see below). Obedience to the laws is to most men

[2] In this relation is applicable what *Gaius* says, III, 194: "Neque enim lex facere potest, ut qui manifestus fur non sit, manifestus sit, non magis, quam qui omnino fur non sit, fur sit et qui adulter aut homicida non sit, adulter vel homicida sit. At illud sane lex facere potest, ut perinde aliquis poena teneatur atqui si furtum vel adulterium vel homicidium admisisset, quamvis nihil eorum admiserit."

a matter of habit, without any reflection. They get, as a rule, no clear notion of the why and the wherefore until they get into temptation to transgress the law, and then they discover after careful self-examination the *purpose* behind every "why."

The same is true of the performance of ethical duties as of legal obligations. When I give alms to a poor man, it is not because he is poor, but in order that I may help a person in need. The signification of the particle "because" is merely to call forth the term "in order that."

The above deduction, which aims essentially at the idea that every reason may be converted into a purpose, might be objected to on the ground that the contrary is just as possible. Instead of saying: I buy a house *in order to* live in it, I need only change my expression and say, *because* I have need of it to live in. The objection would be well founded if I had in mind the possibility of a different form of expression in language. My meaning, however, is not that every reason may be expressed in language as purpose, but that it really is a purpose. In the phrase, "have need of," the purpose concealed in language comes to view again, and so in all other cases.

The second objection stated above (p. 10) to the absolute necessity of a purpose, was the possibility of unconscious and purposeless action. The objection was answered even before it was raised by the proof given above (p. 6) in the case of the animal, that there is no need of consciousness in volition and hence not in purpose. The insane person also acts (so far as his doings may lay claim to this name), not without purpose. His actions are distinguished from those of the rational person, not by the want of purpose, but by the peculiarity and abnormity of the purpose; and I might assert that the last remnant of his human quality as compared with animality appears in this very fact that he sets himself purposes which go beyond the purely animal life, and of which the animal would therefore not at all be capable — in the caricature the man in him is still recognizable.

Even habitual action, in which we no longer do conscious thinking at all, is still purposeful action. Habitual action represents in the life of the individual the same phenomenon as morality and customary law do in the life of a people. In both, the individual as well as the people, a more or less clearly conscious or felt purpose originally called forth the action, but the frequent repetition of the same action from the same motives and with the same purpose, has bound together purpose and action to such a degree that the purpose has ceased to be a consciously perceptible element of the voluntary process.

My development of the law of purpose is now concluded, and as a result we carry away with us the principle, that volition and volition with a purpose are synonymous terms, and there are no purposeless actions. Although language makes use of this expression, it does not denote the absence of purpose in general, but of intelligent purpose. I name as an example the torture of animals. It is objectively purposeless, *i.e.*, not demanded by any purpose in life; subjectively, however, it is not purposeless, for the torturer has a purpose, namely, to feast on the torments of the animal. Opposed to purposeless action, which takes the wrong *purpose*, is inappropriate action, which selects the wrong *means*.

II. *External Stage in the Voluntary Process: the Law of Causality.* The internal stage of an action ends with the resolution, the act by which the will relieves itself of further balancing, and puts an end to the state of irresolution. Next in order comes the performance of the resolution — the deed. By means of the deed the will enters the kingdom of the external world, and comes under the rule of its laws. In place of the law of purpose, the will is now subject to the law of causality — not merely in the negative sense that it can do nothing against this law, but also in the positive sense that it needs the co-operation of the latter to realize itself. He who throws himself down from a tower in order to commit suicide transfers the carrying out of his resolution to the law of gravity. And if it is only a word that he has to speak, merely the word "yes," at the altar by which he enters into marriage, he counts upon the vibrations of the air carrying the sound to the ear of the other person. In short, every action, whatever its content, requires the co-operation of natural laws. Therefore the success of every action is conditioned by the right knowledge and application of these laws ("naturae non imperatur nisi parendo"). If the bullet falls to the ground before it reaches the goal, this fact proves that the person shooting took less powder than nature demanded to carry the bullet to the goal. In every action we have nature by our side as a servant, who carries out all our orders without refusal, provided these have been given in the right manner.

This external action of the will is apparently identical with other processes of nature. Whether the stone falls from the roof, or a person throws it down, whether the word or the thunder sets the sound waves of the air in motion, seems to be quite the same from the standpoint of nature. In reality, however, it is quite different. The falling of the stone and the rolling of the thunder are effected by nature itself, by means of antecedent causes. The throwing of the stone and the speaking of the word, on the contrary, are acts in which nature has no part, a force enters her dominion over which she has no power, — the human will. The human will denotes the limit of her empire; where its dominion begins, hers ceases. Cause and effect, which follow each other in the world of sense like waves in endless succession, break against every human will. Over the latter the law of causality has no power, but only the law of purpose. The will is free in relation to nature; it obeys not her law but its own. But whereas nature has no power over the will, the latter has power over nature; she must obey the will whenever it so desires — every human will is a source of causality for the external world. Thus the will may be designated as the end and beginning of the movement of causality in nature — will means *the maintenance of one's own causality over against the external world.*

This independence of the will on the law of causality, or its freedom in relation to the external world, does not mean, however, that the will can withdraw into itself as into a strong fortress, which will protect it against all assaults from without. The external world knows its hiding place and often knocks at the gate with rude hand, asking for admittance, — nature with hunger and thirst, man with threats and violence. But if the will itself does not open the gate, the besieger cannot come in, and if a strong will guards the fortress, then the whole world may storm it, without accomplishing anything. There are no terrors and tortures which man has not applied to bend the will; but the moral power of conviction, the heroism of duty, of personal love, of religious faith, of love of country, have defied them all — the witnesses in blood of the inflexible strength of the will are numbered in millions. To be sure the witnesses of the weakness of the human will are numbered in milliards, but they do not refute our statement, for we did not mean to say that external influences cannot affect the will *mediately* (by means of psychological pressure, p. 2), but that they have no *direct* (mechanical) power over it, or, which is the same thing, that the will is not under the law of causality, but under the law of purpose.

Therefore the will is the truly creative force in the world, *i.e.*, the force which produces out of itself. It does so primarily in God, and by way of imitation also in man.

The lever of this force is *purpose*. In purpose is concealed man, humanity, history. In the two particles "quia" and "ut" is reflected the opposition of two worlds: "quia" is nature, "ut" is man. In this "ut" he has the whole world in reversion, for "ut" signifies the possibility which exists of establishing a relation of purpose between the external world and the ego, and to this relation there are no bounds set either by the ego or the external world. With "ut" God gave man the whole earth, as the Mosaic story of creation (Genesis I, 26, 28) makes God himself announce it.

CHAPTER II

THE CONCEPT OF PURPOSE IN ANIMALS AS POINT OF DEPARTURE FOR THE PROBLEM OF PURPOSE IN MAN

§ 1. THE MECHANISM OF THE ANIMAL WILL. — § 2. SELF-RELATION IN PURPOSE. — § 3. REALIZATION OF THE CONDITIONS OF EXISTENCE THROUGH THE WILL.

In the preceding chapter we have arrived at the result: no volition without purpose; but we do not yet know what purpose is, for the concept with which we satisfied ourselves for the moment, *viz.*, the direction of the will toward a future state which it intends to realize, is inadequate and must be replaced by a more fitting one.

§ 1. *Mechanism of the Animal Will.* We can facilitate our search or make it more difficult according to the point at which we begin. We may look for purpose where it has attained its full development: in the market of life, in the varied and confusing tumult of human endeavor. Here, however, we should have but little prospect of mastering it so readily, for in Protean fashion it changes its form there unceasingly. But we may also look for it in a place where it appears in a very simple form, so that we cannot fail to recognize it, I mean in that stage where it first emerges in creation: in the low stage of animal life. Here we will try to take hold of it.

Let us therefore put the question, "What is purpose?" with regard to the animal. Let drinking be the process in the life of the animal, which shall give us an answer to our question. We wish to know the elements which are contained in this process.

The animal drinks, the animal breathes. Both processes are vital functions of the animal, indispensable for the preservation of its life. Yet they are essentially different. Breathing takes place involun arily, it takes place also in sleep; drinking is voluntary, and unthinkable in sleep. Nature has reserved to itself the effecting of the former, which takes place altogether according to the law of causality; the latter she has handed over to the animal, and it is accomplished by an act of will on the part of the animal, *i.e.*, it comes under the law of purpose. However imperious the incitement to drinking may be which nature calls forth in the animal by means of thirst, it may be overcome by a counter incitement that is greater; a well trained dog will not drink until his master permits.

But this means, in other words, that drinking takes place in the animal in the form of self-determination. *Self-determination*, accordingly, is the first element which we derive from this process.

Why does the animal drink? You may answer, because it feels thirsty. But we have shown above (p. 10) the incorrectness of this answer. If drinking is really an act of the will in the animal, it cannot, according to the law of purpose established in the last chapter, result from a "because," but from an "in order that."

Shall we then have to answer instead, that the animal drinks for the purpose of self-preservation? This answer is both true and false. It is true from the standpoint of the purpose of nature. In the plan of nature as she has actually formed the animal organism, drinking is an indispensable means for the preservation of life. But this purpose of nature is not at the same time that of the animal. For the purpose of nature the copulation of the animal is also indispensable, but when the animal undertakes the act it has not in view the purpose of preserving the species, it merely follows its impulse, it desires to put an end to the discomfort which it feels. In both cases, when it drinks and when it copulates, it serves the purpose of nature, but it serves it only by serving itself, *i.e.*, two purposes coincide, the general purpose of nature and the individual purpose of the animal (Chap. 3).[1]

The purpose of drinking from the standpoint of the animal is therefore not self-preservation; hence, it is incorrect to think of the instinct of self-preservation as a motive that influences the animal itself, one might with equal right speak of an instinct of the preservation of the species. The animal, which *knows* nothing of its self, but only *feels* it, cannot have the thought of preserving its self as something valuable. The motive which nature sets in motion in order practically to bring about self-preservation is a different one, *viz.*, the feeling of pleasure and of discomfort. The discomfort which the animal feels when it is about to perform an act according to the demand of nature is nature's summons to the undertaking of the act; the pleasure which the animal feels when it has done what it should is nature's reward. Pleasure from the standpoint of nature means, in every living being, that it is in harmony with nature; discomfort, pain, agony, means that the animal is in disagreement with nature.

§ 2. *Self-relation in Purpose.* The purpose which the animal pursues in drinking is therefore not that of

[1] To this opposition of general and individual purpose, or objective and subjective, I return in the second volume (first section n. 16), where I treat of the teleology of the ethical. I designate there the subjective determining reason, which is different from the purpose of the objectively ethical (the ethical norms), by the term motive. The criterion of ethical conduct is the agreement of the subjective determining reason with the objective purpose of the ethical.

self-preservation, but that of terminating the discomfort which it feels. The impulse to its purpose is given to the animal accordingly by its own inner state, it comes to it not from without but from within. We have thus found the second element to be derived from the process in question, *viz.*, the purposive reason residing in the subject himself, the inner necessity ("solicitation" ["Sollizitierung"] many call it) of setting this purpose to itself.

The animal turns to the water; it knows from experience that the water can quench its thirst. In directing its faculty of desire to the water it establishes a practical relation between itself and the water, and this is the third element in the voluntary process, *viz.*, purpose-relation or self-relation. This relation, however, expresses itself in the animal in the form of a feeling of its dependence upon the water, of its being conditioned by the latter. It is the same element which we shall find later (Chap. 12) in man as Interest.

Purpose-relation effects the transition from the cause of volition to *purpose*. To express ourselves concretely, the discomfort of the animal (the condition occasioning volition) calls forth in it the desire to remove the same (first beginning of purpose). It recognizes in the water the means for attaining this purpose (purpose-relation); the hitherto undetermined volition acquires thereby a determined direction. The expression of the inner state of the subject in this stage of the voluntary process is the feeling of dependence.

After the animal has taken the water to itself, the purpose is attained, *i.e.*, its relation of dependence upon the water has ceased. But it has not merely ceased, it has changed into its opposite. The water, which till now had the power over the animal and determined the latter, has now come into the power of the animal, and is determined by the latter, it has become the servant, *i.e.*, the means for the animal's purpose. The concept of means consists therefore in the purposive dependence of the subject upon it.

§ 3. *Realization of the Conditions of Existence through the Will.* Let us now combine in a formula the essential features resulting from our consideration of the voluntary process in the animal, adding thereto the element of the external deed discussed above (p. 16). Our formula will then be: (1) the removal of (2) the inner feeling of dependence (3) through one's own power (4) by means of acting upon the world of sensible matter. The third and fourth elements of this formula (self-determination and external deed) have no further interest for our purpose of comparing the voluntary process in man with that of the animal; the first and second, however, are extremely important. In these two seems to be contained the principle that the reason and the purpose of the will reside in the animal itself, the movement of the will starts from the animal and returns to it again; in other words, the animal does everything for its own sake.

Is this principle true?[2] It has been derived from a process where it fits, but there are in the life of the animal other processes to which it does not apply. The animal feeds and protects its young, and many even risk their lives for them. The animal therefore acts not only for itself but also for others. Our formula therefore which represents the animal as acting for itself, and thus realizing nature's purpose of its self-preservation, does not by any means exhaust the essence and the function of the animal will in the plan of creation. Nevertheless we shall for the present adhere to this

[2] I maintained it in the first edition.

formula in the consideration of the human will, which follows, in order to see how far it will be adequate for an understanding of human will.

In man we designate the exclusive tendency of the will to one's own self as egoism.[3] The following investigation is meant to show what part egoism plays in the human world, what it is able to accomplish, and where it fails. After we have learned the whole extent of its powers, we shall have an opportunity, in studying the theory of the ethical (Chap. 9), to form a conception of the phenomenon of acting for others, which seems quite inexplicable from the standpoint of egoism.

[3] The reason why the expression is not applied to the lower animals will be stated in connection with the discussion of the ethical element (II, n. 12).

CHAPTER III

EGOISM IN THE SERVICE OF ALTRUISTIC PURPOSES

§ 1. COINCIDENCE OF THE PURPOSES OF THE ETHICAL WORLD. — § 2. NATURE. — § 3. COMMERCE. — § 4. ORGANIZED AND NON-ORGANIZED PURPOSES. — § 5. THE STATE AND THE LAW.

§ 1. *Coincidence of Purposes.* How can the world exist under a regime of egoism, which desires nothing for the world, but everything for itself alone? The answer is, the world exists by taking egoism into its service, by paying it the reward which it desires. The world interests egoism in its purposes, and is then assured of its co-operation.

This is the simple device by means of which nature, as well as humanity and the individual man, gain control of egoism for their purposes.

§ 2. *Nature.* Nature wills the existence of humanity. For the realization of this will it is necessary that the individual man preserve the life which nature gave him, and hand it down to others after him. The self-preservation and propagation of the individual are therefore necessary conditions for the attainment of nature's purpose. How does she attain this purpose? By interesting egoism in it. This she accomplishes by offering the latter a premium in case it does what it should, *viz.*, pleasure, and by threatening punishment if it does not do what it should, or does what it should not, *viz.*, pain. If by exception the two fail of their effect, nature is powerless. If the sum of physical or moral pain which life holds out to a man is greater than the sum of pleasures or enjoyments which it offers him, life is no longer for him a good, but a burden, and as everyone throws away a good which has turned into a burden, so the egoist throws away his life — suicide is in such a case the inevitable conclusion to egoism. Whether there is not another standpoint upon which a man may place himself in such a case is a question which we shall have occasion later to investigate; as far as nature is concerned the man justifies himself before her simply by saying: the premium which you have offered me for preserving my life is too small in comparison with the pains and agonies which you have laid upon me, it is your own fault if I return to you a gift which has no longer any value for me, and which I am not in duty bound to retain; we two stand merely on terms of mutual give and take.

But nature has taken care that those cases in which the account tells against her shall be very rare and isolated; she has so regulated the average relation between pleasure and pain in life that the former regularly has the preponderance. If nature had not done this, or if it were possible that the relation should change so that pleasure should be less than pain, nature would have the same experience as an employer of labor who reduces the wage of his workmen beyond measure, and is left without hands; the world would die out in the second generation.

Nature also can win man for her purposes only by setting in motion the lever of his own interest within him. She herself has chosen this way; if she had not wanted it she would have had to make man different from what he is. As he is, she has no other means of making him serviceable to her purpose than by appealing to his own interest. This interest she has given him in the form of pleasure and pain. By means of pleasure and pain nature is able to guide us in the paths that we should follow, by means of these two she unites our interests to her purposes. He who does something for the sake of the pleasure, or forbears because of the evil consequences, acts for his own sake, but he carries out at the same time the orders of nature. If there is anything which confirms me in the belief of purpose in nature, it is the use she makes of pain and pleasure. Imagine them absent or interchanged, associate pain with nourishment and pleasure with death, and the human race would disappear in the first generation. If there were no purpose of nature at the basis of the feeling of pleasure, why has she attached it only to the voluntary and intentional functions of the human organism, why not also to the involuntary? Why does not the circulation of the blood and respiration cause man the same pleasure as the satisfaction of hunger and thirst? He who holds that matter forms itself without purpose or plan has no answer to this question. It would be incomprehensible why pleasure, left to pure chance, should have made its appearance at one point of animal life, and not also at another, why it should not have attached itself just as well to the coming and going of the teeth, the growth of the hair, as to nourishment and copulation. But nature economizes pleasure — she grants it only where she cannot do without it, only as a premium for something for which she has need of animal or man. In the same way does she employ pain. Pain, too, does nor appear without plan, but is just as much calculated by nature as pleasure. An interruption of the normal functions of our organs which does not threaten the continuance of life, as, for example, the interruption of seeing and hearing by the closing of the eyes and ears, is not connected with any pain, but the retention of the breath produces at once discomfort. Pain serves in creation as a warning of danger.

§ 3. *Commerce.* Nature herself has shown man the way he must follow in order to gain another for his purposes: it is that of *connecting one's own purpose with the other man's interest.* Upon this principle rests all our human life: the State, society, commerce, and intercourse. The co-operation of a number of people for the same purpose is brought about only by the converging of all the interests upon the same point. No one perhaps has in view the purpose as such, but every one has his own interest in view, a subjective purpose which is quite different from the general objective one, but the coincidence of their interests with the general purpose brings it about that every one in taking pains for himself at the same time becomes active for the general purpose.

Where such an interest is not present originally, it must be created artificially. Let us take the simplest case of an individual who needs the co-operation of another in order to attain his purpose. The extension of my factory requires the cession of a piece of land on the part of my neighbor. Every one knows that the only prospect I have of coming into possession of the land is by purchase. By means of my offer of purchase I create artificially in the person of my neighbor an interest in the realization of my purpose, provided I offer him an amount such that his interest in relinquishing his claim to the land is greater than in retaining it. If he demands more than my interest amounts to, then there is no agreement in our respective interests, and the purchase does not take place. Only when the price is high enough to make the sale of the land more advantageous for him than its ownership, and low enough to make the purchase similarly advantageous for me, is the point reached where the two interests are in equilibrium, and the consequence is the conclusion of the contract of sale. The fact of the conclusion of the contract contains the proof that according to the judgment of the two contracting parties the point of identity of the several interests has been reached. The judgment might have been erroneous, the subjective conviction or the objective state of the interest might change later, it nevertheless remains true that at the decisive moment the two parties were subjectively convinced of the coincidence of their interests, otherwise they would not have come to an agreement. Agreement of wills in a contract ("consensus") means agreement of the parties concerning the complete identity of their respective interests.

As it is not the objective interest but the subjective judgment of the presence of the latter that is decisive, all the means which are capable of calling forth this judgment are just as much calculated to bring about an agreement as those which aim at the objective establishment of an interest. Hence the value of business eloquence in the making of contracts — he who speaks well pays less or gets more than he who speaks poorly. The buyer lowers the value of the article, *i.e.*, he seeks to convince the seller that the latter has an interest in giving up the article for the price offered; the seller praises it up, *i.e.*, he seeks to convince the buyer that his interest requires he should take it for the price asked; each of the two parties endeavors to prove the existence of an interest for the other which he does not properly value, and experience shows that the eloquence of daily life is not without its reward.[1]

[1] Closely connected with this is the juristic concept of "dolus" in the making of contracts. The purpose of "dolus" consists in bringing about a conviction of interest; not, however, by means of business eloquence, which is fully tolerated by the law (Dig. 4. 3. 37: Quod venditor dicit ut commendet), but by the display of false facts calculated to bring about the decision of the other person, hence by aid of lies.

The circumstances just described form the basis of all intercourse, not merely commercial, of which I am thinking especially, but also social. The purposes of social life also can be attained only by moving the other side with a lever of interest, except that the interest here is of a different nature from that which is employed in commercial life. Here it is the interest of entertainment, distraction, pleasure, vanity, ambition, social consideration, etc. But without such interest, here also, no person can be moved, no society is thinkable, even in the social sense, unless the guests find their advantage therein. By lending their presence they show that such an interest — even though perhaps the negative one of a social duty — exists in their person.

§ 4. *Organized and Unorganized Purposes.* I have so far had in view the case of individual purposes for the realization of which one needs the co-operation of other persons; and it has been shown that egoism, or letting the other person's interest share in one's own purpose, is a sure means of securing this co-operation. The same holds true of the purposes of the group.

These are of two kinds: those for the pursuit of which there is an apparatus created by a confirmed and regulated union of members having a similar aim, *i.e.*, *organized purposes;* and those which have no such system, but depend entirely upon the free efforts of individuals, *i.e.*, *unorganized purposes.* As the latter have no particular interest for us, I confine myself to giving a few examples.

I. *Unorganized Purposes.* 1. *Science.* Science unites all its members into an invisible community. They all exert their powers for the purposes of science, and the total result of the co-operation of all its disciples consists in the preservation, extension, and increase of science. The form of this activity is on the whole completely free, for although there is an organization in science, *viz.*, the organization of *teaching* in the form of institutions of learning, and that of *research* in academies, it needs no saying that such organization is not meant to replace the spontaneous movement of science. Nor could it do so, even within the boundaries of a single State, not to speak of the higher unity of science, which embraces the whole world.

Such universal sovereignty comes to science of itself. How? By its own power and force of attraction. But this is only another way of expressing the interest which determines every individual to devote himself to it; we might in the same way designate the force of attraction of money as the lever of commerce. In both cases, in commerce as well as in science, it is the purely self-regarding interest of the individual that produces the activity, except that the interest in science is incomparably more complex; consisting as it does in the inner satisfaction which it yields, the feeling of duty, of ambition, of vanity; the living it offers; and after the failure of all other motives besides, that of mere habit; to be secure from the dread of *ennui*. He who does not in some way find his advantage in science, will not work for it, any more than will a laborer whom the pay does not attract. In a place where, and at a time when, the rewards of science offer no incentive, the latter will look in vain for disciples.

2. *Political Parties.* As a second example of unorganized co-operation for like purposes which interest brings about, I name the political party, whose guarantee for the co-operation of its members rests merely upon the existence of a union of interest and the intensity with which this is regarded by the several members.

II. *Organized Purposes.* Organized purposes are so extensively represented in our modern world as to make it scarcely necessary to cite examples. To the jurist I need only mention such forms of organization as associations, trade guilds, partnerships and corporations to remind him of the infinite wealth these purposes embody. Let me select from their number an example which will be especially instructive from our point of view — the formation of a joint-stock company for the purposes of building a railway. Of all the shareholders, no single one perhaps is interested in the objective purpose of the railway, *viz.*, the opening of a new route of communication. Government alone in granting the privilege has such purpose in view (for the government alone interest and purpose are one), and yet even there artificial stimulation may have been necessary ere the undertaking could be set in motion. Of the shareholders one has in view the permanent investment of his capital; the other buys shares only to sell them again immediately; the third, a wealthy proprietor of landed estate, or manufacturer, buys in the interest of facilitating the realization on his products or manufactures; the fourth because he owns shares in a rival company; the fifth, a municipality, because it is a condition of influencing the selection of the route of the proposed road which will be favorable to it. In short, everyone has his special interest in view, no one thinks of the purpose, and yet the same is perhaps furthered in this way more surely and quickly than if it had been pursued by the government directly.

§ 5. *The State and the Law.* The organization of purpose attains its highest point in the State, not in the Church. The latter, from the nature of its purpose, is, from the point of view of *organization*, far inferior to the State; namely, in reference to what is the purely external element of the machinery by which the purpose is realized.

The organization of the purpose of the State is characterized by the extended application of law. Does this mean that the lever of egoism or of interest in this sphere is inadequate or superfluous? Not at all, for the law itself, even though it carries necessity on its banner, must after all appeal to interest, *i.e.*, to *free* action in accordance with one's own choice; it attains its purpose in most cases only by bringing interest over to its side. The criminal is not concerned about the purpose of the State or of society, he is guided in his deed solely by his own purpose, by his lust, his greed or other viciousness, in short, his interest. But it is exactly this interest of his with regard to which the State calculates what means for protecting itself against him it has, by punishment. For the State says to him: follow your interest, but see to what side the balance inclines when I put punishment in one of the scales. If the instrument so often fails of its purpose despite the fact that the punishment is made severe enough, this is due in most instances to the fact that the threat of punishment is after all no more than a threat, the psychological effect of which in every case depends upon the criminal's calculation of the chances of his discovery.

But not every law carries punishment with it. The law which commands the debtor to pay his debt, or the possessor of an article belonging to another to return it to its owner, threatens no punishment. What determines these persons to do what they should? To be sure they have no penalties to apprehend, but other disadvantages await them (legal costs). If despite this prospect so many legal actions are preferred by those who know that they are in the wrong, the reason is the same as above in the case of the criminal, the hope that for lack of evidence the law will not succeed in reaching them.

But although in this case the law to a certain extent still finds in interest an ally, there is a point where the possibility of such alliance ceases, and where direct compulsion alone can accomplish the thing desired. Interest will not determine the accused or the condemned to betake himself to the inquest chamber or the house of correction, or to mount the scaffold — direct compulsion is necessary. Similarly must compulsion be employed when dealing with the condemned debtor who is not willing to pay the debt of his own accord (a levy upon his property).

The apparatus which the State employs for realizing its purposes is exactly the same as that which nature applies to the fulfilment of her objects. It is based upon a two-fold manner of compulsion, a direct or mechanical, and an indirect or psychological. The circulation of the blood, digestion, etc., nature effects in a mechanical way, she takes care of the matter herself; and similarly the State manages the infliction of penalties, the execution of civil sentences, and collection of taxes. Other functions and activities, on the other hand, both nature and State have left to the initiative of the individual himself. In fact those activities in general which are not essential to their purpose, they leave uncoerced — they form the individual's free (physical and legal) domain. Those activities, however, which are essential to their purpose, both have secured by the indirect compulsion of psychological pressure.

Unity of purposes and interests on both sides is the formula whereby nature, the State and the individual gain power over egoism. Upon it rests the wonderful phenomenon of the human world, that a force directed to the lowest purposes brings about the highest results. It wills itself alone, its poor evanescent ego with its paltry interests, and it calls into being works and structures compared with which the ego is like a grain of sand in comparison with the Alps. Nor is the counterpart to this wanting in nature. In the chalk cliffs of the Infusoria, we find a similar marvel; where an animal so tiny as to be imperceptible to the naked eye creates a whole mountain. The Infusorium is egoism — he knows and wills only himself, and yet creates a world!

CHAPTER IV

THE PROBLEM OF SELF-DENIAL

§ 1. THE IMPOSSIBILITY OF ACTION WITHOUT INTEREST. — § 2. INTEREST IN SELF-DENIAL. — § 3. CONTRAST OF SELF-REGARDING AND NON-SELF-REGARDING ACTION. — § 4. SELF-DENIAL AND UNSELFISHNESS. — § 5. PLAN OF INVESTIGATION: SYSTEM OF HUMAN PURPOSES. — § 6. THE DIFFERENT SPECIES OF SELF-ASSERTION.

§ 1. *Impossibility of Action without Interest.* The preceding development has shown that action for others is not beyond the capacity of egoism. But this was based on a very important assumption, namely, that in action for others there is involved action for oneself.

This assumption holds good for countless actions of our life, but who would venture to say that it is true for all? Does the mother desire anything for herself when she sacrifices herself for her child? Or the Sister of Mercy, who risks her own life at the bedside of one suffering from the plague, in order to save the life of another? He who knows no other motive of human action than egoism will find insoluble riddles confronting him in human life. His own admission, that he is not himself capable of such acts of self-denial, must force from the egoist the acknowledgment that there are other motives of human action in the world besides egoism.

Language designates the sentiment from which these actions proceed as *self-denial;* the agent in his action desires nothing for himself, but for another. The possibility of such action is not a contradiction of the law of will proved before to be one with the law of purpose.

Self-denial, too, contains something of future desire, but it is a desire that reaches out for others, not for oneself. Still, in the phrase "for others" lies the difficulty! He who has never reflected on this matter will not comprehend why we see in this the most difficult problem of the human will. What can be more simple? such a one will aver: experience shows us self-denial daily. The egoist alone, in whose narrow soul the thought of a sacrifice for others finds no room, can object thereto. Yet daily experience also shows us that a stone falls. But to see a phenomenon and to comprehend it are two different things; science required thousands of years before it understood the fall of a stone. To the psychologist a disinterested action, a deed done for others, contains no less a problem than does for the physicist the fall of a stone, nay, rather, the problem is even more difficult. To him this fact is not a whit less wonderful than if water were suddenly to rise up a mountain. A recent philosopher [1] declares that sympathy is a mysterious fact — but yet how far inferior still is sympathy, a mere feeling, in comparison with practical self-denial; an act done for others at the expense of ourselves!

Yet not all philosophers have looked at the matter in this way. To the mind of one of the greatest philosophers of all times, Kant, the matter presents not the least difficulty. His concept of duty contains the postulate of absolute self-renunciation; man must fulfil his

[1] *Schopenhauer*, "Die beiden Grundprobleme der Ethik" (2d ed. Leipzig, 1860), p. 209, 229. It is "something of which the mind cannot give an immediate account, and the causes of which cannot be found by experience." It is "the great mystery of ethics, its primitive phenomenon and the boundary stone beyond which metaphysical speculation alone can venture to proceed." This attempt of a metaphysical explanation he makes pp. 260–275. I think I shall be able in the sequel to come to the same result in a simpler way.

duty without any reference to himself, *i.e.*, not for the sake of a subjective purpose, or motive, but for the sake of an objective one (p. 21, note). Kant's *categorical imperative*, upon which his whole ethics is based,[2] makes the demand upon the will that it set itself in motion without any interest; its movement is to be caused solely "by a formal principle of volition in general, taking no account of any effect to be expected therefrom" (p. 20). The will is "deprived of all such incentives as may arise from obedience to any law, and there remains nothing therefore except conformity to the law of actions in general, which alone must serve the will as its principle" (p. 22). The *imperative* excludes "every admixture of interest as a motive" (p. 60).[3] The moral law must "not be sought for in the nature of man (subjective), nor in the circumstances of the world (objective). Not the least thing must be borrowed from the knowledge of man, *i.e.*, from anthropology" (pp. 5, 6).

The bare concept therefore is to drive the man to act and nought else. Kant in fact does expressly protest against all "moral sentimentality" (p. 211): "the feeling of pity, and soft-hearted sympathy . . . is even irksome to right thinking persons" (p. 257); "man's ethical standpoint is respect for the moral law" (p. 212). The sympathetic person must not take pity upon the poor by reason

[2] See his "Grundlegung der Metaphysik der Sitten" and "Die Kritik der praktischen Vernunft." The citations in the text refer to the edition of the complete works of *Kant* by *Rosenkranz*, vol. VIII.

[3] The same idea is expressed even more pointedly by *Fichte* in his "System der Sittenlehre." For a selection of passages from it see *Schopenhauer*, "Grundprobleme," p. 181, for ex. "I am only an instrument, a mere tool of the moral law, and not at all an end. . . . The body must be nourished and its health protected for no other purpose than that one may be an efficient tool for the advancement of the end of the reason."

of a stir of sympathy; the dutiful must not fulfil his duty for the sake of an inner peace; his sole motive must be simply a respect for the formal concept of conformity to law. All this in order that the categorical imperative may appear in all its glory as accomplishing everything.

If it only could![4] You might as well hope to move a loaded wagon from its place by means of a lecture on the theory of motion as the human will by means of the categorical imperative. If the will were a logical force, it would be obliged to yield to the power of a concept, but it is a very actual existence which you cannot budge by purely logical deductions, and one must have actual pressure to set it in motion. This real force which moves the human will is interest.

Let us examine whether the case is different in self-denial; whether the will, according to Kant's demands of it, can set itself in motion without interest.

I make sacrifices for my children, for my friends, for a common purpose, but not for the Shah of Persia, not for the building of a temple in India. My self-denying motive is not impelled blindly, finding every purpose equally acceptable; for it criticises and discriminates between purposes. They must all have some definite reference to me if I am to warm up to them. The Protestant does not contribute to the Pius Association, nor the Catholic to the Gustavus Adolphus Association; I would not do for a total stranger that which I do for a close friend.

This idea language brings out, as is well known, by such expressions as, to become interested, to take part in a thing. This is not yet the place more precisely to determine wherein such becoming interested consists,

[4] *Kant* himself has so little confidence in it that he admits (p. 97) that, "The human reason is altogether unable to explain how pure reason without other motives . . . can be practical for itself."

and on what it is based. This can be done only at the end of our investigation (Chap. XII); for the present let us accept the idea thus expressed by language, which we may suppose as understood by all.

Being interested in a purpose, or briefly, interest, is an indispensable condition for every action — action without interest is just as much an absurdity as action without a purpose; it is a psychological impossibility.[5] The interest may be never so slight, but some interest there must always be, if the purpose is to have power over the will.

§ 2. *Interest in Self-denial.* If interest links the purpose to the agent, and if conduct is not thinkable without interest, then self-denial must come under the category of action *for oneself.* In this case, apparently, it would no longer be what it assumes to be, and those moralists would be right who maintain that the motive of every human action is egoistical.

Yet such conclusion were too hasty. Self-denial also presupposes interest, but it is of quite a different kind from that of egoism, and language is quite right when it makes a sharp distinction between the two, and opposes "unselfish, disinterested, self-denying" sentiment to "egoistical, self-interested, self-seeking."

§ 3. *Self-regarding and Non-self-regarding Acts.* In the case of egoistic action for another, the effect which the agent produces by his action for the other is such an indifferent matter to him that he would prefer to attain his purpose without it; it is merely a means for his purpose. In self-denying action, on the contrary, the effect *is* the purpose which the agent has in view; if it cannot, or can no longer, be attained, he forbears the act. No one will leap into the flame or into the water in order to

[5] *Schopenhauer*, "Grundprobleme," p. 165, "An act of will without interest is will without motive, hence an effect without a cause."

save a person who is already burned or drowned — he may take his own life in despair on account of their death, but this we do not call self-denial, for it is not action for another. That which does refer to the agent himself in an act of self-denial is solely the feeling of having helped another in need, of having caused him joy; it is the reflex of another's fortune, another's joy shining back in one's own soul. He is content with a minimum part thereof, and in this very height of unpretentiousness lies the beauty, the sublimity of self-denial. It is no inward satisfaction with his own good deed for which the agent strives; such may arise from merely a cold conformity to duty without any warmth of heart. His satisfaction arises with the success of his deed in the person of another, with complete banishment of thoughts of self; it is just joy in another's good fortune.

Reward there is after all, the egoist will exclaim; and hence egoism again! Let such egoist try to discover for himself what satisfaction *he* will get! The reward which the hero obtains who, in order not to let the battleship or the fort fall into the hands of the enemy, is blown up with it, would very likely offer small temptations for him: a few minutes or seconds of inner satisfaction purchased at the expense of one's whole life — in truth a dearly bought pleasure, the egoist would think! The price and the gain are here in the same proportion as if a man, in order to warm himself, were to feed the fire in the stove with banknotes. But the egoist calculates too well for this; self-denial is a luxury for him which he cannot afford, and in his heart of hearts he regards it as folly when he meets it in others, or tries to adjust it to his own standpoint by introducing ignoble and egoistic motives. That such motives as vanity, expectation of gratitude, appreciation, etc., *may* enter is just as incontrovertible as it is undoubted that they *need* not.

§ 4. *Self-denial and Unselfishness.* Language knows beside *self-denial* also the term *unselfishness.* Whether the two expressions are wholly synonymous, or whether they contain some slight difference in shade of meaning, I shall leave undecided. Nevertheless, I want to call attention to the fact that in reality such a difference exists between them and that it would be well to use these expressions accordingly. We can distinguish two kinds of unselfish action: those from which egoism is completely separated; those which afford the self neither advantage nor yet disadvantage, and those which exact from it a sacrifice, some denial of its individuality. For the latter the proper expression would be, self-denial; for the former, unselfishness. Let me remind the jurist of the form in which the contrast is expressed in law. Of non-self-regarding acts (acts of liberality) the following, according to the conception of Roman law, come under the category of the *unselfish, viz.*, gratuitous contracts (gratuitous delivery of a thing for use, "commodatum," "precarium"; gratuitous keeping of an object belonging to another, "depositum"; gratuitous care of another's business, "mandatum," "negotiorum gestio"); under the category of self-denial comes gift ("donatio" with its subdivisions, "pollicitatio" and "votum"). Gift is the juristic form of proprietary altruism, sacrifice of property rights.[6]

[6] In testamentary dispositions there is no self-denial *psychologically. Juristically* they are distinguished from gift by the fact that while both of them signify an increase in the property of the beneficiary, the latter alone involves a diminution of the property of the giver. We may apply to them what the Roman jurist says of one of their subdivisions, "mortis causa donatio": "(magis) se habere vult, quam eum, cui donat," Dig. 39. 6. 1. pr. In donation "inter vivos" the case is reversed: "magis eum quam se habere vult." Psychologically this expresses the truest distinction between the two species of gift.

It results from the foregoing that there is no action for another in which the doer does not at the same time desire something for himself. In egoistic action, that which the agent expends is, according to the standard of human estimation, in equilibrium with that which he acquires; in unselfish action there is a lack of proportion between the two, which may be so great as to make the act, from the point of view of egoism alone, inexplainable. This circumstance compels us to recognize that egoism is not the only motive of human will, that there is yet another motive besides. By naming it, whether self-denial, unselfishness, power of sacrifice, love, devotion, sympathy, goodwill, etc., we have not yet *comprehended* it, and as long as this is so, our question concerning the meaning of purpose in human will still waits for its solution in vain.

§ 5. *System of Human Purposes.* Whereto shall we look for information? Within the depths of our own heart? There is only *one* way, I believe, which will lead us safely to the goal, and that is to look for the solution of the problem in the real world. There must be gathered what these two motives really signify to the world, and what part they take in the movement which we know as human life. When we know what they signify there, we shall have comprehended them.

Human life in *this* sense, *i.e.*, the life of the species man, not of the individual, is the sum total of all human purposes. Hence the task to which we apply ourselves in the sequel takes the form of a *system of human purposes.* I say system, which means: I want to place these purposes not merely side by side in a superficial fashion, but I want further to make the attempt to discover the inner connection which subsists between them. I want to show how one joins itself to the other, the higher to the lower; and not only this, but at the same time produces the other out of itself and as a consequence of its own nature, by a stringent necessity.

I will impose upon myself only one limitation. The work is addressed solely to the jurist, and this has determined me in subordinate matters hitherto to introduce a number of things which have interest for him alone. The like consideration furthermore guides me in setting the external limitations and giving the inner form to the system of human purposes. It is intended not for the psychologist, but for the jurist. Best perhaps I can express what is now floating before my mind when I say that this is to be a theory of *practical* life, sketched not for its own sake, but solely with the purpose of finally answering by its help the question, Wherein does purpose in the human will consist?

§ 6. *The Different Species of Self-assertion.* The purposes of human existence in general fall into two large groups; those of the individual, and those of the community (society). This contrast we place as the basis of our presentation. This does not mean that in the manner of those holding the theory of the Law of Nature we wish to isolate the individual, separating him artificially from his historical connection with society, and then to present over against such merely theoretical being-for-himself of an individual, his actual life in society and being-for-others. We consider the individual in the position which he actually holds in the real world, but in picturing his life to ourselves we separate from it those purposes by which he holds in view solely himself, and not society, *i.e.*, any other person or a higher purpose. These purposes, which proceed from the agent and return to him, we designate, as is well known, by the term *egoistic*. Of these only *three* deserve emphasis for the purposes of our investigation. I comprehend them all under the name of *individual* or *egoistic self-assertion*, and discriminate between them as *physical*, *economical*, and *juristic* self-assertion in accordance with the three directions in which the purpose of self-assertion is realized by them. I avoid the expression *self-preservation*, because usage refers it exclusively to the first class.

The purposes of the second class, of life in society, which embrace also the problems of the State, I designate as *social*. The interest which these have for us lies not in themselves, but solely in the manner in which society and the State induce the individual to co-operate in their realization. The activity of the individual for these purposes of society is fittingly designated by the term social. The motives which prompt such social action by the individual are of two kinds. The first is egoism, with which we are already familiar. The means by which the State and society gain the mastery over this motive are reward and punishment. The second motive is that which contains in itself the solution of our problem of self-denial. It is the feeling on the part of the agent of the ethical destiny of his being, *i.e.*, his feeling that existence was given to him not merely for himself, but also for the service of humanity. In so far as the individual obeys this feeling and thereby realizes the higher purpose of his being, he asserts himself. I shall therefore designate all action coming under this point of view, as *ethical self-assertion of the individual*.

In the following chapter (V) we first turn our attention to *egoistical* self-assertion. The transition to social action will be brought about by a consideration of *Society* (Chapter VI). We shall then take up the *two egoistic levers* of social movement, *Reward* (Chapter VII) and *Compulsion* (Chapter VIII). The first belongs more particularly to *business*, the second to the *State*, and the form it takes constitutes *Law*.

Then follows *ethical* self-assertion, which presupposes

the existence of morality, and consists in viewing morality as the ideal condition of life of the subject — complete identity of the subjective purpose with the objective. To understand this subjective attitude to objective morality, it is necessary to analyze the latter, and show how the subjective conception and realization of it agree with that theory of the will which has been developed in the foregoing discussion, and which knows only action of the subject for his own sake. To this problem will the ninth chapter be devoted, — *The Theory of Morality.*

After having determined the concept of ethical self-assertion, we shall take up the two forms in which it shows its activity; the *Feeling of Duty* (Chapter X), and *Love* (Chapter XI).

Having in this way reached the aim we set ourselves above (p. 43), *viz.*, to gain an idea of all the purposes for which man can become active, we shall thereupon at the end of the first part again take up the question of the will which was interrupted above, in order to bring it to a conclusion by analyzing the two concepts, *Interest* and *Purpose* (Chapter XII). The application to *law* of the results gained in this whole first part of the book will be left for the second part.

CHAPTER V

THE PURPOSES OF EGOISTICAL SELF-ASSERTION

§ 1. PHYSICAL SELF-ASSERTION. — § 2. ECONOMIC SELF-ASSERTION. — § 3. PROBLEM OF PROPERTY. — JURISTIC FORM. — § 4. CONCEPT OF RIGHT AND DUTY. — § 5. WORK. — § 6. EXCHANGE. — § 7. CONTRACT — THE LAW. — § 8. JURISTIC SELF-ASSERTION.

§ 1. *Physical Self-assertion.* Egoistical self-assertion has for its basis the thought of egoism, *viz.*, that the individual exists for himself, and has the purpose of his existence in and of himself. Of the three directions or kinds of self-assertion which we distinguished above (p. 44) the *physical* contains the lowest form in which purpose first appears in man; it takes us back to the stage in which we first meet it in animate creation, — the stage of the animal.

The first object of will is pointed out by nature to man quite as much as to the animal, — it is the preservation of his own existence.

Discomfort and pain teach him what is repugnant to his nature, and urge him to its avoidance; comfort and pleasure and the feeling of health furnish him with the assurance that he responds rightly to the conditions of his life. But the manner in which man meets this problem assumes with the aid of the human intellect a form different from that in the animal. I mean not only knowledge and culture of the finer conditions of life, but the retrospect which is granted him into the past and the prospect into the future. The physical self-preservation of the animal is with few exceptions calculated for the next moment — once their hunger is stilled most animals care not for the coming day — and the animal's sense of this is, as a rule, guided only by his own experience. In man, on the contrary, it is based not only on his own experience, but also on that of others, and not merely on the experience of a few individuals, but on that of the whole race; and in his case it is not exhausted, as in the case of the animal, in a concern for the present, but in the present it is already thoughtful of the future, especially in the way of securing his future means of subsistence. This concern for the coming day, called forth by the bitter experiences which humanity underwent at a time when nature no longer offered unsought everything in sufficient abundance, is the original practical motive of *property*, *i.e.*, of efforts directed not merely to the acquisition of the momentary need, but to the acquisition and storing up of means of support not needed until the future.

§ 2. *Economic Self-assertion.* This brings us to the second class of self-assertion, the *economic*. Of this we find in the animal world only slight, isolated tendencies. In accordance with its conceptual and historical origin, it is connected with the purpose of physical self-preservation, and in the same measure as the purposes of life are advanced it also acquires higher aims and problems. Securing the future life becomes securing one's future life in comfort; procuring the necessary and indispensable prepares the ground for what is dispensable but agreeable; the satisfaction of the palate is followed by that of the eye, the soul, and the intellect. Everywhere property takes its stand by the side of culture, ever informing of new wants and purposes, as the ready servant who procures the necessary means for everything. There is no purpose, no problem belonging to individual, society, or State, which would not be furthered in the most effective way by property; there is no virtue, no vice, either of the individual or of the nation, which could not find expression in property. The manner in which a man uses his property is one of the surest standards for judgment of his character and degree of culture — in the purposes for which he spends his money he reveals himself. The means by which he earns it lie only too often not in his power, but the manner in which he spends it, as a rule, is a matter of his free resolve. No fine phrase, nor sublime speech, nor outpouring of feelings in words and tears has such convincing force as the dollar which issues from the pocket; a man's cashbook occasionally tells more concerning his true character than his diaries.

§ 3. *Property.* This promotion of property from its original function of securing the physical existence to this its all-embracing mission of civilization and ethical significance would not at all have been thinkable if it had not continually retained, exclusively or predominatingly, its original function of prolonging physical existence for a considerable fraction of the population. The power of property in the hands of him who has more than is needed for securing his physical necessities or even a comfortable living depends upon others having less; who, being obliged to work in order to supply what they lack, must seek in continuous employment the means of subsistence.

§ 4. *Right and Duty.* The purpose of life's maintenance produced property — for without property there is no secure future for existence; the purpose of the two conjoined leads to Law — without law there is no securing life and property.

The form by which law, or right regarded objectively, affords its protection to both interests is, as is well known, by right in the subjective sense. To have a right means, there is something *for us*, and the power of the State recognizes this and protects us. Now that which exists for us may be,

(1) *Ourselves*. The legal expression for this is the right of *personality*. The ethical ground of this concept is the principle, man is an *end in himself*. The slave is not for himself, but for his master; he is not an end in himself, but exclusively a means for the purposes of others.

That which exists for us may be,

(2) *A Thing*. The expression which designates this relation of the thing to our purposes is the right to the thing, or ownership in the widest sense.[1]

That which exists for us may be,

(3) *A Person*. He may exist for us either as a personality in its entirety,—with reciprocal relations (the legal relations of the *family*), or in reference to particular acts (right "in personam").

That which exists for us may be finally,

(4) *The State*. The legal expression for this subserviency of the State to our purposes is *citizenship*.

Opposed to Right is *Duty*. The former tells us that there is something for us, the latter that *we are for another*, but not in the sense that the entire purpose of our being is exhausted in it—in that case the relation would be slavery—but in the sense that this subserviency forms only a particular incident in the purpose of our being.

Accordingly, the position of a person in the world depends upon three conditions, the two from which he derives his right, and a third upon which the world bases his duty to it:

[1] This is the sense in which the philosophers and political economists generally use the expression. It then embraces property in the sense of the jurist, possession, rights in things belonging to another, and the right of succession.

(1) *I exist for myself;*
(2) *The world exists for me;*
(3) *I exist for the world.*

Upon these three concise statements rests the entire scheme of law, and not merely that of law, but the whole ethical world-order, our private life, life in the family, business relations, society, the State, international intercourse, the mutual relations of peoples, those living contemporaneously as well as those long departed (Chapter VI).

§ 5. *Work.* Let us return now to property, the occasion of this interpolation. The concept of property contains from the legal point of view the principle that nature exists for the sake of man.[2] But nature does not *present* her gifts, human labor and exertion are needed to win them from her. If a person's own force is not sufficient, he must have the help of another, which in the long run he can succeed in obtaining only in return for equivalent service by remuneration. The law recognizes the necessity for this extension of property to the labor-power of others by granting its protection to contracts directed thereto. So in addition to the *thing*, *work* too is introduced into the system of proprietary right.

Work keeps step with property, which has gradually raised itself to ever higher purposes from the most pressing, but at the same time the lowest, purpose, of care for physical life. Work, too, begins with the most primitive form, *viz.*, the cultivation of the field and the procuring of that which belongs to physical existence; and it advances with the progress of culture to ever higher achievements and problems.

§ 6. *Exchange.* The laborer takes money in exchange for labor power, the other party takes labor power in

[2] The saying of the Roman jurist: "Omnes fructus rerum natura hominum gratia comparavit," Dig. 22. 1. 28 § 1.

exchange for money; both have more need of that which they receive than of that which they have. Reward is the means by which the surplus labor power which otherwise would remain idle or but imperfectly realized, is directed where it can find the best use in the interests of the laborer as well as of society. The same process is repeated in the case of things, when one thing is exchanged for another (contract of exchange in the legal sense) or for money (purchase). On both sides the process is based upon giving that for which one has either no use at all, or not the right use, in return for that which one may better use. Exchange as a form of commerce has therefore as its object the directing of every thing where it will do that for which it was intended. No thing permanently remains where it misses its economic destiny to serve man; every thing finds its right owner; the anvil finds the blacksmith, the fiddle the musician, the worn coat the poor man, a Raphael the picture gallery.[3] Exchange may be defined as *economic providence*, which brings everything (object, labor power) to the place of its destination.

In speaking of the destination of an object, we have transferred a concept which according to our own doctrine is limited to persons, *viz.*, the *concept of purpose*, to a thing. Is not this inconsistent? The answer is ready at hand.

Our use of this expression indicates that the person sees in the thing an available means for his purposes; he therefore puts into the thing as its destination, its

[3] To be sure, within the sphere where it can seek at all. A Raphael can seek its owner in the whole world, the anvil can look for him only among the blacksmiths of the neighborhood. The same is true of labor power. The ordinary factory laborer cannot look so far as the trained technician, the seamstress not so far as the opera singer, the village schoolmaster not so far as the scholar.

purpose, that which he himself wants to make of it. He substitutes his subjective intention for the objective availability of the thing. The economic purpose of things is nothing else than the availability for human purposes which the things exhibit from the standpoint of the subjective economical consciousness of purpose, whether this availability was present in them from the beginning, or was attached to them by human labor. Usefulness, availability, fitness, destination, purpose of a thing, and whatever other turn of expression one may use, depend upon the operation proved above (p. 22), in connection with the investigation of purpose in the animal; *viz.*, reference to the self, or reference to purpose. These terms, however, are based not upon a concrete judgment, but upon an abstract, *i.e.*, upon a universal and generalizing judgment which is independent of the particular case. The purposes of *things* are nothing more than the purposes of the *person* by whom they are applied — a gradual extension of the horizon of purpose in *man* signifies historically the same fact for *things*.

As the contract of exchange brings to each party that which possesses for his purposes a relatively higher availability than is present in what he has himself, it may be designated from the standpoint of the person as an act of *economical self-assertion*. And the business of exchange, which contains the regulated order of these single acts, may accordingly be designated as the system or organization of the economic self-assertion of man. The more the business of exchange develops, the wider the domain over which it extends, and the greater the quantity of goods, skill, etc., which it can realize, the more feasible does the economic self-assertion of the individual thereby become, and the more is it facilitated and furthered. A new article of trade furnishes thousands of people bread; the opening or shortening of a road, the perfection of means of transportation, a cheap freight rate,—in short, everything which serves to make it possible for things and labor power to seek employment in wider circles, spreads life and well-being in regions where otherwise want and misery would rule; a man who would formerly have starved becomes a well-to-do man.

§ 7. *Contract.* The form of exchange is the *contract.* The jurist defines contract as the union of two minds in an expression of the will ("consensus"). From the *juristic* standpoint this is perfectly correct, for the element of the contract which creates obligation lies in the will. But for us who have in view through this whole investigation, not the will as such, but the determining element of it, *viz.*, purpose, the matter assumes another, and as I believe, more instructive form. When purpose determines the will, then the circumstance that the wills of two or more persons meet in the same point ("convenire," "conventio," "überein-[zusammen-] kommen," "Übereinkunft") contains the proof that their purposes or interests meet in this point, that the intended action in the future, whether of one party or of both, is calculated to attain this coincident purpose. With the delivery of the object sold in return for the price agreed upon, both the buyer and the seller attain what they intend. Through the contract they give evidence of the coincidence of their interests (p. 28), not, however, as an object of theoretical knowledge, as is the case when they are aware that their several speculations are dependent upon the occurrence of one and the same combination of circumstances, but as the practical aim of a co-operation for which they both unite.

But the interests which now meet may subsequently diverge. In such a case the one party, whose interest has in the meantime become different, will wish that the performance of the contract remain unfulfilled, whereas the other party, whose interest has remained the same as at the conclusion of the contract, is just as eager to have it carried out as before. Now if the law did not step in with its constraining power, the law which upholds a contract once concluded, the former understanding would not come to execution on account of the want of present agreement of interests. The recognition of the binding force of contracts, considered from the standpoint of the idea of purpose, means nothing else than securing the original purpose against the prejudicial influence of a later shifting of interest, or of a change of judgment touching his interest on the part of one of the parties. In other words, it means that *a change of interest has juristically no force.*[4] He who insists on carrying out the original contract proves thereby that his interest has remained the same; the opponent, who refuses, proves that his interest, or his judgment thereof has changed; if the same thing happens in the case of the other party, the contract is not carried out, the interest determines the execution as well as the conclusion of all contracts.

The *person*, *i.e.*, the purpose of his physical self-preservation, produced *property*, *i.e.*, the purpose of the regulated and assured realization of that purpose. The two together lead again to law, *i.e.*, to the securing of

[4] Where the law exceptionally allows the extinction of a contract by reason of a later change of circumstances (for example, notice given of the cessation of agency or of the dissolution of partnership; demand of the restitution of a deposit before the expiration of the time agreed upon; extinction of a contract for hire; Cod. 4. 65. 3.), it makes the maintenance of the contract for the party entitled to the above privilege a pure question of interest. Not the former condition of the interest, but the present, is made to be the determining factor for him — a form of the contractual relation which dogmatic jurisprudence names, it is true, in special cases, but does not take into consideration in the general theory of contract.

their mutual purposes, otherwise solely dependent upon the physical strength of the subject, by the power of the State. The concept of law includes therefore two elements; a system of *purposes*, and a system of their *realization*. As person and property presuppose the law, so does the law presuppose the *State*. The (practical) motive (impulse) of purpose, not the (logical) motive (implication) of the concept, presses with necessity from one to the other.

§ 8. *Juristic Self-assertion.* The law embraces the person on all sides of his existence. The assertion of this position granted him by the law we call the *juristic self-assertion* of the person. This self-assertion extends to everything that the person is and has — life, honor, property, family, legal status. In reference to property, it seems to comprehend the whole of economic self-assertion. But the two do not coincide. The purpose of economic self-assertion, *i.e.*, of acquisition of property, is not the *right* to the thing, but the thing itself; otherwise no thief would steal, for theft does not give him the right, but the thing. The *value* of the thing, therefore, controls the purely economic purpose of the acquisition of the thing, and the means put forth in attaining this purpose. This applies to the thief also — he will not expose himself to the same danger for a farthing as he will for a thousand dollars, any more than a laborer puts forth the same exertion for one dollar as he does for ten. The same point of view holds for the economic preservation of the thing — one does not stake ten dollars to procure a dollar — for the maintenance of the *thing*, therefore, the economic value of it is quite decisive. But for the maintenance of the *right* to the thing it is not sufficient; it *may* be, but it *need* not. The struggle for the right to a thing may, for example, take a form in which it involves a person's sympathies.

In this case it is no longer a question of the *thing*, but of the *person*, of his self-assertion as a holder of rights; the economic element is just as immaterial in the matter as in a violation of the law which is aimed directly at the person, *viz.*, an insult to one's honor. The detailed treatment which I have devoted to juristic self-assertion in my "Kampf ums Recht" (7th ed. Vienna 1883),[5] excuses me from a lengthy exposition in this place.

We have now reached a conclusion. The consideration of the three directions of egoistical self-assertion has brought before us not merely the main purposes of individual existence turned toward itself, but it has shown us at the same time in these individual purposes the practical impulse of the concept of purpose. It presses ahead irresistibly from one concept to another, from person to property, from these two to law, from law to the State — there is no halt in this evolution of the idea of purpose until the highest point is reached.

We learn from this that when we placed ourselves in the foregoing upon the standpoint of the individual, this did not mean, as we have already remarked above (p. 44), that we considered it thinkable to isolate the individual by himself — in that case we should have had no right to place the two dicta, "The world exists for me," and "I exist for the world," beside the first, "I exist for myself." What we did was to indicate the attitude which the individual takes toward the world,

[5] I am innocent of the frequent caricature of my opinion as if I held that one should carry on a lawsuit for every disputed right, for I have stated with sufficient clearness the conditions under which alone I regard it a duty to assert one's right. But of what use is all objective clearness when there is subjective darkness in the mind of the reader; when people presume to judge a work, who cannot read, who do not know when they get to the end of the book what they read at the beginning, and impute absurdities to the author for which they should hold their own careless reading and thinking responsible?

when he considers the latter solely from the point of view of *his own* interest. How this interest in making the world serviceable to it at the same time makes itself thereby serviceable to the word, will be shown in the sequel.

CHAPTER VI

LIFE THROUGH AND FOR OTHERS, OR SOCIETY [1]

§ 1. SOCIAL FORM OF HUMAN EXISTENCE. — § 2. THE UNINTENTIONAL INFLUENCE OF ONE UPON THE OTHER. — § 3. CONTINUATION OF INFLUENCE BEYOND LIFE. — § 4. THE RIGHT OF INHERITANCE IN ITS RELATIONS TO THE HISTORY OF CULTURE. — § 5. SOCIAL LIFE AS A LAW OF CULTURE. — § 6. CONCEPT OF SOCIETY. — § 7. DIFFERENCE BETWEEN SOCIETY AND STATE. — § 8. PROBLEM OF SOCIAL MOVEMENT.

§ 1. *Social Form of Human Existence.* Our whole culture, our whole history, rests upon the realization of

[1] In the first edition, this chapter began with a discussion, of the complete untenableness of which I have become convinced in the meantime, and I can scarcely comprehend now how I could have allowed myself to be carried away by it. It had as its subject the statement that an animal uses other animals only as means for its purposes but does nothing for their purposes, and that herein lies one of the main differences between animal and human life. The proofs to the contrary, for example the care of animals for their own young and even for the helpless young of other animals, are so clearly evident that there is no need at all of mentioning them. Even the idea of society, *i.e.*, of a regulated living together in common for the purpose of pursuing common ends, already appears in the animal world, and even the idea of an experience of the species, which I formerly denied. Animals, too, at least some, learn one from the other, communicate their experiences to each other and apply them. For animals also history is a teacher. My former opinion that the animal has its experience only for itself, and that with every animal the same game begins over again to end with it again — without result for the species — may apply to some classes of animals; in the general way in which I maintained it, it is simply untrue.

individual human existence for the purposes of the whole. There is no human life which exists merely for itself, every one is at the same time for the sake of the world; every man in his place, however limited it may be, is a collaborator in the cultural purposes of humanity. Even if he is the most insignificant laborer, he takes part in one of its problems, and even if he does not work at all, he helps along in his every day speech, for by doing this he helps to keep alive the words of the language handed down to him, and transmits them in his turn. I cannot imagine a human life so poor, so devoid of content, so narrow, so miserable, that it is not of some good to some other life; even such a life has not seldom borne the world the richest fruit. The cradle of the greatest man often stood in the poorest hut; the woman who gave him life, who nursed and cherished him, has done humanity a greater service than many a king upon his throne. What can a child be to a child? Often more than parents and teachers combined. In playing with his companions the child often learns more things and more useful for practical life than out of the "teachings of wisdom and virtue." In the ball of his comrade which he tries to appropriate he makes the first practical acquaintance with the concept of property, and the deterring impression of the bad habits of his comrades preaches to him his first morals.

§ 2. *Unintentional Influence of One upon the Other.* No one exists *for* himself alone, any more than *through* himself alone, but every one exists at the same time *for* others, just as he exists *through* others, it matters not whether consciously or unconsciously. Just as a body radiates the heat which it has received from outside, so man radiates the intellectual or ethical fluid which he has breathed in the cultural atmosphere of society. Life is a constant "inspiration," literally, breathing in: receiving from the environment and giving back to it; this holds true equally of physical and spiritual life. Every relation of our human life contains such an element of "being for each other," most conditions of life contain a reciprocal or mutual element. The wife exists for the husband, but at the same time the husband for the wife; the parents for the children, but the children also for the parents. Servants and masters, master workmen and journeymen, the laborer and the employer of labor, friend and friend, the community and its members, the State and its citizens, society and the individual, nation and nation, and the particular nation and humanity — who can name a relation in which the one does not exist for the other and the latter, at the same time, also for the former? And quite apart from these permanent relations which make up the standing forms of our life, what does not man sometimes effect by his mere existence, by his example, by his personality, — nay, by a word uttered at random! In short, wherever I turn my glance, everywhere is the same phenomenon; no one exists for himself alone; every one exists at the same time for others, let us say, for the *world*. Only his world, as well as the measure and the duration of the influences which he exerts upon it, is different from that of others. The world of the one ends with his house, his children, friends, clients; the world of the other extends also to a people, to humanity.

§ 3. *Continuation of Influence beyond Life.* The fruit of one sort of existence for society is summed up in the amount of potatoes, coats, books, etc., which man has furnished it, whereas the fruit of the other kind, the activity of a great poet, artist, technician, scholar, statesman, may assume dimensions which mock at all attempts to measure them. For, whereas with the ordinary man death quickly destroys the traces of his existence, the existence of a historical personality unfolds itself only after his death to its full power and majesty, to ever wider and richer effects. Hundreds and thousands of years after the ashes of the great man have long been scattered to all the winds, his spirit unceasingly works for the cultural purpose of humanity. Homer, Plato, Aristotle, Dante, Shakespeare — and who can name all the heroes of the spirit, of art and of science of whom the same is true? — all of them are still standing today in our midst, with living, unimpaired, nay, increased power — they have sung, taught, thought for all humanity.

§ 4. *The Right of Inheritance in its Relations to the History of Culture.* With this continued influence of an existence after it has itself come to an end, we touch upon that form of existence for others upon which the security and the progress of our whole culture depends. The juristic expression for this is *Inheritance.* The idea of the right of inheritance is, the fruit of my existence does not end with me, it benefits another. The jurist knows the right of inheritance only so far as it has *property* as its object, inheritance signifies for him only the economic output of the person, the sum of his life expressed in dollars and cents; but for the historian and the philosopher the concept of inheritance extends as far as human culture. The institution of succession is the condition of all human progress; succession, in the history of culture, signifies that the successor works with the experiences, with the spiritual and ethical capital of his predecessor — history is the right of inheritance in the life of humanity.

§ 5. *Social Life as a Law of Culture.* There are therefore two directions in which "being for others" is carried out; the influence of our existence upon our contemporaries, and upon posterity.

The measure of the two gives us the standard for the value of human existence, of individuals as well as of nations. The concept of value is, as is well known, relative; it means the fitness of a thing for some purpose. When applied to human life the question of value is, what benefit to society accrues from it? And society measures the value of human life accordingly. A criterion of the value which society puts upon our life is its knowledge of our *name*. Our name *in* the world extends as a rule so far, and lasts so long, as our significance *for* the world. When the names of historical personalities continue, it is merely the proof that the personalities themselves are still alive for the world. For the continuance of a historical name, *i.e.*, fame, is not merely a tribute of gratitude which the world pays, but denotes continued activity by its bearer. How great intrinsically any one was is quite an indifferent matter to the world; it asks for and retains only what he was to it. In the book of history *name* signifies, as once "nomen" did in the Roman housekeeping book, the entry of a debt. The genius who did nothing for the world will have not the smallest item to his credit in the account book of history. That the familiarity of a name is a sign of the significance of its bearer, holds also for the small, and even the smallest orbit of civic life. Here, too, the knowledge of a name extends only so far as society feels the significance for itself of its bearer. The name of the ordinary laborer in a factory is known only to his comrades and neighbors, that of the owner of the factory is known in the entire district.

A celebrated name is therefore an evidence not merely that some one has *become* something to society or the world, but also that the latter is *aware* of it — it is the acknowledgment of its debt through the issue of a bill of exchange for acceptance. The debt exists also without the bill of exchange, but the bill of exchange gives the claim the character of incontestable validity. Its value depends not upon the honor and recognition with which it is redeemed, but upon the assurance which it gives its bearer that his life has not been lost to humanity. Society does not inquire whether he was actuated by ambition, fame, or the desire to serve humanity, it looks solely to the result, not to the motive. And she is right in doing so. For in crowning those also who were merely interested in the reward which she pays them, she makes sure of them, too, for her purposes; only he can grudge them the wreath which she hands them, who envies the laborer his pay — the laurels never fall into any one's lap without trouble and merit; they require as a rule the stake of one's whole life.

All that I have said so far of individuals holds true also of nations. These also exist not merely for themselves, but for the other nations, for humanity.[2] And with them also the influence which they exert upon others is not limited to their lifetime only, but extends to the most distant times according to their importance and their services. The art, the literature and the philosophy of the Greeks, the law of the Romans, forms to this very day an inexhaustible source of our education. The models of the beautiful, the noble, and the mighty which they have left us in their works of art, their thoughts, their deeds, and their men, still bear new fruit every day on receptive soil. All the civilized nations of the world helped to form our culture of today; if we could dissolve our present culture into its elements, and follow them up to their first beginnings, we should get a list of nations, and upon it names of peoples such as no documentary history records.

[2] For a further development of this idea, see my "Geist des römischen Rechts," Vol. I, p. 6 ff. (4th ed.).

To confirm this conviction in us, the status of modern investigation is sufficient, which is only in its first beginnings of a cultural history of humanity; the future has large gains in store in this field. For our purpose, what we already know, and what takes place daily before our eyes, is quite sufficient to warrant the statement that the principle, "Every one exists for the world," is just as true of nations as it is of individuals. In it we possess the highest *cultural law of history*. The cultural development of humanity is determined according to the measure in which it realizes the above principle, and we need only infer from what history *does* to what she *desires*, and prove the *manner in which* she attains what she desires, in order to find in the above principle the highest law of all historical development, and in the realization of the same the destiny of the human race. Until this purpose is realized for the whole human race, history has not attained what she desires.

The discussion hitherto was directed to proving the actual validity of this law; we now add the question of the *form* of its *realization*.

A glance at the world around us teaches us that this form is of two kinds, free and forced. Whether I shall use my head or my hands in the service of society or not is a matter of my free choice: he who is liable to serve in the army is not asked if he will serve. Whether and what I shall give away of my property to others during life, or bequeath by will after death, depends upon myself; the payment of taxes and assessments to the community and the State, and the leaving of the entailed portion to my children, does not. The sphere of force coincides with that of the law and the State; not, to be sure, in the sense that the State compels all the purposes which it pursues — art and science cannot be forced; and yet the cultivation of both is counted among the purposes of the modern State — but in the sense that the State raises the means at least which it needs for these purposes by force.

Of voluntary actions which we undertake for others, some take place from the standpoint of society without any, or at least without much, interest; others again are quite indispensable to society. Whether a person does anything for his friends, or whether he contributes to some collection, is indifferent to society; but that the farmer shall deliver grain, the baker bread, the butcher meat, that society shall always find hands and brains ready for all needs and purposes, artisans and day-laborers, merchants, clergymen, teachers, officials — this is of the greatest interest to her, and all the arrangements and habits of life depend upon this presupposition. What assurance has she that this presupposition will always be realized? This is the question of the organization of society. It will be necessary, in order to answer it, that we first come to an understanding about the concept of society, which we have already used before but have not yet explained. When this has been done we shall consider the levers which society sets in motion in order to carry out her task.

§ 6. *Concept of Society*. The concept of society is, as is well known, modern; it came to us, so far as I know, from France. The fact that everybody uses the expression, whereas there is anything but general agreement concerning the conceptual meaning thereof, shows that there must be at its basis an idea which our present thinking must absolutely have, but which has yet to make its way into complete conceptual clearness. As the matter has not yet taken its final shape, and everyone has his own view of the expression, I also may be permitted to do the same and bring it into connection with my point of view concerning action for others.

A society ("societas") in the juristic sense is a union of a number of persons who have combined for the prosecution of a common purpose, and hence every one of them in acting for the purpose of the society at the same time acts for himself. A society in this juristic sense presupposes a *contract*, directed to its construction and regulation — the social contract. But actual society, namely, co-operation for common purposes, is found repeatedly in life without this form. Our whole life, our whole intercourse, is in this actual non-juristic sense a society, *i.e.*, a working together for common purposes, in which everyone in acting for others acts also for himself, and in acting for himself acts also for others. Upon this mutual advancement of purposes rests, according to my opinion, the concept of society. Society must accordingly be defined as the actual organization of life *for* and *by* others and (since the individual is what he is, only through others) as the indispensable form of life *for oneself;* society is therefore really the form of human life in general. Human life and social life are synonymous. The ancient Greek philosophers recognized this perfectly; there is no saying which expresses the social nature of man more concisely and more fittingly, than the designation of man as ζῷον πολιτικόν, *i.e.*, *social* being. The city (πόλις), *i.e.*, city life with its constant mutual contact and friction, is the condition and the author of all culture, not merely political, which the Greek word at first suggests, but of each and every kind — intellectual, ethical, economic, artistic — in short, of the entire development of the nation. It is society that makes the above statement true (p. 51), "The world exists for me." But this statement can be true only by means of the antithesis: "You exist for the world," the world has the same claim upon you that you have upon the world. The measure in which the first of the two statements is realized in the life of the individual is synonymous with what is called social position, *viz.*, wealth, honor, power, influence; the measure in which the individual makes the second principle true in his life determines the worth of his existence for society, or in its widest extent, for humanity. If it were not that daily experience and history contradict such an opinion in the most glaring fashion, one might believe that the motive and the problem of every social order must be to bring about an equilibrium between the two principles. It may be that the distant future carries in its bosom what the development of things hitherto has not been able to mature.

§ 7. *Society and State.* It follows from this that the concept of society partly coincides with that of the State. But only in part; namely, in so far as the social purpose requires the intervention of external force for its realization. But it needs it only in small part. Commerce and trade, agriculture, manufacture and industry, art and science, the usage of the home and the customs of life, organize themselves essentially. Only occasionally does the State interfere with its law, so far as it is absolutely necessary to secure against violation the order which these interests have evolved independently.

§ 8. *Problem of Social Movement.* But geographically, too, the sphere of society does not coincide with that of the State; the latter ends with the boundary posts of its territory, the former extends over the whole earth. For the statement, "Everyone exists for the other," is true for all humanity, and the march of social movement is constantly advancing to realize this geographically in ever widening extent; to gain new peoples constantly for co-operation; to make all lands, peoples, forces, goods, useful for its purposes. To make the work of the individual, whether it be of the hand or the brain, as useful as possible for others, and thereby indirectly also for himself, to effectuate every force in the service of humanity — this is the problem which every civilized people must solve, and with regard to which it must regulate all its economies. Production alone and manufacture, in short, work alone is not enough. Work alone constitutes only one part of the problem, the second part consists in finding the man who will best realize the purpose of the labor product — if possible to look for him over the entire surface of the earth. Most of the inventions of modern times move in the two directions indicated by these two problems. Some have work itself as their object, its simplification, perfection, facilitation; the others have as their object the utilization of labor by means of commerce; the forwarding and transmission of what the first has produced for society — (whether it be the fruit of his field, the work of his hands, the product of his mind or his imagination) — to the proper purchaser, *i.e.*, to the one for whom the product has the greatest value and who will therefore pay the highest price for it. If we picture to ourselves all the means which the inventive mind of modern civilized peoples has created for the purpose just named, since the time of the Middle Ages, we have a right to maintain that nowadays no power which has the capacity to be useful to humanity is lost for its service; every one finds its proper application in our times. The press carries the thought which deserves it from one point of the earth to the other without delay; every great truth, every important discovery, every useful invention, becomes in a very short time the common property of the whole civilized world, and commerce transmits to all the inhabitants of the earth what she produces at any point, in the Tropics as well as in the Frigid Zone. This makes it possible for the commonest laborer to do good thousands of miles away. Quinine, which the Peruvian laborer gathers, causes the recovery of hundreds in our midst — the merit of the preservation of a life upon which depended the future of a whole nation, or a new era of art and science, is due in the last instance perhaps to the whale-hunter who procured blubber for the consumptive. The laborer in Nuremberg and Solingen works for the Persian; the Chinese and the Japanese work for us; thousands of years hence the negro in the interior of Africa will need us as much as we need him, for the man of science, who opens the interior of Africa, is followed very soon after by the merchant and the missionary, who establish enduring connections.

This therefore is society, namely, the realization of the truth of the principle, "Every one exists for the world, and the world exists for every one."[3] Having determined this concept we now return to the question which we asked above, *viz.*, What guaranty does society possess that every one will do his share in realizing the principle upon which her whole existence depends, namely that the individual exists for society? The following discussion will give the answer to this question.

[3] For the objections to this concept from the juristic standpoint, see Vol. II, no. 18. That the concept of society cannot be avoided even in legal theory will be shown in Chapter VIII, where I reduce the interests protected by the law to the subject of their purpose (individual, State, society). But the most valuable application of this concept will be found in the second volume in connection with the analysis of the concept of the ethical, and in the third volume in connection with the realization of the ethical (social system of coercion). [The third volume was never written. — *Translator.*]

CHAPTER VII

SOCIAL MECHANICS, OR THE LEVERS OF SOCIAL MOVEMENT

1. THE EGOISTIC LEVERS—REWARD. — SOCIAL MECHANICS. — COMMERCE. — § 1. INSUFFICIENCY OF BENEVOLENCE FOR PURPOSES OF COMMERCE (LIBERAL CONTRACTS AND BUSINESS CONTRACTS; ROMAN SYSTEM OF COMMERCE IN EARLIER AND LATER TIMES). — ALL COMMERCE FOUNDED UPON EGOISM. — § 2. THE PRINCIPLE OF COMPENSATION. — THE TWO PRINCIPAL FORMS OF COMMERCE — THE FIRST: EXCHANGE (DIFFERENCE OF PURPOSE ON BOTH SIDES) REAL PERFORMANCE AND CONSIDERATION. — § 3. PROGRESS FROM REAL CONSIDERATION TO REWARD. — § 4. PROMOTION OF REWARD TO EQUIVALENT. — § 5. ORGANIZATION OF WORK IN THE FORM OF A VOCATION. — § 6. CREDIT. — § 7. IDEAL REWARD AND ITS COMBINATION WITH ECONOMIC REWARD (SALARY, HONORARIUM; MAINTENANCE IN CONTRAST WITH REWARD). — THE SECOND PRINCIPAL FORM OF COMMERCE: PARTNERSHIP (IDENTITY OF PURPOSE ON BOTH SIDES). — § 8. ASSOCIATION; PUBLIC SPIRIT; DEFECTS OF THE SECOND PRINCIPAL FORM. — THE BRIGHT SIDES OF COMMERCE; ETHICAL SIGNIFICANCE OF COMMERCE.

Social Mechanics. This is the picture of society as life presents it daily to our eyes. Thousands of rollers, wheels, knives, as in a mighty machine, move restlessly, some in one direction, some in another, apparently quite independent of one another as if they existed only for themselves, nay in apparent conflict, as if they wanted mutually to annihilate each other — and yet all work ultimately together harmoniously for *one purpose*, and one *single* plan rules the whole. What compels the elementary forces of society to order and co-operation; who indicates to these their paths and their motions? The machine *must* obey the master; the laws of mechanics enable him to *compel* it. But the force which moves the wheelwork of human society is the human *will;* that force which, in contrast to the forces of nature, boasts of its freedom; but the will in that function is the will of thousands and millions of individuals, the struggle of interests, of the opposition of efforts, egoism, self-will, insubordination, inertia, weakness, wickedness, crime. There is no greater miracle in the world than the disciplining and training of the human will, whose actual realization in its widest scope we embrace in the word society.

The sum of impulses and powers which accomplish this work I call *social mechanics*. If these were wanting, who would assure society that the moving forces upon which she counts might not one day refuse their service, or take a direction hostile to her purposes; that the will might not one day at this or that point rise in revolt against the role assigned to it and bring the whole wheelwork to a standstill? Temporarily such standing still actually takes place at individual points; yea, even shocks which seem to threaten the entire existence of society, just as in the human body. But the vital force of society is so strong and indestructible that she always quickly overcomes these disturbances; in place of anarchy, order as a rule at once steps in again — every social disturbance is only a search for a new and better order — anarchy is only a means, never an end, something temporary, never anything permanent; the struggle of anarchy with society always ends with the victory of the latter.

But this means nothing else than that society possesses a compelling power over the human will; that there is a *social* mechanics to compel the human will just as there is a *physical* mechanics to force the machine. This social mechanics is identical with the principle of leverage, by means of which society sets the will in motion for her purposes, or in short, *the principle of the levers of social motion.*

There are *four* such levers. Two of them have egoism as their motive and presupposition; I call them the *lower* or *egoistic* social levers; they are *reward* and *coercion.* Without them social life cannot be thought, no *commerce* without reward, and no *law* or *State* without coercion; they represent therefore the elementary assumptions of society; the necessary impulses which can nowhere be wanting and are not wanting, though their condition be ever so rudimentary or degenerate. Opposed to these are two other impulses which have not egoism as their motive and presupposition, but on the contrary the denial thereof; and as they come into play not in the lower region of purely individual purposes, but in the higher region of universal purposes, I call them the *higher;* or, since, as I shall show later (Chapter IX), society is the source of morality, the *moral* or *ethical* levers of social motion. They are the *Feeling of Duty* and of *Love;* the former the prose, the latter the poetry of the moral spirit.

Of the two egoistical levers, coercion holds psychologically the lowest position. Reward stands psychologically a degree higher, for reward appeals to the freedom of the subject; it expects its success exclusively from the free resolve of the latter. In an indolent person reward fails of its purpose, whereas coercion proves its power over him also, for it either excludes freedom entirely, where it operates mechanically, or limits it, where it operates psychologically (p. 17). Coercion addresses itself to man at his lowest; it denotes the lowest point of social mechanics; which should therefore in reality begin with coercion. But the point of view from which we have to consider those two levers is not the manner of their psychological influence upon the individual, but their practical significance for society; and if we apply the point of view of social formation to the two motives as a standard of measurement, there can be no doubt that the social organization of reward — commerce, is to be designated as lower in comparison with that of coercion — the *law* and the *State*. Hence an exposition which has made it its task to rise from the lower to the higher in its consideration of society, must begin with reward, as we are going to do.

Commerce. Commerce is the organization of the assured satisfaction of human wants, which is based upon the lever of reward. This definition of the concept embraces three elements; the *need* as the *motive*, the *reward* as the *means*, and the *organization* in mutual relation of these elements as the *form* of commerce. This organization is, as perhaps no other element of the human world besides, the natural product of the free development of purpose; it is the dialectics (not the logical dialectics of the concept, in which I do not believe), but the practically compelling dialectics of the purpose, which has produced out of the two factors of need and reward in gradual progress the immeasurable wealth of formation which we know by the one word, commerce. And there is no more grateful task for the thinker interested in the practical than to follow the ways of purpose in this matter, and to observe how from the simplest germ there have gradually arisen by a compelling necessity ever higher forms and structures. I will make the attempt to bring to view this dialectics of purpose, by seeking out for all the phenomena of commerce those points in which they proceed from it as branches and twigs from the trunk, from the foot to the crown; at the same time pointing out the determining reasons which produced the particular impulses. The economic side of the question is entirely foreign to my investigation, which is purely social in its nature, and I am only interested in the *arrangements* upon which the security of the satisfaction of human want is based for society, but not in the *laws* according to which the methods of commerce are regulated. The contents of the problem before us will naturally assume a juristic form, which is inseparable therefrom.

The decisive position which I shall constantly keep in mind in the following consideration is that of the *security* of the satisfaction of human wants; it shall be the standard by which I intend to measure all the phenomena of commerce.

Want is the band with which nature draws man into society, the means by which she realizes the two principles of all morality and culture, "Everybody exists for the world," and "the world exists for everybody" (p. 51). Dependent as he is upon his fellowmen through his need, and the more so as his need grows, man would be the most unhappy being in the world if the satisfaction of his need depended upon accident, and he could not count with all security upon the co-operation and assistance of his fellowmen. In that case the animal would be an object of envy to him, for the animal is so made by nature that when it comes into possession of the powers destined for it by nature it needs no such support. The realization of the mutual relations of man for her purpose; the elimination of accident; the establishment of the security of the satisfaction of human need as a basal form of social existence; the regulated, assured and substantial system of actions and methods which minister to this satisfaction, keeping equal step with the need — that is *commerce.*

The simplest form of satisfaction of a need, in man as in the animal, lies in his own power. But whereas in the animal, need and power coincide, this is not the case in man. It is this very disproportion between the two, this insufficiency of his own power, which is the cause by means of which nature forces him to be a man; namely, to look for man, and in association with others to attain those purposes to which he is alone unequal. In his necessity she refers him to the outside world and his fellows. Let us now investigate how he makes use of others for the satisfaction of his wants.

§ 1. *Insufficiency of Benevolence for Purposes of Commerce. Benevolence* and *beneficence* mean *wishing* and *achieving* the *good* of another for this one's own sake, without benefit to oneself. These, therefore, presuppose the sentiment of disinterestedness and unselfishness. That a system of commerce cannot be built upon such a motive is so evident that we need waste no words in discussing it. Nevertheless, this does not exclude the possibility that benevolence may after all exercise a certain function, even though a limited one, in the purposes of commerce. Let us see whether this is the case and to what degree.

Liberal Contracts and Business Contracts. If the question were how far the *juristic* scope of benevolence extends, we should have to answer, quite as far as that of egoism, for the scheme of *gratuitous contracts* (*liberal, by courtesy, friendly*) contains a completely fitting counterpart to that of *onerous contracts* (*egoistic, business contracts*). One may add·

	For Pay	*Gratuitously*
(1) An Object	Purchase, Exchange	Donation
(2) The Use		
(*a*) of an Object	Usufructuary Lease; Ordinary Lease	Loan for Use ("commodatum"), "Precarium"
(*b*) of Capital	Loan on Interest	Loan without Interest.
(3) Performance of Service	"Operæ Illiberales"; Contract for Services	Gratuitous Agency ("mandatum"), Deposit, Voluntary Assumption of Another Person's Business ("negotiorum gestio")

So every business contract has a gratuitous contract corresponding to it, and thereby we might suppose the significance of benevolence in commerce is sufficiently proven. But from the fact that benevolence also makes its *appearance* in the domain of law, and has a share in its forms, it does not yet follow by any means that it has any *practical significance* worth mentioning in the purpose of commerce.

The contracts of the first column are based on no other presupposition than money — whoever pays the most money gets the object, whether he is personally known or not. Those of the second column, on the contrary, presuppose certain personal relations or individual qualities, which give rise to a given act of benevolence [1] — we do not give presents to, nor do we lend to or serve every Tom, Dick and Harry, but we consider the person; and this influence of the personal element

[1] Especially the relation of friendship. This element is frequently emphasized by the Roman jurists in those contracts: "affectio," Dig. 3. 5. 3 § 9, 39. 5. 5; "officium amicitiæ," 42. 5. 23; "officium atque amicitia" 17. 1. 1 § 4. The service which is rendered is a favor, a benefit: "beneficium," 13. 6. 17 § 3.; "liberalitas," 43. 26. 1 § 1, 2 § 2; "liberalitas et munificentia," 39. 5. 1. pr.

makes benevolence useless for the purpose of commerce, which requires complete indifference of person. (See below.)

The initiative which, in all acts that one requires from another for the satisfaction of one's needs, proceeds from the one who feels the need is called in business contracts, *offer;* in gratuitous contracts, *request;* in charitable contracts, *begging;* and these three expressions indicate sufficiently the difference of the personal relation existing in the three cases. *Offer* requires no special individual relations or qualities beyond being aware, in general, of the inclination of the other party to make the contract; but the two other forms of initiative do. A *request* for which the justification is sought by the person who makes it in his poverty and need of help is called begging, and the gift which is granted out of such regard, from sympathy and pity, is called *alms* (*juristically* not distinguished from a gift "donatio"; the difference being simply *social* in its nature); and in the contemptuous judgment which language passes in this term lies expressed the uselessness of *this* sort of help for the purposes of commerce. Assistance which must be bought at the price of personal humiliation is the exact opposite of that which, as we shall see later, constitutes the highest and most beautiful aim of commerce, *viz.*, the independence of the person. This humiliation, it is true, is absent in *request*, but request has a very narrow scope in reference to the thing as well as the person. One cannot request *everything* — there is a point where requesting passes over into begging; — and one cannot request *everybody*, unless the content of the request is limited to such favors as every one can grant without the least exertion; such as courtesies of the street, a request for information, etc. These alone are free from all personal discrimination, and in so far stand on the *same* line as acts of business intercourse — every one has the right to require them and feel assured that they will be granted. But on the other hand the measure of these favors in respect to content is so very scanty that they vanish into nothingness in comparison with the wealth of purposes which commerce has to satisfy. Beyond this minimum of application, request as well as the prospect of its fulfilment is connected with individual personal relations (friendship, neighborhood, acquaintance, relation of dependence, etc.), and even when these are present, its scope is still so narrowly limited that the impossibility of basing any purpose of commerce upon self-denial (favor) instead of upon egoism (reward) is quite evident.

Roman System of Commerce in Earlier and Later Times. I feel the necessity of making an objection to my own view here. The theory advanced is taken from the consideration of our present life, and is true of the stage of development of commerce in the present. In these days money has driven favor entirely from the field as a mode of commerce. But it was not always so. There were times when one got services for nothing which now one can get only for money, and that too not only in cases where there were special personal relations, but in general and with no limitation. At this time, then, favor actually constituted a *factor in the life of commerce*, and exercised a *function* therein. Similar conditions are still to be found among uncivilized peoples of today in reference to hospitality; and in regions thinly populated they are found among civilized peoples also.

The objection is perfectly correct, and I do not regard it as a waste of time to dwell on it a little longer, for it is well calculated to give a better insight into the life of commerce. Yet it will be advisable for our purpose to make clear to ourselves in a concrete historical form what was the condition of society to which this refers us. I know of no better choice — quite apart from the special relation which the object has for the jurist — than to present clearly the contrast between paid and gratuitous services as it practically existed in ancient Rome for centuries; and then to join to this an account of the transformation which the thing underwent in later times. The historical excursus which I shall thus insert will not be fruitless for the purposes of our investigation.

The difference between paid and gratuitous work in ancient Rome coincides with that between manual and intellectual; the former service alone extended the hand for pay, the latter did not. The conception which lay at the basis was not peculiarly Roman, it is found among all peoples and individuals upon a low level of culture, for it is nothing else than the practical application to work of the c udely material mode of viewing things peculiar to them. Bodily work is a fact subject to the observation of the senses by all persons. The subject who is engaged in it feels it, the third person sees it, and not merely the work alone as an act but also its product, its permanent result. This alone gives it a claim to reward; in the first place because this is the only work that costs sweat, and in the second place because, according to crude ideas, this is the only work that produces things.[2] Intellectual labor, on the other hand, is not

[2] This idea is expressed in language, where the expression "Geschäft" [business] (from "schaffen" — to create) is restricted to work in the above sense. Work ("Arbeit") is connected with production ("Schaffen") and property ("Vermögen"). In Latin: "opera," pains, effort; "opus," the product of work, "opes" and "c-opia," wealth, property. In German: "Arbeit" ("arb," "arbi," "arpi." Slavic, with letters interchanged, "rab-ota," Polish "robota") work, and "Erbe" ("arbja," "arbi," "arpi," "erbi," "das Erbe" — inheritance — property, wealth), "Dienen" (serving) and "Verdienen" (earning).

regarded as work, for it seems not to fatigue the person, and apparently costs him no trouble.[3] What right can a man have to ask of us remuneration, whose whole work for us consists in thinking; whose service to us is merely speaking? Words cost no money — he who gives them is paid with the same coin in return; he is thanked with words, and with "divine reward," but he gets nothing.

This conception which is still prevalent today among common people was originally found everywhere. In ancient Rome it was regarded so seriously that it was considered ignoble to receive pay for intellectual work. Manual labor alone was paid for and therefore also despised. For reward ("merces") puts it on a level with merchandise ("merx"); it is offered for sale ("locatur" from "locus")[4] and bought like the other; the paymaster takes the man along ("conducere" to lead along with) just as he takes the thing which he buys ("emere" — to take). The expressions for hire are exactly the same for free men, slaves, and things. The servant or laborer is considered as a temporary contract slave; his service involves social degradation ("minis-

[3] The idea is expressed in Latin: "otium," leisure, "negotium" (*Festus*: quod non sit otium), business. He who has an occupation, a business, has no leisure, and *vice versa*.

[4] "Locare," to display, to exhibit, is synonymous with public offer for sale. In *Plautus* the cooks stand exhibited in the market place and are taken home by the one who arranges for a meal. Conversely in the case of "opus," "locatio," *i. e.* public bidding, takes place on the part of the one who is looking for one to take it upon himself ("conducit"). The German language borrows the expression "Gewerbe" (trade, industrial pursuit) from the same idea of exhibiting, seeking for work. "Gewerbe" means "werben," *i. e.*, "suing for" work and pay. It is not applied to intellectual professions, any more than the terminology of hire ("merces," "locatio," "conductio") was extended to them in Rome.

terium"),[5] for it binds him to do things to which a free man should not give himself, and which he should leave to the slave ("operae illiberales").[6] The service of the free man is no "ministerium," but a "munus '; it consists not in corporeal but in intellectual activity, and it is rendered not for the sake of reward, but out of goodwill ("gratia'), without pay ("gratis"). It is a favor ("munificentia," "beneficium," "officium"), which is worthy of a free man ("l ber," "liberalitas"), and which produces in the other party the obligation to thank only, ("gratiae," "gratum facere" — "gratificatio"). The "munus" may be returned on the other side ("remunerari"), under certain circumstances even in money, but this compensation is no "merces," but "honor," "honorarium," an honorary present which does not prejudice the honor of either party.[7] If special skill or knowledge is necessary for the service, then it is an excellence, a virtue (ἀρετή — "ars"), which is an ornament for the free man ("ars liberalis"); the trouble he takes to learn it is not "labor," "opera," but "studium," an object of striving ("studere") for its own sake.

Such is the ancient Roman conception. Agriculture,

[5] From "minus," "minuere," "ministerium," *i. e.*, lowering, in contrast with "magis" "magister," "magistratus," *i. e.*, elevation above the social level of the ordinary citizen.

[6] *Cicero*, "De Officiis" I, 42. "*Merces* auctoramentum servitutis." The earnings, he says here, of all hired labor are dirty: "quorum operae, non quorum artes *emuntur*," Similarly the gain of all manual laborers ("in sordida arte versantur"), of peddlers and even of shop keepers. Hence "*sordidum*" — the pay of the broker, Dig. 50. 14. 3.

[7] Dig. 11. 6. 1. pr " . . . ad remunerandum dari et inde honorarium appe lari." Its value lies not in the money but in the intention — a conception which appears again in the "honorare" of bequests ("legatum"): The respectable person is more concerned about the recognition, the honor ("honor legati," Dig. 27. 1. 36. pr.) than about the money, no matter how eager he may be to get it.

placing money, wholesale business, are respectable; every other branch of industry has a taint attaching to it. Intellectual power, talent, knowledge is a good which everyone who values honor must place gratuitously at the disposition of his fellow-citizens and the State. The State official receives no salary (only subordinate service is paid, so far as it is not provided for by public slaves); magistracies are purely posts of honor ("honores"). Neither does the calling of jurisconsult ("jurisconsultus"), so entirely indispensable to Roman life, bring any income.

For ancient Rome this conception held an eminently social significance. I do not mean this in the sense that it determined the social position of the individual and the distinction of classes, but in reference to the function of the gratuitous services in commerce. In Rome the gratuitous services covered essential needs of society and the State; the condition of both rested for hundreds of years on the presupposition that such services could be safely depended upon at all times to the needed extent without pay; just as drinking-water with us — indispensable, and yet at the same time free.

Now what was it that made the Roman give his services free of charge? Was it benevolence, unselfishness? We do not know the Romans very well if we believe this. No! The Roman did not relinquish all reward for his services, only it did not consist in ringing coins, but in a good which had no less a power of attraction for the man of the higher classes than money for that of the lower, *viz.*, honor, prestige, popularity, influence, power. This was the price which the prominent public character regularly had in mind when he did anything for the people; and he measured the value of magistracies accordingly. The purely ecclesiastical posts, those of the "rex sacrificulus," of the "flamines," etc., which bestowed no power, enticed him so little that whereas in the "honores" the men sought the office, here the office sought the men.

It was not therefore self-denial, but the familiar principle of egoism, upon which in Rome the assurance of those services was based which were indispensable to the State and society; except that the reward which was expected was not *economical* in its nature, but *ideal.* At the same time this phenomenon so strange to our days of replacing the prosaic motive of money by more ideal motives has a peculiar fascination for us.

But the thing, in addition to its ideal side, had also a very serious practical reverse side.

A calling which brings only honor but no bread is closed to the man of no means. So it was in Rome. Service of the State and jurisprudence actually constituted the monopoly of the well-to-do. One of the most prominent jurists in the time of the early emperors,[8] who had devoted himself to this science without means, had to buy this venture in the choice of his profession by being obliged to receive support from his auditors. Where science has not yet won its *right, i. e.*, its claim to compensation, the *gracious gift* takes the place of compensation.

This defect brought about the fall of the entire system, and the innovation, in the transition to the pay system, meant great progress socially. The revolution took place first in science, and this was brought about by foreign influence. The Greek teachers in all branches of art and science, the "rhetores," "grammatici," "philosophi," "mathematici," "geometrae," "architecti," "paedagogi," and whatever other names those teachers may have had who made pilgrimages to the world city in great numbers to try their fortune there, and who betray their

[8] *Masurius Sabinus*, Dig. 1. 2. 2 § 48.

Greek origin in their names — all brought considerable knowledge and skilled hands. But their pockets were empty and their stomachs were hungry, and necessity forced them to defy Roman prejudice and accept money for instruction. So these accustomed the Roman to a spectacle hitherto new to him, of seeing science earn a living; and theirs is the merit — for it was a merit — to have conquered the national prejudice, and to have won for art and science their legal status on Roman ground. For so we must regard the circumstance that the law did not apply to science the humiliating form of "actio locati" and "merces," but created for it a new form, the "extraordinaria cognitio" of the praetor over the honorarium — the procedural expression of the fact that art and science were not placed on the same line with manual labor.[9] The private honorarium was followed later by compensation to teachers from the funds of State and community.

Jurisprudence too was not left without a trace of the revolution. Greek influence brought about a division in the legal profession which had been quite unknown in ancient times; between the purely practical or business profession and the purely scientific or theoretical. The former is represented by the "pragmaticus," the jurist with a Greek title, and patterned after a Greek model, a kind of jurist that was quite foreign to ancient Rome. He is a business man who is ready to serve every business interest for money, a juristic *commissionaire*, or agent, good for everything. The second branch of the profession is represented by the jurist with the *Roman* title ("jurisconsultus"), and in the ancient Roman style, the man of science, who holds to the traditions of ancient times and disdains to make a source of profit out of

[9] That this formula was meant as a distinction and privilege follows from Dig. 50. 13. 1 § 6. 7.

science. He gives his service gratuitously to every one who desires his advice or instruction, but with lofty reserve he keeps far away from the quarrels of the market place and the tumult of business life. He waits until he is consulted; is highly esteemed by public opinion, and regarded far superior to the jurist of mere bread and butter. The highest goal of his ambition in the time of the emperors was the bestowal of the "jus respondendi," which stamped him as the official juristic oracle of the people. The incompatibility of compensation with the scientific calling of the jurist was so firmly axiomatic to the Roman jurist that as late as the third century in the time of the emperors, when the revolution above mentioned had been carried through in all the disciplines, one of them denied the teacher of law his claim to a honorarium.[10] Nay, even the public compensation, which all other publicly appointed teachers had been for a long time receiving, was still denied the teacher of law in the time of Constantine; and, apparently, it was not until the period of decadence from Constantine to Justinian that he was assigned a salary.[11]

As Rome owes to the Greeks the appropriation of pay to art and science, so she owes to the provinces the

[10] *Ulpian* in Dig. 50. 13. 1 § 4. 5. "... est quidem res sanctissima civilis sapientia, sed quae pretio nummario non sit aestimanda nec dehonestanda." The teachers of philosophy also share in this doubtful distinction. It is said of them, "hoc primum profiteri eos oportet mercenariam operam spernere," as if a philosopher could live on air! Both are only allowed to accept a honorarium offered voluntarily, "quaedam enim tametsi . . . honeste accipiantur, inhoneste autem petuntur."

[11] In Cod. 10. 52. 6. of Constantine, the "mercedes ac salaria" do not refer, as the Glossators assumed, to honorarium, but to public compensation (Dig. 50. 13. 1 § 5). The decisive addition, "doctores legum," which is wanting in the original text of the code in Cod. Theod. 12. 2. 1, was made by the compilers of Justinian. This will justify the conclusion in the text.

introduction of salary in the service of the State. The custom of the aediles spending more than the sums set aside by the senate for the public games so that they were obliged in many instances to cover the enormous deficit out of their own means, had become so prevalent in the last century of the Republic that whoever did not want to ruin his chances with the people and destroy his political future dared not economize during his aedileship even if he spent his entire income upon it. In return, however, the public sense of ethics allowed him to recoup himself as provincial governor. Legally he received merely the equipment that pertained to his station, later he received in place of this a sum of money ("vasarium"); but as a matter of fact his post was an indemnification for the costs of the aedileship and municipal magistracy. It was an authority issued to him to recover, on leaving the service of the State, the investment he had spent when he entered it — a letter of marque issued by the people and senate upon the provinces — and if one were not too clumsy in collecting it he had nothing to fear. The emperors found it more advisable to take the business of plundering the provinces into their own hands, and to this end to redeem the undesirable competition of the provincial governors by a salary. This is the origin of salaries in the later period of State service at Rome. It was soon extended from this to all imperial officials, whereas in the republican magistracies, which had become insignificant, the old order remained.

The preceding account proves that for many centuries Roman society was able to maintain an important branch of its public service solely by means of the ideal rewards of power, influence, honor, prestige; but that it was obliged in later times to call to its aid the economic reward of money. When I say, "to call to its aid," and not "to put in place of the former," it is in view of an opinion which I shall not be able to prove until later (§ 7); namely, that the kind of money reward which appears in the two spheres mentioned represents not a simple case of economic reward but forms a union of economic and ideal rewards.

§ 2. *All Commerce Founded upon Egoism; Principle of Compensation.* Compensation in the world of commerce is only a particular application of a general idea, which pervades the whole human world, the idea of retribution ("Vergeltung"). Beginning with *revenge*, the return of evil for evil, the idea of retribution in its development always rises higher and higher until finally, risen above the region of human existence, it finds its highest conclusion in the idea of a divine retribution and justice. Let us try to get a clear understanding of the content of the term by reference to its linguistic derivation.

The German word "gelten" expresses equality of value. In the original transitive sense, now retained only in the composite words "entgelten" and "vergelten," it signifies the granting of equality. In the intransitive sense, it denotes the existence thereof, hence the German word for money, "Geld" (originally "Gelt"), means the thing that is equal in value (intransitive), and the thing that equalizes value (transitive). The oldest use of the expression that is historically traceable ("gëltan," "këltan," "gildan") goes back to heathen worship (J. Grimm, "Mythologie," p. 34). With his thank-offering the man paid (German "galt") the god for the good which came to him, with the expiatory offering he paid for the evil committed by him. Our present usage employs the term "Vergelten" (retribution) in this sense, and distinguishes it from "Entgelten" (compensation). The latter expression is appropriated in legal phraseology for the equalization of a service, whether promised beforehand or to be expected under the circumstances ("*entgeltliche* Verträge" — onerous contracts). The former expression is used for the return of evil for evil, and good for good, which was not contemplated originally.

Organized compensation ("Entgelten") in social life becomes business intercourse or commerce; organized retribution ("Vergelten") of the socially evil becomes criminal justice. The *State*, *public opinion*, and *history* are divided in the retribution of the socially *good*, but the ideal culminating point of the concept of retribution in *both* good and evil is reached in the idea of *divine justice.* There is no idea which man feels to be so compelling as that of compensatory equalization. What the basis of this is, whether it is innate in man, or like many other ideas which we regard as innate, is only a result of historical development, does not here concern us, and we shall take up the question in its proper place.

But whatever be the final source to which the idea of equalization must be traced, there can be no doubt that egoism alone is the impelling motive of its realization in commerce. Commerce is a complete system of egoism, and nothing more. I do not mean to indicate in this a defect of commerce or a failure, but a virtue; it is the element upon which its greatness and strength depend, and according to the perfection of this element the height of the development of commerce is determined. The more it succeeds in basing the guaranty of the satisfaction of human wants exclusively upon egoism in all relations of life, and in replacing benevolence and unselfishness by self-interest and the desire for gain, the more perfectly does it fulfil its task.

I am aware that this eulogy of egoism will arouse opposition in every one of my readers who has not thought over the matter carefully. Egoism in commerce, he will object, is a necessary evil, but where it has not yet found its way it must not be summoned, and we must be glad that we can get along without it. Let the reader make the trial himself in a special case.

Let him suppose he has the choice between a journey into a land where he can find hotels everywhere, and into one in which there are no inns at all, but where this want is replaced by a general hospitality. Where will he prefer to guide his steps, provided there are no other circumstances to influence his choice? I doubt not that he would decide for the country of inns.

Hospitality is a fine thing, truly; one which opens the door to the weary wanderer, and the poetic charm of the thing must not at all be denied any more than the poetic charm of robber-knights, robbers, and lions; yet for practical life safe streets are better than unsafe; oxen and police officers are better met than lions and robber-knights; and an inn is better than hospitality. For an inn gives me the certainty of a reception, which I have not in hospitality; and my money spares me the humiliation of a request, of accepting a favor, of giving thanks — my freedom and independence on the journey lie in my purse. Therefore it means an advance which can hardly be overestimated when inns are established in an unpopulated region where hitherto the stranger was obliged to beg his accommodation. Then only is a land of this kind really opened to the travelling public — and the innkeeper becomes no less important for travel than the merchant is for the business of exchange; both of them guarantee the easy and assured satisfaction of a certain class of human wants; they contain in them the *commercial* organization of this satisfaction; *i. e.*, a system built upon the principle of compensation.

The transition from gratuitousness to compensation

or from favor to business, that was shown in this example, has been carried out in many other relations, and is still taking place under our own eyes. Every one who helps in this transition deserves well of society, although he earns for his services blame rather than recognition from the great majority. Most people see only the unpleasant side of the innovation, *viz.*, that they must hereafter pay for that which before they had for nothing, without noticing to what degree the disadvantages of the change are outweighed by the advantages. I cannot forbear from the task of bringing these advantages into fuller light.

Money alone is really able to solve the problems of intercourse, *i. e.*, to establish completely a thorough system for the assured satisfactions of human wants. The completeness of the system depends partly upon its extensiveness. Money satisfies all needs, the noblest as well as the lowest; and to any extent required, great and small. Partly the working of the system depends upon the fact that the requisite conditions for the satisfaction of all imaginable needs are reduced to the single one, infinitely simple, ever constant and wholly calculable, *viz.*, *money*. There are statements which seem so commonplace that one is almost afraid to make them, and yet if one wants to make a thing perfectly clear one must not always omit them. An example of this is *the perfect emancipatory power of money*. Favor has many conditions, money has no other conditions than money. A favor must be asked for with reserve, with tact; it has its moods, its humors and antipathies; it may turn away from the very person who needs it most, or at the time and in the circumstances when it is most indispensable, and though it were always willing it retains its narrow limitations. Money knows nothing of all this. Money knows no dignity of person; it does not indulge in moods; has no times when it is less accessible; and finally it knows no limit where its willingness becomes exhausted. Egoism has the liveliest interest in being at the service of *everybody, at all times, to any extent.* The more we demand of it the more it does, the more we ask of it, the more willing it is. Nothing would be more unbearable than if we had to depend upon favor for everything that we need, it would be the lot of the beggar! Our personal freedom and independence depends not only upon our *being able* to pay but also upon our *being obliged* to pay — our moral as well as our economic independence depends upon money.

The Two Principal Forms of Intercourse: First, Exchange (Difference of Purpose on Both Sides). The difference between compensation and gratuitousness is not exhausted by money, the consideration may consist of other things besides, *viz.*, of objects or personal service (p. 77). All such compensatory contracts are denominated in the terminology of the jurists, *onerous* or *bilateral* contracts; the gratuitous are called *liberal, lucrative* or *unilateral.* The psychologically inevitable condition of the process in the former is the conviction of both parties that what each receives is more valuable to him than what he gives; each party not merely tries to gain, but is convinced that he does gain. Without this conviction, even though objectively it is not in accordance with fact, no exchange can take place. The objective designation of the consideration as *equivalent*, however true it may be, as will be seen later, from the standpoint of business intercourse, is decidedly incorrect when looked at subjectively from the point of view of the parties. A consideration which is for the party nothing more than an equivalent, *i. e.*, equal in value to the original service, has psychologically no force to effect an alteration of the existing conditions. To do this there is need of a preponderance, of a *plusvalent;* not in the objective sense to be sure, but in the subjective; both parties must be convinced that they gain by the exchange.

It may happen that this is really true for both. He who sells an object for which he has absolutely no use for a moderate price improves his economic position, for he gets something useful in place of something useless, and the buyer, too, is a gainer, who buys the thing cheaply. This possibility of mutual gain in a business transaction depends upon the difference of need on the two sides; each of the two parties has, by reason of his peculiar need, an individual standard for measuring the value of the two articles or acts which form the object of exchange; one which differs from the standard of the other, and so it happens that each one gains without the other losing.

This therefore is the logic of the bilateral contract; *viz.*, each one looks for his own advantage and knows that the other does the same, and the law admits their right to do so.[12] It allows egoism free play, so far as the latter does not make use of prohibited means for the carrying out of its purpose.

The relation of two parties to each other, based upon egoistic motives on both sides as seen in business life, is called the *business attitude.* Opposed to this is the *attitude of grace or favor, i.e.*, the relation of the two parties in liberal contracts (p. 77), in which both are

[12] Dig. 19. 2. 22 § 3. "Quemadmodum in emendo et vendendo naturaliter concessum est, quod pluris est, minoris emere, quod minoris sit, pluris vendere et ita invicem se circumscribere, ita in locationibus quoque et conductionibus juris est." The nature of a relation of trust and confidence (agency, guardianship, partnership, etc.,) gives rise to the opposite state of affairs. Here "dolus" begins as soon as one pursues his own advantage, whereas in business relations there is no "dolus" unless one pursues his own advantage by means of a conscious suppression of the truth.

agreed that one does the other a favor. To this difference of position Roman law attaches important consequences. For example, in reference to the dissolution of the relation, the measure of "culpa," the obligation of warranty, infamy.

The process in onerous contracts, objectively considered, is that of changing the place of the objects or acts on the two sides. Each of the two things or acts seeks the person with whom it can better attain its destiny, for whom therefore it has a relatively higher value than for its present owner; and accordingly it changes its present place for another. The expression *Contract of Exchange*, which the jurist uses only for the exchange of two objects,[13] applies to all values that form the object of intercourse: articles, money, service. The German expression "Verkehr" (business intercourse) is derived from the idea of their turning from one place to another — ("Kehren" — to move, to turn). The same is true of the German word "Wandel" in the phrase "Handel und Wandel" (literal meaning of "Wandel" is walking, going, and in the phrase just mentioned it means trade). The corresponding term in Latin, "commercium," is borrowed from goods, merchandise ("merx," "mercari"), and emphasizes the element of community between the parties ("com-mercium") which is caused by it. Intercourse ("Verkehr") is therefore synonymous with intercourse of exchange ("Tauschverkehr").

But commerce ("Verkehr") does not coincide in life with Exchange ("Tauschverkehr"). It embraces rather two groups of business transactions of which only one has as its motive the exchange of acts, whereas the other,

[13] In connection with the Roman concept of "permutatio." "Mutuum," loan, is connected with "mutare" (movitare, to move). Linguistically it is characterized as *change* of place (of the fungible object, with agreement of subsequent return).

on the contrary, has as its motive the union of persons for a common purpose. The business of exchange presupposes a *difference* of need on both sides, and accordingly also a difference in the means whereby the need is to be satisfied, *viz.*, in the mutual services. Opposed to this is the case where the needs of both parties are *identical*, where their interests coincide for one and the same purpose. Now if each of them can attain the purpose by himself alone as easily and as surely as in combination with the other, there is no reason urging him to co-operate with his neighbor. The case is different when the purpose exceeds the powers of a single person, or when the combined pursuit of it gives a prospect of economy in the means to be expended, or greater security in the attainment of the purpose. In this case it is to the interest of both to unite their forces and means. The juristic form of this is the *Contract of Partnership*. Like the contract of exchange in the wider sense given to it above, so the contract of partnership embraces not any particular contract, but a peculiar sphere of contract in commerce. Like the other it contains a fundamental form of commerce, which is of unlimited application, I mean that of *association*. The principal difference between these two fundamental forms of commerce is based upon the contrast of *difference* and *identity* of purpose. In exchange the purpose of the one differs from that of the other, and herein lies the reason of their *changing;* in partnership the purpose, the aim, is the same, and that is why they *unite*. There is not and there cannot be a third form; for an alternative which makes the purpose bringing the parties together other than either the same or different is inconceivable. It is evident that partnership belongs to onerous contracts, or which is the same, that here too the principle of compensation is in force.

Of these two fundamental forms, that of exchange is inferior, and hence historically the older. It is the primitive form of commerce, from which the term itself is derived. The most limited understanding sufficed to see the use of exchanging two things or acts, but the idea of a common business operation was the work of an inventive and thoughtful mind; and even in such a mind it became possible only at a certain stage of business development.[14]

This relation of the two fundamental forms of commerce gives us the order of the following exposition. We shall turn first to the lower and older form, and shall try to present clearly and in the proper order the various elements and formative principles contained therein in which the force of purpose has become developed and realized.

§ 3. *Reward (Money). Real Performance and Consideration.* The simplest formula of bilateral contract is the immediate satisfaction of mutual needs. Each one of the two parties receives the object or act which he needs. The contract, therefore, performs the same

[14] "Societas" as actionable contract belongs in Rome to the later business law ("jus gentium"), whereas sale in the form of "mancipatio," and loan in the form of "nexum" go back to primitive times. To be sure, this does not mean that there were not actually contracts of partnership even before the introduction of the "actio pro socio," whether non-obligatory and founded purely upon mutual good faith ("fides") or fear of public opinion (infamy in case of disloyalty), or concluded with legally binding force in the form of "stipulatio" (verbal agreement). To attempt to place the origin of partnership back in the ancient family life of the Romans I regard as an error. So far as brothers and sisters continued after the death of the father their life in common as theretofore, it was legally under the protection of the "act. fam. erciscundae." And even later the relation of co-succession was not brought by the Roman jurists under the point of view of partnership any more than was that of joint ownership.

function for both, and I shall call this form of exchange contract by the name of *equality of function.*

But this simplest form of contract is at the same time the most imperfect, for it presupposes that each party possesses and sells the very thing that the other wants, a condition which seldom obtains, and which would make commerce exceedingly slow and clumsy, if it could not free itself therefrom. The means by which it did free itself from the condition above mentioned contains one of the most ingenious ideas of man[15] — *money.* The service which it renders commerce is so clear and evident that I shall waste no words upon it, and shall limit myself to a single observation.

I have defined commerce as the system of the satisfaction of human wants. Is the definition good for money too? Does money satisfy the wants of him who does something for it? Not actually, but potentially. In the money which the buyer pays him for the thing, the seller gets the means for the satisfaction of his wants; and he only has to find the right person who is able to do it, to obtain the most unlimited freedom of choice in respect to all forms and modes of satisfying his wants (time — place — persons — scope). Money does not

[15] I cannot refrain from inserting here for non-jurists the exposition of the Roman jurist (*Paulus*) in Dig. 18. 1. 1. pr. "Origo emendi vendendique a permutationibus coepit. Olim enim non ita erat nummus, neque aliud merx, aliud pretium nominabatur, sed unusquisque secundum necessitatem temporum ac rerum utilibus inutilia permutabat, quando plerumque evenit, ut, quod alteri superest, alteri desit. Sed quia non semper nec facile concurrebat, ut, cum tu haberes, quod ego desiderarem, invicem haberem, quod tu accipere velles, electa materia est, cujus publica ac perpetua aestimatio difficultatibus permutationum aequalitate quantitatis subveniret, eaque materia forma publica percussa usum dominiumque non tam ex substantia praebet quam ex quantitate nec ultra merx utrumque, sed alterum pretium vocatur."

therefore satisfy the want immediately, but it confers an absolutely sure title to the subsequent satisfaction of his want; a title respected by all. The difference between exchange in the narrower sense and purchase consists therefore in the fact that in the former the satisfaction of the mutual wants takes place in one and the same act, whereas in a contract of purchase it falls into several acts; the buyer alone, not the seller, receives in this case immediately that of which he has need.

And so in contradistinction to the above formula of bilateral contract, which rests upon *equality of function*, there is another based upon *difference of function*, in which the one act brings about the actual satisfaction of the want, and the other only the potential. Or, which is the same thing, there is on the one side a real or individual act, and on the other an ideal or abstract thing, *viz.*, money. We get therefore the following schema, already given above (p. 77), which includes now all conceivable contracts of exchange in the wider sense.

Real Performance	Money	Contract
(1) Permanent Cession of a Thing	Price	Purchase
(2) Temporary Cession		
(*a*) of a Thing	Rent	Contract of Lease
(*b*) of Capital	Interest	Loan
(3) Service	Wages	Contract of Service

(*Honorarium, Salary*). *Progress from Real Consideration to Reward.* It is desirable to have a definite expression for the function which money performs in all these cases. The term equivalent is not suitable, for it emphasizes a value relation of the two acts to each other which has nothing to do with money as such — a thing can also be the equivalent of another (see above). I will permit myself to use the concept of remuneration ("Lohn"), which is regularly identified in scientific usage with wages, but which has a much wider signification in ordinary usage, as is well known. I propose to use this term for all the three cases of performance involving money which were mentioned above. I shall therefore understand by the term remuneration in the wider sense not merely the wages of labor, but also the purchase price, rent, and interest. The concept of remuneration in the first sense (wages) will also be extended later on (§ 7) to ideal remuneration, as opposed to economic, *i. e.*, money, and to mixed remuneration, which combines ideal with economic. By this means the concept of remuneration becomes so general that we may designate remuneration, as I have done in the title of this chapter, as the motive or lever of all commerce. To be sure, we are guilty of the inaccuracy of considering only the perfect form of exchange (in return for money), and leaving aside the imperfect form of two real performances as on the whole insignificant for commerce.

But has not the concept lost perhaps its definiteness, and at the same time its usefulness, by this extension of its meaning? I believe not. Money and real performance are the two forms of compensation, of the equalization of one act by the other, which are opposed to each other by the nature of the case. Now although it may be necessary from the standpoint of the jurist as well as the political economist to distinguish in the function of money between wages, price, rent and interest, these differences are of no consequence in the question which we have proposed here, and which we have to answer, namely, how does commerce effect the satisfaction of human wants? The only answer to this question is, it effects this *immediately* or *mediately;* immediately by a real performance, mediately through money; and for this function of money we need an expressive term. The remuneration which the workman receives does not satisfy his want immediately, it only gives him the means thereto. The same is true of price, rent, interest in reference to seller, lessor, lender. Whether it is immediate necessity that impels the one to work, the other to sell, the third to let; or whether it is only the desire to realize in a suitable manner their labor power, their articles or their capital, which causes them to do these things, makes no difference as far as the character of the money is concerned which they get by those transactions. In the one case as in the other the money does not satisfy the want immediately, it only makes subsequent satisfaction possible.

§ 4. *Equivalent.* The concepts remuneration and equivalent do not coincide. The equivalent may consist in something other than remuneration (real performance), and remuneration may be *no* equivalent; it may exceed the amount thereof or fall below it. By equivalent we understand the equality between an act and its consideration, measured by the value of goods and acts as established by experience in commerce. How the standard is formed and on what it is based is a question of political economy, which we need not discuss; our object is directed merely to proving the gain which accrues to intercourse from the promotion of remuneration to equivalent.

The fixing of remuneration in a particular case is a matter of individual agreement, and the law recognizes egoism as the determining factor and a just one.[16] The conception from which the law starts is that each of the two parties has in mind his own advantage, each one endeavors to use the disadvantage of the other man's

[16] Dig. 4. 4. 16 § 4. "In *pretio* emptionis et venditionis naturaliter licere contrahentibus se circumvenire." Dig. 19. 2. 22 § 3. " . . . ita in locationibus quoque et conductionibus juris est." Cod. 4. 44. 10. "dolus emtoris . . . non quantitate pretii aestimatur."

position in his own favor. This disadvantage may rise to a position of actual duress, when the highest degree of want on the one side coincides with the exclusive possibility of satisfying it on the other. In this case there remains no other choice for the party in need than to accept the conditions dictated by the other party. The drowning man will promise a fortune, if necessary, for a rope; the man dying of thirst in the desert will give his pearls away for a skin of water; Richard III in Shakespeare offers "a kingdom for a horse" — the most insignificant thing gains the highest value if one's life depends upon it.

Is this, then, the fruit of egoism, which has been so glorified by us, namely, pitiless exploitation of another's need! Does not this result, which outrages every moral feeling, force us to declare our whole theory of egoism bankrupt, and to admit frankly that it cannot rise to the demand of commerce, which is to procure the regulated and assured satisfaction of human want? Must we not confess that society needs a fixed principle by which to be guided in order that egoism, which is insatiable by nature, may have imposed upon it from outside the restraint which it does not bear within itself?

The egoism of the one is opposed by the egoism of the other; the former endeavoring to take as much as possible, the latter to give as little as possible. The point of indifference or the zero point where the two produce equilibrium is the *equivalent.* Equivalent is the equilibrium effected by experience between performance and consideration; it is an amount of remuneration (of a specific performance) in which both parties come to their right, and neither of the two loses. Equivalent is the realization of the *idea of justice* in the domain of *commerce.* For justice, simply and intelligibly expressed, is nothing else than that which suits *all*, where *all* can subsist. Accordingly, to enforce as much as possible the principle of equivalence in all relations is one of the chief problems in the life of commerce.

How does society solve it? Does it solve it by law? If it is true that it is a problem of justice, then it seems inevitably a legal problem; for what justice demands must be realized by law. According to my opinion, however, it is not so, but when it is made out that the interest of *all* demands a certain order, we must still consider first whether the interest is not strong enough to establish the order by itself. In this case there is no need of a law — no law finds it necessary to prescribe marriage and to forbid suicide.

Now, does commerce possess the means to realize the idea of equivalent out of its own power? On the whole, this must evidently be the case; no law prescribes the prices for the laborer, manufacturer, shop-keeper, etc., and yet they observe a price. Evidently not from disinterested motives or as social doctrinaires in order to realize the idea of equivalent, but because they cannot do otherwise. Who compels them? No one else than their own egoism. Egoism forms in this case its own corrective. And it does this in a two-fold manner. First, by means of competition. The egoism of the seller who tries to force too high a price is paralyzed by the egoism of another who prefers rather to sell for a moderate price than not to sell at all, and the egoism of the buyer who offers too little is paralyzed by that of another who offers more — *competition is the social self-adjustment of egoism.*

But no matter how true this may be on the whole, there may be special cases or peculiar relations in which competition is temporarily or even permanently excluded. The only innkeeper, physician, apothecary in the place has no competition to be concerned about, and even when there is more than one it may happen that a person who has need of their services finds himself in such a position that he can address himself to one of them only, and must submit to the conditions laid down by him. The surgeon who has completed the operation, but has not yet stopped the flow of blood, has the patient in his power, and similarly the innkeeper at whose place the patient is staying. Who or what prevents them from asking an extravagant price for the completion of the operation, and the continuance of the lodging? If they count on future patients and guests, it is regard for their own advantage. As the egoism of the one holds in check the egoism of the other by means of competition, so in this case egoism holds itself in check. The egoistic exploitation of the present is opposed by a regard for the future. The egoist balances the two possible advantages against each other, and sacrifices the advantage of the moment, no matter how great it is, in order to secure the smaller but permanent advantage for the rest of his life. Concern for the future is the individual self-regulation of egoism in those cases where competition, *i. e.*, the social regulation, fails to act.

But in order to be able to look into the future one must have an eye to do it with, and the eye of most people is so dull that it does not carry them beyond the present. Others again have such a weak will that they cannot resist the temptation to sacrifice the future to the present moment, and it is even possible that one enormous extortion [17] outweighs the loss of the entire

[17] I use the expression here and in the sequel not in the criminal sense, but in the economical, to denote the exploitation of the condition of necessity of another for the purpose of raising the price or the compensation above the equivalent. Carried on systematically or as a matter of business, extortion becomes *usury*. We must

future, or even that it may seem practicable to practice extortion as a permanent business (usury). Here the protection which egoism offers against itself fails, and when the dangers which egoism threatens assume a serious aspect there is nothing left to society but the means whereby it always tries to ward off the dangerous excesses of egoism, *viz.*, *the law.* The laws which thus curb the excesses of egoism in commercial intercourse are: legal tariffs of charges; laws limiting the rate of interest; penalties for usury, etc.[18] Experience has shown that many of these attain their purpose very imperfectly, and the public opinion of our time, in favor of freedom of trade, looks upon them with disfavor and would prefer to set them aside entirely on the ground of bein a hindrance to business, as in fact has been done with many of them already. There will be need of more numerous and bitter experiences before people will become aware again what

distinguish between extortion and *fraud.* The former speculates on the opponent's condition of necessity, the latter on his ignorance of the real price or his disinclination to make the disproportion between the latter and the price demanded a subject of unpleasant discussions.

[18] The different legislations vary extraordinarily in this connection. The ancient Roman law directed its attention almost altogether upon usury; the later Roman law added some other matters (extortion on the part of the physician, Cod. 10. 52. 9, Dig. 50. 13. 3; on the part of the lawyer, the so-called "pactum de quota litis" and "palmarium" 2. 14. 53, 50. 13. 1 § 12. Cod. 2. 6. 5, prohibition of the "lex commissoria" in case of pledge, rescinding a contract of sale on the ground of the so-called "laesio enormis," and many other instances). Mohammedan law no doubt went furthest in the opposite direction. It imposes a duty upon the vendor to state the true value, and allows only tradespeople to reserve a profit for themselves over and above the value of the object. It forbids entirely auction sales, where the price can be easily raised above the real value. *N. von Tornauw,* "Das Moslemitische Recht," (Leipzig, 1855), p. 92, 93. This regulation reminds one of the prohibition of interest in the canon law.

dangers to society individual egoism, freed from all bonds, carries with it, and why the past has found it necessary to put a check upon it. Unlimited freedom of trade is a license for extortion, a letter of marque for robbers and pirates with the right of holding up all who fall into their hands — woe to the victim! That the wolves cry for freedom is easy to understand. But when the sheep, as has often been the case in this question, join in the cry, they only show thereby that they are sheep.

The authority which I thus claim on behalf of legislation is in no conflict with my fundamental conception of commerce as the system, based upon egoism, of the satisfaction of human wants. I do hold firmly to the view that egoism is the motive power of all commerce, and that it alone is able to solve the problem. The idea of replacing it by coercion is so impossible that one should try to think it out if only in order to become the better aware how inseparably the success of labor is connected with the reward of free service. To regulate work by coercion instead of by reward would mean to change society into a workhouse, and to limit the national work to the work of the hands, for only the hands can be coerced, not the spirit. But even in manual labor coercion cannot take the place of remuneration. Coercion makes egoism an antagonist to work; reward makes it an ally; for when work is not free the workman has an interest to work as *little* as possible; when the work is free his interest is to work as *much* as possible. In the former case he deceives his master, in the latter, himself. Coercion is effective only so long as the whip is in sight; remuneration works continually.

But though I am convinced that there is no other motive power of commerce than egoism, I am just as firmly persuaded on the other hand, that society has the right to check the excesses of the selfish motive when these become dangerous to the success of society. In my eyes there is no error more serious than the idea that a contract as such, as long as its content is not illegal or immoral, has a just claim upon the protection of the law. In the second part of this work I shall have occasion to combat this error; here I content myself with a protest. It is the right as well as the duty of society to set its own interests against those of individual egoism. But the interests of society are directed to that which suits not only one particular person but all; which enables all people to subsist; and this is, as has already been remarked above (p. 101), nothing else than *justice*. Justice is above *freedom*. The individual exists not only for himself, but also for the world (p. 51) — therefore *freedom*, that which is expedient for the individual, must be subordinated to *justice*, which is for the advantage of all.

The social problem just treated, of the advance of remuneration to equivalent, or of the realization of the idea of justice in commerce, is closely connected with a phenomenon to which I now pass; the significance of which, however, is not at all exhausted by the fact that it has this one problem to solve.

§ 5. *Organization of Work in the Form of a Vocation, Business or Trade.* By vocation ("Beruf") in the social or objective sense, in contradistinction to the individual or subjective sense of the word, *i. e.*, the subjective qualification, the inner voice, which "calls" ("vocare," "rufen") a man to a task, we understand a definite kind of activity, for which the individual puts himself permanently at the disposition of society: his *social post*. If the vocation is combined with the economic purpose of the subject to make his living thereby, it is called a *trade or business*. A trade or business is therefore a branch of work *for which* and *from which* the individual intends to live. In the phrase *for which* we have the relation of the business to society; in the phrase *from which* we have its relation to the subject. The individual solicits ("wirbt") from society ("Ge-werbe") in order to gain thereby; he serves ("dient") it in order to profit ("verdienen") himself. This brings no discredit according to our present ideas, which are essentially different from those of antiquity (p. 81). It is dishonorable neither to the most eminent nor to the most lowly. Work is no disgrace, and neither is the acceptance of pay for the work of one's vocation. We are in the habit of seeing a dishonorable element only when one allows himself to be paid for a service which does not constitute his vocation. When a porter takes a man from the station to the hotel, every one finds it proper that he should want to be paid for it. In any other person we should call it mean. Why? The one makes his living from these services; they belong to his vocation, and pay for the work of one's vocation is, in the eyes of society, an equivalent not merely for the particular service, but at the same time for the adoption of a vocation which is useful to society. This ensures his permanent readiness thereto; and only he who lives *for* the work shall live *by* it.

He who takes up a definite business declares thereby publicly his fitness and inclination for all services connected with it. The public receives the assurance that every one who needs him can count on him, and he gives every one the authority to call upon him.[19] His own

[19] If he does not possess the ability he is a bungler, who does not belong to the trade, and whom an intelligent social policy commands to keep at a distance in the interest of business as well as in the interest of the public. This was the aim of the master-piece among artisans in the old organization of the guilds. The same purpose is intended at the present time by the State examinations of lawyers, notaries, physicians, druggists, midwives, teachers of private institutions, etc.

interest, to be sure, and the spur of competition guarantee as a rule his readiness; but both motives may fail sometimes, and what then? Has he a right from a sense of comfort or ill humor to refuse the man who needs his services? Has the innkeeper a right to refuse the stranger; the shopkeeper, baker, butcher to refuse the customer; the apothecary, the physician to refuse the patient; the lawyer the client? Every true man of business has the feeling that he has *not* the right; he is aware that he would suffer in public opinion. Why? No one finds fault with the owner of a house if he does not want to let or sell his vacant house. Why, then, should we find fault with the business man when he withholds his services from those who desire them? Because by the adoption of his particular vocation he has given society an assurance, which he is not making good. All those who pursue a public business are public persons, *i. e.*, they exist for the public, and are in duty bound to serve them. Public opinion sees in their vocation *a position of obligation toward society.*

Therefore it withdraws its respect from the business man when he neglects his business, when he is lazy or unreliable, no matter how respectable he may be otherwise. It declares him incompetent and puts a low estimate upon him if he does not understand his business, whereas it respects the competent business man, even if in other respects it may see a good deal to object to in him. And this standard of social service by which it measures him is also his own. It is that of the "honor" of the competent business man, his "honor" does not allow him to neglect his business, to deliver poor work, etc. What has honor to do with business? The answer is: honor in the objective sense (the respect of the world) is the recognition of the social worth of the person; in the subjective sense it is one's own feeling and the actual living up to his worth.[20] Honor is determined by those elements which fix the value of the person for society, and hence also his special social task. The tasks of the artisan, the physician, the lawyer are different, but to summon up all one's powers in their fulfillment is counted to them all as an honor; to neglect them, as a dishonor. A good artisan will find it just as incompatible with his honor to deliver careless work as a conscientious physician or lawyer to leave his patients or clients in the lurch. Whoever does so makes his name suffer. But "name" ("Ruf") and "calling" ("Beruf") are very closely connected. The manner in which a man responds to his vocation is that which society as a rule throws into the scales first in judging a person; and according to this it determines his ability, *i. e.*, his fitness for society.[21]

It is part of the egoism of society that it does not ask what the man is *in himself*, but what he is *for it*. To be *nothing* to society, to live only for one's self is no satisfactory mode of existence, to be sure, but at least a tolerable one; but not to be to society what one is *meant* to be, *i. e.*, to be incompetent, is a feeling so oppressive and worrying that it cannot be completely compensated for by anything else. Whereas, on the contrary, loyal, energetic fulfilment of the duties of one's vocation is able to keep one up even under hard blows of fate. It keeps before him the fact that even if his life has been robbed of its worth and charm for himself, it still has at least worth and significance for others.

Duty represents that side of vocation which addresses itself to society; the pecuniary return represents the

[20] For a justification of this definition, see Vol. II, p. 502 and Vol. III, in connection with the Social System of Coercion ("Soziales Zwangsystem"). [See above Ch. VI, note 3. — *Translator*].

[21] For the connection of the concept of ability with that of virtue, see II, no. 19.

side which addresses itself to the individual. And although the latter aspect may now and then, in the case of a particular person who does not need the pay, be without any significance, still it is so influential and decisive in its total effect that it is this which makes the relation and the person what experience shows they are and are meant to be. He who devotes himself to a definite vocation pledges thereby to society his entire existence for the purpose of carrying out the task undertaken by him; and so *its* interest becomes *his* interest. If he wishes to prosper he must devote to it his whole power, his ability and knowledge, his thinking and feeling, his will and endeavor. He must not wait until society expresses a need, he must anticipate it; he must guess its wishes and thoughts even before they are uttered. He must teach it wants or forms of satisfying them which it did not know before; like a sick-nurse he must know how to listen to every breath of society, and like a physician he must know how to feel the lowest pulse beat of the social need, and to diagnose it. Skill or the lack of skill in judging of the social need, always different and infinitely varying in place and time, signifies for him wealth or poverty.

What has been said so far shows sufficiently the great importance of a vocation for social life. Every vocation represents the organization of the mode of social activity represented by it, and hence contains for society a guaranty of the assured, regulated and constant satisfaction of this need. Commerce, we may say, has not actually fulfilled its task until it has produced a vocation for its service. Therefore the extension and perfection of the organization forms the standard for judging the stage of development of commerce. The lack of a particular vocation in the economic system of a given time is a proof that the corresponding need was not yet felt then to the extent of producing an assured form of satisfying it. In a country in which there are ten or a hundred times more distilleries than book stores, circulating libraries, and educational institutions for women, the need which the population feels for brandy is evidently far stronger than its desire for spiritual nourishment and the education of women. The presence or absence of a particular vocation, its numerical representation, in general its statistics, form an absolutely trustworthy index of the intensity of the need corresponding to it. Where the need is not felt at all or not in the requisite measure, the vocation as an organized branch of industry is impossible, but where it has sufficiently extended itself, the vocation is not slow to make its appearance. The same is true here as when nature awakens in the spring. So long as there is not the necessary heat, no tree sprouts; but as soon as the sprouting takes place, it is a proof that the necessary amount of heat has appeared. If the economic system is what it ought to be, then the aggregate of human needs on the one side must find a counterpart, completely adequate to it, in the system of organized branches of industry on the other side. At the present time there is probably scarcely anything that is wanting in this connection. Man just as he is, as he thinks and strives, with all the needs of his body and mind, with all his interests, the lowest as well as the highest — what wish, what desire can he utter for the satisfaction of which there is not ready at hand some kind of vocation? There is only one limit, and this a natural one, which stands in the way of the absolute carrying out of that organization, and that is the *immovable* object. There are all sorts of commerce, from trade in rags up to that in art, but there is no trade in immovable objects.[22] If one wants to buy or farm real estate,

[22] Accordingly our Commercial Code restricts the concept of commodity to movable objects. Similarly the Roman law restricts the concept of "merx" to the same things, D. 50. 16. 66.

or rent a dwelling, he must apply to a private person; there is nowhere in the world a merchant who deals in estates or houses. The first step in this direction towards organization has been made by building societies in great cities who build houses for the purpose of selling them; or dwellings for workmen for the purpose of letting them; a branch of industry which probably has a great future before it.

A peculiar kind of vocation is the *business of the middle-man*, as I might call it, *i. e.*, the mediation between those who are looking for objects or services and those who are able to furnish them (brokerage, intelligence office).[23] In many relations in which commerce still contents itself at the present day with the middle-man's agency, it will probably in the course of time replace it with more direct methods of doing business. The business of providing money is clearly tending that way. The simplest and therefore also the original form of dealing in money is this, namely, that he who needs money seeks the private person who is in a position to advance it to him. The next form is when both apply to the middle-man, who negotiates the raising as well as

[23] In Rome the business of the middle-man was very completely organized in the most various directions in the time of the Empire. In money transactions it existed long before that time. The banker ("argentarius") undertook the agency, lending out the moneys entrusted to him (either in his own name or in the name of the lender), collecting the interest and crediting it. Later was introduced the broker (D. 50. 14. 2: "proxeneta faciendi nominis, ut multi solent"). The business of the broker in Rome was, as the language indicates ("proxeneta," "proxeneticum," "philanthropia," "hermeneuticum" 1. 3. *ibid.*), of Greek origin. In the time of the Empire there were in Rome, just as with us, special intelligence offices for positions of all kinds, D. 50. 14. 3: "sunt enim hujusmodi hominum (ut in tam magna civitate) officinae." They were even more needed there than with us now, where the same purpose is served by advertisements in the public papers.

the investment of the money. In the last form the lender gives up his money to the banker who undertakes to lend at his own risk, and relieves his client from the trouble of search and from the risk of loss. Banking is the most complete form of dealing in money, and the advantage for all three persons involved is so evident that it is likely it will gradually in the course of time suppress the two imperfect forms.

We started in our preceding discussion from the view that the formation of the various vocations runs parallel to the development of human needs; and the view is confirmed by experience. But no reason has yet been given why a particular need should be satisfied precisely in the form of a particular vocation. I am almost tempted to omit it, for everybody knows the reason; namely, the division of labor. The advantage which this brings to the workman as well as to society is so plain that it could not have escaped the notice of man even in the lowest stage of the development of commerce. In the time in which A produces $10a$ in his special business, and B $10b$ in his, A would perhaps produce only one b, and B only one a. When the one limits himself to a, and the other to b, and both then interchange a and b, the former gains $9a$, the latter $9b$, and this gain of $9a + 9b$ is of benefit not only to them, but, in the cheaper price of the two products, ultimately to the entire public. No sailor would be so foolish as to make his own boots, and no shoemaker would be so foolish as to make his own coat. Each of the two knows that he will be better off if he buys them, and that both of them save labor power in directing it exclusively to one particular branch of work.

I sum up the above discussion in the statement that a vocation signifies the social organization of the work as well as of the satisfaction of a need.

But this does not by any means exhaust the significance of vocations for the economic system; for we have a second and a third principle associated with the first.

The second is, a vocation is *the organization* of reward. The organization of reward consists in its promotion from the vacillating and accidental character of a rate measured according to purely individual estimate to the uniformity and certainty of a universal standard of value. In other words, it is the advance from a purely individual standard of measurement to the realization of the *idea of equivalent.* The influence which the vocation exerts in this respect is twofold; it *determines* the amount of the equivalent, and it *secures* the practical maintenance of the same. It accomplishes the former by fixing, on the basis of constantly repeated experience, the measure and the costs of the work necessary to produce the service. Only he is able to do this who has devoted his whole power and his whole life to the problem. He alone knows what work costs; and the possible errors in his experience, which may be due to the influence of special individual factors, are rectified by the experience of all the other people. Thus current prices are the product of the experience of the entire trade, *i. e.*, of thousands and millions of individuals, who have figured on the problem and are constantly figuring on it anew. It is not the particular isolated job which they take into consideration, but the job in connection with the whole of life, as an aliquot part of it, hence with reference to the necessary preparation thereto, to the continual readiness for service that business demands, and the involuntary stoppages in work caused thereby, etc. The honorarium of the physician and the lawyer must pay not merely for the prescription or the opinion, but also for the period of study; the pay of the porter, of the cab-driver, of the midwife must indemnify these persons for the involuntary waiting which is necessarily connected with their business — the customer must pay for the time when the porter stands idle on the street corner, when the cab-driver sleeps on the box, and the midwife has a holiday. In the case of the day laborer alone this does not hold good; the daily wage is for him in reality just what he calls it, the wage of the day, *i. e.*, the *equivalent* of the particular *period of time* which he gives up, without any reference to a time of preparation or waiting outside of it.

As the branch of industry *determines* the right amount of the equivalent, so it *secures* the actual maintenance of the same. He who has occasion to perform a service, or to sell or let a thing, only sporadically, may demand for it the price that he can get; but he who makes a regular business out of certain services, or out of selling or letting, has an interest in taking the price which is his due (p. 102).

Accordingly the vocation may be designated the regulator of compensation. The compensation which it fixes is in the long run always the right one, *i. e.*, an amount which corresponds to the service, and hence fair and just for both parties. Society has the most vital interest in preventing remuneration from being reduced below its proper measure, for a just price is the condition of a just work. The vocation itself must suffer when it does not get its right. Therefore he who lowers the prices below this measure is not a benefactor of society, but an enemy thereof, for he attacks the foundation of the entire vocation or business, *viz.*, the equilibrium established by experience between work and compensation. His purpose in the matter, whether he does it for his own profit, or in order to make a sacrifice, is of no consequence. The popular instinct correctly appreciates the social danger of such a proceeding. On this basis rested the social ostracism of the unlicensed artisan in the era of trade guilds, and the license of persecution which the system recognized ("Bönhasenjagen"). The man belonging to the craft exercises his business openly in the workshop or in the shop, the unlicensed artisan does it secretly and by stealth,[24] and is hunted down like the hare in a kitchen garden; both depending upon others for their support. The pay which business yields is due to him who has devoted himself to it, for pay is the equivalent, as has been shown above (p. 114), not merely of the particular work, but of the *entire vocation*, from which the work proceeds; the equivalent for training, preparation and personal and material readiness to serve. Every branch of industry has developed by experience an equilibrium between burdens and advantages, duties and rights. He who appropriates the advantages alone, without taking upon him the duties of the vocation, disturbs this equilibrium and endangers the branch of industry; he is a social freebooter whom society has all reason to suppress. The cheap prices which he offers are a Greek gift; they are the cheap prices of the poacher — in another man's preserve hunting is cheap.

Persecution of the unlicensed artisan ("Bönhasenjagen") has disappeared along with the constitution of the guilds to which it belonged, but the thought which was expressed therein, *viz.*, the inadmissibility of competition from people who do not belong to the business, is in my eyes so true that a healthy social policy should never lose sight of it. Competition *within* the business regulates itself, competition from a point *without* the business

[24] In a corner ("Winkel"), hence the term "Winkelschreiber" (lit. corner writer — obscure writer, penny-a-liner) and "Winkeladvokat" (lit. corner lawyer — petty fogger); or on the floor ("Boden," "Bön"), hence "Bönhase" (lit. floor hare — bungler, interloper).

is like a race in which some one who has not taken up his post together with the rest at the point of departure, jumps in at a later place to gain a handicap with which to wrest the prize from the legitimate competitors who have to cover the whole course.[25]

There is still a *third* point remaining in the consideration of the social significance of the vocation. It is the advantage which the organization of industry gives to society by securing the necessary talent.

As long as it was considered dishonorable at Rome to receive pay for intellectual work, the service of the State and the cultivation of science formed the monopoly of the rich; talented persons without means found the access to either practically closed (p. 84). The circumstance that both subsequently became *vocations* open to the people, was a step in advance not only for the individual, but also for society. We like to reassure ourselves with the proposition that genius overcomes all difficulties, but genius also needs bread in order to live, and if the vocation promises him no bread because it has not yet developed into a trade or business, he must choose another which will give him this certainty. The musical genius of the nineteenth century has his bread assured him by his music; the musical genius of the fourteenth century had to beg his in the castles and palaces of the great. But begging is not for every one, and many a one at that time may have preferred to be a respectable shoemaker or tailor to becoming a wandering

[25] A case in point is presented to us in the question recently ventilated in Austria, whether judicial officials enjoying a pension should be allowed to practice law. According to my opinion, decidedly not! I can see in it only a disorganization of the legal profession. If the pension which the government allows to retired judicial officials is too small, it must be increased, — but from the government's *own* pocket. The above measure allows them the increase at the expense of the lawyers.

musician. Nowadays a genius is not likely to be lost to the world. Wherever he emerges he is noticed and moved to the place where he finds his proper appreciation, and the latter gives him at the same time his bread. A Catalani, a Paganini, a Beethoven, can never in our days become anything else than what they have become. In the middle ages, if they had disdained to become ballad singers or fiddle scrapers, they would have had to take up a respectable trade. In a time which is not prepared for a genius, genius is a curse — an eagle in a narrow cage who, when he moves his wings with boldness and force, breaks his head against the iron bars. In the present time, however, which has smoothed the paths for genius in all domains of art and science, the genius has himself to blame if he does not become a source of happiness to himself and of blessing to the world.

What has caused this change? The assurance of pecuniary return by means of a vocation. The vocation gives to the competent person who follows it the promise of a competent support. At the present time Hans Sachs would not find it necessary to make boots in order to write poetry, Spinoza would not have to grind lenses in order to be able to philosophize. Art and science have advanced so far that they can offer an adequate living to every one who brings with him a sufficient amount of endowment. The charity of the great, upon which art and science had to depend in former times, is replaced by the salary and the honorarium (§ 7).

§ 6. *Credit.* Credit is the consummation of the development of the system of exchange. It is demanded by the purposes of commerce, so that it must always necessarily appear when commerce reaches a certain development. Without credit commerce would be the most perfect and most awkward thing in the world — a bird without wings. In order to move, it must have the wings of credit, and as the bird's wings grow as soon as it comes out of the egg, so do the wings of commerce, *i. e.*, credit.

Political economists, whom it behooves to define the concept of credit, are not at all agreed as to its meaning,[26] and this circumstance has determined me to assist the problem on my own part from the juristic side, by enlisting the support which the Roman law, from which the term credit has been borrowed, gives us also in reference to its content. And so in the first edition of this work I gave a lengthy presentation of the legal development of the subject in Roman law. In rereading the passages in question I am convinced that I overshot the mark, and I have therefore subjected it to a revision and abridgment, confining myself to what is essential and absolutely necessary.

By the term "credere" in the wider sense, the Roman jurists understand the giving up of a thing to another with the obligation of its subsequent return; and the Roman Praetor used in his edict the expression "res creditæ" as a title comprehending all contracts belonging to this category.[27] To this relation of establishing an obligation by *giving* was attached linguistically as well as historically the term and the concept "creditor," for that was originally the only mode of establishing the obligation, as we shall prove later (Chapter VIII, § 5).

"Creditor" was the one who had given something,

[26] A summary of the various opinions is given by *Knies*, "Der Kredit, Erste Hälfte" (Berlin, 1876). I regard the view of the author as incorrect, and it is for this reason especially that I decided to devote more space to an analysis of the idea of credit than I should otherwise have done.

[27] D. 12. 1. 1, " . . . credendi generalis appellatio est, ideo sub hoc titulo Praetor et de commodato et de pignore edixit, nam cuicumque rei adsentiamur alienam fidem secuti mox recepturi quid ex hoc contractu, credere dicimur."

and "debitor" the one who had received something ("creduere," "credere" from "dare"; "debere" from "habere").

But the development of the Roman obligation gave a wider content to the thing itself and correspondingly a wider meaning to the expression "creditor." In the new law every obligee is called "creditor" even if he gave nothing,[28] and every obligor is called "debitor" even if he received nothing; the mere contract, concluded with legally binding intention, is sufficient to make the parties "debitor" and "creditor" respectively.

In this later stage of the development of obligation, therefore, the "res creditae" form only a particular, though a widely comprehensive category of obligatory contract. This again is divided into two classes according as the giving up of the thing transfers the thing merely *de facto* (possession) or *de jure* (ownership); in the first case, with the obligation of returning *the same thing*, in the second, of returning a *similar* thing (*specific* and *generic* determination of the object of return; in short "species" and "genus").

To this contrast there attaches a practically very important and influential difference for the creditor. In the first case where he retains the ownership, and in most cases also the *juristic* possession, he is thereby much more effectually secured than he is in the latter, where he gives up both. In addition to the action "in personam," which the law places at his disposal, he can institute actions to recover possession and ownership, the latter even against third persons; nay, according to ancient law, he can even procure for himself the thing by force. His legal attitude to the thing is exactly the same as if the thing were still in his possession; this "credere" is *juristically* connected with very little risk

[28] D. 50. 16. 10–12.

for him. As examples of this we have the giving up of a thing for the purpose of care-taking ("depositum"), or for temporary use, whether paid for or gratuitous (usufructuary lease, ordinary lease, "commodatum").

It is quite different in the second case. Here the creditor loses entirely his remedy against the thing itself, since he transferred to the debtor possession and ownership, and has only his obligatory claim to fall back upon. The debtor can transfer the thing which he has just received, immediately to another, and if he is not able, when the time comes, to meet his obligation, it is the creditor's loss. The insecurity which in this case threatens the creditor presupposes therefore on his part a much greater confidence in the debtor ("credere" in the sense of belief) than in the first instance, and it was probably this consideration which induced the Roman jurists to assume for this category a higher kind of "credere"; which they designate by the expressions "in creditum ire" or "abire," "in credito esse," "in creditum dare, accipere."[29]

Such a "credere," which according to the preceding discussion presupposes that the thing to be returned is only generically determined, is possible even with regard to commodities which differ individually too much for indiscriminate exchange or convertibility. In commerce, however, it is found only in those commodities in which proper generic designation gives adequate assurance that exactly the same value will be returned as that which has been given. This is the basis of the juristic concept

[29] D. 12. 1. 2 § 1, 19 § 1; 14. 4. 5 § 18; 16. 1. 19 § 5; 19. 2. 31. "Suum esse" is designated, as contrasted with "in credito esse," as a sign, "quod vindicari non possit," D. 34. 2. 27 § 2. "In credito esse" is therefore synonymous with the problem of property. In cases of the first kind the creditor has the "suum esse" remaining to him and thereby the prosecution thereof by "vindicatio."

of *fungible* things in contrast to *non-fungible.* In the former the generic determination is the rule, in the latter it is a rare exception. This idea of fungibility, *i. e.*, of the equality of value of particular things, reaches its highest degree in money, which the Romans designate as "certum" in the highest sense. Money is therefore, quite apart from the other reasons which lead to the same result, singled out by its nature to represent the main object of "credere" in the above sense. All other objects put together, which are in themselves available for this purpose, cannot bear the remotest comparison with money in reference to this mode of their economic application. In this form "creditum" attains its greatest importance for commerce, and the older Roman law distinguished it from the others by special rules. To get our modern concept of credit we must start from this form.

Money alone is the object of credit in our modern sense. The shopkeeper who gives goods on credit does not credit the goods — that would mean that he wanted to get them back — he credits the price.

But not in all cases where money is handed over with the condition of its subsequent return do we speak of giving credit. When a man prior to his departure deposits his available funds with a banker in such a manner that not the coins ("depositum regulare") but the amount should be returned to him in the future (so-called "depositum irregulare"), he undertakes, it is true, an "in creditum abire" in the Roman sense, and he puts himself legally in exactly the same position as if he had given him the money as a loan. But this case must not be brought under the point of view of credit in the commercial sense, and Roman jurists, too, distinguished it from the case of loan. The consideration which led them to do this was the difference of motive in the two cases. The depositor gives the money for his own sake, the lender for the sake of the other. In both cases, it is true, the receiver can dispose of it for his own purposes, but in the one case it is only the effect of the handing over, in the other it is the purpose of it. The same relation exists in the case where one hands over to his agent the money required to carry out some business or to defray expenses. He transfers the ownership to him, and relies upon him to apply the money in accordance with his orders. But this, too, is not giving credit; the latter presupposes that the transaction is in the interest of the receiver.

The crediting of money in the interest of the receiver may take place in two ways: in the form of an *independent* contract by the handing over of money, *i. e.*, a loan, and on the occasion of *another* contract by crediting the sum of money which he owes as a result of it. This may take place immediately on conclusion of the contract or, by granting an extension of the time of payment, not till later. The most frequent occasion for this is found in the conclusion of a contract of sale. If the credit of the selling price is made a condition, we speak of a purchase *on credit*, or time. This is just the case of which we think in the first place when, in everyday life, we speak of credit and trust. Under this form comes the credit which the shopkeeper allows to his customers, and the credit which the merchant needs for his operations. If he needs a loan of money it shows that he has not sufficient credit in the business world; for the right kind of business man credit should take the place of loans.

Now Roman law offers a conception for this form of credit, which I wish to communicate to the reader and apply for our purposes. This indeed is my sole reason for inserting here the entire discussion concerning Roman law. It may be expressed briefly in the words that every case of credit contains an *accessory loan* undertaken in connection with the principal transaction.

If a buyer has not the money to pay the purchase price, he must find some one who will lend him the money — a loan must make the contract of sale possible. Now the seller can give him the loan just as well as anybody else,[30] and he does this when he trusts him with the price. He does it not out of benevolence, but in his own interest, in order to make possible the sale at the price demanded by him. If he found a buyer who would take the thing for cash at the same price, he would not give the credit; in business no one gives credit who does not profit thereby. Even in the case where the seller does not stipulate interest on the price, and receives therefore no interest as a matter of form, he gets it as a matter of fact. For it is in the price; and the merchant who sells "on time," allows therefore quite consistently to the buyer who does not wish to avail himself of it, a reduction for cash (deduction, discount).

The juristic process of crediting the purchase price must therefore be thought of in this way, *viz.*, that the seller in the capacity of lender turns over the purchase money to himself in his capacity as seller,[31] and the price is thus paid.

[30] A counterpart to this is found in D. 19. 2. 15 § 6, where the passenger advances the fare to the boatman before the termination of the voyage in the form of a loan ("vectura, quam pro mutuo acceperat"), an accessory loan, which serves subsequently, after the termination of the voyage, as a payment of the fare. The recipient pays it to himself in his capacity of sailor.

[31] Juristic manipulations of this kind are not rare among the Roman jurists. [So, for example, the guardian in his capacity as debtor of his ward must pay to himself in his capacity as the latter's representative, *i. e.*, he must enter it on the ledger as paid, D. 26. 7. 9 § 5. Another example in D. 12.1. 15]. For the technique of the law they cannot by any means be dispensed with.

In order that the process here assumed should find its correct juristic expression, there would be need of a special juristic transaction for the purpose of changing the purchase debt into a loan debt, and we should know very little of the old Roman law if we could not maintain with the greatest assurance that it has given the transaction this form. The solemn transfer of ownership ("mancipatio") offered no opportunity for this. Credit had therefore to be brought either into the form of loan ("nexum") corresponding to our promissory note, or into the form of a literal contract,[32] or a verbal contract.[33] After the formless contract of sale had become actionable, its binding force was extended also to the subsidiary agreement whereby the purchase price was credited. The negotiation of the credit, though a distinct transaction, *viz.*, the subsidiary loan, thus became superfluous.[34] Procedurally this found its expression in the fact that a credited selling price was sued for under the "actio venditi." The old conception of the purchase price as a loan to the buyer is still traceable in the rule that he has to pay interest on it from the moment of the delivery of the object.

The foregoing exposition has had for its object to make clear the *juristic form* of credit, as it is found expressed in Roman law, in order by this means to prepare for the following discussion, which is concerned with its social-economic significance.

[32] An example in the celebrated case of fraud in *Cicero*, "De Officiis," III, 14: "nomina facit, negotium conficit."

[33] That credit assumes thereby the form of a loan is expressly recognized in D. 14. 6. 3 § 3. "Si in creditum abii . . . ex causa emptionis . . . et stipulatus sim, licet coeperit esse pecunia mutua."

[34] The possibility, however, of changing the purchase debt afterwards into a loan by means of a simple contract still remained, D. 12. 1. 15.

We start from the proposition which served to introduce the subject of credit above (p. 118), *viz.*, that without credit commerce would be the most imperfect and most unmanageable thing in the world. The purpose of commerce demands credit so greatly that its necessity will appear everywhere with compelling force.

The purpose of commerce consists in the satisfaction of human wants. The form in which this satisfaction is carried out is the contract of exchange in the widest sense, *viz.*, something done or given for something else. Therefore, since money has become the normal form of equivalent for all things desired, commerce means the procurement, by means of money, of something done or given.

But suppose the person in want of something has no money. In this case if he is not in a position to procure the satisfaction of his need by the sale of his belongings —and that too perhaps only with the greatest loss— he would not be able to satisfy his need, and he would be denied bread, upon which the lives of his children, as well as his own life, are dependent. Even if he had the most certain prospect of getting the money soon, he becomes temporarily indigent.

This gap which the system of exchange in the above form leaves open is filled by credit. Credit assists the need of the present by applying to the future.

The need of the present may be helped in the first place by a friend. But friendship and benevolence do not constitute a factor of commerce (p. 83). The lever upon which it counts and must count is egoism, which has the advantage that it never fails.

The loan of a friend is gratuitous, that of an egoist is paid; he requires interest. In this way the loan subordinates itself to the principle of the system of exchange, *viz.*, performance for a consideration. Interest is the equivalent for the temporary handing over of capital. Time is money, in reference to the money's, as well as the man's power of acquisition.

But even with this condition attached, the person in need receives the money only when the lender is confident that he will get it back later. The *economic* "credere" of the money has as its presupposition the *moral* "credere" in the person. Credit is belief in the domain of economics; the believers are the creditors.

The lender as the possessor of funds, which he puts at the disposition of the borrower, we call *capitalist*, and the funds, *capital*.[35] If the present has more than it needs, it lays by, under good management, a surplus for the future — it *saves*. When these savings become more than is generally used up by normal individual need, we call them *capital*. Capital is the surplus of economy which has withstood victoriously the attack of constant need. It follows from this that the concept is relative. A sum of three hundred marks, or even of thirty, may be capital for a poor man, *i. e.*, a saving perfectly secure from these attacks. For a rich man, ten or a hundred times this sum may not yet be capital, for capital begins where expenditure need no longer claim all that is available.

Now as trade in merchandise brings the object from the place where it does not fulfil its function of serving

[35] The designation "caput" for the sum lent (in the sense of the principal thing as opposed to the interest, the secondary thing) dates from the time of the later Roman Empire; the earlier term was "sors." Like the expression "caput," so the modern terms, capital, capitalist, involve the economic exploitation of money by means of interest. When we are not thinking of the latter, we speak of money. The function of capital is to bear interest. A capitalist in the eminent sense of the term is the man who can live on his interest (income ["Renten"], hence "Rentier" [a person living on his income]).

human need to the place where it does, so trade in money does the same with regard to capital. Interest is the lever in this process. It draws money from the place where it has accumulated without finding economic employment to the place where it is wanting and needed. Superfluity in one place and want in the other compensate each other; what the one has too much of comes in handy to the person who has too little. The economy of the past, present and future is equalized and divided between two persons. The past falls to the capitalist; for he had to save to be able to lend; the present and future fall to him who borrows the money; the present in the form of a deficit, the future with the task of covering this deficit by an eventual surplus. In the economic world we find a similar phenomenon of equalization to that represented in the cosmic world by the equalization of heat over the various seasons, regions, land and sea.

But the loan of the capitalist who lends us money, whether he gives it himself or opens a credit for us with another, is not the only means by which we can relieve our need. With this is associated the second species of credit, mentioned above (p. 123), in connection with another contract, *viz.*, the giving credit for the *sum* of money in contradistinction to giving cash. The principal occasion for this is offered by the contract of sale, and in view of this we will designate this species as *merchandise credit* in contradistinction to the *money credit* of the loan, following in this the usage of ordinary life, which speaks of "taking goods on credit." That juristically it is not the goods but the purchase price which is given on credit, has been remarked above (p. 122).

In the legal sense the price is credited only when there is an agreement to that effect. If this is not the case, then the purchase, even if the seller allows the goods to be taken away without receiving payment, is, legally speaking, a purchase for cash. The giving credit is in this case purely a *de facto* arrangement, a contractual "precarium," to which the seller can put an end at any moment, and which does not therefore involve, according to the Roman law, the ownership of the object purchased. The latter presupposes payment or contractual credit of the price. But this distinction is without particular significance for the economic function of credit in our present business life, which is the only thing to be taken into account in the following investigation. Actually, pure credit *de facto*, where the seller can, if he chooses, demand the price of the goods immediately after delivery, or send a bill and insist on its payment, but does not do so, plays a scarcely less important role than credit in the meaning of the law.

Merchandise credit in the wider sense is distinguished from money credit by the fact that the latter is demanded by the nature of the business itself — a loan without credit is a contradiction in terms — whereas in purchase it is an accidental addition which may be wanting. The contract of sale began as a sale for cash, and it is only in the course of development that sale on credit became associated with it. The idea of credit first saw the light of day in the loan which is exclusively based upon it, and it was only later on transferred from it to the contract of sale. Even without the historical evidence which the Roman law presents in support of this proposition (p. 125), we should find ourselves driven to it from general considerations. The born lender is the capitalist, who has amassed money by his savings, and his interest is to find another with whom he can turn it into profit in the form of interest. The lender tries to get rid of his money, whereas the seller tries to get it, and frequently he is so far from being at the same time a capitalist that on the contrary the want of money is not seldom his only motive for selling.

What causes him to credit the price? Evidently nothing but his own interest. If he can sell just as advantageously for cash as on credit, he allows no credit. He allows it only either to make possible a sale which would otherwise not have taken place at all, or to get a higher price. In either case the contract of sale must pay for the credit which he allows.

In giving credit the seller undertakes economically the role of the lender, of the capitalist. He saves the buyer the necessity of procuring the money he needs from the capitalist, who is the special man for the purpose, and does himself what originally the latter alone did, *viz.*, to put at his disposal the money which he needs, and which is required for the conclusion of the purchase. That is, he lends it to him, not as the other, in the form of an independent loan, but as an accessory loan, which is inserted as a constituent element in the contract. Whether it assumes the juristic form of a loan, as was the case in old Roman business, and as happens with us in the business of merchants by the drawing of a bill of exchange, is indifferent so far as the *economic* view of the transaction is concerned. The seller does actually exercise the function of a lender. The interest, without which the capitalist does not make the loan, is found by the seller, in the absence of express stipulation, in the amount of the price, which is set higher, in view of the credit allowed, than it would be in a sale for cash.

Looked at in this way, money credit and merchandise credit come under the same point of view, *viz.*, the loan. Money credit is an independent, open loan; merchandise credit is an accessory, latent loan. The practical significance of the transference of credit from loan to contract of sale cannot be estimated too highly; it belongs to the number of those business factors of prime importance which have given an exceptional form to the entire system of commerce. By admitting credit into the business of merchandise, exchange has received that complete form of which it is capable, beyond which it is capable of no further progress.

In order to appreciate properly the significance which merchandise credit has for commerce, we must distinguish, I think, two applications of it. The one belongs to private (not mercantile) exchange, the other to mercantile transactions; credit which the *private man* (non-merchant) takes, and credit which the merchant takes. The former I shall call *private* credit, the latter *mercantile* (or *trade*) credit.

Contracts of sale concerning movable things in which private persons are on both sides form the exception in business intercourse; as a rule the other party is a merchant (in the widest sense of the word), who makes a business of buying and selling; a shopkeeper, a dealer in old clothes, an innkeeper, a bookseller, an artisan, a banker, etc. In comparison with the enormous number of contracts of sale which are daily carried out in this form, those in which one private man sells to the other vanish almost into nothing. In the life of many persons years, even a whole lifetime, may pass without the occurrence of such a case, and when it does happen once, the sale is as a rule for cash. Only the breaking up of a household in case of death, of change of place, etc., brings the private man into the position of appearing as a seller of movable property, and the sale takes place as a rule in the public form of an auction sale. On such an occasion the question of credit confronts him likewise. It is an experience with which the Romans already were familiar that one can get higher prices in auction sales on credit than for cash, and this was the basis in Rome of the organization of credit in auction sales. It consisted in assigning the giving of credit to the "argentarius," the Roman auctioneer, who was, by reason of his personal knowledge, the proper man to judge the solvency of the particular bidder, and who undertook the giving of credit on his own risk for a certain percentage of the entire income, exactly like the modern auctioneer who undertakes the "del credere" on a certain commission, and after deducting this pays the owner the entire amount at once in cash. The private person wishes as far as possible to have nothing to do with the giving of credit, and leaves it to the business man.

In the sale of immovable property, the case is quite different from what it is in the sale of movable. Here credit is the rule. A portion of the price is paid; the other portion, as a rule the larger, remains on the estate, bearing interest and secured by reservation of the title or by mortgage. The seller advances the buyer the sum, which the latter would otherwise have to borrow from some one else, and assumes the economic function of the lender. This case of credit comes under the point of view of *real credit* in contradistinction to *personal* credit. It has nothing in it of credit in the sense of trust. In demanding real security the seller shows that he has no trust in the buyer; he lends him indeed ("credere" in the economic sense), but he does not trust him ("credere" in the moral sense).

We, therefore, may say that in a private sale credit in this latter sense has a very subordinate role; in a thousand cases of credit given by the merchant there is perhaps not one given by the private person. The private person makes sure of his object, and he can and must do so, for he does not make a living from the sale as the merchant does, who in order to increase his sales is obliged to call in the aid of this artificial means of inducement, and with whom the loss which he suffers in a particular case is distributed over a large number of cases and thereby neutralized. As his business makes it necessary for him to give credit, the advantages of giving credit pay for its risks — the merchant insures himself.

We must distinguish between the private man and the merchant in reference to the persons to whom credit is given. As regards the creditor himself there is no essential difference, to be sure; he tries in both cases to make possible by means of it the closing of a deal which would otherwise perhaps not have taken place, and he risks in the one case as much as in the other, except that the risk assumes greater dimensions with the merchant. But in reference to the other party, credit exercises an essentially different function in the two cases, which I think I can fittingly express by the terms *consumers' credit* and *trade credit.* The former finds its motive and its measure in the immediate need of the thing which is given on credit. The condition of a lack of money to cover the cost is here the exception, not the rule. The management of private affairs should be so arranged, and is as a rule so arranged, that there is no need of credit with the shopkeeper, baker, butcher, etc. The respectable housekeeper makes no debts, does not live on credit, just as he is not in the habit of giving credit himself. Cash payment is the principle of a well ordered household, the necessity of credit is a proof of disturbance — whether due to improvidence or to misfortune — of the normal relation.

The case is quite different in trade credit, where it is not a question of obtaining the thing for the purpose of satisfying one's own want, but for the purpose of selling it. The respectable merchant may receive credit without losing his standing, and he must do so; he would not be a merchant if he did not utilize it for his operations. The sale of his goods must furnish him the means with which he covers the purchase; he must buy more than he can pay for at once. Credit constitutes an essential and absolutely indispensable factor and lever of his business management; the measure in which he enjoys it is the criterion of his competence and importance in the mercantile world. The distinction between the *normal* form of private management and business management may be expressed in two words, *cash payment* and *credit.*

As a matter of fact, however, the use of credit even in private affairs has increased in a manner which hardly bears out the last proposition. It is not limited by any means to the compelling occasion which first called it into life, *viz.*, the want of cash money — I might call it in this form *emergency credit*—but it is given and taken where this condition is not at all present. There is many a place and many a business where it is forced upon the customer against his will; cash payment is refused as if it were dishonorable for the seller to accept it; a bill can scarcely be gotten from him before the time when he is in the habit of presenting it. In place of immediate payment or immediate presentation of the bill, the custom has arisen of presenting it periodically at certain dates. Wherein does the motive of this consist? In the first edition of this work I placed it in the facilitation of the mode of payment which is effected thereby for both parties — the burdensome and annoying small, daily payments at the grocer's, baker's, butcher's, are replaced by periodically recurrent larger ones — and designated it accordingly as the *credit of convenience.* I am now convinced that this conception does not wholly cover the object which is aimed at in the matter. The credit of convenience is at the same time calculated to cover the emergency credit; it is meant to save customers to whom the latter would apply the embarrassment of asking for it, which would perhaps keep them from buying altogether. In order that it may be given naturally to those for whom it is specially intended, it is given to *all*. The arrangement must be general in order to offer its service to those for whom it is intended.

Such is credit in the domain of private life. But the full development of its force it attains only in the domain of mercantile life. A private person who has an income of a thousand a year will not under proper management take more than a thousand a year on credit, but even a responsible merchant who owns ten thousand often does business of a hundred thousand and more. The function which mercantile credit exercises does not consist, as it does in private credit, in making harmless the momentary inequality between the need and the means, but in affording the business man the possibility of using another's capital for his business in order to be able to speculate with it. Hence we may designate this form of credit as *credit of speculation*. The goods which are delivered to him without payment constitute for him a sort of loan of capital (money value instead of money), the credit which he receives is meant to strengthen his resources; it is given in view of the success which it helps to bring about.

But the advantages which credit offers to the mercantile business must be dearly paid for. Credit exposes the otherwise hardy constitution of business to a serious danger, to periodic disturbances and interruptions of its normal functions of life. Credit is similar to narcotics. A proper use tends to stimulate the powers of man, to animate and increase them, but when used to excess they produce instead of refreshment, relaxation and weakness. The same is true of credit in trade. If it is used properly, it raises the powers of the individual above the ordinary scale and stimulates commerce, but when used beyond measure its effect is devastating; destroying those who take it as well as those who give it. In regard to spirituous intoxication, our language describes the condition of involuntary expiation decreed by nature for excess in the use of liquors by the term "katzenjammer." In commerce it is called a "business crisis"; in more recent times the term "crash" also has come into use. Crash is the economic "katzenjammer" resulting from excessive use of credit — "Schwindel" (swindle, vertigo) plays a great role in both.

The cause of this danger lies in the fact that credit operates with another man's capital. Of the sum *x* which the dealer on credit stakes on the card, only one-tenth *x* perhaps belongs to him, and the other nine-tenths to B. If the undertaking succeeds, the whole gain accrues to him; if it fails, then the risk exceeding one-tenth *x* does not fall on him but on others. If the whole *x* were his own, he would bear the entire risk himself and would therefore be more cautious in staking it. Credit is a means of encouraging risks — the less a man has, the more advantageous it is for him to speculate, if he finds people to give him credit.

With credit in business we have reached the highest stage of the system of commerce which is based upon economic reward, that term being understood in the widest sense as above explained (p. 98). But economic reward is not the only form in which society applies the concept of reward for its purposes; there is still another to which we will now pass on.

§ 7. *Ideal Reward and Its Combination with Economic Reward.* Our language does not limit the concept of reward to that form of it alone which we have been considering till now, namely, money; for it uses it also in a moral sense for every good which falls to anyone's share as compensation for a meritorious act. For example, it speaks of the reward of virtue, of diligence, etc. Whether this wider concept of reward has any significance for *commerce* will appear in the sequel; that it has importance for *society*, cannot be a matter of doubt. Reward in this wider sense forms the counterpart of punishment. Society punishes him who has wronged her; she rewards him who deserves well at her hands.

The use which society makes of reward nowadays is far behind that of punishment; she has taken in this respect, in comparison with antiquity, a considerable step backward. In Rome reward and punishment, as the two means at the disposal of society for the carrying out of her purposes, were regarded by the sociologist as fully equal. A Roman jurist does not hesitate on the question of the final purpose of the law to put reward on one and the same plane with punishment.[36] This is highly significant! What has the jurist to do with reward? Nowadays, nothing; nowadays, punishment alone is confided to him, a *legal* claim to reward for distinguished and unusual merits belongs to no one. But this very thing reflects the enormous difference between the Roman world and our own, *viz.*, that public reward in Rome had not as with us a merely social significance, but a *legal* significance. The *law of reward* — an idea unfamiliar to us — corresponded in Rome to the *law of punishment* (criminal law). Nay, it is not saying too much to maintain that up to the codification of the criminal law at the end of the Republic, the law of reward was more clearly defined than the criminal law. The criminal law was administered by the Roman people with a freedom which verged on arbitrariness.[37] Whether

[36] D. 1. 1. 1 § 1. ". . . bonos non solum metu poenarum, verum etiam praemiorum quoque exhortatione efficere cupientes."

[37] See my "Geist des römischen Rechts," II § 25 (4th ed., p. 46 ff.).

they should recognize a penalty, and which one, was always a matter of their free choice. But whether the general deserved a triumph or an ovation, whether the soldier had a claim to the "corona muralis," "civica," "castrensis," "navalis" — the military decorations of the Romans — was a matter of detailed regulation, and might even furnish a cause of action.[38] To the triumphs and olive wreaths of the Olympic games, to the mural and civic crowns of antiquity correspond, according to their character, our decorations of today; our titles and ennoblements. But these are not a matter of right, but of supreme grace or favor, and the notion that they represent the undoubted proof of distinguished social merit is nowhere more effectually guarded against than at the source of their bestowal, because there the operative motives, levers and considerations are best known. They can be often compared with apples which cannot be reached by those who stand at a distance, but fall in the laps of those who sit under the tree, or who are in a position to be able to shake it. Whether this form of the matter will in course of time give room to another; whether the same revolution will take place in the State's system of reward as has taken place in its penal system, by an advance from subjective choice to fixed rules and law, which would be no more than a return

[38] *Val. Max.* II, 8, 2 " . . . judicium, . . . in quo de *jure* triumphandi . . . actum." The whole eighth chapter in this writer treats "de *jure* triumphandi." For an action in claim of a "corona muralis," which is said almost to have led to a military uprising, see *Livy*, 26, 48. For the "jus civicae coronae" see *Gellius*, VI, 5 § 13. There were other rewards of a juristic nature which were connected with definite conditions, for example, the attainment of complete civic power and of "patria potestas" for an "imperfect citizen" (Latini Juniani, Ulp. III, Gaj. I, 66), the "jus liberorum," so important in connection with the right of succession and otherwise — the premium of a fruitful marriage.

to the method of antiquity — this I leave to every one's own opinion; I for my part believe in it. Whether it is reward or punishment (the function of both being simply the realization of the idea of justice) that errs, *i. e.*, misses the right man and finds the wrong one, is equally incompatible with the idea of justice.

But it is not the personal representative of sovereignty alone who rewards social merit; there is an impersonal power besides, *viz.*, public opinion and also history, which rectify the errors which the former may have committed. They have honors to confer with which the favors of the ruler cannot even remotely compare. For those which he controls are of an exceedingly evanescent character; they are buried with their bearer — naïve vanity hits the nail on the head when it fastens those decorations to the coffin! But the laurel around Dante's temples is ever green and will never fade; one leaf of it outweighs wagon loads of grand crosses.

The species of reward which I have considered just now I designate as *ideal* reward. I call it ideal in contradistinction to material reward (money), which bears its value in itself, whereas the ideal value depends solely upon the ideas which are associated with it. What are three horsetails, a peacock's feather, a ribbon in the buttonhole, for him who does not know what they signify, and what are they even for him who does know but puts no value upon such honors? External marks of honor possess no higher value for their owner than he himself puts upon them; money, on the contrary, retains its full value, its economic power, even in the hands of him who values it slightly. It is of the greatest interest to society that ideal reward should stand in the highest possible estimation. The higher the value which is put upon it, the more effective is the lever which society therein possesses for the achievement of her purposes.

We have defined commerce (*supra* p. 74) as the system of the regulated and assured satisfaction of human wants. In these wants, however, are counted not only those of the body, such as eating and drinking, clothing and shelter, but for a certain portion of the population also the ideal interests of art and science. He who satisfies these fulfils thereby a purpose of commerce; the artist and the scholar therefore serve commerce no less than the farmer, the artisan and the merchant. Art and science, too, go out on the market and offer their treasures for sale; the painter his picture, the sculptor his statue, the composer his symphony, the scholar his manuscript. By this means, it might seem, they place themselves on a line with all others who hold their products or manufactures for sale, *viz.*, the farmer, the manufacturer, the artisan, and tread the economic level of business life. They accept reward for their work, consequently it is wages ("Arbeitslohn"), and whatever applies to the one group applies to the other.

It is by all means necessary to free oneself from this view. Not indeed because it degrades art and science, but because it distorts the truth in such a way as to prevent one understanding the reality. The true view recognizes two spheres of social work. In the one, money constitutes the only purpose and is the lever of all operations which take place therein; in the other, the individual by his efforts has another aim in view besides money making. To the second sphere belong art and science, the service of the Church and the State. Language with its fine discrimination has correctly grasped the difference between the two spheres. In the one it calls the reward "wages" ("Arbeitslohn), in the second it carefully avoids using this expression and replaces it by other terms. The writer, composer, physician receives no "pay" ("Lohn") or "wages" ("Arbeitslohn"), but a "honorarium," the official receives "salary" ["Gehalt," "Besoldung"] (in case of extraordinary compensation, "remuneration"), the lawyer, "fees" ("Deserviten"). This is no mere politeness of expression, meant to conceal the fact that the receiver works for money, nor is the difference in designation merely aimed at the contrast of physical and intellectual work. According to my mind, it is meant to express the relation of the reward to the work. Reward constitutes for the ordinary workman the sole motive of his work, whereas the physician, lawyer, artist, scholar, teacher, preacher, government official, unless indeed he is a mere workman, seeks the motive of his activity and his satisfaction by no means exclusively in the money, but also in something superior; if the usage of language had its basis in mere etiquette, science would have every reason to free itself from it, for it would in that case rest only upon an ancient prejudice, which is quite obsolete nowadays, that there is something dishonorable in accepting pay for work (p. 81). Where the pay is purely return for labor, an avoidance of this expression on account of the social position of the receiver would be just as senseless as if one wanted to call purchase money, rent, interest, operations in stocks in case of persons of high standing, by a different name from that they bear among persons of lower rank. Language is too intelligent a thing to lay stress upon matters so absolutely irrelevant.

The essence of salary and all other similar forms of reward depends upon the combination of economic and ideal reward. They add to the two species of simple reward, *viz.*, the purely economic and the purely ideal, still a third, which is composed of both; I will call it the *mixed*. It is conceivable that in this combination the two elements are only united as in a mixture without mutually affecting each other. In this case the principles of wages would apply fully to salary also. That this is, however, not the case, but that the combination influences the economic reward in such a way that under certain circumstances not the least trace is left of that which constitutes its essence, the giving of an equivalent for the work — of this anyone can convince himself who wishes to make a trial in the three relations mentioned: art, science, and public (State, Church) service.

Is the high compensation of a Catholic ecclesiastical prince an equivalent for his work? Does the difference, often so great, between the salary of the president of a board and that of the other board members correspond to the difference in value of their labor power, or the difference in the measure of their exertion? Is the honorarium of the writer or composer always regulated according to the value of his writing or composition? Schubert gave away many of his immortal compositions for almost nothing, while at the same time and in the same place Strauss, the composer of waltzes, received hard cash for his waltzes.

Is it the money that guides the hand of the painter, the sculptor, the poet, the scholar? Cornelius sacrificed many years of time and trouble in the Villa Bartholdi in Rome without any pay, only for the sake of bringing fresco painting into favor again, and yet he was a man altogether without means, and found himself often in the most pressing need. Alexander von Humboldt lost his entire fortune in the service of science, and many a scholar spends half a lifetime of effort on a work which often scarcely brings him enough to pay for the paper, the ink and the oil. Does a shoemaker, a tailor, a manufacturer, a merchant, work many years for nothing solely for love of his work? The honorarium of the artist, the poet, the scholar, is not a wage; it lacks the most essential characteristic of wage: equivalence (p. 101). It may be high where the work is easy, low where the work is hard, and may be wanting entirely where the work reaches the highest grade. And these are not merely single instances; there are entire branches of scientific literature which find themselves in the position of being obliged to do without any honorarium, and they give actual proof of being able to do so, as for example the natural sciences. Here the special journals exist without paying their contributors, and the cost of independent treatises with engraved illustrations not infrequently must in part at least be defrayed by the author.

The lever therefore which sets the talent for art and science in action cannot be found in economic reward. But there exists a reward with which the economic is allied, and which sometimes takes its place entirely, and that is, the *ideal*.

I distinguish two kinds of ideal remuneration: *external* and *internal*. By the first I understand the reward which is paid by society or the power of the State (p. 138): fame, recognition, honor; by the second I denote that satisfaction which a work itself affords; such is the delight in intellectual work *per se*, the charm of proving one's power, the joy of discovery, the pleasure in creating, the consciousness of having done a service to the world, of having utilized one's faculties for the welfare of humanity. The social effectiveness of ideal reward presupposes a subjective susceptibility to it, *viz.*, the ideal sense. Peoples, ages, individuals who lack this sense will never achieve anything great in the domain of art and science — the ideal flourishes only on ideal soil. The typical motive for art and science without which they cannot fulfil their calling is idealism, the typical motive for business is the desire for gain. An artist who cares for nothing else than the gain, who has no other interest in the work which he creates than that it should be paid for, is a somewhat superior type of artisan, and will never create a real work of art — where the interests of gain and art clash he will give preference to the former. The counterpart of this man who allows himself to be guided by economic motives in an ideal sphere, is the business man who should wish to pursue ideal interests instead of gain in the economic sphere. Both have missed their vocation; they pursue within it an aim for which it is not intended; the former should have been an artisan, a merchant, or manufacturer; the latter an artist or scholar. Business must be pursued in a businesslike manner, the ideal in an ideal manner; and this way lies the success of the individual and of society. By this it is not of course intended to give expression to the foolish idea that the ideal and the practical are opposites which are incompatible in the same person, so that he who feels called upon to represent the former must be unpractical, and he who represents the latter must be inaccessible to the ideal. Experience shows the truth of the contrary in both domains, and in reference to the practical man, art and science have every reason to think gratefully of their advancement, frequently made only through those sacrifices by which booksellers and art dealers of the higher type have made their works possible.

In art and science the equivalent of the performance, which according to the preceding discussion is a union of the ideal and the economic reward, varies greatly, and the establishment of a fixed scale, such as is possible in pay for work, would be an impossibility. The case is different in the service of the Church and the State. Here we are presented with a system of reward in which the two component elements, the economic (salary), and the ideal (rank), rise in a uniform progression from the lower stage to the higher. There is here a carefully thought out and systematically arranged scale of rewards. The principle of remuneration here is the official estimation of the importance of the office for the purposes of the State, and in monarchies also for the person of the ruler — the degree which each one occupies within it can be estimated by the salary and rank. Supplementary to this *ordinary* system of reward there is besides an *extraordinary* reward, which is measured in accordance with the merits of each case as it occurs; economic reward in the shape of remuneration; ideal reward in the shape of a title of honor (in contradistinction to the official title), and a decoration.

But not in all cases where the State, to which I confine myself in the sequel — for the same conditions essentially apply to the Church and the municipalities alike — not in all cases where the State pays for the services rendered it, does the remuneration belong to the above described system of rewards. The clerk in the chancery does not receive a "salary" but "pay" ("Lohn") in the sense of wages; the common soldier receives no "salary," but compensation ("Löhnung"), and many services the State does not pay for at all. If we turn over in our mind all the services which are rendered to the State, we shall find that they rest upon two levers, *compulsion* and *reward*. We will briefly formulate these.

I. *Compulsion*. Certain services, as for example that of the soldier, the juror, the witness, the State compels. These constitute a civic duty just as much as the payment of public taxes. What determines the application of compulsion in these is not the indispensable nature of the service. Judges and military officers are quite as indispensable as jurors and common soldiers, and yet the latter are compelled, the former are not. The reason is two-fold. First, because every one not affected by special disabilities is capable of performing these services, and also because by reason of their temporary duration no one is hindered because of them in the choice and pursuit of a civil vocation. Service of the State, on the other hand, in the professional sense of the term presupposes a fitness to be gained only by long preparation, and the permanent and exclusive devotion to it demands the pledge of one's whole existence. This is a sacrifice which the State cannot without being unjust impose arbitrarily upon this or that person, but which it must make dependent upon the free choice of the individual, and make possible by granting a livelihood (see below). Where an indemnity is granted for those compulsory services also (the compensation of the soldier, the fees of the witnesses, the allowances of the jurors), it does not come under the point of view of reward, but under that of living expenses during the time of service (see below).

II. *Reward.* This takes a three-fold form:

1. *Purely economic reward, or wages.* Wages for services rendered to the State are those of the industrial, inferior and dependent services; and not merely the temporary (those of the men in the offices paid by the day, of the day laborers and workmen in the construction of public works), but also the permanent (those of the clerical employees). The scale fixed for their payment, which is often in crying disproportion to the salary of the officials, shows that theirs is a purely economic remuneration, an equivalent for the work. But their case is in the popular mind already affected by the ideal element. A faint reflection of the splendor of State service falls also upon the chanceries and offices, gilding the pens and the inkstands. The most insignificant member of the personnel of the chancery feels elevated by the thought of being a member of the great machinery called the State — there is need only of a title: actuary, secretary, councilor of the chancery, to raise the sense of his own dignity to the greatest height.

2. *Purely Ideal Reward.* Those positions in which the equivalent for the service consists solely in the position of power and honor which is connected with them, are called *posts of honor, offices of honor.* Having comprehended in ancient Rome the entire upper sphere of the State government (the "honores"), they gave place in later Rome to paid service of the State (p. 86 f.). In modern Europe, after having been restricted for centuries to the sphere of the service of the Church and the municipality, it is not until recent times that they again recovered a highly influential position in the unsalaried popular representation. Where the representative of the people receives an allowance, the post falls under the next following category.

3. *Mixed Reward.* If the service is of a permanent nature, the economic reward granted for it is called salary, "Besoldung" (payment), "Gage" (remuneration); if it is of a temporary nature, like that of a popular representative, or an official who has to execute a commission, it is called a per diem. In both cases, in my opinion, it comes under the same point of view, *viz.*, that of support befitting one's station during the time of service. The State exempts the incumbent of the post from the care of earning his livelihood, permanently in the former case, temporarily in the latter. In the case of per diem payments no one will doubt it; they are from their nature nothing but expense allowances, and their amount is therefore determined not by the character of the work, whether it be hard or easy, but according to what is demanded to maintain the recipient in a manner befitting his station. This point of view is quite clear in the various classes of per diem allowances. That it applies also to salary can be shown I think with a conclusiveness leaving nothing to be desired, and I do not regard it as superfluous to furnish the proof,

since the political economists have brought salary under the concept of wages, which, in my opinion, is erroneous.

Salary is not wages, *i. e.*, it is not an equivalent for service, for it often remains exceedingly far behind the measure determined by business as the value of work. Banks and other private enterprises have often offered government officials whom they desired to take into their service many times, in many cases as much as ten times, the salary which they had hitherto received. Evidently, then, the latter was no equivalent for their work. I believe the same is true regarding the rate of salary of most clergymen and teachers; it is sometimes even below the income of a subordinate official — there are sextons and beadles who are better off than the clergymen and professors placed above them. The matter is most plain in the case of the military officer. It is impossible to see in his pay an equivalent for the life which his oath to the flag obliges him to risk. For the rich the pay is scarcely more than pocket money. The money comes so little into consideration that they would serve without any pay, and it is only the circumstance that the rich alone are not enough to cover the need of officers which makes it necessary for the State to pay a salary at all.

Wages of labor vary according to the quality and amount of the work; the skilful and diligent worker earns more than the unskilled and slothful. In the service of the State this circumstance exerts no influence in reference to the *salary;* every official of the same category, whether eminent or mediocre, receives the same amount. The difference of calibre between individuals may determine promotion and remuneration of a special kind (p. 145), but it exerts no influence upon salary. For the salary is as a rule fixed by law and does not accommodate itself to the individual, as wages do to so considerable an extent. Whilst the latter fluctuate according to supply and demand, the former remains quite stationary for entire periods, the influences to which labor and wages are subject having no power over salary. If the laborer is incapacitated his wage ceases; in the case of an official his salary continues as pension. A capable business man must have earned so much by the time he reaches old age as to have repaid the capital which he had to spend in preparing for his work and to have acquired enough to be able to live. That with an official this is not as a rule the case, is known. His salary hardly yields support befitting his station for him and his family, not to speak of sufficing to repay the original investment, or to allow provision for old age. And when one of our first authorities in political economy [39] applies to the service of the State the otherwise self-evident postulate that work must cover its own net cost, I think I have two reasons to oppose to this statement. *First*, that so far as I can judge this is actually not the case. An official who does not want to give offence by declining to incur the expense of his station imposed upon him for himself and family by his position and by custom, is not in a position to save anything. *Secondly*, that we need not and must not make this requirement in the service of the State. The original investment of the official is paid for by the fact that he enjoyed the life-long advantage of being an official, an advantage which he has over every business man, and for which he does not pay too high by the loss of his invested capital. The advantages of official position lie partly in what I designate as ideal reward: social position, rank, power, influence, character of work, and partly in the superiority of salary to wages. Being inferior to the

[39] *Engel*, "Über die Selbstkosten der Arbeit, zwei Vorlesungen," (Berlin, 1866).

latter in reference to amount, it makes up amply for this disadvantage by the following qualities: lifelong security, independence of all business disturbances and temporary incapacity, increase with advancing age, pension in case of complete disability to serve, the service of the State being practically an insurance institution.

These advantages explain how it is that in spite of the comparatively low salaries, the service of the State exercises even from the economic point of view so great an attraction. Of all those who have to work no one receives a smaller loaf, but at the same time no one gets a surer one and one less mixed with bran than the government official. To demand that the salary should pay his invested capital is nothing else than to invest capital in an annuity and demand that it be repaid at death.

For this reason, because salary as a rule yields no surplus above one's need, and does not make it possible to accumulate a capital, the son of the public official or military officer without means, if it were not for other enabling circumstances which I shall mention in the immediate sequel, would not be able to enter upon the vocation of his father. He would have to pass over to the industrial class, and the grandson would be able with the capital which the son has acquired to apply himself again to the vocation of his grandfather. For the interest of the service this change would not be advantageous. Sons of official and military families bring to the service views more conformable, and a temper more suitable to the vocation than sons of business people. To be sure, they also bring onesidedness and prejudices, but even in combination with these the endowment which they bring into the service from their parents' house is, after all, more valuable for it than the freedom from prejudice of the "homo novus." Now experience shows that these classes on the whole recruit themselves from their own numbers, even more so than the considerations indicated would seem to demand. There are two factors which make this possible. One is the free public preparatory institutions for certain branches of the public service (military academies, colleges for army surgeons, theological seminaries, boarding schools, foundations, etc.), as well as the facility for study by means of stipends, free board, etc. The second factor is the rich wife. She constitutes an important factor in the present system of the government service, a scarcely less important requirement than the passing of the examinations. Care is taken that the procuring of it shall not be too difficult — the daughter of the rich manufacturer or merchant becomes the wife of the military officer or State official; *she* brings *him* the money, *he* brings *her* social position, both are benefited.

We have so far brought out the negative fact that salary is *not* wages; let us now convince ourselves that the positive side of salary consists, as was stated above, in providing support befitting the station.

Wages, in the widest sense, give more than a mere livelihood;[40] salary gives nothing more than that. But note that it provides a livelihood *befitting one's station*, and this element is the key to the understanding of the entire matter of salary. What is "befitting one's station" is determined by the *rank* of the office, and this in turn is determined by the *power* connected with the office. It is not the greater or less measure of knowledge and experience required for the capable management of the

[40] This opinion, which was proved in a convincing manner by *Adam Smith* in his famous work, Vol. I, ch. 8, was attacked to be sure by the well-known theory of *Ricardo*, according to which labor wage should allow only what is absolutely necessary to support life, but it was surely not refuted by it.

various offices that determines the amount of the salary. In that case the ablest would receive the highest salary. But we cannot sufficiently warn the reader against seeing in salary the proper equivalent for anything, whether it be knowledge, or talent, or industry. Salary aims at nothing more than support according to one's station. He who has to incur greater expenses than another by reason of the importance of the office which he fills receives also more liberal means from the State for the purpose. And according to the State's classification of offices, not that is the highest which requires the greatest measure of knowledge and exertion, but that which bestows the greatest power, and hence bespeaks the greatest confidence. The State follows in this case the naïve popular opinion, which is imposed upon more by power and influence than by ability and knowledge. A minister, general, ambassador, nobly born but, as was formerly often the case in our small German States with their flourishing system of family influences, at the same time incapable, enjoyed among the masses much higher consideration than the most distinguished military officer or government official of lower rank. Great respect is indispensable to the complete effectiveness of a high position, and the latter again is conditional on the corresponding rank, title, salary.

The power, and thereby also the authority, of the State reaches its culminating point in the person of the monarch, and in a constitutional monarchy there corresponds to this the pecuniary endowment which is constitutionally attached to royalty; I mean the civil list. The idea of maintenance befitting the station is here so evident that there is no need of saying anything further about it.

I sum up the result of the preceding discussion in the

statement that salary is regulated according to position and not according to work done.

As a secondary element in the determination of salary is added a fair regard for the increasing need of support with advancing age. The unmarried does not need so much as the married; the first years of marriage, in which the expenses for children do not amount to very much, require less than the later when the children are grown up. That is why the salary grows with the years, which would otherwise not at all be justified in view of the unchanged amount of official work and the diminution rather than increase of capacity for work with advancing years.

If salary is intended to remove from the official anxieties for the means of existence, this extends also to his wife and children, for the possession of a family pertains to complete existence. In the pension of the widow this accessory function of salary appears in its independence and receives official recognition. The pension, that paid to the widow as well as to the official himself, is characterized as a continuation of the support after the cessation of service. If salary were wages, then pension would be an unwarranted abuse, which no conscientious financial administration would tolerate; but if on the contrary it is that which I conceive it to be, then pension is only its last corollary.

From the purpose which salary is intended to carry out there proceeds the obvious limitation by which an official is not permitted to pursue a business. If salary were wages like any other, there would be no reason why the State should forbid its official to obtain an increased income for himself by means of an additional business; we might, on the contrary, suppose that the State would welcome such effort on the part of the official thus to supplement an inadequate salary. But as the object of the salary is the granting of a livelihood by the State, apart from other considerations (division of activity, dependence upon the public, injury of social position) the pursuit of a business would justify the charge against the State that it does not give its servants that to which they have a just claim. That regard for an undiminished conservation of his working power for the service of the State is not the only ground of the prohibition is clearly proven from the fact that the same applies to the wives of the officials as to the officials themselves. The wife of a president may not keep a fancy goods shop; the wife of a mayor must not engage in the vegetable business; the husband who would tolerate such doings would thereby soon lose his own position.

My last argument I derive from the relative lowness of salaries. The salary never exceeds the limit of support in accordance with the station, whereas wages often go far beyond it. There are high salaries, but even the highest do not give more than, and often hardly as much as is necessary for living in a manner becoming one's station. No minister's salary approaches the income of a celebrated opera singer, of a famous surgeon, etc. Therefore an official in the service cannot save anything, cannot even have repaid to him the capital invested (p. 149). An artisan, a manufacturer, a merchant, who has not saved anything in the course of a long life and strenuous activity, has shown thereby that he did not understand his business, or that he managed badly. An official who acquired a fortune in the service of the State shows on the contrary that he either denied himself what he should have had, or appropriated what he should not have. In normal relations an official who entered the service without money leaves nothing but a wife and children, and not seldom also debts. The accounts of the State are correct only when his finances disappear with his death. And we must admit that the State well knows how to calculate. If any blame can be attached to it in reference to its regulations concerning salary, it is surely not that of exceeding the measure of support befitting the station, but rather that of falling below it. And this perhaps in a manner which not merely contains an injustice toward the individual but in a great measure also runs counter to the true interest of the service. A starvation diet may in certain circumstances be clearly called for, but whether it is the right means for developing a feeling of duty and the ideal sense may be doubted.

An interesting confirmation of the view developed above is furnished by the Roman nomenclature for the various compensations received for public service in Roman times. The pay of the subaltern officials is the only one which is designated as real pay for work ("merces");[41] for every other compensation the language emphasizes the purpose of maintenance.[42] Thus, for example, in military service we have the "stipendium," the "aes hordearium," the "salarium," the "congiarium,"[43] and in the later civil service the

[41] Lex Cornelia de XX quaestoribus I, 2; II, 33. (*Bruns*, "Fontes Juris Romani Antiqui," ed. III, p. 79), *Cicero*, Verr. III, 78.

[42] The item "Wohnung" (residence, lodging), which plays such a great role in the modern subject of salary (official residences, allowance for rent, real allowance) is not represented in the following list. Our modern expressions, such as "Gehalt" (salary), "Besoldung" (compensation), "Gage" (wage), "Remuneration," "Deputat" (allowance), unlike the Roman, contain no reference to the purpose. This can be seen only in "Teuerungszulage" (allowance for high cost of living).

[43] 1. "Stipendium" from "stips," which signifies in the usage of the later language a small financial support, but, to judge from its connection with "stipula" (blade of corn), it seems to have signified originally grain. Here we see a similar transition from the primitive

"annona," the "cibaria," the "sportula," the "viaticum," the "vasarium,"[44] and likewise the "salaria" of the public teachers of art and science.

All the special features of salary point to this concept of sustenance which we have suggested. To what extent it corresponds to the nature of the relation is clear. He who devotes himself to the service of the State or the Church must not have in view the acquisition of money, but his vocation. In order, however, that he may devote himself to it entirely, the State and the Church relieve him of the care for his sustenance — the declared purpose of salary consists in making possible economically an undivided devotion to one's calling.

Our investigation of the concept of reward is thus brought to a conclusion. It has led us to a relation which the usual meaning of the word "commerce" does not embrace, *viz.*, the service of the State and the Church, but which in reality is quite similar to it. Like commerce it represents the system of satisfying a want of society, and as in the former so here, too, the system depends upon the lever of reward, except that the reward assumes here quite a peculiar form. Whether a private

object of value of the husbandman, *viz.*, grain, to money, as it has taken place in cattle ("pecus" — "pecunia"). 2. "Aes hordearium," Gaj. IV, 27: "pecunia, ex qua hordeum equis erat comparandum." 3. "Salarium" — salt allowance paid in money. 4. "Congiarium" — originally a definite measure of oil, wine, salt.

[44] In "annona" and "cibaria" the meaning is plain; "sportula" signifies the fruit or food-basket, then in the time of the empire the fees of the bailiff; "viaticum," travelling expenses; "vasarium," a lump sum for the equipment of the provincial governor, which was formerly given to him in kind. The element of conformity to a man's station which I emphasized in salary is here expressly attested. See references in *Th. Mommsen*, "Röm. Staatsrecht," I, p. 240, note 2, p. 241, note 4, where (p. 244, *et seq.*) more is to be found concerning these expressions.

person employs a physician, an architect, etc., or whether the municipality or the State appoints him, in both cases it is a question on the one side of the satisfaction of needs, and on the other of the economic exploitation of services, *i. e.*, of the fact of a contract of exchange in the wider sense, and therefore of an act of commerce (p. 74).

Over against *exchange* as one fundamental form of commerce we placed above (p. 95) a second, *viz.*, *Association*. Let us turn to it now.

§ 8. *The Second Principal Form of Commerce; Association.* The contract of exchange presupposes a *difference* in purpose; the contract of association, an *identity*. Considered from the point of view of economic movement, the result of the former contract consists in the fact that two values, whether objects, money, or services, change places with each other. What the one had *before* the contract (even though, as in service, only potentially, and as a still unpicked fruit of personal power) the other has *after* its performance. In association, the movement of persons and things which participate in it is of a converging nature; they all steer toward the same goal; the goal as well as the way is the same; the final gain is a common one.

Why do I combine with another with whom I finally have to share profits? Is it from benevolence? Commerce knows no benevolence; all business contracts are built upon egoism, and so is association. This does not mean that the motive of benevolence may not sometimes come into play in business association also; this is doubtless just as possible as that one may out of good-will sell or let a thing below the price; it means merely that association, according to its function and meaning in commerce, serves not benevolence, but egoism. No egoist will share with another what he can have for himself. If he does share, it shows that he makes out better in sharing the profits of a common business than if he had transacted the business by himself.

Certain purposes exceed the means of the individual to such an extent, and are so dependent upon the united exertions of many, that isolated pursuit is altogether out of the question. For such, association is the only thinkable and the necessary form. Among these must be counted all such purposes as, at the present day, form the problem of political or religious communities or of the State. At a time when such communities did not exist, the one who desired to pursue such common purposes was obliged to look about for associates. Before these purposes, for example, public safety, laying out of streets, schools, care of the poor, appointment of preachers, building of churches, assumed the forms of political or ecclesiastical functions, they were pursued in the form of free association, as is still the case at the present day among the inhabitants of North America. For all these purposes the individual has only the choice of either renouncing them entirely or pursuing them in the form of combination with others. There are other purposes on the contrary which, to judge from experience, can be just as well pursued by individuals as by societies, for example, mercantile business and industrial enterprises. The motive which determines the individual to look about for an associate in these consists in the fact that he is in want of one or the other of the requirements necessary for the undertaking, which he can complete by inviting another person. He possesses by himself the required knowledge and business connections, but he has not sufficient capital, or conversely, he has the capital but not the technical knowledge; or he has both, but not the credit in the business world or the required business connections, etc., whereas another finds himself in possession of that which he lacks, and is ready to place it at his disposal. In the contract of exchange, the difference of purpose has corresponding to it a difference in the services rendered by the two parties (p. 95); in association, the identity of purpose is compatible with the difference as well as identity of the means contributed by the individuals.

This combination of the required means by getting the assistance of another is, however, possible not only in the form of association, but also in that of a contract of exchange. If a person possesses the money required for the undertaking but lacks the technical or mercantile knowledge, he fills the want by the employment of an engineer or a bookkeeper, etc. If he lacks sufficient money he adds to it by borrowing from the capitalist; in short, everything that is necessary for the undertaking can be procured just as well by contract as by association.

What it is that in such a case decides for the one or the other form cannot be stated in general terms. One is driven by circumstances to the choice of partnership because those to whom he applied demanded a share in the profit, or for the sake of security have insisted upon control and co-operation in the undertaking. Or he may think to avail himself more certainly of the zeal and the industry of the persons whom he needs if he allows them to share in the business. Another finds himself in a position to undertake the business on his own account and sees his advantage in choosing this form. What the legal consequences are which attach themselves to the choice of the one or the other form,—the influence of the person invited upon the management of the business in the one case or his lack of influence in the other; the community of profit and loss in the former case, restriction to the compensation stipulated once for all in the latter — this is so well known to every jurist that I shall say no more about it.

Association is, as has been remarked above, a self-serving relation, *i. e.*, a business contract; it belongs to the system of egoism, not to that of benevolence (p. 77). He who enters thereon desires his own advantage, and not that of the other — he who intends the contrary puts partnership upside down, just like the man who makes use of a contract of sale to make a gift to the buyer.[45] But the position which egoism attains in partnership is essentially different from that which it has in contracts of exchange. In the latter the interests of the two parties are at the opposite poles — the more disadvantageous the purpose is for the buyer the more advantageous it is for the seller, and conversely. The policy of each party can be resumed in the following proposition: *his* loss, *my* profit; no one can find fault with me for caring for myself only and not for him (p. 93, note). Every one must speak for himself in these relations. The case is quite different in partnership association. Here one's own interest goes hand in hand with the interest of the other; the latter cannot suffer without the former suffering also: *his* advantage, *my* advantage; *my* advantage, *his* advantage. If, therefore, partnership is to attain its purpose, this thought of the solidarity of interests of both parties must serve as a guiding star. He who makes use of the partnership relation to pursue his own interest instead of the common advantage acts against the basic idea of the whole institution — think

[45] Such an upside-down partnership the Roman jurists designate after the model of Æsop's fable a "societas leonina," D. 17. 2. 29 § 1, 2, and declare it null and void, *ibid.* 5 § 2, "donationis causa societas recte non contrahitur." On sale as a means to gift, see D. 18. 1. 36, "pretium . . . donationis causa non exacturus non videtur vendere." Cod. *ibid.* 4. 38. 3, ". . . emptioni *sui* deficit *substantia.*"

of such a method of action as universal, and for commercial purposes this relation would be practically eliminated. A disloyal partner is an enemy in one's own camp. Therefore his punishment according to Roman law is infamy, whereas the practice of deception in contracts of exchange was not thus branded.[46]

Association therefore, although called into being in the service of egoism, raises the demand, seemingly quite incompatible with its nature, to regard that which belongs to the other with the same care as one's own. By this means it throws a bridge between egoism and self-denial, and indicates the point of neutralization where both become one.[47] Contract of exchange, gift,

[46] The Roman jurists clearly recognized this fundamental difference between partnership and all other relations. Partnership is in their opinion a sort of fraternal relation ("societas jus quodammodo *fraternitatis* in se habet," D. 17. 2. 63. pr.). The principle of equality, therefore (not external mechanical equality, but internal, *ibid.* 6, 29. pr., 80), holds in partnership, in contrast with the freedom of reciprocal taking advantage which is recognized in contracts of exchange. Fraud in entering into partnership makes it null and void (D. 4. 4. 3 § 3, 16 § 1); conviction of fraud is punished with infamy; even after the extinction of the relation, the "socii" owe each other consideration at the execution (the so-called "benef. competentiae"); while the relation exists they are responsible only for "diligentia quam in suis rebus." All these rules, with the exception of infamy, are found again in the dotal relation between husband and wife (remedy against overreaching, D. 23. 3. 6 § 2; nullity on account of fraud, D. 24. 3. 22 § 2; "benef. comp.," D. 42. 1. 20; "diligentia quam in suis rebus," Cod. 5. 14. 11. In *business* contracts *not one* of these rules holds.

[47] In Chapter IX, where I explain psychologically how egoistic intention changes into ethical, this idea will afford us the most valuable service. The disinterested attention of the will to the interests of other persons is prepared in those relations in which those interests coincide with one's own. Here it gets accustomed for the first time to see itself in the other, it is the "stratagem" of the ethical, by means of which it inveigles the will into its own camp without the latter becoming aware of it; — a bit of pedagogy of the ethical world-order.

association, are the three types which exhaust the relation of the will to interest in the sphere of the law. In the contract of exchange the will desires its own interest at the expense of the other person's (egoism); in gift the will desires the other's interest at the expense of its own (self-denial); in association it desires its own interest *in* the other's by furthering its own interest in the other's and the other's in its own: partnership equalizes all opposition between its own interest and the other's.

Now if in the form of association it were merely a question of association in the sense it has in private law, in particular of trade partnerships, the ethical advance of the will therein would have little significance for society. But association in the juristic sense is only a particular case of a more general concept. We gave it only as a type, as with contract of exchange and gift. Just as behind contract of exchange in the narrower sense lie all the relations of exchange and all commercial intercourse, and behind gift all liberal contracts and the whole system of benevolence (p. 98), so behind partnership association there stands an entire system of similar relations; all societies, fellowships, unions, from the lowest to the highest, including those of the State and Church.[48] We embrace them all in the one word *association*.

[48] The German language uses the particle "ge-" to denote relations of community (Old High German "ga," "gi," "ka," "ki," "ke"), "Geselle" (companion), "Genosse" (comrade), "Gemeine" (community), "Gefährte" (mate), "Geschwister" (brothers and sisters), "Gemahl" (spouse), "Gevatter" (intimate friend), "Gehilfe" (helpmate), "Gesinde" (domestic servants). For the first fundamental form it uses the particle "ver" (Old High German, "far," "fir," "fer," "for" — away, forth), "vertauschen" (to exchange), "verkaufen" (to sell), "vermieten" (to let), "veräussern" (to alienate), "verschenken" (to give away as a present), "versetzen" (to pledge), "verleihen" (to lend), "versprechen" (to promise). The Latin language uses for the first relation "con" ("communis," "coheres," "correus," "confidejussor," "collega"), for the latter "trans" ("transdare" — "tradere," "transferre," "transigere," "transscribere").

Association. Association is a form of the most general applicability, and is in fact that which I stated above (p. 95): the second of the *fundamental forms* of social existence.

I know of no human purpose, with the exception of family life, which could not be and has not been pursued in the form of association. Everywhere there appears beside the individual a community aiming towards the same goal; for many individuals this form is the only possible one; for others it is the only one that adequately meets the purposes of their existence.

If we begin with the lowest purpose which is possible for individual life, *viz.*, the satisfaction of the *bodily wants*, we find already the competition of the union with the individual in the form of co-operative societies. It is continued for the satisfaction of the social instinct in the social unions (clubs), beside the private entertainments of a social nature. In the system of industry it grows to immense numbers in the form of manufacturing and trading associations, banks, etc. There exists scarcely a branch of industry which has been able to escape association. Now come the various interests of *instruction*, *education*, *art* and *science*, *benevolence*, which, although they are nowadays either exclusively or principally taken in hand by the State, were originally simply a matter of association, and in many cases have remained so to this day in competition with State provision. It is hard to tell where the activity of societies ceases — even when we are dead there is a society that finally takes care that we should be laid under the ground, and that those whom we leave behind us should not starve.

And now consider the highest forms of association: of Church and State, with the municipalities, corporations and unions which belong to them. Outside of the inner life of the family and the emotional relations of the individual, the entire wealth of human purposes comes to its realization in the form of association. Without any substantial nature of its own, being nothing but a form, and a form of unlimited extent, it puts itself at the disposition of society as a ready receptacle to take into itself almost every content of which human life has need.

And it gains new content constantly, whether it be that the forms already existing, expecially the municipality and the State, are enriched by taking on new aims hitherto pursued in another form, or that new associations are established for the pursuit of new or old purposes. What future this form still has in store our imagination can hardly grasp in detail, but it does not require the gift of prophecy to know that institutional progress as well as the progress of law will move principally in this direction. The one half of the law, the law of exchange, the Romans developed so completely that the modern nations have been able .to supplement it only in certain directions (law of bills of exchange, insurance, maritime law, etc.), but this leaves them all the more to do for the contents of this second part of the law. How far we are still behind is shown in the history of stock companies during the last decade. Under the eyes of our lawgivers the joint-stock companies have been transformed into organized agencies of robbery and deceit, whose secret history covers more baseness, dishonor, villainy than many a penitentiary, except that the thieves, robbers and swindlers instead of lying in irons are bedded in gold.

Public Spirit. I now resume the thought which I merely touched upon above (p. 160), *viz.*, the peculiar combination of one's own purpose with that of another which is characteristic of partnership or, as I shall hereafter call it, association, in contradistinction to all other contractual relations. The other person's interest and one's own here appear as one, for he who furthers his own end at the same time furthers his partner's interests, and *vice versa*. The subjective condition of the will corresponding to this objective character of the interest and postulated thereby is *public spirit*. Public spirit embodies a very interesting phenomenon. I do not mean so much in respect to its effects, as in respect to its origin. For him who is not content to consider social phenomena merely as given facts, but is impelled to investigate their causes, the existence of public spirit contains a problem well calculated to challenge reflection. Public spirit within the system of egoism is a phenomenon just as strange as a flower on a bare rock — from where does either draw its nourishment?

Public spirit is merely a refined form of egoism; the egoism of the man who sees far enough to know that the foundations of his well-being rest not only upon the conditions immediately connected with his own person, but also on those which he shares with others. Public spirit is egoism directed to that which we have in common with others (*common* interests as distinguished from *particular* interests), and it is tested by subordinating the latter to the former, by risking one's own to further the common cause. This phenomenon I regard from an ethical point of view as exceedingly worthy of notice. Not so much because it reveals egoism living side by side in peaceful harmony with its own negation, self-denial, but because the hardest problem of ethics, *viz.*, how comes man, *i. e.*, the egoist, to self-denial, obtains a solution which to my mind is of mathematical certainty. Self-denial does not come down to us from heaven as a being of a higher order to put an end to the barren course of earthborn egoism, but it is born on earth from the bone and sinew of egoism, the product of a process which takes place within egoism itself. The further development of this idea must be postponed to the discussion of the theory of ethics (Chap. IX), as it would take us beyond egoism to which we have to confine ourselves here. Here it is sufficient to have indicated the point from which we shall have to start later.

The simplest form of association is partnership, in the sense of the Roman law. The several members share in the common undertaking in the same way as they do in their own; whatever takes place, takes place through all of them; there is no resolution, no act in which they do not all co-operate. The extreme contrast to this is represented by the joint-stock company. Here the members have nothing to do with the management, which they surrender into the hands of persons who may be members, it is true, but need not be. Here, therefore, the two elements which in the normal form of right coincide in the one person entitled, *viz.*, interest and control, are separated in such a way that the shareholders have the interest without the control, and the board of directors the control without the interest. Such a separation may also occur elsewhere as is well known. The reason in every case is that the owner of the right is permanently or temporarily unable to perform the necessary acts of disposal, either by reason of the lack of personal qualification (minors under a guardianship), or on account of absence; or through the excessive number of persons entitled. The law designates this relation as *representation*.

Two cases are here to be distinguished from one another. The one in which the representative is given the power merely to execute a decision made by his principal without having any power of disposal himself, and the other case in which he is intended to make decisions in place of the person represented, such being either incapable of or prevented from making them himself, in which case, therefore, the representative is given the power to dispose of the affairs of the other. Here he *administers*, *i. e.*, he exercises the power in the other's place, and hence is designated as *administrator* (also *manager*, *director*). Such an administrator, in the legal relations of the individual, is the guardian (curator and ward); and the administrator of a whole estate (the trustee in bankruptcy). In the relations of association, of joint-stock companies as well as of all corporations, etc., it is the board of directors. Two elements characterize his legal position: the power of disposing of another person's right, and the duty to exercise it solely in the interest of the person represented.

In the last element lurks the serious part of the relation. As long as one's own interest sits at the helm of the right the interest is not sacrificed; but as soon as the rudder is confided into strange hands, this guarantee which one's own interest gives fails; and there is present the danger of the helmsman directing the course whither his own interest and not the other person's leads him. The position of an administrator contains a great temptation. Exciting his desire by the constant touch into which it brings him with another's property, it opens to him as to none other an opportunity to appropriate it — no thief finds it so easy to steal as the administrator of another man's property, no swindler can commit a swindle and hush it up so easily as he. Therefore there is need of the greatest guaranty in this place, where the danger is greatest. How the law meets this requirement in the case of guardians and administrators of public property and public interests, *i. e.*, the officials, has no interest for us here. That it has not been equal to it in reference to the administrators of joint-stock companies, no one who understands the matter will have any doubt after the experiences of recent years. What value the account which the board of directors give to the general meeting has is seen in the circumstance that cheating and deception has in no way been prevented by it. You might as well think of protecting a minor by making the guardian give him an account. That there is need of other means here is clear, and I am convinced that the legislation of the future will succeed in creating measures of safety by means of criminal and civil regulations. Our present law presents a yawning gap in this matter. The joint-stock company in its present form is one of the most imperfect and menacing institutions of our whole law. Most of the evils which broke upon us in the last years in the domain of business can either be directly traced to this source or are at least in intimate connection with it. I do not at all here wish to take into account the deeply demoralizing influence, poisoning in their very marrow the principles of honor and honesty, which the business of stocks has exerted. I want to estimate it here merely from the economic point of view, and cannot now suppress my conviction that however high you may place the resulting advantages for commerce, the curse which the joint-stock companies have brought upon us is incomparably greater than the blessing. The devastations which they caused in private property are worse than would be the case if fire and flood, failure of crops, earthquake, war and hostile occupation had conspired to ruin the national welfare. If we compare a price list of the time since the last panic (1873) with a similar one taken from the period of the formation of the joint-stock companies, the judgment thus derived will condemn our whole business of stock speculations beyond the possibility of palliation. We are presented with the picture of a battlefield or of a cemetery — lakes of blood, corpses, graves — marauders, grave diggers — the latter alone are well off, for they alone have profited! If the desolating effects of the joint-stock companies had been confined to the immediate participants, we could satisfy ourselves perhaps by saying that they should have been careful, although their stupidity does not give the right to deceive them, nor their carelessness the right to rob them. But all society is affected by the misfortune. The joint-stock companies have accomplished the feat of disturbing in all directions, in the most unwholesome way, the equilibrium upon which the whole order and security of our business intercourse is based. In buying and renting they have destroyed the equilibrium between price and goods; in speculation, the balance between profit and loss; in production, that between demand and supply. No business man pays for a thing more than it is worth. We are not afraid even that the greatest business houses will, merely to make business, buy dearer and sell cheaper than others; that they will produce more than is needed; that they will ignore in daring speculations the right relation between risk, profit and loss — the simple calculus of egoism prevents all this in their case. And yet the joint-stock companies have disregarded all principles of ordinary business. What is the explanation? It is that the directors operate with other people's money, that therefore the regard for their own interests — this so invaluable regulator of all business — is not present with them; and the feeling of duty, which is the only thing that can take its place, is an altogether unknown quantity to a great many people. What does a board of directors care in launching an undertaking whether they pay for materials and labor power in excess of their value? They pay out of another's pocket, and they have no interest to wait until they can get them at a suitable price; their interest is to set the enterprise going as quickly as possible. What is another's money? Seed that is scattered! If it sprouts, very good, a brilliant speculation — not seldom the matter is so arranged that the leaders of the enterprise appropriate it for themselves; if it does not sprout, the owner bears the loss. The business of stocks is the counterpart of credit; in both, one operates with other people's capital. Everything I said above (p. 135) of the latter holds in even a greater degree of the former also.

The problem which I have so far tried to solve consisted in demonstrating the apparatus of which society makes use, by means of the lever of egoism, to satisfy its need; not, however, as a given and ready-made system, but as a process gradually developing under the influence of the idea of purpose. Having arrived at this point, I will finally attempt to convey an idea of the social problems which commerce realizes in its sphere more or less perfectly. They are the following: —

(1) *Independence of the Person.*
(2) *Equality of the Person.*
(3) *The Idea of Justice.*

(1) *The Independence of the Person.* Independence does not mean so much, as is commonly supposed, to have as few needs as possible (this is an independence for which in my opinion no one need be envied; the animal is far superior to man in this respect, and the uneducated to the educated); but rather to be able to satisfy one's needs. In so far as commerce makes this possible, the service which it thereby renders to human society may be designated as the establishment of human independence. We must not object that the condition attached to this service, *viz.*, the possession of money, virtually removes this advantage again; for however

true it may be that commerce is worthless to us without money, it is just as true that money has no value without commerce. Of what use are to us mountains of gold among a savage people where we can buy for it nothing of that which makes life valuable, whereas at home the smallest sums are sufficient to procure for us the noblest enjoyments? In a civilized land the wage of the most insignificant laborer is sufficient to procure for him the labor products of thousands of men. A farthing which we pay fetches us things from all ends of the world, and sets for us innumerable hands in motion. If it is true that no work is done for nothing in commercial intercourse, that as buyer of an article I must pay for all that was required for its production, from the first moment when the material left the earth to the last when it came into my hands, then in the few farthings which I pay for a cup of coffee and a newspaper, I contribute to all the costs which were necessary to produce them. In the coffee I contribute to the ground rent of the owner of the plantation — to the costs of production — to the costs of transportation on the sea, the insurance premium, the hire of the crew — to the profits of the ship-owner and importer, the commission of the agent — to the tax, the costs of transportation on the railroad — to the profits and business expenses of the shopkeeper and the owner of the coffee-house. And this is only the coffee; in the sugar and milk the calculation begins over again. In the case of the newspaper I pay with my farthing for the owner of the paper, for the printer and his men, for the manufacturer of the paper, for the whole editorial personnel, for the correspondents, for the telegraphic dispatches, for the post, for the newsboy. The items for which I pay in all these cases assume dimensions which defy all calculation and imagination. But only he who is quite devoid of judgment can believe that they are not contained in infinitesimal form in my farthing.

The phenomenon here presented is based upon three institutions which we owe to the perfection of our present system of commerce, *viz.*, the division of labor, the undertaking of work for an indefinite number of future customers, and the extension of trade over the whole earth. The treasures of Crœsus would not have been sufficient to procure him a cup of coffee and a newspaper if he had wished to undertake for himself individually all the operations which are necessary for the purpose. A poor man today is served for a few pennies by more people in all parts of the earth than Crœsus could conjure if he had wished to empty all his treasure chambers.

(2) *The Principle of Equality of the Person.* Commerce knows no respect of persons; whether high or low, known or unknown, native or foreign — all in its estimation are alike; it regards the money alone. This complete impartiality of the intercourse of exchange toward persons — a self-evident consequence of egoism, which is concerned about gain alone — is socially of truly inestimable value; for it gives every man, whoever he may be, provided he has the money, the certainty of satisfying his wants, the opportunity of living in accordance with the cultural conditions of his time. There is nothing which can deprive a man of his position in commerce. The State may take away from him freedom and honor, churches and societies may reject him, but commerce will not exclude him. A man may be good for nothing else; people may avoid his company and contact with him, but he is always good enough to do business with. Money represents a check drawn on society, *i. e.*, on the support of others, and this check is always honored and never refused.

This complete indifference of business as regards persons is synonymous with the equality of persons in business relations. There is no sphere of life where the principle of equality has been practically carried out with such perfection as in business. Money is the true apostle of equality. Where it is a question of money, all social, political, religious, national prejudices and oppositions lose their force.[49] Shall we approve this, or shall we deplore it? This will depend upon the point of view. If we look at the motive, there is not the least reason for praise; for the motive is not humanity, but egoism. But if we regard the result, I can only repeat here the same remark which I made on p. 34; that egoism in serving itself serves the entire world. Thinking only of itself and its own advantage, it realizes in its sphere, without suspecting or wishing it, a thought which it otherwise opposes wherever it can, *viz.*, the thought of the equality of persons.

(3) *The Idea of Justice.*[50] The idea of justice is the equality which is demanded and measured by the interests of society between a deed and its consequences for the doer, *i. e.*, between an *evil* deed and *punishment*, and a *good* deed and its *reward*. This is nowhere realized in the latter direction to the same extent as in the sphere of commerce. In business intercourse each party receives

[49] The present time, it seems, must refute this statement of mine. In Paris the stirring up of the national hatred against Prussia by the press has led, in addition to the various other outbreaks in which it manifests itself, also to placards in many shops bearing the legend "on ne vend pas aux Prussiens" (we do not sell to Prussians). I can see in this only a foolish demonstration, which like many others carries the impossibility of its practical execution on its face. Will any one of the demonstrants ask a buyer whom he recognizes as a German whether he is a Prussian, Bavarian, or Austrian? The power of money will make itself felt in these shops also, and those placards will neither become general nor permanent.

[50] I discuss this more fully in another place. Here I touch upon it only so far as it comes into consideration for the present purpose.

on an average, by means of the consideration, as much in return as he has given. His pay, in wages and price of commodities, is on an average an equivalent representing the economic value of the service rendered at the time (p. 101). The equivalent may therefore be defined as *the realization of the idea of justice in the economic sphere.* The fixing of punishment is something arbitrary and the effect of a positive determination by the State. The standard which the State applies in awarding punishment is highly elastic and unreliable. The fixing of the equivalent, on the other hand, is the result of the most careful investigations and experiences, constantly renewed by all those interested. Reward is as sensitive as the mercury in a barometer; it rises and falls at the slightest changes in the economic atmosphere. If I ask myself where the idea of justice is *most perfectly* realized in our social institutions, the answer is: in business. If I ask where it is realized the *earliest*, the answer is again: in business. Business and its remuneration found their suitable form earlier than did the State and its punishments. If I ask finally where it is realized *most uniformly* in the whole world, I get the answer a third time: in business. Law and punishment may have a different form on this or that side of the frontier line, but prices and compensations know no State boundaries; although, to be sure, positive regulations of the State, by duties and taxes, may prevent their complete equalization in different States.

The application of the concept of justice to compensation reveals the explanation of a peculiar psychological phenomenon. I mean the resistance of many persons who are anything but miserly to paying more for a thing than it is really worth, even when the difference is scarcely worth speaking of. The cause of their resistance lies not so much in avarice (as the unthinking imagine), but rather in their feeling of right; which cannot bear the thought of being obliged to give the opponent what is not his due. It is not the economic motive which calls forth their resistance, but the moral. To free themselves from the suspicion of avarice, and to give a proof that it is not the money as such that concerns them, they often add immediately thereafter acts of a purely disinterested generosity. They fight for a penny and give away a dollar.

The three ideas which I have now explained in their application to business are the highest problems of morality which ethics knows, and commercial intercourse has realized these problems in a manner with which the methods used by the State in dealing with them cannot at all compare. Long before the State arose from its couch, in the morning twilight of history, trade had already completed a good part of its day's work. While the States were fighting one another, trade found out and levelled the roads that lead from one people to another, and established between them a relation of exchange of goods and ideas; a pathfinder in the wilderness, a herald of peace, a torchbearer of culture.

CHAPTER VIII

SOCIAL MECHANICS, OR THE LEVERS OF SOCIAL MOTION

2. EGOISTIC — COERCION

§ 1. FORM OF COERCION IN ANIMALS. — § 2. MAN — INTELLIGENCE ADDED TO FORCE (SLAVERY, PEACE, LAW); — THE POSTULATE OF FORCE IN THE VARIOUS PURPOSES OF THE INDIVIDUAL. — (§ 3. PERSON, PROPERTY; § 4. FAMILY; § 5. CONTRACT; BINDING FORCE OF CONTRACTS, THEIR FORM IN ROMAN LAW). — SOCIAL ORGANIZATION OF FORCE (§ 6. PARTNERSHIP; § 7. SOCIETY; § 8. STATE) — § 9. THE FORCE OF THE STATE. — § 10. LAW. — THE ELEMENTS OF THE CONCEPT OF LAW: COMPULSION. — § 11. NORM, CONTENT. (§ 12. THE CONDITIONS OF SOCIAL LIFE). — §§ 13, 14. POSITION OF THE INDIVIDUAL IN LAW. — § 15. SOLIDARITY OF HIS INTERESTS WITH THOSE OF THE STATE.

The second lever of social order is Coercion. The social organization of reward becomes trade; coercion organized makes the State and Law. It is in the latter forms of organization that commerce attains its final fulfillment; reward must have law behind it.

By coercion in the wider sense we understand the realization of a purpose by means of mastering another's will; the concept of coercion presupposes in the agent as well as in the passive object of coercion a voluntary subject, a living being. Such mastery of another's will is possible in a two-fold manner (pp. 11, 12, 34): *Mechanically* (mechanical, physical coercion, "vis absoluta"), when the resistance which the foreign will opposes to our purposes is broken by summoning physical power superior to its own. This is a purely external process of the same kind exactly as when a man removes a lifeless object which is in his way. Language denotes the process in both cases as *force*, but for the application of force to a living being it also uses the expression coercion, evidently in view of the fact that even though at first force moves only the body, it also indirectly moves the will, since it hinders it in its free self-determination. It is in this sense, for example, that we speak of a strait-waistcoat ("*Zwangs*jacke") in the case of the insane; of the carrying out of a coercive measure ("*Zwangs*vollstreckung"); of a bankrupt sale ("*Zwangs*versteigerung").

In contradistinction to mechanical coercion we have the *psychological*, in which the resistance of the foreign will is overcome by itself from within. We have shown above in what way this is done. In mechanical compulsion the act is undertaken by the person compelling; in psychological, by the person compelled. In the one case it is a question of breaking the resistance of the will negatively, here it is a positive changing of its motion; a difference which outwardly does not show, but is of great importance psychologically as well as juristically. We have an example of this in robbery, and the forced transfer of ownership.

According to the difference of the purpose to be attained, namely, according as it is negative or positive, coercion is *propulsive* or *compulsive*. The former has for its object the prevention, the latter the undertaking of a certain act. Self-defence is propulsive, self-help compulsive.

This is the formula of coercion which we thought it proper to lay down by way of introduction to the following discussion. Therein we shall examine the organization of coercion for the purposes of society. It depends on the realization of the two concepts, *State* and *Law:* it requires the establishment of the *power* which shall exert the force of coercion, and the laying down of *rules* for the right exercise of the same.

Such organized coercion does not, however, by any means exhaust the application of coercion for the purposes of society. In addition to *political* coercion, there is still another, unorganized, which historically everywhere preceded the other, and asserted itself everywhere along with it. I call this the *social*. Political coercion has for its object the realization of *law*, social coercion has for its object the realization of morality. The theory of morality (Chapter IX) will present the *system of social coercion* as a development in connection with this question.

In what follows I shall make the attempt to trace the two concepts of State and Law to their earliest conceptual beginnings; and in the same way as I have done in the system of commerce in reference to reward, I shall attempt to present the genesis of these two concepts as a necessary result of the practical impulse of the concept of purpose. The gain which I promise myself from this is in my eyes two-fold; first, the conviction of the continuity of the development of the idea of purpose in human society, and, secondly, the advancement of knowledge of the complete State and Law.

It is without doubt a great advance of modern philosophy of law as distinguished from the earlier Law of Nature that it has recognized and forcibly emphasized the dependence of law upon the State. But it goes too far when, as Hegel in particular does, it denies the scientific interest of the conditions before the State came into existence. The independent existence of the living being dates from its birth, but science goes beyond that to the first beginnings of life in the mother's womb; and the history of the development of the embryo has proved itself one of the most fruitful and most instructive sources of knowledge.

Therefore in law also science must not be hindered from making the embryonic state of law the object of investigation, and it stands to the credit of the advocates of the Law of Nature that they were not satisfied with the mere facts of the law and the State but raised the question, whence are the two? But the manner in which they solved the problem, in making the historical State originate in a contract, was a mistaken one. This is a pure construction without regard to actual history; a history of development, which did not take the trouble to investigate the development itself. Against such a solution of the problem the criticism which the modern philosophy of law opposed was perfectly justified. But the problem itself has not been thereby removed, it retains its full claim to a solution; and if the historian of comparative jurisprudence and the philosopher will join hands, the history of the development of law will in time be no less instructive to us jurists than that of the fœtus has become for the comparative anatomist.

The earliest commencement to our investigation extends in the case of coercion further back than in reward. Reward originates in man, coercion is already found in animals. It appears in its lowest form among animals; in its highest in the State. Let us try whether we can fill the interval between the two with an unbroken chain of intermediate links.

§ 1. *The Animal. Force.* We apply the concept of force ("Gewalt") equally to inanimate and animate bodies; we speak of the force of the storm, of the sea, of the falling body; and of violence ("Gewalt") which one animal enforces against the other. Outwardly alike, the processes are inwardly quite different. When the storm uproots the tree, or when the sea breaks through the dam, it is the law of causality alone which is carried out; but when one animal overcomes the other and kills it or devours it, it does it for a purpose. Such action, therefore, does not come under the law of causality but under the law of purpose. But the purpose which force serves in the animal is the same as in the world of man: the preservation and maintenance of one's life. Force follows out its purpose in the animal, in man, and in the State. The effects of force depend on the predominance of power; everywhere in nature the stronger lives at the expense of the weaker. But occasion for the application of force is offered only where the conditions of life on the two sides clash, and the weaker refuses to subordinate his share of life to that of the stronger. This leads us to coercion.

Psychological Coercion. In comparison with the use of physical force, its employment denotes a very great progress. An inanimate weaker body cannot avoid the thrust of the stronger body, but a weaker animal may escape by flight from the stronger; and by thus leaving the path open to the opponent who disputes the same with it, it preserves its own life. An animal, a man or a people which avoids the stronger, establishes, by subordinating the conditions of its own life to those of the other, a "modus vivendi" between itself and the other. Accordingly, to yield to coercion becomes a means of self-preservation for the one coerced. The weaker dog, which without waiting for the fight leaves the bone to the stronger, sacrifices the bone in order to save its life. Force is the maintenance of one's own purpose by means of denying in principle and suppressing in fact the purpose of the other. Coercion makes compatible both purposes by means of intelligence and the resulting submission of the one threatened. Force means *negation* of the will, coercion is the *restriction* thereof. That the animal has the degree of intelligence to understand a mere threat on the part of the other, and to get out of its way, has become in the hands of nature one of the most effective means of making possible the co-existence of the weaker with the stronger. To the weaker, to whom she denies the strength of withstanding the attack, she gives as a compensation intelligence to withdraw himself from it.

The case of coercion which we had till now before us we designated above propulsive coercion, and this kind predominates in the animal world to such a degree that we might be tempted to regard it as the only one. But the animal world, too, knows some cases of compulsive coercion. The most interesting case is that of the predatory excursions of ants, in which one tribe, ordered in battle array under the direction of its officers, takes the field against another tribe. The lot of the vanquished is not annihilation, but slavery; the vanquished enemies are compelled by the victors to work for them.

§ 2. *Man—Self-control of Force.* Life of the stronger at the expense of the weaker, annihilation of the latter in conflict with the former,— such is the form of life in the animal world; assured existence also of the weakest and the poorest by the side of the strongest and mightiest, —such is the form of life in the human world. And yet man historically found no other point of departure than the animal; but nature equipped him in such a way that he was not only able, but compelled, to raise himself to the higher stage in the course of history. If the play of the world's history were renewed a hundred and a thousand times, humanity would always come to the same point where it finds itself at present, *viz.*, the law; for man cannot but establish such conditions as make community of life possible.

The history of force on the earth is the history of human egoism, but this history is summed up in the fact that egoism becomes wiser by instruction. In respect to egoism's use of force for its purposes, such learning consists in its coming to comprehend how it must use force in order to make the power of others not merely harmless but useful to itself. At every stage in which he finds himself, from the lowest to the highest, guided by his own interest, man uses his progressive intelligence to increase his force as well as to moderate it. That humanity to which he rises is in its origin nothing else than the self-control of force, as dictated by man's own correctly gauged self-interest.

The first step in this direction was slavery. The victor who spared the life of his vanquished enemy instead of slaughtering him did it because he understood that a living slave is more valuable than a dead enemy. He spared him for the same reason that the proprietor spares his domestic animal; the "serv-are" of the "servus" took place for the purpose of "serv-ire."[1] But even though the motive was purely egoistic — all the same blessed be egoism, which recognized the worth of human life, and, instead of destroying it in wild fury, possessed sufficient self-control to preserve it for itself, and hence for humanity. Recognition of the economic value of human life was the first beginning of humanity in history. The Romans call a slave "homo" — he is a human being who is nothing more than a human being, *i. e.*, a human animal, a working animal, not a subject of rights ("persona"). This the citizen alone is, but this "homo"

[1] Roman etymology (passages in *Schrader*, "Instit." on 1. 3. de jure pers. § 3.), which although linguistically mistaken, contains a correct idea objectively.

signifies nevertheless the first rise of humanity to humaneness. In slavery for the first time is solved the problem of the co-existence of the powerful and the weak, of the victorious and the vanquished.

In the course of time humanity finds gentler forms — the lot of the weak in comparison with the strong becomes in the progress of historical development always milder. The conquered people is not led into slavery, it pays tribute; it buys itself free; it is incorporated with the conquering people, with inferior rights, and finally with equal rights; in short, the fight ends with a contract which regulates the relations of both parties and allows the weaker to remain *free*, *viz.*, a contract of *peace* ("pacisci" — to come to an understanding, "pax" is peace). Peace involves the acknowledgment of freedom in the person of the opponent, for one concludes no contract with a slave. What determined the strong man, before the opponent lay as a slave at his feet, to place his sword in its sheath and offer him fair terms? Was it humanity? It was no other humanity than that which induced him to spare the life of the subdued enemy, *viz.*, his own interest. The prospect of probable or perhaps certain victory if he continued the fight was obscured by a regard for the price at which it must be bought. The question of the continuation of the fight took the form of a pure question of interest. Thus: is it more advantageous to buy more at a high price, or less at a fair price? Does the additional profit pay for the additional costs? To compress a body into a volume of x inches a force y may be sufficient, but to bring it into $x-1$, $y+10$ may be necessary. Does it pay to exert a force of 10 in order to gain 1? Such forms the beginning of the calculation made by every successful enemy. If he possesses enough self-control to give a hearing to his intelligent consideration instead of his passion, he will prefer in his own interest not to arouse his opponent to a desperate struggle by proposing unacceptable terms, with further prospects of exertions and sacrifices on his own part, which stand in no true relation to the profit that is aimed at. The excess of pressure beyond what is bearable avenges itself by a recoil. There is no need of humanity to induce force to maintain the right measure. Mere politics is sufficient.

We have thus indicated the manner in which force without the help of any other motive than its own interests arrives at law. The form in which law appears here is, as has already been remarked, *peace;* the settlement of the fight by establishing a "modus vivendi," which both parties recognize as binding. Force thus sets a limit to itself, which it desires to respect; it recognizes a norm to which it intends to subordinate itself, and this norm approved by itself is *Law.* Whether it actually observes it is immaterial for the significance of the process which has thus been accomplished; it can trample the law under foot, it can carry on as it likes just as before, but the law has been placed in the world once for all, and this fact can never be undone again. It has laid down a rule for its conduct, and set up a standard by which to judge it, unknown before. If it tramples under foot the work of its own creation, it is no longer *force* that does this, but *despotism*—which is force qualified by opposition to law.

The process which we have here outlined gives the impression of an *a priori* construction, but in reality it is derived from a consideration of history. In the sphere of international relations it is repeated at the conclusion of every peace. Every peace contract puts law in place of the temporary struggle by force. The motive which determines the victor to do this is the one given above; law relieves force, which desires rest for its own sake and renounces further advantages which stand out of all proportion to the means that have to be spent for their attainment. The process has equal significance for the development of law in the interior of States; it makes public law as well as private. Whoever will trace the legal fabric of a people to its ultimate origins will reach innumerable cases where the force of the stronger has laid down the law for the weaker. The origin of law from force by means of self-limitation has not merely an historical interest but also an eminently philosophical one. It is an error which in my eyes characterizes our entire modern conception in ethical matters, that being in possession of institutions, views and concepts gained by the work of many thousand of years, we carry over our own ethical view into the past. This is true also of the conception of the relation between law and force. To be sure, we cannot get away from the observation that the actual relation between the two which we have before us has not existed always. But the question lying so near at hand, whether the difference in external relation had not in the past a corresponding difference in inner conception, is not asked. We cannot imagine that that which is to us quite certain and evident could ever have appeared to man in a different light. He might not yet indeed, we think, have recognized the truth with full clearness, but in any case he must have had an imperfect idea of it, obscurely felt it. The "idea" of law, we imagine, began its work at that time; and although the hindrances were many which it met with in its historical realization, still it was this idea which set man in motion and drove him irresistibly farther; in short, the historical progress of law is not a matter of *quality* but of *quantity*. That law and force are opposed, that force must be subordinated to law, this man has felt correctly from the very beginning,—his innate feeling of right having taught him this. And if force yielded in the course of history to law, this has its ultimate reason in the compelling power of the idea of law over the human spirit.

Such is the picture of the history of the development of law as drawn by current conception. But this picture is nothing but a projection of our present ideas into the past; historical facts present a quite different picture. It is not to the ethical conviction of its nobility and majesty that law owes the place which it holds in our modern world, but to the final results of a long process of development, and not to the beginnings thereof. The origin is naked egoism, and it is only in the course of time that it has given place to the ethical idea and the ethical sentiment. How the latter could have proceeded from it will be shown in connection with the treatment of ethics (Chapter IX). Here it is a question merely of the proof that egoism could have arrived at law without the help of ethics.

The problem which egoism has to solve consists in bringing together the two elements which make up the concept of law, *viz.*, norm and force; and this is possible in two ways, — *norm arrives at force, force arrives at norm.*

The first way is the one which I shall present more particularly below (§ 6: Self-regulation of Force in Partnership). The common interest which all have in the establishment of order calls the norm into life; and the preponderance of the power of all over that of the individual assures to it the power requisite for maintaining itself against the opposition of the individual. The private form of the relation is *Partnership:* a union of equals for a common purpose, and the practical maintenance of it against the particular interest of the individual.

The political form of it is the *Republic*. Here the point of departure is not pre-existent power as in the second method, but the norm comes first and power later. The other method is the one mentioned above, — force first, norm next; law originating from the power of the stronger, and in its own interest limiting itself by norm.

These are the two ways in which egoism arrives at law by means of its own compelling power, two out of many ways leading from the domain of egoism into the kingdom of ethics. Serving itself, it works here as elsewhere, without knowing or willing it (Chapter III), for the establishment of the ethical order. It builds the edifice of law into which later, when it finishes its work, the ethical spirit enters to set up its kingdom there. It could not do it if egoism had not prepared the path; the ethical spirit always comes in the second place, egoism everywhere occupies the first. Where the rough work has first to be done, egoism alone has the strength to do it.

It is egoism, as was shown before, which leads force to law by our second formula. Force arrives at law not as at something foreign to it, which it must borrow from the outside, from the feeling of law; neither does it arrive at law as to something superior to which it must subordinate itself with a feeling of its own inferiority. Force produces law immediately out of itself, and as a measure of itself, *law evolving as the politics of force*. It does not therefore abdicate to give the place to law, but whilst retaining its place it adds to itself law as an accessory element belonging to it, and becomes *legal force*. It is the opposite relation of that of today which we know as the *rule of law;* here force constitutes the accessory element of law. But in this stage, too, of the development of law the relation of the two sometimes changes about. Force suddenly gives notice of its refusal of obedience to law, and itself lays down a new law—the *coups d'états* of the political power; the revolution from above which is the counterpart of that from below. There it is organized, here it is unorganized force, which rises up against the subsisting law. Legal theory finds it easy to condemn these acts; yet this very disturbance of the normal relation ought to give it occasion to look upon the latter with different eyes from what it has been accustomed to. Law is not the highest thing in the world, not an end in itself; but merely a means to an end, the final end being the existence of society. If it appears that society cannot maintain itself under present legal conditions, and if law is unable to render it the proper assistance, then force must step in to do what is demanded; — these are the conditions of necessity in the lives of peoples and States. In conditions of necessity, law ceases in the lives of peoples and States as well as in the life of the individual. In regard to individual necessity, this is recognized by the law itself,[2] and up to a certain point it has happened similarly with States, and alterations in systems of government have taken place accordingly. In case of necessity a dictator was named in Rome, the guarantees of civil freedom were set aside, law receded, and unlimited military power stepped into its place. Corresponding measures at the present day are the right of the government to declare a state of siege, and to issue provisional laws without the co-operation of the estates of the realm; such measures acting as safety valves, to enable a government to remove the distress by course of law. But

[2] Imperial Criminal Code, art. 54: A criminal act is not present if, without being a case of self-defence, it is committed in a condition of necessity for which one is not responsible, and which cannot be avoided in any other way, in order to save the agent or one belonging to him from present danger to life or limb.

neither *coups d'états* nor revolutions are any longer effected on the ground of law. It would be a self-contradiction of law to allow them; and from the standpoint of law they must be absolutely condemned. If this viewpoint were the highest, the judgment concerning them would thereby be sealed. But life stands superior to law, and if the case be actually one such as we have here presupposed, a political condition of necessity, constraining us to choose either law or life, the decision cannot be doubtful: force sacrifices law and rescues life. These are the *saving deeds* of the power of the government. At the moment when they are committed they spread fear and terror, and are branded by the advocates of law as a criminal outrage against law's sanctity; but they often need only a few years or decades, until the dust which they have raised has settled, to gain vindication by their effects. And thereupon the hatred and curses which they brought upon their author turn into gratitude and blessings. Judgment concerning them is involved in their results; from the forum of law where they are condemned they make an appeal to the tribunal of history—the court which has always been recognized by all nations to this very day as the superior and indeed highest—and the judgment which is thence delivered is the final and decisive one.

We have thus indicated the point where law emerges into politics and history, and where the judgment of the politician, the statesman, and the historian has to take the place of that of the jurist. He knows only the standard of positive law; but they show that whilst law remains indeed applicable to normal relations, from which it was derived, it is an impracticable thing frequently by which to measure unusual relations, for which it was not intended beforehand and could not be. It is, if we are not afraid to use the term *law* here, by the exceptional *law* of history that the existence of law is, as a rule, made practically possible. Force, in its sporadic emergence upon its original historic mission and function, appears as the founder of order and the organizer of law.

In this sense I am not afraid to speak in favor of force, and free myself from the traditional juristic and philosophic conception. Neither of these in my eyes does justice to the significance which force has in the world, and which, as I add, it rightly has. In the relation between law and force they would lay all stress upon the former whilst assigning to the latter merely a dependent position as mere servant, obliged to take its orders from law and carry them out blindly. But here the reckoning is made without the host; force is no will-less creature, as according to this view it would have to be. Force both knows what it is and feels it; it demands the same regard from law as law from it. The relation is not one of servant and master, but that between husband and wife. They must have a mutual regard for each other in order to live in harmony.

Force can, if necessary, live without law, and of this it has actually given proof. Law without force is an empty name, a thing without reality, for it is force, in realizing the norms of law, that makes law what it is and ought to be. If force had not prepared the ground for law, if it had not broken the resisting will with iron fist and accustomed man to discipline and obedience, I should like to know how law would have been able to found its kingdom; it would have built on quicksand. The despots and inhuman tyrants who chastised the nations with iron rods and scorpions have done just as much for educating mankind in law as the wise lawgivers who set up later the tables of the laws: the former had to come first in order that the latter might appear.

This was the mission of force, even of the wildest, rudest, and most inhuman kind in the earliest periods of humanity. It accustomed the will to subordinate itself and recognize a superior over it. Not until it had learned this did the time come for law to take the place of force; for earlier, law would have had no prospects of success. And actually this relation of force and law also corresponded to the conceptions of the people in that stage. These did not look upon force with our eyes; they saw nothing improper in such a condition; nought detestable and damnable, but only what was natural and self-evident. Force as such made an impression upon them and was the only kind of greatness they could appreciate. Force ("Gewalt") and "mighty" ("gewaltig") were synonymous to their minds; and that is why instead of detesting the violent characters of their rulers, who made them feel them in unmerciful fashion, they extolled and glorified them, even as they despised the weak and gentle. They had an instinctive understanding that there is need of an iron fist in a wild time to force resisting wills to common action, that there needs a lion to tame wolves, and took no offence at his devouring the sheep and the lambs. If we conceive the people in that stage as equipped with our modern feeling for right and humanity, it would indeed be a riddle to us to understand how they could allow such cruel deeds as history reports of their rulers in inexhaustible plenty. But the riddle is solved by the fact that the ethical standard for judging these things, with which we quite unhistorically equip them, was quite a foreign thing to them. In the lack of this feeling lies the compensation by which history made these unbearable things bearable; they saw in such doings nothing else than the elemental sway of the forces of nature. They thought of them as of death by wild beasts. For physical sufferings they lacked the moral after-taste which makes those deeds for us so horrible.

Thus we see that force played *actually* a quite different role at the origin of the social order from what it does in the ordered state of law. It did this because it had a different mission. But this is not all. Force besides was *viewed* and *judged* subjectively by the people in a different fashion. For this last remark I claim universal truth in the history of morality; and I cannot sufficiently emphasize it; not merely in order to correct the *historical* error which the opposed view commits,[3] but in order also to remove from Providence the charge of complete *ethical* despair which this view contains for history. Those epochs of humanity which had to endure force because it alone was able to solve the problems of that time, *viz.*, to break the intractable will of the individual and educate him for life in a community—those epochs had an understanding for that which was suitable for their time just as we have for that which is suitable for our time. Our present conception, our aversion to force, would have appeared to them in fact incomprehensible; it would have seemed to them proof of senile weakness in us. But if *they* could not have understood *us*, we can and ought to understand *them*.

If truly we might boast of such understanding I could have spared the preceding discussion, but as is clear from what has preceded, we are very far from having it. I consider it a fundamental error of our prevalent conception of law that on account of the ideal element of its content it has too much left out of consideration the very real element of personal energy; an error against which

[3] I shall explain my attitude toward it later, first in Vol. II, p. 108 (*nativistic* theory of ethics), then in Vol. III (critique of the sense of right). [See above Ch. VI, note 3—*Translator*].

I have already frequently had occasion to speak.[4] The ideal of law is the clock-work, which runs its regulated course, into which no disturbing hand enters. How far the actual picture which history presents to us of law is removed from this will be clear from what has been said before. Law cannot dispense with energy. Law cannot do without it in reference to its concrete *realization*. For where its protective institutions fail, the person entitled to a right must enter the lists for it with his own power. Examples of this are: defence in case of need; self-defence; instances of permitted self-help, and war. Neither can law dispense with it in reference to its abstract *formation* — the process of legal evolution is not a matter of mere *knowledge*, as in the case of truth, but the result, too, of a *struggle* of *interests;* and the weapons by which the fight is won are not reasons and deductions, but the actions and the energies of the national will. Even though force may in the course of time assume more and more frequently forms which are compatible with the order of law, still instances happen even in a well-regulated legal environment where it refuses obedience to law, and as naked energy, whether by governmental *coups d'états* or popular revolutions, accomplishes the same work as it did formerly, when it first built up the social order, and *laid down the law*.

The following exposition has for its purpose to study force during this first building up of the social order. Not historically, as history has nothing more to say

[4] First in connection with the history of the origin of Roman law in my "Geist des römischen Rechts," Vol. I, § 10 (establishment of rights by personal energy), and in other places of this work, for example, Vol. II, § 25, 35, then in my "Kampf ums Recht" (1st ed. Vienna, 1872, 7th ed., 1884). My own insight into the significance and justification of energy in law I owe, I think, to Roman law. No other law forces it so irresistibly upon the mind of the man who has eyes for it as this law of the most energetic people in the world.

about these first beginnings, but from the point of view of *purpose*. We must prove that the purposes of human existence postulate force for their realization. We shall imagine man as thrown exclusively upon the resources of his own energy. We shall then present to him the purposes of his purely individual existence, according to the measure of the urgency and indispensability to which they lay claim for him. We shall do this in order that, after we have gained an insight into the insufficiency of a purely personal and unregulated force, we may rise to its organization in a political form. Our objective point is the State and the Law; our starting point the individual himself.

§ 3. *Propulsive Coercion in Law — Person, Property.* The first relation in which the purpose of human existence postulates force is personality. When its existence and life are threatened by foreign attack, it defends itself and repels violence with violence (*propulsive* coercion). Nature herself, in giving man life and implanting in him the impulse of self-preservation, requires this conflict. Every being she has created must maintain himself by his own power; the animal as well as man. But while such defence in the animal is purely a physical process, in man it assumes an ethical form. Man not merely defends himself, but he recognizes that he has a right to and must. From this point of view we call the act *self-defence* ("Notwehr"). Necessary defence is both a right and a duty; a right in so far as the subject exists for himself, a duty in so far as he exists for the world. For this reason the term obligatory self-defence may be applied to man, but not to an animal; for the animal lacks conscious reference of its existence to itself and the world. To deny or curtail man's right of self-defence is to degrade him below the beast.[5]

[5] And yet it has been done! See concerning it my "Kampf ums Recht" (7th ed., p. 90). The Romans with their healthy common

But the self-protection of the person embraces not merely what he *is* but also what he *has*, for having is extended being (p. 52); and here again language hits the nail on the head in using for it the expression self-defence ("Selbstverteidigung"). For the person defends, in that which it has, its *self* — its own complete ego, extended into the sphere of property.

Having is, as is well known in law, two-fold in species, "de facto" (possession) and "de jure" (ownership); and accordingly force, in its application to the maintenance of what one has, likewise assumes a double form. It takes the *defensive* in reference to maintaining the "status quo" in the holding of a thing; and the *offensive*, in reference to the recovery of a thing which has disappeared "de facto." In civilized epochs the law allows the person entitled to use force in the first case only; in the second case, on the other hand, it directs him to have recourse to the law, by inflicting severe punishment upon the use of arbitrary power in this direction (*self-help* in contradistinction to *self-defence*). For the subject who is thrown upon his own resources, and receives no aid from the State, as we are supposing, such a distinction is not yet present, and propulsive coercion extends equally to both cases.[6] Whether I ward off the person who seeks to gain possession of an object belonging to me, or take it away again from the person who obtained possession of it — in both cases the purpose of the force exerted is propulsive in its nature, for it has for its object the negative attitude of the opponent in reference to that which I call my own.

Granting that this is so, it will be objected, what does this difference matter? For positive law such wide

sense teach: "vim vi defendere omnes leges omniaque jura permittunt," D. 9. 2. 45 § 4.

[6] I proved it for the ancient Roman law in my "Geist des römischen Rechts," I § 10.

extension of the concept has not the slightest significance. I admit it has no significance for present law. But the case is different for the history of the development of law. I, at least, have discovered by a consistent investigation of the concept of propulsive coercion in its entire extent the meaning of a phenomenon in ancient Roman law, which one usually passes by without notice; whereas it agrees fully with the broad concept of propulsive force, as laid down here. Measured by the modern standard, every appropriation of an object in the possession of another on the part of the one entitled to it would be characterized as self-help. The ancient Roman people looked upon it differently; they saw in it nothing abnormal, but something self-evident. But the point of view which enabled them to do this was no other than the above of propulsive force, from which the consequence of its legal permissibility drawn by them followed of itself. From this conception we can explain the form which the protection of possession and ownership took in old Roman law. The possessor is entitled to use force not only against the person whom he himself allowed temporarily "de jure" or "de facto" possession, but also against the one who took it away from him against his will. And this force (and here lies the decisive point) is not brought by the Romans under the point of view of recovery of possession, but under that of maintenance.[7]

[7] In juristic terms the "interdictum uti possidetis" and "utrubi" were "interdicta *retinendae* possessionis." The recuperatory function of this interdict was a simple consequence of the idea of propulsive coercion as the force directed to the maintenance of what belongs to one. The "interdicta unde vi" and "de precario," on the other hand, were forms of *compulsive* coercion. They concluded with a demand for restoration, *i. e.*, for a positive deed of the defendant, whereas all interdicts enjoining "vim fieri, veto, quo minus . . ." were based upon *propulsive* coercion, *i. e.*, they imposed nothing upon the defendant, but prohibited resistance against the self-help of the plaintiff.

In the same way the victorious plaintiff in an ancient procedure of vindication was entitled to take the object in dispute by force; the verdict given enforced no act on the part of the defendant, as in later procedure, but merely decided the existence of the plaintiff's ownership. The practical consequence of this was self-evident; the plaintiff realized his right by expelling the defendant. There was no need of any activity on the part of the latter, and hence absence or death of the defendant did not exclude the realization of the judgment in the vindicatory procedure, whereas the case in the realization of a personal claim was different. Here an action of the condemned was necessary for the purpose.

§ 4. *Compulsive Coercion — The Family.* In personality the subject is still limited to himself, in property he passes beyond himself to the object; for both of these relations *propulsive* coercion suffices. Both in the family and in the contract the subject forms a relation to the person — permanent in the former case, temporary in the latter. This progress of the relation conditions also the means required for its maintenance, *viz.*, the elevation of propulsive coercion to *compulsive.* The master of the house who establishes the family must have the authority in the house, if it is to remain; and nature herself has indicated this position for him in its essential outlines — in relation to his wife, by the superiority of his physical strength and by the greater amount of work which falls to his share — in relation to the children, by the helplessness and dependence in which they are for years, — the influence of which, even after they are grown up, remains in the same relation in which it was formed during that period.

Thus nature herself has determined the family relation to be one of superiority and subordination; and in making every man without exception pass through the latter relation, has provided that no one shall enter society who has not already learned this lesson of superiority and subordination, upon which relation the existence of the State depends. The family is for every man the preparatory school to the State; for many nations, as is well known, it was even the model of the latter (*Patriarchal* State).

I shall not now add any more to the subject of the family relation, as I have here to consider it merely from the point of view of compulsive coercion. The concepts of Duty (Chapter X) and Love (Chapter XI) will bring us to it again.

§ 5. *Compulsive Coercion — Contract.* Not every contract requires compulsive coercion for its security; a contract of sale or exchange which is at once carried out affords no room for it, since it leaves nothing to be gotten by coercion. It must not be objected that the buyer has to be protected in the possession of the object, and the seller in the possession of the money. For this there is no need of compulsive coercion, propulsive being sufficient. For a state of intercourse which is limited to this simplest form of exchange, *viz.*, a cash business, compulsive coercion would be unnecessary. But this immediate fulfillment on both sides, which makes compulsive coercion unnecessary, is not practicable in all contracts. It is not practicable in a loan — the lender must precede with his performance; the consideration, *viz.*, the payment of the loan, can only follow later. It is not practicable in a contract of lease — whether the rent is paid before or after permission is given to use the object; one of the two parties must come first with his performance and wait for the consideration. Thus certain contracts necessarily presuppose the postponement of the performance on the one side, *i. e.*, its promise.

Promise denotes a very great progress in comparison

with the lowest form of contract above mentioned. By putting mere speech ("ver-sprechen" [German for promise] — speaking in favor of the person addressed, p. 162, note), the word, in place of the act, it frees the contracting parties from the hampering presupposition of immediate payment and possession. It makes it possible for them in their business transactions to take their future payment as the basis of operations, and discount the future. A promise is the emancipation of the contract from the fetters of the present, and is an order on the future for the purpose of defraying the needs of the present.

But in order that the word shall take the place of the act, there must be security that it will be exchanged for the act at the proper time; or as language, applying the idea of pledge to this case, expresses it, that the word pledged or pawned shall be redeemed. This is the "*fulfilment*" of the promise; the word that was empty hitherto becomes "*full*," the mere *thought* of the future act becomes a *reality*. The guarantee for such fulfilment depends upon coercion. The necessary condition for the creditor's accepting the promise of the debtor is that the latter should authorize the creditor to coerce him. It is demanded not only by the interest of the creditor, but just as much by his own interest. If the *creditors* did not desire promises to be actionable, the *debtors* would have to do so.[8]

The juristic expression for this effectiveness of the promise is the binding force of contracts. The contract "binds" the debtor, the latter is "bound" by his word if he can be forced to "keep" it, *i. e.*, if the fulfilment can

[8] The same legislative point of view applies here as is enacted in D. 4. 4. 24 § 1 for minors, "ne magno incommodo . . . afficiantur nemine cum his contrahente et quodammodo commercio eis interdictur (interdicto?)".

be compelled by external force. The figure by which the German language as well as the Latin views promise is that of a bond by means of which the creditor holds the debtor firm. The bond is tied ("contrahitur" — "contractus"), loosened ("solvitur" — "solutio"), the condition of the debtor is that of being bound ("Verbindlichkeit" [German for obligation] — being bound in favor of another, in Latin "obligatio" from "ob" — the German "ver," *i. e.*, toward, and "ligare" to bind, and "nexum" from "nectere" to bind, to chain).

The binding force of a promise is not a thing that comes to it from the outside; it is inevitably posited in the practical function of it. If a promise were not binding, loan would be as good as useless in business intercourse; only a friend would then be able to get a loan. Contracts of service and lease would be stricken from the list of contracts, for who would be foolish enough to give his services, or allow another the use of his object, unless he were certain of receiving his pay and his rent? Who would be foolish enough to pay the latter in advance if he must expect that the promised act might remain undone? Barter and purchase alone would be possible in the primitive and extremely constraining form of immediate fulfilment.

In view of this practical indispensableness of the binding force of contracts it is scarcely conceivable how the doctrine of the Law of Nature could have considered it so difficult a problem, for the solution of which some have expended the most violent efforts, while still others have altogether despaired of reaching any solution. The question became a problem only because the element of purpose in it, *i. e.*, the function of promise in business, was altogether left out of sight, and the attempt was made to answer the question merely from reasoning on the nature of the will. Furthermore, they presupposed a purposeless volition, and argued not concerning a will that wishes to attain to something in the world and hence makes use of proper means for the purpose, submitting to consequences demanded by its own volition, but concerning a will that knows nothing of the conditions of its own volition. It forgets in the next moment after it has concluded the contract that the success of what it wills is a matter not of temporary but of continued volition. From this purely subjective point of view, which considers only the possibility of voluntary acts in the individual, we certainly cannot prove why the same man who willed a thing today should not be able to will its exact opposite to-morrow. But the very point of view is altogether inapplicable to the above question, which is not a psychological one, but a problem practical and juristic. It involves not what the will *can* do in itself, but what it necessarily *must* do if it is to attain its purpose in the world. By its purpose we mean not all it may conceivably propose to itself, including the most foolish and senseless things, but such purposes as are compatible with those of the others in whose community it has its being. How far this is the case is a purely historical question. The middle ages recognized contracts as valid which we today simply reject, and the same relation will always be repeated. To answer the question of the binding force of contracts by an abstract formula is no better than to do the same in reference to the question of the best form of government. Rights of contract and forms of government are facts of history, which can only be comprehended in their relation to history, *i. e.*, to the conditions and needs of the time when they arose. By abandoning the firm ground of history and undertaking to answer the question from the nature of the subjective will, abstracted from society and history, the doctrine of the Law of Nature deprived itself of all prospect of solution. Whether it maintains or denies the binding force of contracts, it is equally mistaken in both cases, because it is in sharp contradiction with the real world. The real world can neither affirm nor deny the question; and can only answer it according to its required purposes at the time being.

I doubt whether any other legal system proves this statement so strikingly as the Roman law. In connection with purpose, contract rises from one stage to the next, even from the lowest to the highest; and this without skipping any intermediate step. We might suppose we had before us not a historical but a conceptual development of the concept of contract, so coincidently do the two grow. This circumstance induces me to insert here the history of the development of Roman obligation. I shall only offer thereby in a different form what I have to give, *viz.*, the inner conceptual development of compulsive coercion in the contract — concept and history move in perfectly parallel lines.

According to the conception of the ancient Romans a mere promise ("pactum nudum") produces no action,[9] *i. e.*, the idea of the binding force of a promise is quite foreign to ancient times. The legally enforceable character of a promise, *i. e.*, its actionability ("actio"), is conditioned by the fact that the creditor performed some act for or gave something to the debtor. The obligating reason of the promise depends upon the act ("res") of the other party; no one promises who does not have to, namely, in order to get something himself. Every promise is therefore a promise of a subsequent act by reason of a previous act that was received, or is juristically assumed to have been received. The word

[9] D. 2. 14. 7 § 4, " . . . nuda pactio obligationem non parit." *ib.* 7 § 5, " . . . regula: ne ex pacto actio nascatur." Paul. Sent. Rec. II, 14. 1, "ex nudo pacto inter cives Romanos actio non nascitur."

without "res" is an empty word which obligates no one; it acquires a binding force only through the substantial element of possession in the person giving it.

This is the ancient Roman conception which controlled for centuries the history of the development of Roman obligation, and which is testified to in language the moment we make our first entry into this sphere. Etymology, that guardian of the primitive popular conceptions, sketches ancient Roman obligation for us in the following manner.

A debtor ("debitor") is he who has something from another ("de-habere" — "debere," "debitor"); creditor ("creditor") is he who has given something ("duere" — "dare," "creduere," "creditor"); a debt is money which was given to the debtor ("aes alienum"). All three concepts therefore, — debtor, creditor, debt, — point, in accordance with their linguistic form, back to the idea of having something from another.

From this realistic point of departure Roman obligation now develops in such a way that it gradually overcomes the substantial element of "res," until it finally has freed itself from it entirely, and given rise to mere contract as such.

In order that the reader may understand the following outline of Roman contracts, which proposes to arrange them in the order of their conceptual and historical sequence, I will preface the following observation on the terms to be used.

A business transaction which is carried out by an immediate performance on both sides, I call bilateral real business; a transaction in which the performance of one party comes first, while the consideration does not follow at once, but is only promised, I call unilateral real business; a transaction in which neither party performs any act forthwith but each only promises, I call bilateral promissory business; and a transaction in which only one party promises without any consideration being promised or granted upon the other side, I call unilateral promissory business. If besides I add that unilateral real business occurs in Roman law in a double form, *viz.*, with effective and imaginary previous performance (merely juristically assumed), we have the outline of obligatory business transactions, which in my opinion contains the historical gradation of Roman obligation.

I. *First Stage.* — *Bilateral Real Business.* The simplest form of contract, economically as well as juristically, is contract of exchange, and sale with immediate execution (cash). In ancient Roman law this stage is represented solely by solemn sale ("mancipatio"). There is no special form peculiar to exchange; the stage of exchange seems already superseded in the law of contract.

II. *Second Stage.* — *Effective Unilateral Real Business.* The first demonstrable case of obligation to a future act in the old Roman law is the solemn loan, known as "nexum," distinguished by the immediate personal execution which belongs to it. We might call it the promissory note of the ancient Roman world. The obligating power of the word, which here as everywhere in Roman law the person must speak who is to receive the right by the act, depends upon the antecedent act on his part.

With this solemn form are connected the formless loan, and, in the further course of development, the other real contracts, named as well as unnamed. All of these hold firmly to the ancient Roman idea that the debtor is not obligated by a word, whether his own or another's, but by the combination of word and performance. For this reason, only such individual is entitled to an action in one of the unnamed contracts who has carried out his part of the contract; before this is done the contract is not binding on either party, the word only acquiring force when a real performance is joined to it.

III. *Third Stage.—Imaginary Unilateral Real Business.* Obligation develops further from this basis by keeping formally to it, but in reality freeing itself therefrom. This takes place first in loan ("nexum"). The old effective payment (sale "per aes et libram") is transformed into a mere imaginary act, so that one who had not received anything in reality could establish a debt by means of an imaginary loan in which the giving was limited to a piece of brass. With this was connected the "literal" contract, in which a sum is charged on both sides as "given" and "received," while there was no need of actual giving. As in the former case the real act was replaced by an imaginary act, so it is replaced here by acknowledgment; a process of the same kind as occurs in the history of the bill of exchange, in the substitution of the actual payment of the value by the value clause ("value received"). The last step in this direction is represented by the verbal contract of Roman law. In form it contains not the slightest reference to a previous performance supposed to have taken place, which seems to have been altogether eliminated in it, though according to the juristic idea it lay at the basis. Verbal contract may be defined as a receipt of value received with accompanying promise of a subsequent act on one's own part. The verbal contract is the last off-shoot of the old Roman concept of obligation, and appears only as an artificial operation. In it the force of the original idea that an obligation to an act can be established only by a corresponding antecedent act, is already to such a degree weakened as to have become simply an embodiment of the abstract power of obligation of the will.

IV. *Fourth Stage.—Bilateral Promissory Business.* The obligating force of a promise as such, without the support of a previous act, formally certified or merely assumed, as was the case historically in verbal contract, comes to actual recognition only in the four consensual contracts of Roman law. Of these, however, only three, *viz.*, sale, lease and partnership, belong to the category of bilateral promissory business; whereas the fourth, "mandatum," comes under that of unilateral promise (see below). In comparison with the other forms of obligation of Roman law, they appear as highly limited exceptional cases, which were taken over into Roman law from international private law ("jus gentium"), and do not therefore by any means justify the conclusion that the old Roman conception was superseded in them and abolished in principle. Neither the Roman people nor even Roman jurisprudence ever rose to the thought that consensus as such has in it a juristically binding force. Nowhere does the latter give the slightest hint that this corresponds really to the nature of the thing; never does it make an attempt to extend those four exceptional cases. On the contrary, it guards anxiously the old boundaries and warns against overstepping them as a serious danger.[10]

V. *Fifth Stage. — Unilateral Promissory Business.* This is the last step in the development of actionable promises which Roman law took, and it is perhaps the most interesting of all. Whereas in all previous stages obligation remains in the service of the purposes of commerce and hence of bilateral egoism, it makes itself free from it in this stage, and rises to the thought of benevolence and self-denial; or to speak differently, liberal or gratuitous contracts (p. 76) are joined to the onerous as actionable.

[10] D. 2. 14. 7 § 5. " . . . hoc non valebit, *ne ex pacto actio nascatur*," a turn which is repeated four times in this passage.

These, too, like onerous contracts become possible in two forms; in the form of immediate performance, and in the form of promise. The object of both may be the permanent cession of property value (donation, alms), or temporary service by object or person.

We now have the formula required to embrace the various cases and forms of liberal contracts, and at the same time a standard of measurement which we may apply to every positive law. When I apply it to the Roman law, I do so in the first place, naturally, in order to complete the development just outlined of the concept of promise in Roman law. But here, too, I am not so much concerned about Roman law as about the advancement of the knowledge of the law in general, and for this reason I do not limit myself to liberal promise but combine with it a consideration of liberal real performance in the conviction that only by this means will the peculiar significance and function of the former be manifested with the greatest clearness.

(1) *Liberal Real Performance.* A gratuitous service is juristically a purely indifferent thing; as *such* it gives rise to no question of right, and therefore science had no reason to stamp it with the seal of a legal concept.[11]

Gratuitous delivery of a thing for use, however, touches law at least in so far as it contains the obligation to return the object. To enforce it Roman law has the "interdictum de precario," the "condictio certi" in loan without interest, and the "actio commodati."

The effect by which a gift makes itself felt in law consists in the transfer of ownership, a result which it shares with each onerous transaction in transfer of ownership. It is not therefore necessary for the jurist to use

[11] Juristic questions can be connected with it only by the accession of special circumstances; for example, "dolus," erroneous assumption of obligation, D. 12. 6. 26 § 12, or "negotiorum gestio."

the concept of gift in order to explain it. To speak in juristic terms, gift comes into consideration only as the motive of transfer of ownership. The difference between paid and gratuitous transfer of ownership is not juristic in its nature but economic; for gift is, from the juristic point of view, completely covered by the concept transfer of ownership. This Roman law also recognizes perfectly in reference to "traditio." The theory of "traditio" knows no difference between a paid and a gratuitous transaction. The case was quite different, however, in that form of transaction which according to the old Roman law transferred Roman property only, *i.e.*, such as may be prosecuted by vindicatory procedure,[12] *e.g.*, in "mancipatio" of "res mancipi." The only reason stated which may determine the owner to a transfer of ownership is sale. For the transfer of a "res mancipi" by way of gift the old law had no form, *i.e.*, the idea of gift is not given legal expression to — an ancient Roman was not in the habit of making gifts.[13] If, nevertheless, one desired to do so, he could do this only by wrapping his gift in the form of "mancipatio," imaginary sale. The importance of this phenomenon he only can fail to recognize who in the forms of the law sees mere forms, and not the expressions of real ideas. For him who agrees with me in the opposite

[12] The establishment of this view I must reserve for another place (the second division of the third part of my "Geist des römischen Rechts"). The effect of *Roman* property ("dominium ex jure quiritium") consisted in "vindicatio." Its transference to "res nec mancipi" did not come till later. In ancient times its protection was restricted to "act. furti," which was directed, however, not only against the thief, but also against the receiver of stolen goods (Gaj. III, 186: "furtum conceptum").

[13] So *Polybius* literally, 32. 12. 9, where he tells of the generosity of P. Scipio toward his mother: "Unheard of in Rome, for in this city no one gives away of his own accord any of his belongings to another as a present."

opinion, "mancipatio" contains the proposition that the most ancient Roman law knows no gratuitous transfer of ownership, but only paid.

Thus, gift was forced by the law itself to conceal itself in the form of another transaction, and pretend to be what it was not in reality. The fact that we meet the same phenomenon also in other laws at a lower stage of development,[14] leaves no doubt possible, according to my opinion, of the reason of this phenomenon. It was not the limitation of the legal *form*, which was adapted only to the most important cases of transfer of ownership, but the limitation of human *egoism*, which had not yet been able to rise to the idea of gift.

This ancient national conception of gift continued to influence for many centuries the attitude of legislation and jurisprudence. In forms of law it shows itself in the limiting determinations of the "lex Cincia," and in the prescription of "insinuatio" of the time of the emperors. In juristic theory it discovers itself in traces which will be indicated later. Even in the classical

[14] So, for example, in Lombard law in which it was a fixed legal rule that a gift, especially when conditional on the death of the giver, was valid only if the donee handed over to the donor a compensation ("Laungild" — "Lohngeld"). *Stobbe*, "Reurecht und Vertragsschluss nach älterem Deutschen Recht," (Leipzig, 1876), II, p. 16. Two other examples, which I owe to Prof. *Ehrenberg*, are "manumissio per denarium" according to the Frankish law, in which the slave about to be manumitted offered a "denarium" for his freedom, which the master (in order to indicate the character thereof as a merely imaginary payment) jerked out of his hand with a fillip, and the establishment of a relation of dependence (whether one of complete ownership or of lesser dependence, for example, a relation of vassalage) by means of an imaginary consideration (designated in the sources as "pretium"). According to Turkish law gift, except where there is a relation of kinship, becomes irrevocable only through a gift in return. *Von Tornauw*, "Das Moslemitische Recht," (Leipzig, 1855), p. 145.

period of Roman jurisprudence we meet with a conception of gift which would do honor to the most sober egoism: gift is a sort of exchange; one makes a gift in order to receive a gift in return.[15] The only point where liberality comes to the surface within the law is the testament. But let us not deceive ourselves about the true worth thereof. The liberality of the last will and testament is psychologically far removed from liberality among living persons. What one donates, he sacrifices, he takes away from himself; what he gives in his last will, he gives only because he cannot keep it himself; or more correctly, he does not give at all, but, as language fittingly expresses it, he "leaves," *i.e.*, he leaves it behind because he must. If he does not dispose of it, it falls to the legal heir without his assistance; the testament only gives him an opportunity of putting other persons in his place. The value of such generosity must not be put very high. It happens not rarely that an incorrigible miser, who had not the smallest gift to spare during his lifetime for charitable purposes, relatives and friends, bequeaths the richest legacies and makes the most splendid foundations. These bequests may be very valuable for the beneficiaries and for society, but psychologically they have not the value of a gift:—the gift of the cold hand is compatible with an ice cold heart; it is not a gift of one's own, but from the purse of the legal heir.[16] Only the gift of the warm hand feels warm.

Such is testamentary liberality in its true shape. But even the paltry residue of liberality which still remains

[15] D. 5. 3. 25 § 11, ". . . ad remunerandum sibi aliquem naturaliter obligaverunt, velut genus quoddam hoc esse permutationis."

[16] Its psychological character is very well described by the jurist in D. 39. 6. 1. pr. ". . . habere se vult, quam eum, cui donat, magisque eum, cui donat, quam heredem suum."

after this analysis was too much for the Romans. Law had no independent form for it in which it could appear as such, but they borrowed for it the forms of business intercourse. For the heir they borrowed the form of "mancipatio" — his institution is made in the form of a purchase of the estate. The heir, or some other person in his place ("familiae emptor"), buys the estate. For the legatee they borrowed the form of "legatum per damnationem" (the obligation on the part of the heir to transfer to the legatee the quiritarian ownership in a thing), *i.e.*, of the strict form of debt, of the debt of loan ("nexum"). Thus we may say that the ancient Roman law possesses no particular form specially intended for liberality, either as "inter vivos," or testamentary. It employs for the purpose the forms of business intercourse. For gift it uses "mancipatio"; for a promise of gift, "stipulatio," verbal contract (see below); for institution of an heir, "mancipatio"; for a legacy, "nexum."

(2) *Liberal Promise.* A liberal promise becomes actionable in a manner quite different from an onerous promise. The actionability of the latter is a requirement of commerce; on the other hand, that a liberal promise be actionable is a thing not at all demanded from the standpoint of business — whether it be admitted or rejected by the legislator, trade and commerce will not feel it. Juristic formalism alone, which is attached solely to the abstract concept of promise, can see a contradiction in the fact that the same legislator who grants the power of enforcement in onerous promise denies it in liberal.

The possibility and necessity of distinguishing between onerous and liberal promise, which is here emphasized, is confirmed in the fullest measure by the Roman law. For the former it had long possessed a rich supply of forms; whereas, for the latter, it had not a single form. The first case in which it resolved to equip liberal promise also with legal effects, was that of a promise of gratuitous service ("mandatum");[17] and this, too, happened in such a manner as plainly to show that the Romans were clearly aware of the difference between the two species of promise, and little inclined to abolish it in favor of any abstract concept of promise. He who hires out his services is bound to the contract, but the mandatory who performs them gratuitously can withdraw if he has reasons,[18] the consideration that it is a courtesy to which he pledged himself mitigating the strictness of the pledge. But the courtesy in this case stands upon a peculiar footing; it is still partly in the sphere of business; and it is just in this circumstance of the semi-commercial character of "mandatum" that I see the reason which made it actionable. Even in a pure business negotiation, which has as its impulse not benevolence but egoism, regard for that good understanding with the other party, which is demanded by self-interest, may require that the one should take an order from the other without asking to be paid for it. This is not a service of a friend in the real sense of the term, but of that peculiar variety of it which the business world designates as a business friend. In services of greater importance the Roman gave and expected a honorarium, and jurisprudence saw so little that was offensive to the nature of the relation, that in case of a previous

[17] In the seventh century of the city at the earliest. See my "Schuldmoment im Römischen Privatrecht" (Giessen, 1867), p. 34, 35, ("Vermischte Schriften," Leipzig, 1879, p. 192). A very special case is presented in the promise of gratuitous service made on oath by the freed slave at the moment of receiving his freedom. Its actionability was based on the presence of a *consideration*, *viz.*, the freedom which is granted to him, D. 38. 2. 1. pr. "ad *remunerandum* tam grande beneficium"; 12. 6. 26 § 12 " . . . natura *debet.*"

[18] D. 3. 27 § 11, 22 last §; 17. 1. 23–25. Similarly the "sequester," 16. 3. 5 § 2, and the "arbiter," 4. 8. 9 § 4, 5; 10; 11. pr.; 15; 16. pr.

stipulation concerning it, it even declared the "actio mandati" as admissible.[19]

A promise of temporary gratuitous cession of an object or of capital was, according to my opinion, not binding even when clothed in the form of "stipulatio," verbal contract.[20] Only the promise of a gift was given by law the force of obligation; but it was necessary for this purpose to clothe it in the business form of verbal contract, just as the gift of an object in "res mancipi" had to find refuge in the form of "mancipatio" (p. 208). That the reason for the want of a proper form lies here

[19] D. 17. 1. 6. pr. "Si remunerandi causa honor intervenit, erit mandati actio." The business character of "mandatum" cannot be expressed more clearly than is done here. A friend does not stipulate for a compensation for a service, and there can be no action for consideration in an essentially gratuitous contract. One must have a very imperfect idea of the Roman "procuratores" to believe that they submitted to all the cares and hardships of their office out of mere benevolence. The contrast between the "procurator" and the friend is expressly brought out in 17. 1. 10 § 7: "qui non *animo procuratoris* intervenit, sed *affectionem amicalem* promisit . . . mandati *non* teneri". Compare with this the opposite case in 3. 5. 42: "*rogatu* . . . *mandatu*," and for "act. mandati contraria," see 16. 3. 1 § 14 " . . . *suaseris* . . . *mandasti*," and 50. 14. 2, "*monstrat* magis nomen quam *mandat*."

[20] The Roman judge could not give judgment for specific performance, but only for the interest. But in such a case he would scarcely have recognized its "honesta causa" (D. 47. 2. 76 § 1). I am inclined to apply to this the saying of 22. 1. 3 § 4, "non sine rubore desiderabitur." See also the statement in 43. 26. 14, " . . . nullo eo nomine actio civilis est, magis enim ad donationes et beneficii causam, quam ad negotii contracti spectat precarii condicio," and the manner in which the jurist in 39. 5. 27 upholds the gratuitous permission to use a dwelling in the special case, "officium quadam *mercede* remuneratum Regulum." Of "precarium" we know that the agreement it should last a definite period was not made effective even by the fulfilment of the precarium, and the defendant was not granted a plea against earlier notice to vacate, 43. 26. 12, "sed nulla vis est huius conventionis, ut rem alienam invito domino possidere liceat."

also in an objective disinclination to the business itself, follows from the plea granted by the "lex Cincia" in both cases to a business irreproachable in form. In consequence a special form for gift in the law of things as well as in the law of obligations is not found in ancient Roman law.

Not until Justinian does the promise of gift attain to independence of form. The necessity of clothing it in the business form of verbal contract, which was in force till then, was abolished by him, and the simple, formless contract ("pactum") in which gift presents itself as that which it is, is put in its place. Roman law had therefore existed over a thousand years without granting juristic recognition to the promise of gift as such; a fact so significant for the Roman conception of gift that it needs no further commentary.

What determined Justinian to break with it? According to my opinion it was the influence of the Christian conception.[21] We need only cast a glance at the mass of charitable foundations named in the constitutions of the Christian emperors to be convinced of the measure in which Christianity, however high or low we may in general estimate its ethically rejuvenating influence upon the decadent Roman Byzantine world, undeniably exercised a morally ennobling effect at least in one direction. We speak of its stimulating influence upon beneficence and liberality. It is only with the coming of Christianity that the virtue of charity arose in history to the rank of a factor socially influential and significant. Not only did the beautiful calling of mitigating the misery of entire classes of society fall to its lot, — a social problem which commerce guided by pure egoism leaves every-

[21] The Constitution in which he makes this disposition mentions expressly the Christian institutions, Cod. 8. 54. 35 § 5, " . . . piis actibus vel religiosis personis."

where unsolved,—but at the same time the world mission to assist in laying the foundations of the Christian Church by supplying the requisite economic means. To make this possible, Christianity had to overcome the egoism of Roman law. And it has a right to boast of it,—it is through Christianity alone and by means of Christian doctrines that beneficence and love have come to their full right in legislation as well as in life.

Roman law knew of two cases only in which gratuitous promise was equipped from ancient times with binding force. These were "votum" and "pollicitatio," a *vow*[22] to the gods and to the community. But even here, when in contact with the highest that the Roman knows, his deity and his fatherland, he does not fail to betray the trait of egoism; does not forget to make his account with both. "Votum" is for him only a sort of nameless real contract with the deity.[23] It is not a pure, disinterested promise of gift, but an act for the sake of a consideration; its binding force, too, is supported by the "res." And "pollicitatio" also does not obligate without further ado as pure liberality.[24] It is in force only when motived by a special reason ("justa causa"). This may be either because the community has given or is to give something,[25] or (and here, judging from the language,

[22] Liberality in favor of a *purpose*, in contradistinction to that in favor of a *person*, *viz*., *gift*.

[23] According to the formula, "do, ut facias," help me, and I will give you! To be sure, this is nowhere expressly said, but it can be inferred with certainty according to my opinion from the many formulae in *Brissonius*, "De Vocibus ac Formulis," lib. I, c. 159, fl. All "vota" are conceived conditionally.

[24] D. 50. 12. 1 § 5, "qui non ex causa reipublicae pecuniam pollicentur, liberalitatem perficere non coguntur."

[25] D. 50. 12. 1 § 1. "Si quidam ob honorem promiserit decretum sibi vel decernendum vel ob aliam justam causam, tenebitur ex pollicitatione." In forming the expression "pollicitatio," they had in mind

we probably have a later extension) on account of a heavy misfortune which befell the community, or when, a beginning having been made of carrying the promise into execution, it thereby becomes a reality and the mere word has assumed the form of a deed.

I add a third case to these two, but again for the purpose of stripping it of the appearance of liberality with which it is clothed. It is the promise of "dos." The regular form of it was, until late in the time of the emperors, the verbal contract. It therefore took on a business form, and the Roman jurists maintain the business character of "dos" (in contradistinction to gift) even for the man who receives it. This they justify by the statement that the man has to bear the burdens of marriage, and the purpose of the "dos" is to give him such contribution as is due from the wife.[26] At the same time there was unilateral promise ("dotis dictio") in certain cases; the same form, therefore, as in "votum" and "pollicitatio." But the business element in contradistinction to the purely liberal asserts itself here also in the fact that this form was limited to the assumption of an antecedent debt;[27] and thus here also it was the "res" which served as the basis of the promise. Not

the case of an antecedent performance on the part of the community. "Polliceri" is "pote" (strong, powerful) "liceri" (to offer, to bid), "pollicitator" is he who has made the highest bid to the community for something which it grants him (honor). It is therefore again real contract, "do, ut facias." The obligation undertaken by the bidder is actually designated (*ibid.* 6. pr.) as "aes alienum," and in 3. pr. as "quasi debitum."

[26] In place of all other passages I shall name only D. 44. 7. 19, where the "lucrativa causa" of "dos" is expressly rejected and the idea of consideration is emphasized.

[27] "Dotis dictio" can be made by the wife, by her debtor, or her father, Ulp. VI, 2, *i. e.*, by persons who are already obligated either "civiliter" or "naturaliter," and hence do not give it as a gift.

until the Christian period is the promise of a "dos" as such, *i. e.*, without the business form of verbal contract, recognized by Theodosius and Valentinian as actionable.

We have now come to the end, and after the long digression which we permitted ourselves, we now return to the path which we followed earlier. The point where we left it was the question of compulsive coercion (p. 198), and the reason we quit it was in order to get a firm historical point of support for this question. The result with which we return consists in the recognition that the impelling motive in obligation is not an abstract idea of will, or, which is the same thing, a formal concept of promise, but the practical purpose. But the concept of purpose is highly relative; its practical form in law is conditioned and determined by that which is felt as a condition and aim of life. And this too not by a particular and peculiarly formed individual, but by the typical individual of this definite period, *i. e.*, by the whole of society. To secure this content, these purposes, answers to the interests of everyone, for without them no one can live; and in granting them the form of obligation in order to secure them, the law only protects the conditions of life of all society.

We have not yet, however, advanced, in the development so far of our discussion, to the concept of law. We are still occupied with the concept that is introductory to it, *viz.*, the individual coercion demanded by the purpose of the realization and security of the necessary conditions of life. But everything we have found so far leads us inevitably to the law. It presupposes the juristic formation of the entire content of purpose developed so far, which the individual would have to pursue by his own power if we imagine him thrown upon his own resources. Every one of the purposes which he feels according to the general standard above given as essential to life, demands coercion. Such demand, however, presupposes law as systematized coercion.

§ 6. *The Self-regulation of Coercion.* — *Partnership.* We have made the attempt in what has preceded to go back to the ultimate motives of coercion in civil society. Now, whatever form the State may give to it, however extended may be the application which it makes of it for its own purposes, the ultimate germ of coercion as a social institution, the beginnings of its foundation as an organization, lies in the individual; the purpose of existence of the individual cannot be realized on earth without coercion. It is the first, and in it lies therefore the primitive germ of *law*, as *legal force* (p. 187).

But by showing that coercion is indispensable we have not yet gained much; the decisive point is the assurance of its *success.* Of what use to the owner or creditor is the authority of realizing his right by coercion, when the preponderance of force is found on the side of the opponent? Under such conditions the exercise of his right of coercion takes the form of a two-edged sword, whose sharpness is directed against himself. The whole question of the social organization of coercion is connected with the problem of *bringing the preponderance of force on the side of right.*

We can answer the problem easily enough by saying that this matter is attended to by the State. Why, then, call it up as a problem? I do not want to disturb anybody's comfort who is satisfied with this reply, but I for my part cannot be content with it, if I am to do justice to the problem of presenting clearly the unity and continuity in the conceptual development of coercion in civil society, from its first beginnings in the individual up to its last conclusion in the State and the Law.

He who does not regard his power as sufficient for maintaining his right against violent injury or deforcement, will look around for help, whether it be in the moment of danger when the right is threatened, or as soon as it is established. Both forms of protection take shape daily before our eyes in international intercourse; in the first case by *alliance*, in the second by *guarantee*. The imperfect development of the idea of right in the life of nations is responsible for the fact that these two rudimentary forms have been retained in this domain from the time of primitive law; forms which everywhere else were made superfluous by the organization of the law which succeeded, and hence were abolished.[28] Both of them contain the first beginnings of the realization of the problem of right; which is, to create a preponderance on the side of right. But only the first beginnings, for the success of either is ever highly problematical. The one who menaces can look around for allies just as well as the one threatened; he who finds the most is the strongest, and it is not right but accident that decides the matter. Guarantee goes a step higher. But its value, too, as the experience of international law has at all times shown, is highly problematical; for who will guarantee the guarantor? As long as his interest goes hand in hand with that of the principal or at least is not opposed to it, there is no strain in their relations; but it is quite different when their interests part; here the guarantee is put to the test, which it only too often fails to stand.

[28] I thought I discovered a trace of them in the private law in the five witnesses of the ancient Roman "mancipatio" and "nexum." See my "Geist des römischen Rechts" I § 11*b* (4th ed.). Their original purpose was according to my opinion that of *assistants* ("testes" from "stare")—assistance not with word alone, *i. e.*, with testimony, but with the hand, with deed.

This seems to indicate for law the way in which it can bring the preponderance of power on its side, and secure the guarantee by self-interest, *i. e.*, by means of reciprocity. This form of reciprocal security of right is the *defensive and offensive alliance*. But this means, too, is not yet the right one, for the opponent also, from whom we have to expect the attack, may make use of the same means. And if he does so, then it is again not right but mere accident that decides; and again the strongest conquers.

These are the facts regarded externally. The case is quite different when looked at from within; and here, indeed, we finally come upon the vital point in the whole organization of right. This consists in the preponderance of the *common* interests of *all* over the *particular* interests of one *individual; all* join for the common interests, only the *individual* stands for the particular interest. But the power of all is, the forces being equal, superior to that of the individual; and the more so the greater their number.

We thus have the formula for social organization of force, *viz.*, preponderance of the force which is serviceable to the interests of all over the amount at the disposition of the individual for his own interest; the power being brought over to the side of the interest common to all.

The form in private law of a combination of several persons for the pursuit of the same common interest is *partnership*, and although in other respects the State is very different from partnership, the formula in reference to regulating force by interest is quite the same in both. Partnership contains the prototype of the State, which is indicated therein in all its parts. Conceptually as well as historically, partnership forms the transition from the unregulated form of force in the individual to its regulation by the State. Not merely in the sense that it contains a combination of several for the same purpose, and thereby makes possible the pursuit of aims which were denied to the power of the individual — an aspect of partnership which, in its high social significance, we have already appreciated above (p.157)—but in an incomparably greater measure in the sense that it solves the problem of creating the preponderance of power on the side of right. It does this by putting in place of the opposition of two particular interests fighting one another without an assured prospect of the victory of right, that between a common interest and a particular,[29] whereby the solution comes of itself. In partnership all partners present a united front against the one who pursues his own interests at the expense of these common interests assigned by the contract, or who refuses to carry out the duties undertaken by him in the contract; they all unite their power against the one. So the preponderance of power is here thrown *on the side of right*, and partnership may therefore be designated as the mechanism of the *self-regulation of force according to the measure of right*.

Against this deduction I must expect to have it objected that the force of an individual partner may after all be stronger than that of all the others put together; and also that a majority may combine in order to pursue their particular interests at the expense of the interests of the partnership. Let my answer be that I put at the basis of my deduction the normal function of society as it is posited by its purpose and intention in intercourse. In this its normal form it actually accomplishes what I credit it with: it creates this preponderance of power on the side of the common interest. It is true that we have

[29] "Quod *privatim* interest *unius* ex sociis . . . ," and "quod *societati* expedit," D. 17. 2. 65 § 5.

to recognize those two possibilities as dangers to which partnership is exposed when the normal conditions are not present. Against the first mentioned danger it offers help in itself, by the indefinite increase in the number of its members. In a society of ten members the individual has nine against him, in a society of a hundred he has nine and ninety, in the society of the State he has millions against him in the form of the State force.

The solution of the problem to which our entire investigation has till now been devoted depends then upon the fact, — and I now may be allowed to exchange the term partnership for society, — that society is stronger than the individual; and that therefore where it is obliged to summon its power in order to assert its right against the individual, the preponderance is always found on its side, *i. e.*, on the side of right.

I do not have to explain why I replaced the term partnership by society. The ambiguity of this word helps to carry over the meaning of my deduction from society in the private sense, which is partnership, to society in the political sense, *viz.*, the State. The admissibility of such transference of a proposition found in one connection to another presupposes that the agreement of the two in name has a corresponding identity also in content; and that it is not accident therefore, but the right recognition of their inner equivalency, that induced language to cover both with the same name. A comparison of private society with political will show the relative similarity of the two. The fundamental features of both are exactly alike, as follows:

1. Community of purpose.

2. The presence of norms, which regulate its pursuit; in the one, in the form of a contract, the "lex privata," in the other in the form of a law, the "lex publica."

3. In their content: their legal status, the rights and duties of the whole as well as of the individuals.

4. Realization of these norms against the resistant will of the individual by means of coercion.

5. Administration: the free pursuit of the purpose with the means at the disposal of society within the limits set by the above norms, and all that is connected therewith, namely, the creation of a special organ for administrative purposes when the number of members is large (board of management, government). Belonging to this is the distinction between those *by* whom and those *for* whom the administration is carried on (functionaries, officials — shareholders, citizens, subjects). Also the danger thence arising of applying the common means in opposition to the interests of the society and in favor of its administrators; a danger to be feared no less in political society than in private (p. 167). Furthermore, and as a means of protection against this danger, the control of the administrators by the society itself (general assembly; assembly of the estates of the realm).

The conceptual transition from private society to political is brought about by an intervening link, *viz.*, public association.

§ 7. *Public Association.* Public ("öffentlich") is that which is open ("offen"). A public garden, river, square, theatre, hall, a public school, lecture, gathering, is open for every one; every one has free admittance, whether with or without pay makes no difference as regards the concept. The Romans derive the designation of the concept from the word "populus"; "populicum," "publicum" is that which is intended for all, for the people, *i. e.*, is open to all.[30] The opposite of "open" is "closed,"

[30] D. 43. 7. 1, " . . . ad usum *omnium* pertinet"; 26. 10. 1 § 6, "quasi *publicam* esse . . . hoc est omnibus *patere*"; Inst. 3. 19 § 2, " . . . usibus *populi*."

"locked"; the opposite of "publicum" is "privatum," "proprium" ("quod pro privo est," *i. e.*, that which is intended for a particular individual), that which every one has for himself alone, and from which he accordingly excludes everybody else. The whole contrast turns about community and exclusiveness of relation, and it forms the cardinal point of public and private law, without, however, being exhausted in the contrast of these two. The difference between a private house and a public hall has nothing to do with law; both are equally private property, but their economic use is different. The one serves for the owner exclusively, the other for the whole public.

The contrast in reference to society is found also in the form of *partnership* and *association*.[31] The juristic distinction between the two in reference to their structure is unimportant for our purposes; we are interested only in the distinction which is conditioned by the difference in their purposes, namely, that of being closed and being open.

Partnership, like all other relations of private law, has the characteristic of being exclusively intended for those subjects who called the legal relation into being (*prin-*

[31] The "universitas" of the Romans. Both expressions, the German as well as the Latin, have the same fundamental notion of the unity of what are distinct ("in unum vertere" — to unite). "Vereinbaren" (to agree) is used only in the objective sense, "Vereinbarung" (agreement) — contract. "Vereinigen" (to unite), on the other hand, is used both in the objective and subjective sense ("*über* etwas sich vereinigen" — "sich vereinbaren," to come to an understanding in reference to something, to agree; "zu etwas sich vereinigen" — "sich verbinden," to unite for some purpose). "Verein" (association) is used only in the subjective sense, To replace the expression "Verein," which is already firmly fixed in the language, by the term "*Genossenschaft*" (lit. comradeship) is to my mind not at all called for.

ciple of exclusiveness). Every one of the several partners, like each joint-owner, has his definite portion, which may be represented in the form of a fraction. Each is a *part-owner;* and in so far as he is that, he is entitled to his part and protected therein quite as exclusively as is the sole owner in the whole of the property which he by himself owns. Every part forms, so to speak, a juristic cell complete in itself. A consequence of this is that a partner does not by withdrawal or death lose the portion which falls to his share from the management of the business up to that time.

The relation is quite different in the case of associations. The legal status of the associate members cannot be expressed in the form of a definite share. They are not called "*part-owners*," but "*members*" ("*Mit-glieder*"); and for this very reason they have no claim, in case of withdrawal or death, to be paid the quota of the joint property which would fall to their share in accordance with the number of members at the time.

The difference in the manner in which the individual members are benefited by a partnership and by an association coincides with the difference between "frui" and "uti." "Frui" is divisible, "uti" is indivisible; or to express ourselves more clearly, in "frui" the competition of a number of persons is represented in the form of definite parts (quotas), every new share makes the parts smaller, every part that falls out makes them larger. "Uti," on the other hand, every one of those entitled enjoys in its entirety. If the thing can be done as, for example, with public roads, then hundreds and thousands may participate without the abridgment of the "uti" of any single one. The former is the relation in partnerships, the latter in associations. When the fruit or the income of a thing is divided among eleven competitors instead of among ten as heretofore, every one of the ten suffers from it; his own part becoming so much the smaller. On the other hand, the advantages which an association offers to its members suffer no diminution by the admission of new members; but, on the contrary, these are rather increased as a rule. A large association is enabled to offer more to its members than a small one. For this reason an association is not merely willing and ready to receive new members, but it welcomes them and must do so. And this is the case whether its purpose be confined to the interests of the individual members (*self-interested associations*), or whether the object of the association is the promotion of general interests (*unselfish associations, associations for the common welfare*). For every addition of new members raises the powers of the association, both of its individual members as well as of the society as a whole, and hence also the means for the prosecution of the purpose; and every addition strengthens the moral element of the association, the inner marrow of it, so to speak, *i.e.*, the belief of the members in its utility and necessity. In short, it strengthens the *raison d'être* and future of the association; promoting an *ésprit de corps*, by flattering the members' vanity, and thus lending new stimulus to their interest and zeal. Therefore the admission of new members is provided for in the statutes of all associations; an association that would exclude new membership would be doomed from the start, by denying itself what is essential to an association: its public and open character. Associations animated by the right spirit rather zealously endeavor to gain new members; every association seeks to expand, to grow as far as possible in power, prestige and influence. *Exclusion* is the essence of partnership, *expansion* is the essence of association. This impulse of expansion is common to all associations, the most important as well as the least important:[32] State and Church, political, ecclesiastical, scientific, social — the State conquers, the Church makes propaganda, associations solicit members. The name is different, the thing is the same.

But there are certain associations, and they existed in great numbers particularly in former times, which were, according to their original plan, intended as associations, and grew up as such, yet later took the form of a hybrid of association and partnership. These are such associations as, to express it briefly in juristic terms, grant their members "frui" in addition to "uti"; as, for example, in a municipality, definite shares in the common lands, forests, etc. As long as in the latter case the communities possessing these advantages are so large that the present members are not injured by the admission of new ones, they have no reason for opposing such admission. But when this is no longer the case, a change necessarily takes place; and the remedy which egoism hits upon is that the old members keep the "frui" exclusively for themselves, and allow the newcomers only a share in the enjoyment of the "uti." In other words, two groups of members are formed within the same association, each with different rights; there are members

[32] In those very associations which live without any serious purposes on trifles only, on names, flags, colors, committees, parade, conventions, vanity, jealousy, this impulse often puts forth the most edifying blossoms. There is a peculiar bit of folly in mankind, a particular "mania sine delirio" which is quite compatible with intellectual health in other respects, *viz.*, the folly of making associations. It takes the place of children's toys in grown-up children. In England, where the impulse of association has developed in the richest and healthiest manner, it seems also to have put forth these delightful excrescences in luxurious plenty (I am referring here to the piquant persiflage of *Boz Dickens* in his "Pickwick Papers").

having full rights and members having only partial rights. This form of the relation is so offensive and provoking to those having the narrower rights that it was always the cause of the most violent conflicts; from the days of the Roman Patricians, who in this manner excluded the Plebeians from the "ager publicus," to our own century. The relation suffers from an inner contradiction; it is a hybrid formation of partnership and association which, as the opposition is irreconcilable, unceasingly fight against each other, until association finally obtains the upper hand.

With association our development of the concept has reached the level of the State. As far as its form is concerned the latter stands on a line with all other associations, though, with the exception of the church, it far surpasses them,—by its social function, and by the wealth of the content with which in the course of its development it equips itself in rising progression. In adding the element of publicity (*i. e.*, of being open to the outside world) to the other elements which partnership already has in common with the State (p. 222), association removes the only difference which still remained between the two. With this last step the organ of association receives that utility and completeness which makes it fit for the pursuit of all purposes of society; for the reception of every content, the richest as well as the poorest. Association is *the form of organization of society in general.* There is no purpose society has to realize for which this form cannot be used and has not historically been used; and there is no purpose which has not, after having been first realized by the individual, finally gained control of this form or will not gain control of it. This form is as inevitably required for social purposes as the exclusive form of private right is required for the purposes of the individual. If a certain relation is intended for individual use, its legal expression is found in closing and shutting it against the outside world, in the principle of exclusiveness; if it is intended for society, it finds its expression in resting open to the outside world, and in admitting every one who is fit to co-operate in the realization of society's objects.

Association belongs to public law, or, more correctly, it is altogether coincident with it, just as private law coincides with the individual. It is arbitrary in my opinion to limit the concept of public law to the State and the Church. It is true that these two embrace a vital content of such wealth and importance that in comparison with them every other association is as a mouse compared with a lion. But mouse and lion are both mammals, and you may turn and twist as you like, you cannot get away from the fact that State and Church are associations for the common welfare. The difference between the particular species is not *structural*, but merely *functional;* it is based not upon a difference in their juristic mechanism but upon a difference in their purpose; it is a difference not of form but of content. We grant that the State — I include in the sequel the municipality also in this term — in the course of its development gradually appropriated almost the entire content of the life of society. Still, always the fact remains that not only was the State's original content in the beginning of history relatively modest, and limited essentially to the maintenance of security within and without, but also that the living needs of society constantly produced new objects, in addition to those which the State had already absorbed. These new purposes, being foreign to the State, led a separate and independent existence in the form of associations until they had attained the necessary degree of maturity; and then they burst the covering in which they had existed hitherto and emptied their entire content into that form which it would seem was intended to take up everything within itself, *viz.*, the State. What was instruction formerly? *A private affair.* What was it next? *The business of association.* What is it now? *The business of the State.* What was the care of the poor formerly? *A private matter.* What was it next? *The business of association.* What is it now? *The business of the State. Individual, association, State*—such is the historical step-ladder of social purposes. An object is first taken up by the individual; as it grows larger it is taken over by associated interests; when it grows to its full size it falls to the lot of the State. If inference from the past to the future be justified, the State will in the final future take up within itself all social purposes. The association is the pioneer which levels the roads for the State,—what is now association is after thousands of years the State. All associations for the common welfare bear within them an order on the State; it is only a question of time when the latter will honor it.

§ 8. *The State. Separation from Society.* After a long and roundabout way we have finally found what we are looking for, *viz.*, the final form of utilizing force for human purposes; the social organization of coercive force: the *State.* We might have arrived at it more easily. It depended only upon ourselves to take up at once the idea of social coercion in the ready-made form of the State. Why the roundabout way? In order to show how and why, so long as right had not extended to the State, we could not solve the problem of right. In the State, right for the first time finds what it was looking for: mastery over force. But it attains its goal only *within the State;* for on the outside, in the conflict of States among themselves, might stands opposed to right in the same hostile manner as, before the historical appearance of the State, the two were opposed to each other in the relation of individual to individual; where the question of right takes practically the form of a question of might.

Starting from the question how society comes to solve the problem which is placed before it (p. 70), I gave the answer in Chapter VII, as first, by means of *reward*, and secondly by means of *coercion*. But the social organization of coercion is synonymous with *State* and *Law*. The State is society as the bearer of the regulated and disciplined coercive force. The sum total of principles according to which it thus functions by a discipline of coercion, is *Law*. By defining the State in this manner I do not mean that this formula exhausts all its activities, and that it is not also something else besides. I have just proven the contrary by showing how the State in the course of its development continually enriches itself with objects previously foreign to it. But no matter how manifold and numerous the purposes may be which it has already taken up into itself — and will yet take up, — there is one purpose which surpasses all the rest and which was directed to it from the very beginning, nay, called the State into being, and which never can be wanting. This is the *purpose of law*, the formation and securing of *law*. All other problems of the State recede into the second place in comparison with this one; neither do they emerge historically until this first and most essential one is settled; and they have its permanent solution as a necessary condition — the cultivation of law is the essential function of the life of the State.

This leads us back to that relation between State and society already touched upon before (p. 67). I believe I cannot express it better than by saying that the State is coercive society. In order to be able to coerce, society takes the form of the State; the State is that form which the regulated and assured exercise of social coercive force takes. In short, it is the *organization of social coercion*. According to this, one might say, State and society would have to coincide; and just as the latter extends over the entire earth (p. 68), the State too would have to embrace the whole earth. But yet the State remains behind society; for the latter is universal, the former particularistic. The State only solves those problems which arise for it within limited geographical bounds (political district, territory); the sphere of its sovereignty ends everywhere with the boundary-posts.

The problem of the organization of social coercion is therefore the point where State and society part; where the former finds itself obliged to remain behind the latter, which knows no boundary on earth. But, as if it knew that its limitations were imperfectly drawn, the State is always extending and widening its boundaries. In the course of historical development the greater community always swallows up the smaller, and when the smaller are swallowed up and only the larger remain, a struggle for life and death is again provoked between them until they, too, are welded into greater political complexes. In this way States are ever increasing in size. From the duodecimo of the small communities of classical antiquity the State swells to octavo; from octavo to quarto; from quarto to folio — every increase denotes the extinction of as many hitherto independent communities. We may censure history because she will not tolerate the small peoples in the lives of nations; because the small ones, if they do not understand how to become big themselves, must make room for the great. We may commiserate the generations which were chosen to experience such catastrophes — history knows why she has inflicted such hardship upon them; and she provides for it that the grief and misfortune of one generation is compensated for in a later one; and not seldom does the grandson bless what the grandfather cursed. The impulse of expansion of States by conquest is society's protest against the geographical limitations which are imposed upon her by the organization of social coercion. Till now there has never been a period on earth when this impulse of extension did not stir in every vigorous nation. Will the distant future bring a change? Who can say? If the small span of time which humanity has lived till now — I call it small even if it should amount to a hundred thousand years or more — if, then, this small span of time permits any inference to be made concerning that infinite time which is still before us, then the future of man seems to consist in an ever progressing approximation of State and society. Though the idea of a universal State, embracing the whole world in the form of a central force, uniting and controlling all the single States in the manner of municipalities — though this may belong to the Utopias of the philosopher, for whom it is easier to follow up ideas to their ultimate consequences than it is for humanity to realize them, — still the approximation of State and society seems assured.

The organization of social coercive force embraces two sides: the establishment of the external mechanism of force, and the setting up of principles to regulate its use. The form of solution of the first problem is the *State force*, that of the second is the *Law*. Both concepts stand in the relation of mutual dependence: the State force has need of the law, the law has need of the State force.

§ 9. *State Force.* The absolute requisite of the State force, demanded by the purpose of the State itself, is the possession of the highest force, superior to every other power within the jurisdiction of the State. Every other power, of the individual or of the many, must be "under" it; and it must be "over" the other. Accordingly language denotes the former side of the relation as *submission* ("Untertänigkeit," "unter-getan," "untertan," "sub-ditus"), the latter as *sovereignty* ("supra," "supranus," "sovrano"), the State force itself which possesses it, as *authorities* ("Obrigkeit"); and the act by which it extends this power over a domain not subject hitherto, as *sub*jection ("*Unter*werfung"), *conquest* ("Er-*ober*-ung"). All other requirements of the State recede before this one. Before this is achieved all others are premature, for in order to fulfil them the State must exist first, and it does not exist until it has solved the question of power in the above sense. Powerlessness, impotence of the State force, is the capital sin of the State, from which there is no absolution; a sin which society neither forgives nor tolerates, it is an inner contradiction: *State force* without *force!* Nations have borne the meanest abuse of State force, the scourge of Attila and the Cæsar madness of the Roman emperors; nay, they have not seldom celebrated as heroes despots before whom they crawled in the dust, feasting with intoxication on the sight of the elemental magnificence of accumulated human power, a wild irresistible might which, like a hurricane, throws down everything before it, while they forgot and forgave that they were themselves the victims (p. 191). Even in a state of delirium, *despotism* still remains a political form, a mechanism of social force. But *anarchy, i. e.*, impotence of the State force is no longer a political form, it is an absolutely antisocial condition; the decomposition, the dissolution of society. Every one who puts an end to it, in whatever way it may be, with fire and sword, the native usurper or the foreign conqueror, does a service to society; he is its savior and benefactor; for an intolerable form of political system is nevertheless better than no system at all. Nor is it easy for nations to get back from a condition of political barbarism to one of political order. It needs an iron hand to accustom them again to discipline and obedience; the transition passes through despotism; which puts the arbitrariness of State force over against anarchic violence. When the Roman people in the period of the civil wars had forgotten discipline and order, the Roman Cæsars appeared, to establish anew the force of the State and replace it in its rights, and terrorism mounted the throne along with them. The horrors and inhumanities in which they indulged were only the orgies of the State force celebrating its home-coming; the bloody proof that it had come into power again and had no force on earth to fear any more. This proof given, then only could moderation make its appearance.

Revolution bears quite a different character from anarchy. Although outwardly similar to it in that it also contains a disturbance of the political order, it is fundamentally different from it, because it does not negate order *in general*, but only the *existing* order. It desires order, but a different one from the one existing hitherto. If it succeeds we call it *revolution;* if it does not succeed, we call it *rebellion*, *insurrection*. In the success of the first lies the sentence of condemnation of the political powers; in the failure of the second lies its own doom.

The preceding investigation *postulates* the predominance of the power of the State over every other power within its jurisdiction, but it has not shown how it happens that there is such predominance — we must now get clear on this matter. One might suppose that the thing can be settled simply by means of our principle mentioned above (p. 220); that the power of all surpasses that of the individual. We based upon this principle the security of the common interest in partnership against the particular interest, because the power of all entered the lists for the former, but only the power of the individual for the latter. The same opposition of interests and of the powers in their service is repeated in the State; on the one side the purpose of the State, the interests of all, and for its defence the force of the State — the power of all; on the other side the particular interest and the merely private power.

But the logic of this opposition of the power of all and that of the individual is valid only when it is an individual or a minority that is opposed to the power of all, but not when it is the majority that is so. For in this case, if the question of power in the State were decided by mere numbers, the predominance of power would necessarily go over to the side of the majority, and then the force of the State would always be powerless against the majority. But the experience of all times has shown that the force of the State may have the entire population against it, and yet be in a position to maintain its own power. Numbers alone, therefore, do not decide the matter, else the force in the State would always be with the majority of the given moment, and the political power would be in a constant state of fluctuation and vacillation. Happily, however, the matter is different. The firmness of the State depends upon the fact that the influence of the numerical element on the question of power is counteracted by two other factors: the organization of power in the hands of the State force, and the moral power which the idea of the State exerts.

The force of the State, as regards its substance, is nothing but a quantum of popular power — physical, spiritual, economic, collected for certain social purposes. And this power, too, as need scarcely be stated, is always much smaller than that which remains on the side of the people. Quantitatively, therefore, the natural bearer of the power, the people, is always superior to the official bearer thereof, the State. But this proportion of the two is essentially altered by the fact that the power of the people is raw substance, whereas that of the State is organized. The predominance of organized power over unorganized is the predominance of the man who has only *one* sword, but well sharpened and always ready, over the one who has several dull ones, and has to look for them when he needs them, and does not know how to use them.

The practical moral for the State is therefore self-evident; it consists positively in the highest possible perfection of the organization of its own forces, and negatively in the prevention of any organization that threatens it on the part of the forces of the people. If every art has its technique, then the State organization of forces may be designated as the proper *technique of the political art;* and if we call that person a virtuoso who has developed technique to perfection, we may also speak in reference to the above species of technique of a virtuosoship of States. Technique is not the highest, for the *idea* stands above it, which it is meant to serve, but it is the condition of the highest. How important it is can be shown by the example of the history of Rome, and by a comparison of the former German empire with that State of modern times which has understood as no other has how best to make up for the insignificance of its forces by an exemplary organization: I speak of Prussia.

This is the positive side of the problem. The negative side of it consists in preventing the organization, dangerous to the State, of hostile elements; or, since organization proceeds in the form of associations, in the use of the proper legal restrictions, and a careful administrative vigilance, for all associations. The forces of associations are qualitatively not different from those of the State, and in respect to quantity there is no element in the associations themselves which puts a definite limit upon the accumulation of forces. The association may have more wealth than the State, and if it extends beyond the limits of the State territory it may have more members than the State. If we consider in addition the fact that the association employs for its purposes the same mechanism as the State, we see the great danger which the former contains for the latter. Being its most efficient aid in the pursuit of social purposes when it stands on the State's side (p. 229), it is transformed into its most dangerous enemy when it takes an opposite direction.

The State is the only competent as well as the sole owner of social coercive force — the right to coerce forms the *absolute monopoly* of the State. Every association that wishes to realize its claims upon its members by means of mechanical coercion is dependent upon the co-operation of the State, and the State has it in its power to fix the conditions under which it will grant such aid. But this means in other words that the State is the only source of law, for norms which cannot be enforced by him who lays them down are not *legal rules.* There is therefore no *association law* independent of the authority of the State, but only such as is derived therefrom. The State has therefore, as is involved in the concept of the supreme power, the primacy over all associations within its domain; and this applies to the Church also. If the State grants associations the right of coercion within their spheres, it holds good only as long as the State thinks this advisable — a "precarium" of the State law which, all assurances to the contrary notwithstanding, can always be taken back by it; for contracts of this sort, contradicting as they do what is essential to the existence of the State, are null and void.[33] The opinion that the will of the individual is sufficient to transfer to another, whether it be individual or association, the power of coercion over himself, needs no serious refutation. If it were well founded, the creditor could reserve to himself by stipulation the right of Shylock, and an association, the entire property of members in case of withdrawal; the State would only have to play the bailiff, who would carry out these agreements. The autonomy of individuals as well as of associations finds its limit in the criticism of the State, which is guided by regard for the welfare of society; to it belong the forces of coercion, and the judgment of the purposes for which it will use them.

As a *second* element upon which the predominance of the State over the elementary power of the people depends, was named above (p. 236), the *moral power* of the idea of the State. I understand by this all those psychological motives which fall into the scale in the cause of the State when we think of the State and the people as in mutual conflict, *viz.*, insight into the necessity of political order; the sense of right and law; anxiety for the danger threatening persons and property incurred in every disturbance of order, and fear of punishment.

We have now concluded our view of the *external* aspect in the organization of the social force of coercion, and turn to the *internal*, *viz.*, the Law.

§ 10. *The Law — Its Dependence upon Coercion.* The current definition of law is as follows: law is the sum

[33] The same thing applies here as the Roman jurist says in D. 43. 26. 12, of the non-obligatory character of such contracts against ownership, "nulla vis est huius conventionis, ut rem alienam domino invito possidere liceat."

of the *compulsory rules* in force in a State, and in my opinion it has therewith hit the truth. The two elements which it contains are that of rule, and that of the realization of it through coercion. Only those rules laid down by society deserve the name of law which have coercion, or, since, as we have seen, the State alone possesses the monopoly of coercion, which have political coercion behind them. Hereby it is implicitly said that only the rules which are provided by the State with this function are legal rules; or that *the State is the only source of law.*

The right of making their own laws (autonomy) for their own affairs, which many other associations besides the State have actually exercised, is not opposed to this view, for it has its juristic reason in the express grant or the tacit toleration on the part of the State; it does not subsist by its own power, but by derivation from the State. This applies also to the Christian Church. That its own conception may be a different one, and the mediæval State may have recognized it; that the "jus canonicum" may have been considered during a thousand years as an independent source of law, can no more be decisive for modern science (once the latter is convinced that this conception is incompatible with the essence of the State and of Law) than the Church doctrine of the motion of the sun around the earth for modern astronomy.

In so far, however, as the Church, without the help of the external power of the State, is able to realize the commandments which it imposes upon its members by the moral lever of the religious feeling, we can say that these rules, although they are devoid of external coercion and hence are not legal norms, nevertheless practically exercise the *function* of legal rules. But if we should want to call these rules law for this reason, we could do the same with every other association, even one that is forbidden by the State; and we should then have to speak of law in a robber band. The jurist who does not want to lose all firm ground under his feet must not speak of law in such a case; for him there is no other criterion of law than the recognition and realization of the same by the force of the State. The true pedagogue may be able, by means of moral influence, by means of praise and blame, to *replace* the rod, but this psychological restraint does not for that reason turn into a rod. If general recognition and actual obedience of certain rules of human conduct were sufficient to lend them the stamp of law, — a point of view from which an attempt was recently made to come to the assistance of the law of the Church, — then morality and ethics would also have a claim to this name. These are not without general recognition and obedience either, and all distinctions between law, morality and ethics would thus be removed. Coercion put in execution by the State forms the absolute criterion of law; a legal rule without legal coercion is a contradiction in terms, a fire which does not burn, a light that does not shine.[34] Whether this coercion is put into execution by the *court* (civil and criminal court) or by the *administrative*

[34] And yet one of our most famous jurists has not recoiled from this monstrous idea of a legal rule without legal coercion. *Puchta*, "Pandekten," § 11, note g, thinks that when legislation removes custom as a source of law, the consequence merely is that "it is deprived of its effect upon the judge." Customary law, therefore, according to him, continues to subsist as law; only the judge does not apply it! You might as well say, when fire is extinguished by water, it still remains fire, only it does not burn. Burning is no more essential for fire than is for law the judge's enforcement of its observance. What misled *Puchta* was the possibility above mentioned of a voluntary obedience to norms within a definite sphere. If this were sufficient to lend the norm the character of a legal rule, then the norms of forbidden association would also be legal rules.

authorities is indifferent. All rules which are realized in this way are law, all others, even though they are actually followed in life ever so inviolably, are not law; they become law only when there is added to them the external element of political coercion.

But there is an objection against the conception developed here which has often been raised, and which *seems* to prove it entirely untenable. The criterion of the organization of coercion for the realization of law fails entirely in *International Law*, and in another division, namely in *Public Law*, it fails at least in so far as concerns the duties of the monarch within an absolute or constitutional monarchy. The observance of the limits which the constitution places upon the *sovereign*, and the fulfilment of the duties which it imposes upon him are not secured by coercion.

What attitude must the theory of law take up in relation to these facts? It may pursue three different courses. The first consists in completely denying to international law and the above-mentioned regulations of public law the character of *legal rules*, for the very reason that they cannot be enforced, and allowing them only that of *moral* precepts and duties. This course was actually taken by some, but the view is altogether mistaken according to my opinion. It is not only in contradiction with *linguistic usage*, which denominates those rules uniformly among all peoples as laws, but it misunderstands also their nature, which language clearly appreciates. All those rules make the same claim upon unquestioning observance as all other legal rules, and their disregard is felt, like the disregard of the latter, as a *violation of law*, and not merely as *immoral* conduct. That this conception is true can be seen in the manner of the popular reaction against a violation of their rights. War and uprising, which are the means used, are the forms of *self-help* in *public law* which, in default of legal protection, the people in defence of their rights take into their own hands, as the individual did for a similar reason in former times in defence of his *private rights.* For the legal character of international law speaks also the circumstance that agreements of nations are not infrequently placed under the guarantee of third disinterested powers, a thing which would have no sense at all in moral obligations. There is, besides, the circumstance that the decision of national disputes is not infrequently given over to the judicial arbitration of a third power; and a *judge*, even an *arbitrator*, presupposes a *legal matter* and a *law* according to which the question is to be decided. The legal character of international law, as well as of the constitutional regulations concerning the monarch, cannot be an object of doubt.

Whereas this view, in order to save the element of coercion in the concept of law, completely denies those rules the character of legal propositions, a *second* view, in order to retain this character, lets the element of enforceability fall in the concept of law. The former sacrifices the element of law, the latter that of coercion. Where this view leads has been shown above. The characteristic mark of distinction between the rules of law and those of ethics and morality is in this way destroyed; under the broad point of view of generally recognized and actually followed rules, which is common to them all, all the three fuse into a homogeneous mass, into a soft pulp.

The *third* course, which I regard as the only correct one, consists in holding firmly to coercion as an essential requirement of law, but with this must be combined the knowledge that the *organization* of it in those two cases meets with obstructions which cannot be overcome.

The organization of coercion cannot keep equal pace here with the legal rule; the latter has the same form conceptually, and makes the same claim upon unquestioning obedience practically as everywhere else; but coercion remains behind the rule. If it desires to become active in order to realize the rule practically, it finds itself limited to the imperfect form which it bore originally, but which everywhere else has made room for the perfect form; it can only use unregulated unorganized force. But just in this, in the self-help of nations for the purpose of maintaining their rights, is found the connection of the two elements of law, the inner one of rule and the outer one of coercion. And he who does not hesitate to date back with me the existence of law even to the epoch of self-help and law of might, which was once lived by all nations,[35] will not be in doubt how to judge the above phenomena. There are cases in which law can absolutely not create the organization of coercion which it ordinarily strives after. In international law this would presuppose the formation of a superior court above the particular nations, from which they would have to take the law, and which would have the power as well as the good will to carry out its sentence with armed force if necessary. We have only to think the matter out clearly to be convinced of the complete impracticability of the idea. What States are to hold this office; which will make them judges of the world? The idea would be wrecked at the outset. And suppose the judges themselves came into conflict with one another. Where would the whole central force be? It would dissolve itself. The case is no different in public law. The highest bearer of force, who is to coerce all the other bearers of the same standing under him, cannot again

[35] I proved it for the oldest Roman law in my "Geist des römischen Rechts," Vol. I, § 11.

have another above himself to coerce him. At some point in the political coercing machine there must be a limit to being coerced, and coercing alone remain,[36] just as conversely at some other point coercing must cease, and being coerced alone remain. In all other organs of the State force being coerced and coercing coincide; they receive their impulses from above and continue them down, just as in clock-work, where one spring drives the other. But the clock cannot wind itself up; for this there is need of a human hand. This hand is in a monarchical form of government, the monarch; it sets the whole wheel-work in motion; he is the only person in the State who coerces without being himself coerced. We may limit his power ever so much, *negatively*, by a constitution (counter-signature and responsibility of the ministers, constitutional oath of the servants of the State, etc.), and we may *positively* try to secure on his side obedience to the laws by means of the moral guarantee of an oath on his part to uphold the constitution, but *positive legal coercion* against him is an impossibility; for he holds the same position in the State as the general in battle. The latter would not be general if another had power over him — there is no higher point above the highest, as there is no lower below the lowest.

The impossibility of having his political duties enforced, which characterizes the status of the monarch, is found also in other positions, for example in that of jurymen in reference to the duty imposed upon them to

[36] The practical Romans recognized it correctly. They allowed no judicial coercion against the bearers of the State force, *viz.*, the judges, as long as they were in office. *Gell.* XIII, 13, "neque vocari, neque, si venire nollet, capi atque prendi salva ipsius magistratus majestate posse." D. 2. 4. 2, "In jus vocari non oportet . . . magistratus, qui *imperium* habent, qui coercere aliquem possunt et jubere in carcerem duci."

judge according to their conviction. For conviction and conscience there is no control and therefore no coercion; the only guarantee of which the law can make use for this duty is the oath. Must it for this reason be designated as moral? The institution of the jury is a legal institution, and that, too, of the very first rank; the fundamental idea is *legal purpose*, and all other regulations which are intended to bring about the realization thereof bear without doubt the character of legal rules. According to *intention*, therefore, the idea of legal duty is applicable also to the obligation of jurymen. Like the obligation of the monarch in a monarchical government, it forms the conclusion of the entire institution, the highest point which the idea of purpose reaches within it; but here again coercion remains behind the idea of law, not indeed because it would not *like* to follow it, but because it *cannot*.

We arrive therefore at the result that there are points within the legal order where coercion fails. If we, nevertheless, confer the character of *legal rules*, *laws*, upon the rules which legislation lays down in reference to them, it is because of a double consideration: first, because the entire institution of which they form only a small part is of a *legal* character, and then because according to the *intention of the legislation* they lay claim to the same unquestioning regard and validity as are realized in all other rules by means of coercion. The monarch who violates the constitution, the juryman who condemns or acquits the accused against his better knowledge, transgresses against the *law*, not against *morality*; though the law cannot reach them.

§ 11. *The Law — The Element of Norm.* The second element of the concept of law is norm (p. 240); the latter contains the inner side of law, coercion the outer.

The content of norm is an idea, a proposition (legal rule), but a proposition of a *practical* kind, *i.e.*, a direction for human *conduct*. A norm is therefore a *rule* according to which we should direct ourselves. The rules of grammar come also under this concept. They are distinguished from norms by the fact that they do not concern *conduct*. Directions for conduct are contained also in propositions derived from experience concerning the element of purpose in conduct, *viz.*, *maxims*. Norms are distinguished from the latter by the fact that they are of a *binding* nature.[37] Maxims are guidances for *free* conduct; their observance is placed in the judgment of the agent himself; that of the norm is not; it designates a direction for another's will, which he *should* follow, *i.e.*, every norm is an *imperative* (*positive* — *command*, *negative* — *prohibition*). An imperative has meaning only in the mouth of him who has the power to impose such limitation upon another's will;[38] it is the stronger

[37] The language expresses the idea of *binding* in this relation· German "Verbindlichkeit" (legal bond, [from "binden," to bind]), Latin "obligatio" (from "ligare" — to bind), the old Roman "*nexum*" (from "nectere" — to bind), "*contrahere*" (to draw the band together, tighten), "*solvere*" (to loosen it), "*jus*" (= that which binds, from the Sanskrit root "*ju*" — to bind, tie; see my "Geist des römischen Rechts," Vol. I, p. 218, 4th ed.).

[38] The idea of imposition is expressed in the language. In Latin in "*lex*" (leg-ere — to lay; "lex publica" — "Gesetz" [something *set down*, statute]; "lex privata" — "Auflage" [something imposed, an order] in a will or contract); in "*imperare*" ("endo parare" — to impose; the imperative refers linguistically as well as actually to an "imperium"), German "*Auflage*" (imposition, injunction), "*Obliegenheit*" (that which is imposed or incumbent upon one, a duty). For the relation of dependence on the part of the subordinate party the language makes use of the terms "*hören*" (to hear), "*horchen*" (to hearken). Thus "die *Hörigen*" (bondsmen), "*gehorsam*" (obedient), "*gehorchen*" (to obey). Similarly in Latin "obedire" from "audire." Transferred from persons to things in "das Gehören" (belonging to) = the thing belongs to me.

will that designates the line of conduct for the weaker. An imperative presupposes a double *will;* it passes from a *person* to a *person;* nature herself knows no imperatives. According as the imperative merely designates conduct in a particular case, or a type of conduct for all cases of a certain kind, we distinguish *concrete* and *abstract* imperatives. The latter coincide with norm. Norm is accordingly to be defined as an *abstract imperative for human conduct.*

The ethical world-order contains three classes of such abstract imperatives: of law, of morality, and of ethics. What is common to them is the social purpose; all three have society as the subject of their purpose, and not the individual. With reference to this purpose, I call them *social imperatives.*[39] In morality and ethics these are laid down as well as realized by *society;* in law these two functions are exercised by the *State*, the former *regularly*,[40] the latter *exclusively*. The difference between the imperatives of the law and those of morality and ethics is that the former have the element of external coercion connected with them by the power of the State and administered by the same.

All coercion presupposes two parties: the one who coerces and the one who is coerced. To which one of these is the coercive norm of the State directed? The question has been raised by criminologists with special reference to criminal laws, and has received a three-fold answer from them;[41] *the people, the judge, the State.*

The latter view would presuppose that one can direct an imperative against oneself. This is incompatible

[39] More of this in Ch. IX, Vol. II, p. 105, 227, 238.

[40] Modified by customary law so far as its validity is not excluded by legislation.

[41] See further concerning it in *Binding*, "Die Normen und ihre Übertretung," Vol. I, p. 6 and fl. (Leipzig, 1872).

with the concept of an imperative, which presupposes (p. 248) *two* opposing wills — a stronger and a weaker. The idea which gave occasion to this view is the obligation incumbent upon the State and recognized by it to prosecute and punish crime; but the form of expression is mistaken.

One may resolve firmly to do some thing, and carry out one's resolution inviolably, and even acknowledge to another one's obligation to do it, but the concept imperative cannot be applied to it without destroying it; imperatives to oneself are a contradiction in terms.

There remain therefore the people and the judge or, since we extend our circle of vision to the whole law, including police and administrative law, the State authorities. To which of these does the law direct its imperatives? Or are they perhaps directed to both?

It is clear in the first place that there are imperatives which are directed exclusively to the authorities. The regulations which govern the organization, the management and the jurisdiction of the authorities, have nothing to do with the private person, and though in some of these one has the right to protest or complain against their disregard, there are also other regulations in which this is not the case; where obedience is secured only by the right of supervision and review on the part of superior authorities. The political coercion for the realization of all these imperatives (laws, ordinances), whether those issued by legislation or by the State force, takes place altogether within the coercive machinery of the State; it is the working of the machine within, without any exertion of force on the outside.

Over against these purely *internal* coercive norms, as I shall call them, are the *external*, the effectiveness of which shows itself passively in the private person, who is held to their observance on the appeal of another private person, or on the initiative of the State force itself by a threat of coercion or of punishment. They find therefore their practical object without doubt in the private person; the latter is to be enjoined to act or forbear in accordance with the norm. In this sense, therefore, we can say that they are directed to the *people*.

But there are doubtless many legal regulations which direct no imperatives at the private person, either in respect to their form or content,[42] and yet they are intended to be applied to him by the judge. I name as an example, in civil law, the propositions having to do with the development of legal concepts; the regulations of the age of majority; concerning the influence of error on acts in the law; concerning the interpretation of laws and acts in the law; in criminal law, the regulations concerning criminal responsibility, and state of necessity. Where is coercion here, which is to constitute the criterion of all legal norms? We are confronted here, it seems, by the necessity of recognizing that there are legal rules which are not imperatives; and thus our whole definition of the legal norm, which identifies it with an imperative wielded by the State force, would fall to the ground.

But the imperative shows itself here also; it asserts itself in the person of the judge, who is expected to apply all these norms. Majority and minority signify this for him — treat the one who is of age differently from the minor; compel the former to fulfil the contracts concluded by him but not the latter. Error, irresponsibility mean this — do not compel the fulfilment of the contract, or the carrying out of the punishment. Interpretation signifies — take the doubtful words in this

[42] I am alluding in this observation to the possibility of divesting the imperatives of this form by raising them to juristic concepts. See concerning this, my "Geist des römischen Rechts," 3 § 41.

sense. The propositions connected with the development of legal concepts signify — recognize the case or the crime, or do not recognize it, and condemn and carry out your sentence accordingly, according as the conceptual elements are present or not.

With the person of the judge, or, more properly, of the authorities, who carry out the imperatives of the State, we have reached the point where the idea of coercion is proven to be absolutely true in law, and valid without exception. The criterion of all legal norms is their realization through coercion by the *State authorities* appointed for the purpose; whether it is that the upper coerce the lower; that they are themselves constrained to coerce; that the judge or the administrators coerce the private person, or that, as in monarchy, the monarch alone coerces without being himself coerced. Considered from this point of view all law presents itself as a system of coercion realized by the State; as the *machinery of coercion* organized and wielded by the State force. All norms without exception come under this point of view; even those to which attention was called above (p. 246) in reference to the ruler and the jury. There coercion fails indeed in its power over the two latter, but they concern there, too, its exercise on others.

If we repeat from this standpoint of our consideration of the State and of law the above question: To whom are the imperatives of the State directed? The answer can only be: to the organs which are entrusted with the management of coercion; from the monarch and the highest pinnacles of the hierarchy of officials down to the lowest levels. Every legal rule, every political imperative is characterized by the fact that some bearer of political force is entrusted with its practical realization. Coercion against the private person, though it belongs to it, is an unsafe criterion of law; coercion which any political authority exercises either within, downward or outward is an absolutely safe one; provided that the imperative is equal to the requirements which the government expects of it.

All such imperatives whether concrete or abstract are *legally* binding on him to whom they are directed; he who does not observe them sets himself in opposition to the law. All State decrees, on the other hand, to which the State itself denies this enforceability by its authorities are not imperatives of a legal kind. They are mere announcements, expressions of opinion, invitations, desires, requests of the State, even if they appear in abstract form in legislation in the midst of other legal regulations. Such, for example, in Oriental law books, are prescriptions of a religious and moral nature, which are not legal norms. It is not the *expression* of a norm by the State that lends it the character of a legal norm, but only the circumstance that it obligates its organs to carry the same out by means of external coercion. A code of morals or a catechism compiled by the State; a direction for study published by a board of examiners; a system of spelling published by the ministry of education, are not binding; none of this has the signification of a legal norm. Only that norm can lay claim to a legal title whose realization by means of coercion the State has imposed upon its organs.

Our result is therefore that the criterion of a legal norm does not consist in its *external* effectiveness in the direction of the *people*, but in its *internal* operation in the direction of the State authorities. The former remains far behind the latter; and we shall therefore, if we wish to express the concept of legal norm correctly in juristic terms, not go wrong, if we define it in reference to its *form* as containing an abstract imperative directed to the organs of the State force. And the external effectiveness, *i.e.*, the observance of the same on the part of the people, as far as there is occasion for it, must be designated from this purely *formal-juristic* point of view (not from the *teleological*) merely as *secondary* in comparison with the other as *primary*. All legal imperatives without exception are directed in the *first* instance to the authorities, the entire civil code, the criminal code; all finance laws, police laws, military laws and ordinances, etc., are nothing but regulations for the management of the coercive force of the State. But so far as the latter is put *actively* at the disposal of the private person for his interests (private criminal prosecution), or so far as it can *passively* be put into execution against him on the basis of such a request to punish an offender or without one, they extend their operation to him also; they *vindicate* him and they *obligate* or *bind* him. In reference to the *purpose* of such norms we may say that they aim at the private person; the above statement that in *form* they are directed solely to the organs of the State force is not invalidated thereby.

But not all legal imperatives of the State force are legal norms; we must rather distinguish between concrete and abstract; the latter alone are legal norms. And even within the latter we have to point out a distinction which is of the greatest importance for the complete realization of the idea of law in society. It is that of the *unilaterally* and *bilaterally* obligating force of the legal norm. The object of the State in issuing a legal norm can be only to bind thereby the one to whom it is directed, but not to bind itself; so that it reserves to itself the privilege in a particular case of disregarding the norm if it so chooses. But it can also issue the legal norm with the object and the assurance of binding itself thereby. With this form only, if it is actually observed, the law reaches its complete stage, *viz.*, the certainty of an unfailing realization of the norm as once laid down.

The exposition following is intended to show these three particular stages in the rise of the political imperative to the complete form of the legal norm.

First Stage.—Individual Command. The simplest conceivable form of command is that of the individual command. Called forth by the immediate need of the particular case, by the impulse of the moment, it emerges only to disappear again at once, exhausting its entire effect in the particular case, without leaving a trace behind. A force which we think as limited to this form of command must always first will itself before setting another's will in action; the latter is related to it as the lifeless instrument which does not move unless it is played by some one. The picture which this lowest stage of the political imperative presents before us is that of the constant exertion and activity of force; force in perpetual motion, solely directed to the moment, to create by a command what it demands.

The concept of an individual command does not require that it be directed to a single individual. Calling out persons of a certain age for the purpose of conscription is an individual command; for it exhausts its effect in and with this particular case, and does not hold good for the following year. Whether all those liable to service are invited singly or through the designation of their class, by means of an announcement affecting them all, is conceptually immaterial. Conversely, the circumstance that the command is limited to a single person is not sufficient to make it an individual command. A judicial order of fine or imprisonment is directed to a single person; yet it is not an individual command, for it has its basis not in a *free, spontaneous* act of will of the *State*, called forth solely by this case, but in a *previous abstract* volition of it — which only appears here in concrete form — *viz.*, in the *law*. Not the will of the judge but that of the law compels the debtor to pay, and sends the criminal to prison; the judge only fills out the blank which the legislator drew up; his command is *concrete*, but not *individual*. The concrete is the *correlative* of the abstract, the individual is the *opposite* of it; the concrete, regarded in its generality, is called abstract; the abstract in its realization becomes concrete. He who makes use of the expression concrete thereby implies the idea that corresponding to the particular which he designates in this way there is a universal which only appears in connection with it. Conversely, he who makes use of the expression abstract implies that the universal which he has in mind can become actual in a particular case. But on the other hand, he who designates a thing as individual desires to express in that term that it is not a mere repetition of a type, of the abstract, but that it denies it in some point which is peculiar to it. Applying this to the commands of the State we say then that only those are to be designated as individual which concern in a particular case a regulation not already provided for in an abstract way, or laid down as necessary by the law, but based upon the free and spontaneous volition of the State force. The individual commands of the State stand therefore on the same line as the abstract; both have as their source and presupposition the same moving force of the State. Only the scope within which they are active is different; in the former it is the temporary instance, in the latter the permanent relation; there it *individualizes*, here it *generalizes*.[43] Our German legal phraseology does not

[43] The latter expression is used by the Roman jurist in D. 1. 3. 8, "Jura non in singulas personas, sed *generaliter* constituuntur."

express this conceptual contrast, whereas the Roman did so early, *i.e.*, it comprehended it consciously.[44]

The expressions which our German legal terminology presents, *viz.*, *statute* ("Gesetz"), *ordinance* ("Verordnung"), *enactment* ("Verfügung"), are, in accordance with the application which usage makes of them, indifferent for the above distinctions. At the same time the language itself seems to have had in mind the idea of the abstract in the formation of the first two, and that of the individual in the third; and it would be desirable that usage should be fixed in this sense. We dispose ("verfügen") of things or persons, over whom we have power; "verfügen" is the Latin "imperare";[45] the fitting in, adaptation and subordination of them to our purposes. The idea which the language has in mind here is a particular act of the use of force which is spent in the temporary purpose. So the State, too, disposes ("verfügt") of its forces; and an enactment ("Verfügung") of it would therefore be linguistically a command which is exhausted in the single case. In this sense we should have to designate as "enactments" ("Verfügungen") of the State those commands which do not consist in a simple carrying out of a prescribed legal norm, in a mere application of some thing already laid down in advance, but which are based upon the free use of the State force adapting itself to the peculiar relations of the single case.

[44] As early as the time of the Twelve Tables we meet with the opposition between "leges," by means of which the Roman people issued a general ordinance, and the "privilegia," by means of which it issues an individual ordinance for or against a particular person, as was the case in the "testamenta in comitiis calatis" and the "arrogationes." The opposition is found again in the *Praetorian Edicts* in the form of "edicta perpetua jurisdictionis causa proposita" and "edicta prout res incidit proposita." In the Imperial Constitutions their division into "constitutiones generales" and "personales" comes at least close to this contrast.

[45] See above p. 245, note 36.

In a State in which the legislative power and the executive are not combined in one person, that is, in a republic and in a constitutional monarchy, in contradistinction to an absolute monarchy, an enactment ("Verfügung") which is opposed to the existing laws is possible only in the form of a law; for the legislative power alone is able to remove out of the way the obstacle which, in the form of a law, stands in the way of the proposed measure. The statute may be compared to the "composition" of the compositor in a printing establishment. Both are types for the purpose of multiplication. The particular cases of the statute correspond to the several impressions of the printed sheet. If it is intended that in a particular impression a given passage should read differently from the "composition," this can be brought about only by the compositor's changing his type for this particular case. The same thing can be accomplished in law in a legal manner only by the legislature excluding for the particular case the legal rule which ordinarily would apply to it, and substituting another for it.

Upon this is based the concept and the indispensableness in State law of the *individual statute*. The individual statute shares in respect to its validity and effect the character of an enactment in the above sense. But whereas the latter can be issued by the executive power of the government, the former necessarily presupposes an act of the legislative power; it is in reality a law, though not abstract but individual; and it is required only in the case when the proposed measure is incompatible with the already existing law. The individual statute is "*contra* legem," the individual enactment is "*secundum* legem."

The distinction between an individual statute and an individual enactment is too little regarded by juristic theory. If it were properly comprehended, we should not meet with the statement that individual privileges, such as, for example, the granting of concessions, rights of corporations, etc., are individual *statutes*. They are such only when they are *opposed* to the existing law; as, for example, a change in the succession to the throne in a given case, or the prolongation beyond the legal period of the protection of copyright, otherwise not. The former I am in the habit of designating as *administrative* privileges, the latter as *legislative*. The former can be issued in a constitutional monarchy by the power of the State alone, the latter only by the co-operation of the estates of the realm. In reference to expropriation, both forms occur in different States. Where legislation has laid down definite principles concerning expropriation, by which it is intended that the government should have the right to undertake the same, (whether it be exclusively through the administrative authorities, or in co-operation with the court), the undertaking of it contains merely a particular act of the application of a law. Only where this is not the case, do we have a *law of expropriation*.

The interest which the individual command possesses for our present purpose consists merely in the fact that it contains the conceptual introduction to the norm. Taking force as our point of departure, as we did above, the individual command presents itself as the first and lowest form employed by force to establish order. It is in this way that the Romans conceive of the beginning of their communal life,[46] and this is the meaning of the Roman "imperium": it is the government free to

[46] So, for example, the description of the jurist *Pomponius* in D. 1. 2. 2 § 1, "Et quidem initio civitatis nostrae populus sine lege certa, sine jure certo primum agere instituit, omniaque *manu* a regibus gubernabantur." So *Tacitus*, "Annals," III, 26, " . . . nobis

do as it pleases; the personality of the magistrate in contradistinction to the legislative power of the people. The people issue the abstract commands, the bearer of the "imperium" issues the individual commands.[47] The history of the political development of Rome exhibits in quite a considerable degree this contrast, the sphere of the "imperium" becoming constantly smaller, that of the "lex" ever larger. Only in times of danger does the "imperium," in the form of the dictatorship, again temporarily take up its old form.

Second Stage.—Unilaterally Binding Norm. The individual command shows us force in a state of continual activity, the abstract command, the *norm*, shows it to us in a state of rest; a single norm takes the place of thousands upon thousands of individual commands; but provision for the obedience of the command is the same here as there.

The change of the individual command for the norm brings with it, therefore, the great advantage of economy of force, of convenience, and of facilitation of labor; and this advantage was sufficiently evident to bring about this progress in practice. Self-interest impelled force to substitute for the imperfect form the more perfect, *viz.*, that of the abstract imperative. Egoism unnoticed guides force into the path of law.

The concepts which are brought to light by this progress are those of *norm*, *statute* and *law;* and here

Romulus *ut libitum* imperitavit," and with general application to all peoples, *Justinus* I, 1, "Populus nullis legibus tenebatur, *arbitria* principum pro legibus erant."

[47] This is also the original contrast between "judicia *legitima*," *i. e.*, "legis actiones," and "judicia *imperio* continentia," *i. e.*, the international judgments based upon the *individual* instruction ("formula") of the "praetor peregrinus," the model of the later Roman formulary procedure.

our next aim will be to master the views which language has expressed in these terms.

The form in which the norm makes its appearance is its statement in public. This is demanded by the purpose in view; for that which is intended to be generally observed must also be made generally known. Our German language has the two expressions, *statute* ("Gesetz") and *ordinance* ("Verordnung"). The former is derived from the idea of setting ("setzen"), and is found again in the expression "Satzung" (*statute*). What does setting here mean? Does it mean the *public* setting, or exposition thereof, so that every one may see it? The element of publicity is in no way indicated. The idea seems to me to be rather the following. Setting means cessation of motion; that which is set down is at rest. In this sense language uses the term "Satz" (sentence) of a thought expressed. In order that the latter may be brought into the form of a sentence ("Satz"), the thinking antecedent to it, the search for the thought or the terms, in other words, the intellectual motion, must have reached its conclusion. In the sentence, thinking comes to rest; it has gained its permanent, fixed form. The same idea of the fixed, of that which has come to rest, appears again in "Gesetz" [statute] (hence also "festsetzen" [to lay down as a rule]), and in the modern "jus positivum" ("ponere" to place, set). The laying down of the rule denotes the end of the search: rest in contradistinction to previous motion; with the statute ("Gesetz") force, which was till then continuously in motion, is set at rest. A related figure is that of *setting up* ("stellen"), which the Latin language uses in "statuere" (hence is derived "statuta," statutes), and "constituere" ("constitutio"), and ours in "feststellen" (to establish). On the contrary, in the term "legen" (to lay), from which are formed "lex" (law) and "Auflage" (impost, injunction), language seems to have had in mind rather the idea of imposing ("auferlegen") than that of simple laying down ("hinlegen"). In "Verordnung" (ordinance) it seems to have thought not so much of the original *establishment* of order ("Ordnung"), as rather of the perfection of the same; to which "Verordnung" adds something.

The content of the law is formed by a *norm* or *rule*. Both terms point to the same idea, *viz.*, determining the direction to be followed. "Norma" is a square; "norma juris" is a legal rule. The word "regere," to determine the direction, has shown itself extraordinarily fruitful for legal terminology in Latin as well as in the modern languages. "Regula" is the impersonal rule, "rex" the personal; "rectum" is that which keeps the right direction, the straight. From this is derived the German "Recht," whereas the Romance languages borrow the designation of law (Recht) from the compound "dirigere" ("directum," "diritto," "droit"); also the German word "richten," which is the Latin "regere" in form as well as in content. The idea at the basis of the word "richten" is that of the way which every one has to follow; it is the "way of law" (legal proceedings), the footpath ("Richtsteig"). He who leaves this way becomes guilty of an "*error*" ("Verirrung"), a "*transgression*" [misdemeanor] ("Übertretung")—he transgresses the law in stepping beyond the right way ("delinquere," "delictum")—a "*lapse*" [offence] ("Vergehen"), he goes astray, and the judge ("Richter") is there to show him the right way. He is judged ("gerichtet") by being guided back in the right direction ("richtige Richtung"). In "crime" ("Verbrechen") alone language has in mind not the direction, but the order; "Verbrechen" (crime) is the breaking ("brechen") of the civil order.

All the concepts above mentioned have that of the

norm as their presupposition. The law sets it up. The judge applies it. Law comprehends all the norms. Offence, crime, misdemeanor, disregard them.

Every norm contains a conditioned imperative, and consists therefore always of the two elements, the *conditioning* (presuppositions, facts of the case) and the *conditioned* (imperative). A norm can therefore always be rendered by the formula, if . . . then. The protasis contains the motive and the justification of the apodosis; the "if" is always a "because," containing the reason which induced the legislator to the given regulation. The proposition that when a "filius familias" contracts a debt he is not liable, takes the following form in the consideration of the legislator, *viz.*, in the peculiar relations of the "filius familias,"I see a reason which excludes his responsibility for the loan. The norm is always and without exception directed to the authorities entrusted with its realization (p. 252 f.), who must prove for this purpose whether the conditions are present in the given case (question of evidence), and then carry the imperative into execution. A norm directed only to a private person and not to the authorities is an absurdity. It is an absolute criterion of every legal rule that in the last instance the authorities are always seen to be behind it, enforcing the same if necessary.

In the concept of the norm as such is involved the condition of binding only the one to whom it is directed, but not also its author. He who lays down the norm can also recover it. In this relation, *i.e.*, in reference to its abstract validity, it is always dependent upon his will — there is no unalterable law. But the author's attitude to the norm as long as it subsists, *i.e.*, in reference to its concrete realization, is a different matter. The intention with which he issues it may be that he means to refrain from any encroachment upon it, and hence to respect the norm himself. In this case, when he acknowledges himself as bound to it, I designate it as a *bilaterally* binding norm. This is the form of the norm in an ordered condition of law; the *sovereignty of the law.* If the object of its author does not go so far as to grant the norm this security of realization independently of his will; if he means rather to bind by it only those upon whom he imposes it, and not himself, I designate it a *unilaterally* binding norm.

This is the shape law takes in the stage of *despotism.* The despot, *i.e.*, the master of slaves, as language characterizes him (from ποτ, "potestas," and δέω to bind, hence master of the bound), has not the object of putting a limit upon himself by means of the norms which he issues; he rather reserves to himself the privilege to disregard them in every case where they prove inconvenient to him. Can we speak of *law* at all in such a condition? In so far as we understand by law merely a sum of compulsory norms, yes. In so far as we apply the standard of that which the law can and should be, *viz.*, the assured order of civil society, no. But the germs of the law in the latter sense are after all already present here also. I mean by this, naturally, not alone the mere form of it, the norm, but also the substantial element of the law, *viz.*, the purposes which it has to realize.

These are first *order*, *i.e.*, uniformity of social action. It may be interrupted, it is true, at any time by arbitrary acts, but so far as this does not happen, there is already order, *i.e.*, a uniformity of action regulated by norms and secured by the fear of authority.

The other element of law is *equality.* It is posited in principle in the norm as such; for every abstract proposition is based upon the affirmation of the equality of the concrete; and no matter how arbitrarily the law of the despot may shape the particular categories for which he issues his regulations, within a particular category he proclaims in principle, by means of every law, the theory of equality. To be sure, he is free to negate it in applying the law, but the fact that he set it up himself is not removed thereby. In the very norm which he himself tramples under foot he expresses his own sentence; and this is the point where the moral element of the legal norm makes itself felt for the first time in the shape of fear of open contradiction with itself, and of self-condemnation; where the thought occurs to its author of respecting the law for its own sake. At the moment when force invites the law to announce its commands, it opens its own house up to the law, and there at once commences a reaction of law upon force. For the law brings with it, as its inseparable companions, order and equality; and whilst at first merely a scullion in the house of force it becomes in the course of time the major-domo.

The third and last element which is realized by the unilaterally binding norm to a certain degree, though not absolutely, is the concept of *right* in the *subjective* sense.

Is there such a thing in despotism? We must distinguish between the merely conceptual possibility and the practical actuality of it; and in reference to the former again between public and private law. A share by the subjects in the authority of the State is excluded by the concept of despotism, just as much as a share by the slaves in the authority of the master is excluded by the concept of slavery; despotism knows no *rights of citizenship*. But the recognition of legal relationships among the subjects is compatible with tyranny and demanded by its own interest in establishing and maintaining a definite system; *i.e.*, private law is theoretically compatible with despotism. It is exactly the same as when the slaveholder prescribes an order to his slaves which they are to observe in their relations among themselves, since he himself is interested therein.

But in this very circumstance lies at the same time the imperfection of this status. Put forth solely by the interest of the master, his order remains even in its execution in constant dependence upon him; the slave who complains of a disturbance of order in his person, of an injustice done him, obtains justice only so far as the master has no interest in denying him recognition. In *this* sense, therefore, there is no private law in despotism; it lacks the security for its realization, which it obtains only so far as the humor, partiality, or avarice of the autocrat do not oppose it.

One might suppose that this danger diminishes in the same measure as the personal contact of the despot with his subjects becomes more difficult and less frequent by reason of the extension of his State's domains; and that therefore security will increase with the size of the empire and distance from the throne. This would be true if the tyrant that sits on the throne did not at the same time occupy the judge's bench. As the master so the servant. The difference is only that the former picks out preferably the great for his prey, and the latter principally the small. The former spares the small because they do not tempt him, the latter spares the great because he fears them. Therefore the powerful find themselves relatively safest at a distance from the throne; the weak in its proximity. Security under despotism is based solely upon the endeavor not to attract attention and not to come in contact with the autocracy; it is the security of the deer, which depends solely upon not being discovered by the hunter.

Under such conditions the development of the feeling of right is an impossibility. If it consisted merely in the *knowing* of the right there would be nothing in its way, but the essence of the feeling for right consists in *willing;* in the energy of the personality that feels itself to be an end in itself; in the impulse of legal self-assertion, which has become an irresistible need, a law of life. But the elevation of the feeling to this power is a matter of deed, and that too not of the individual or of a short span of time, but of the whole nation and of a long historical practice; it is therefore as unthinkable in a despotism as the growth of an oak on a bare rock — soil is lacking. For this reason also there is no advantage in a few individuals becoming familiar with this fact by personal contact with a foreign country or by a knowledge of its literature; it only serves to estrange them from the conditions which they find at home, if they are satisfied merely to know this, or to make them martyrs if they wish to carry their better knowledge out into practice. The attempt to gain the multitude for their cause would be as hopeless as to plant an oak branch on a bare rock, or to introduce the palm in the far north; in the hothouse it may flourish but not in the open. The great multitude under a despotism knows only sentiments of dependence, submissiveness and subjection. The philosophy of life by means of which it gets along with the existing conditions takes shape in a policy of dull, unresisting resignation to the inevitable, which spells apathy. This mood, embodied in dogma, is *fatalism;* the necessity of all that happens, but not the need of a uniform law which, in addition to dependence, embraces for him who knows it and observes it also independence and security. They feel nought but the inevitableness of incalculable chance, of fate, which excludes every possibility of protecting oneself against it, and leaves nothing but blind submission. In the domain of law we designate the condition in which accident rules instead of law, *arbitrariness*, and we pronounce thereby an ethical sentence of condemnation upon it. But we must not forget that we thus apply a standard which is foreign to the stage to which we transfer it (p. 192). As the blind man who knows not light can have no idea of shadow, so neither can he who knows not law have an idea of arbitrariness; an understanding of arbitrariness presupposes one of law.

Third Stage.—The Bilaterally Binding Force of the Norm. We have adopted above (p. 240), the current definition of law which designates it as the sum of the valid coercive norms in a State. But the preceding discussion has shown us how inadequate the two elements of political coercion and the norm are to bring about that condition which we call the *state of law.* What is it that is still wanting? The element emphasized above under the name of bilaterally binding norm; that the authority of the State itself should respect the norms issued by it; that as long as they exist it should grant them actually the all-inclusive validity which has been in principle attributed to them. Only in this way is chance banished in the application of the norms; and in place of arbitrariness comes uniformity, security, reliability of the law. This is what we understand by *legal order*, present to our mind when we speak of the *sovereignty* of right and law; and such is the demand that we make of the law if it is to correspond to that idea of it which we carry within us. It is the problem of the *legal State.*

Law, therefore, in this full sense of the word means the *bilaterally* binding force of the statute; self-subordination on the part of the State authority to the laws issued by it.

Language has given this idea a still sharper turn in the concepts of *arbitrariness* and *justice*. To determine the meaning which language attaches to these means to present the popular side from which they originated.

He who orders his conduct in accordance with right or law acts *rightly* or *lawfully*,—*legally;* in the contrary case he acts *against right* or *law, unlawfully,*—*illegally;* he commits a violation of the law, an *injustice* ("Unrecht").[48] All these expressions permit of application to the State authorities as well as to the subjects. The former, too, may be guilty of conduct opposed to right or law; of an injustice. But the State authorities occupy a different position with respect to law from the subject. The former have the function and the power to *realize* the law, *i. e.*, to force to obedience him who resists; the task of the subjects is exhausted in *carrying it out.* The former have to order other people's acts in accordance with the law, the latter have to order only their own; the former have to command, the latter have to obey. This difference in position lends to the injustice which the State authorities commit, in contrast to that of the subject, a peculiar character; and language has felt this correctly in naming it *arbitrariness.* The subject who transgresses the law acts *illegally* ("gesetzwidrig"), not *arbitrarily* ("willkürlich"). Arbi-

[48] The corresponding Latin expressions are "*justum*," "*injustum*" "*injuria*" from "jus," "*legitimum*" from "lex." "*Rechtlich*" (just) has, as is well known, a different sense, similarly "*loyal*" formed from "lex" ("loi"). Both of these express the *inner* disposition of the *will* in harmony with the purpose of the law—the *intention*, in contradistinction to the *outer* observance of the law, legal *conduct* in accordance with the law, which may be due merely to the knowledge of the coercion which will follow in case of disobedience. The just, loyal man acts lawfully from his inner impulse, even when he does not have to fear the law. *Loyalty* is the aim of the law, *legality* is only a preparatory stage thereto.

trariness is the injustice of the one placed *in authority;* it is distinguished from that of the subject in that the former has the power on his side, whereas the latter has it against him. If the subject instead of violating the abstract norm acts against the *concrete* command of the person in authority, he makes himself guilty of a *violation of the law*, of *disobedience.* Just as the two last expressions cannot be applied to the person in authority, so the expression *arbitrariness* — and as we shall see, that of *justice* also — cannot be applied to the subject.

Etymologically "Willkür" (arbitrariness) is the will which chooses its own content ("kürt" from "Kür," "Kur" — choice), hence freedom of choice. But an essential element therein besides the will itself is the existence of a *law.* The will power which has no law over it is not arbitrary, but simply power. The power of the will becomes arbitrary only when the law appears at its side. Hence there can be no question of arbitrariness in the history of law in the stage of the unilaterally binding power of the legal norm (p. 267); and for this reason we could not introduce it until now. As shadow did not exist before light, so arbitrariness did not exist before law. As a purely negative concept it presupposes the opposite of law, whose negation it is, *i. e.*, it presupposes knowledge on the part of the people of the necessity of the bilaterally binding force of the State norms. In the light of this conception the condition above described of the stage preparatory to law may seem to us like the rule of pure arbitrariness, but we must not forget that we introduce into it in this way an internal element which was foreign to it (p. 192). The negro who is sold by his prince as a slave, or slaughtered in the celebration of a festival, does not feel this as arbitrariness, but as a mere fact. He regards the power which destroys him in the same way as we regard the hurricane or the hail storm. Only he feels arbitrariness in whom the feeling of right is alive, and in the same measure as it is thus alive within him; susceptibility to arbitrariness is the index which measures the development of the moral force, and the feeling for right.

But the significance of the term "Willkür" (arbitrariness, free will) extends further than I have assumed hitherto, where I applied it only to disregard of the law on the part of the State authorities. Our language uses the term in a double sense, in a good ("in bonam partem") and a bad ("in malam partem") sense. In the former sense it is used for an action which the law *permits*, in the latter for an action which it *forbids*. In a physical sense we call a voluntary ("willkürlich") movement that which we ourselves undertake of our own resolve, and not nature in us. The contrast which we have in mind in this connection is our dependence upon the law of nature. "Willkür" (option, free will) in this case is therefore the freedom which we have beside the law of nature. In the juristic sense our older legal terminology used the expression "Willküren" for the voluntary agreements of communities, corporations, etc., which they made to fix the relations subject to their control. "Willkür" in this case was therefore synonymous with freedom *beside* the law; the concept was equivalent to the foreign word autonomy now current in that sense, which has the same meaning etymologically (*αὐτὸς νόμος* — a law unto oneself). Linguistically both denote the same idea; "Willkür" in the good sense and autonomy, both mean the determination of the will *beside* the law.

In contradistinction to this, "Willkür" in the bad sense (arbitrariness, despotism) must be defined as the determination of the will *against* the law; but with the limitation that it is the determination of the will in violation of the law on the part of the one who *commands*, and to whom the very power which he possesses leaves free scope beside the law. The scope of power which the will possesses *beside* the law is therefore the common element in which the two meanings of the term coincide, and this is what the language had in mind when it brought the two applications under *one* concept notwithstanding their difference, which is considerable in other respects.

It is in the latter sense that we use the expression, as is well known, not merely of the State authorities, but of every one who can command, *i. e.*, who has the task and the power of establishing order. So we use it of the father in reference to his children—we accuse him of arbitrariness when he shows preference to one child over another, or when he punishes it without cause. The same is true of the master as against the slave, of the teacher as against the pupil.

But, it will be objected, the father who does this does not transgress any *law*, for there is no law that forbids him. This very fact shows that we must extend the concept of law, if we wish to retain this term, from the legal to the ethical. The ethical determination of the paternal relation prescribes certain norms to the father, as the source of power, to which he is bound according to our ethical feeling. If he disregards them, we designate this disregard of the ethical norms by the same term arbitrariness as we apply to the disregard of the legal norms by the bearers of political authority.

The necessity of extending the conception of the norm in this way is shown in the political relation to which we now return. We speak not only of arbitrary decisions of the judge and arbitrary acts of the government where we apply the standard of positive law, but also of arbitrary laws. But the legislating authority does not stand like the judge and the executive power *under* the law, but *above* it. Every law which it issues, no matter what its content, is in the juristic sense a perfectly legal act. In the juristic sense, therefore, the legislature can never commit an arbitrary act, for it would mean that it has not the right to change the existing laws; which would be a contradiction within the legislating power itself! But just as the father is bound morally, though not legally, to use the power entrusted to him in accordance with the meaning of the paternal relation, so is the legislator bound to use his power in the interests of society. His right, like that of the father, is at the same time a duty; for him, too, demands arise from the task put before him which he must satisfy; norms which he must observe; and he, too, can therefore be guilty of misusing the power entrusted to him.

But not every misuse of power is arbitrariness. A bad or mistaken law is not yet on that account arbitrary. A thing is *arbitrary* only in two cases. First in such decisions as are in their nature "free" and "positive"; *i. e.*, such as require a regulation not prescribed by general legal principles, as, for example, fixing the terms of prescription. Here we use the expression in the good sense mentioned above, *viz.*, as the determination of the will in reference to a point concerning which the will of the legislator is *not* bound by the principles by which, according to our view, he should allow himself to be guided. In the bad sense, on the other hand, we use the expression arbitrary of those legal determinations which imply that the legislator, according to our opinion, has set himself in opposition to the general principles of law. In this case we raise the charge against him that he has disregarded the norms which we consider as binding upon him. We also use the expression *unjust* as meaning the same thing. The category of arbitrary ("wilkürlich") legal determinations embraces therefore two entirely different kinds of acts: *positive* acts, for which there is no binding standard according to our opinion, and *unjust* acts, in which the standard is disregarded.

With the expression *unjust*, which we have purposely avoided using till now, we introduce a concept which stands in closest connection with that of arbitrariness, *viz.*, the concept of *justice* ("Gerecht"). Linguistically it denotes that which *conforms to right* ("das dem *Recht* Gemässe"). If we apply the term "Recht" (right) in the juristic sense to positively valid "Recht" (law), "gerecht" (just) would be synonymous with "lawful" ("gesetzlich"),—"in accordance with law" ("rechtmässig"). Every one feels, however, that it also bears a narrower sense. No one says of the subject who obeys the law that he acts justly, or of him who violates it that he acts unjustly. He who has to obey can no more act justly than arbitrarily. Only he can do either of these two who has to command, *i.e.*, who has the power and the authority to establish order—order of the State, the legislator and the judge; order of the house, the father; of the school, the teacher; in short, every one in authority in relation to his subordinates.[49] The Latin language expresses this thought properly in "justitia"

[49] Our language also makes use of the expressions "gerecht" (just, correct) and "ungerecht" (unjust, incorrect) in a wider sense, which does not interest us here, namely in application to a judgment (scientific, esthetic, ethical) which one utters concerning another person or his acts. Here, too, the decisive characteristics of the concepts emphasized above are found again, namely, in the first place, the superiority of him who judges to the one who is judged—he sets himself up as the other man's judge, he places himself above him—and in the second place, the assumption that he is bound to certain norms which must lie at the basis of his judgment. If he observes them, he judges justly ("gerecht"), if he ignores them, we call his judgment unjust ("ungerecht").

(*i.e.*, the power or the will which "jus sistit," *i.e.*, establishes right and order), whereas our German word "Gerechtigkeit" (justice) does not emphasize the characteristic element. Accordingly justice and arbitrariness are correlates. The former denotes that the person who has the authority and the power to establish order in the circle of his subordinates agrees to be subjected by the norms to which we regard him as bound, the latter that he does not.[50]

We have seen above (p. 271) that this obligation may be of two kinds, *legal* and *moral*. For the judge it is of the former kind, for the legislator of the latter; the former stands beneath the law, the latter above it; the former is directed by justice ("rechtlich") to apply the law, and he is just ("gerecht") if he does it. He is not reponsible for the injustices of the law itself; these fall to the account of the legislator. For the latter, who must set up the law for the first time, the standard of justice cannot be derived from the law itself; he must first seek and find justice in order to realize it in the law. It is desirable to express in language this bifurcation of the concept of justice; and the nearest expression that offers itself is that of *judicial* and *legislative* justice. But the concept of justice, as has been shown above, does not coincide with that administered by the State. The contrast above mentioned cannot therefore be named with reference to institutions which belong to the State only. The most appropriate designation would be *formal* and *material* justice.

The former alone comes within the scope of the present investigation, for we have not here to do with the question whence the State authorities must *take*[51] their norms,

[50] A slight modification follows, p. 275.

[51] I will treat this question in connection with the ethical element (Chapter IX).

but with the consideration that they must *observe* the norms which they themselves set up. The fact, however, that a proper understanding of the species depends upon a knowledge of the genus, imposes upon me the necessity of discussing the concept of justice here, at least in so far as is demanded by our object.

The practical aim of justice is the establishment of *equality*. The aim of material justice is to establish *internal* equality, *i.e.*, equilibrium between merit and reward, and between punishment and guilt. The aim of formal justice is to establish *external* equality, *i.e.*, *uniformity* in the application of the norm to all cases when it is once established. The solution of the first problem is, in the State, the business of the legislator. But he can direct the judge, where the conditions permit and demand it, to apply the standard of internal equilibrium himself. In this case it assumes the character of a *formally* binding standard for the judge. The problem of the judge coincides with the second problem, *administration of justice*. Why it is his problem only, and not also that of all the other organs which are entrusted with the execution of the laws, *viz.*, the *government*, will be shown later.

A decision of the *judge* ("Richter") which conforms to the law we call *just* ("gerecht"). An enactment of the *administrative authorities* in a similar case we do not call just, but *lawful*. In the contrary case we pronounce both alike *arbitrary*. It follows from this that arbitrariness and justice are not simply correlative concepts; the negative does not here coincide with the positive, but reaches out beyond it. The concept of justice is limited to those authorities for whom the determining idea is *equality in the law*, *viz.*, the legislator and the judge. The concept of arbitrariness, on the other hand, permits of application to all the authorities of the State, to every administrative board, and even to the executive power of the government. The latter can act *arbitrarily*, when it obstructs the course of the law, but it cannot act *justly;* for it has no part in the administration of justice (see below). Conversely we apply the concept of justice to God, whereas the idea of arbitrariness is incompatible with His nature. There, arbitrariness without the possibility of justice; here, justice without the possibility of arbitrariness: the two concepts are therefore not coincident.

Is the concept of justice then based upon the principle of *equality* in the law? What is there so great in equality that we measure the highest concept of right — for this is what justice is — by it? Why should law strive after equality, when all nature denies it? And what value has equality independently of any particular content? Equality may be as much as anything else equality of misery. Is it a consolation for the criminal to know that the punishment which has overtaken him will also strike all others in the same position? The desire for equality seems to have its ultimate ground in an ugly trait of the human heart; in ill-will and envy. No one shall be better or less badly off than I; if I am miserable, every body else, too, shall be so.

But the reason we want equality in law is not because it is something worth striving after in itself, for it is not so at all. We see to it that with all the equalizing powers of the law inequality finds its way back again by a thousand paths. But, indeed, our reason for wanting it is because it is the condition of the *welfare* of society. When the burdens which society imposes upon its members are distributed unequally, not only does that part suffer which is too heavily laden, but the whole of society. The centre of gravity is displaced, the equilibrium is disturbed, and the natural consequence is a social struggle for the purpose of re-establishing equilibrium; which under certain conditions becomes a highly dangerous menace, and is always a shock to the existing social order.

Leibnitz finds the nature of justice in the idea of symmetry ("relatio quaedam convenientiae"), and illustrates it by comparing the "egregium opus architectonicum."[52] But the symmetry which he requires seems to be less the practical object of equal distribution of gravity and a resulting fixity of the social order than the æsthetic satisfaction of the feeling for beauty, and the harmonious impressions aroused by such order, as in the case of a work of art. But where it is not a question of beauty but of the carrying out of practical purposes, the determining point of view is not the æsthetic but the practical. Here the demand for equalization can be justified only by proving that the nature of those purposes demands the same, and how it does so. We must prove, therefore, how the problem which society has to solve becomes conditioned by the realization of equality. The Roman "societas" will give us the answer to this question.

The Roman jurists recognize the principle of equality expressly as the leading point of view, as the principle of organization of the "societas," yet not as an *external*, *absolute*, *arithmetical* equality, which would assign every participant exactly the same share as the next one. For they intended an *internal*, *relative*, *geometrical* equality, which measures every share in accordance with each one's contribution.[53] Theirs was not therefore any idea

[52] I take the citation (Leibn. Theod. I, § 73) from *Stahl's* "Rechtsphilosophie," II, 1, 2d ed., p. 253. *Stahl's* own exposition seems to me quite mistaken.

[53] D. 17. 2. 6, 78, 80. To establish equality in this sense is the task of the "boni viri arbitrium," 6 *cit.* The nature of "bonae fidei judicium" involves it, 78 *cit.*

of abstract equality among particular individuals, but that of equilibrium between the stake and the profit; in other words, the idea of the *equivalent* (p. 100) in special application to society. A society which desires to flourish must be sure of the complete devotion of the particular member to the purposes of the society; and in order to have this it must grant him the full equivalent for his co-operation. If it does not do so, it endangers its own purpose. The interest of the injured member in the carrying out of the common purpose becomes weakened, his zeal and energy are impaired, one of the springs of the machine refuses to work, and finally the machine itself comes to a standstill. Inequality in the distribution of the advantages of society, and injury to the individual which results therefrom is an injury to society itself.

It is therefore the practical interest in the continuance and success of society which dictates the principle of equality in this sense, and not the *a priori* categorical imperative of an equality to be realized in all human relations. If experience showed that society could exist better with inequality, such would deserve the preference. The very same thing is true also of civil society, no matter what the *species* of equality which the law has to maintain in order to realize the *practical interest* of that society. The determining standpoint in this matter is not that of the individual, but of society. From the former we arrive at an external, mechanical equality which measures all by the same standard — small and great, rich and poor, children and adults, wise and foolish; and which, by treating the unequal as equal, in reality brings about the greatest inequality ("summum jus summa injuria"). Under such conditions society cannot exist. It would mean practically to deny the differences which actually are and must be within it.

A demand for equality of this sort is no better than were the demand that the various members of the human body should be formed exactly alike. They must be different in order that we may speak of a body. The same is true in the social body. The equality which is to be realized within it can only be relative, *viz.*, commensurateness between capacity to perform and the act imposed; between the problem and the means for its solution; between merit and reward; between guilt and punishment. Its motto reads, "suum cuique"—the "suum" is measured according to the peculiarity of the conditions. This is the basis of the concept of true justice. The equality which it endeavors to attain is the equality of the law itself; the equilibrium between the determinations of the law and circumstances. We call that law just in which, according to our judgment, this equilibrium is present. We call it unjust where it is wanting. That law is unjust which imposes the same burdens upon the poor as upon the rich; for it then ignores the difference in the ability to perform. The law is unjust which inflicts the same punishment for a light offence as for a heavy one; for it then disregards the proportion between crime and punishment. The law is unjust which treats the person of unsound mind like him of sound mind; for it pays no regard to the nature of guilt.

One may admit this and yet deny the practical significance for society of justice in this sense. If ethics does not do so the reason is not because it tacitly means to admit this practical importance, but because the idea of it is quite foreign to ethics. The point of view which the latter adopts for justice is the ethical, the same apodictic imperative of the moral feeling upon which it bases its entire system of morality. I shall come to terms with it when I treat of the theory of morality (Chapter IX), where I oppose to it the practical standpoint of the welfare of society. The result of that discussion will prove decisive for justice as well as for all other questions of morality. But on the present occasion, too, we must not and do not wish to omit emphasizing the practical side of justice. Not in order to treat it in exhaustive fashion, for that is excluded at once by the subordinate significance which the question has for our present purpose, but in order to direct the reader's own reflections to the matter.

The surest way to get a clear view of the matter is to put the question negatively; what is the effect politically, economically and morally of unjust laws? I believe it would not be difficult for the reader to prove the injurious effects in all three directions, and thus arrive at a positive recognition of the measure in which the strength, the welfare and the success of the community depend upon justice.

I select a particular case, not because it is specially important, but because the recognition of the true relation may most easily escape notice in this very case. It belongs to the economic side of criminal justice. I leave the ethical point of view altogether out of consideration, and confine myself exclusively to the utilitarian.

Punishment in the hands of the State is a two-edged sword. If it is improperly used, it turns its edge against the State itself and injures it along with the offender. With every offender which it condemns it deprives itself of one of its members; every time it confines one in prison or in a house of correction it cripples his energy. The recognition of the worth of human life and human strength has an eminently practical significance for criminal law. If Beccaria in his celebrated work on crime and punishment (1764) had not raised his voice against immoderate punishment, Adam Smith would have had to do it in his work on the causes of the wealth of nations (1776). If it had fallen to *his* lot to treat of this matter, he would have brought out the truth that the society which sacrifices the life or the time of its members to the penal purpose without absolute necessity is acting quite as much against its interest as the owner who injures his animal by ill-treatment. As in the primitive times of the human race the recognition of the value of human life and human strength was the first step to humanity, because such recognition determined the victor to spare the life of the captured enemy instead of slaughtering him (p. 182), so the same recognition can and should pave the way to humaneness in the relation of society to an internal enemy. Its own interest properly understood demands the most careful consideration in threatening punishment. Where a fine is sufficient there should be no imprisonment; and where the latter is sufficient there should be no capital punishment. In the first penalty, the guilty party alone suffers loss, society does not. In the last two, society has to purchase the evil which it inflicts upon him at the expense of its own loss; every excess recoils upon itself.

The purpose of the investigation so far was to fix more precisely the meaning of the concepts, arbitrariness, equality, justice, which resulted from our analysis of bilateral norm, and to distinguish their use as applied to the legislator from that applied to the judge, as the sole difference with which we are here concerned. We shall now return to the bilateral norm.

We defined the concept (p. 267) as the *subordination* of the State authorities to the laws which they themselves issue. What here is the meaning of subordination? How can the State force *sub*ordinate itself since, from the very meaning of the term, it has no power superior to it? Or if the subordination consists merely in self-limitation, who will secure it? How do they arrive at the idea of imposing a measure upon themselves, a limitation upon the use of their power? Is this act of theirs beneficial? Is it proper for them to apply it in all directions? Or is there not a sphere in which the unilaterally binding law, and even the individual imperative, has its complete justification?

Such are the questions concerning which we must seek enlightenment. I arrange their contents under the following three points of view:—

1. *Motive.*

2. *Guarantees.*

3. *The Limits* of the subordination of the State authorities to the law.

1. *The Motive.* What motive can induce the authorities to subordinate themselves to the law? The same motive which suffices to determine a person to self-control, *viz.*, self-interest. Self-control pays itself. But in order to know this one must have experience and insight. Those who have no insight learn nothing from experience; one must have insight to understand the teachings of experience, and moral strength to practise them. If we assume these two conditions as given, if we think of authority as joined with insight and moral strength, the problem which we put to the authorities is solved; they make use of the law because they are convinced that their own interest properly understood demands it.[54] As the gardener cultivates the tree which he has planted, so they cultivate the law, not for the sake of the tree, but for their own sake. Both of them know that it must be attended to and cared for if it is to bear fruit, and that the fruit is worth the trouble.

[54] A voluntary confession of absolutism that is worthy of notice is the saying in Cod. 1. 14. 4 of Theodos. II and Valentinian III (429), "Digna vox est majestate regnantis legibus alligatum se principem profiteri, *adeo de auctoritate juris nostra pendet auctoritas.*"

Where the State authorities obey the orders of their own prescription, there alone are the orders secure of their proper effect. Where the law is supreme, there alone the national well-being prospers, commerce and industry flourish, and the innate spiritual and moral force of the people unfolds in its full strength. *Law is the intelligent policy of power;* not the short-sighted policy of the moment, and momentary interest, but that far-sighted policy which looks into the future and weighs the end.

Such policy is conditional on *self-control.* But self-control in the State authorities just as in the individual is a matter of practice. It requires many centuries before the State authorities, starting from the point of unlimited power, which we assumed, arrive, after long vacillation and many relapses to the original manner, at the firm and inviolable observance of the law.

2. *The Guarantees.* There are two, one internal, the other external; one is the *feeling of right,* the other the *administration of justice.*

Just as the sense of order cannot develop in the servant if the master's conduct in reality makes order impossible, so the sense of right cannot develop in the State's subjects if the authorities themselves tread under foot the law which they issue — respect for law cannot win its way below where it is wanting above. The sense of right needs to be realized in order to grow up strong; it cannot develop if the world itself shows a contempt for the demands which it makes. The same is true here as in the sense of beauty, which develops only by the cultivation of beautiful objects; by making trial of itself in the formation of the beautiful. Objective and subjective, internal and external, stand in closest relation, mutually conditioning and advancing each other; the sense of beauty flourishes only in and with the beautiful, the sense of right or law only in and with the law.

The point where the development of the sense of right first begins is private law. The most limited vision suffices to see the sphere of interest of private law; the simplest understanding comprehends what it has at stake in private law. And in confining itself purely to the sphere of its own ego, it arrives at the abstraction of *right in the subjective sense.* This is the point of view from which egoism is able to comprehend, and did begin to comprehend, legal order. It is not right in the abstract that concerns it, but *its* right. Its right, however, does not extend beyond that which immediately affects it.

But egoism is an apt pupil. One of the first experiences it has consists in observing that when it ignores the right of another its own right is ignored and endangered, and that in defending another's right it is defending its own. Private law is that part of the law, the practical significance of which for the community is felt first of all, and in which the sense of right has actually come to be first realized.

In the domain of public law, and strangely enough also in criminal law, the sense of right does not develop until very much later. That it should be so in regard to public law is easily understood; but in criminal law this fact is surprising. Of what use is all the security of private law, if the penal power of the State be not confined within fixed limits? By means of an arbitrary exercise of the latter the State authorities could put to naught the whole private law; they protect it against the private person through the civil judge, but they negate it through the criminal judge. But even though, owing to the unusually stubborn resistance which it meets at the hands of the State authorities, the sense of right does not realize its demand of legal security in these two spheres until very late, once it has arrived at power on the floor of the latter, it is driven irresistibly onward by its own strength, until it finally realizes in its full extent its demand that right be secured.

This is the final point of the development. The objective, actually realized, and the subjective sense of right are both on the same height, and condition and support each other mutually. The security of right depends in the last instance entirely upon the moral force of the national sense of right. *Not* upon the form of government; you may think it out as skilfully as you please, yet we can imagine no form which would as a matter of fact take away from the State authorities the possibility of trampling the law under foot (p. 245). *Not* upon the oaths, by which we think it is secured; experience shows how often these are broken. *Not* upon the nimbus of holiness and inviolability with which theory clothes the law; despotism is not overawed by it. The only thing that impresses it is the real power which stands behind the law — the people, who recognize in the law the condition of their existence, and feel an injury done to it as an injury done to themselves; the people, from whom it may be expected that in case of necessity they will fight for their rights. I do not mean to say that this low motive of fear is the only thing which induces the State authorities to observe the law. I mean only that it is the last and extreme motive which does not deny its services even when the higher motive of respect for the law for its own sake fails. The security of the law in the upward direction is situated similarly with its security in the downward direction. The fear of the law must be replaced by respect for it. But where this is not the case there still remains fear as the last resort. And in this sense I designate the fear which the State authorities have of the reaction of the nation's sense of right as the ultimate guarantee of the security of the law, and I do not fail to see either that when once the sense of right has attained to its full influence among the people, it will not fail to exert its purely moral influence upon the powers of the State also.

Accordingly the security of the law depends ultimately on nothing else except the energy of the national sense of right. The power and prestige of the laws stand everywhere on the same level with the moral force of the sense of right; a lame sense of right in the nation means an insecure law; a healthy and strong sense of right means a secure law. The security of the law is everywhere the work and the merit of the people itself. It is a good which history does not give as a *gift* to any people. It must be won by every nation as the reward of a painful struggle often accompanied with bloodshed.

The value of security for the law is so evident that it may seem superfluous to waste words concerning it; and in reference to its value for the external order of life, particularly for trade, commerce, business, this is not really necessary. For no one need be told that the value of things does not depend solely on their real utility; that the value of soil, for example, does not depend on its fertility alone, nor that of property, claims, etc., on their amount, but essentially upon the legal and actual security of their maintenance. If it were not so, real estate in Turkey would have the same value as with us; but the Turk knows very well why it is more advantageous for him to transfer his estate to the mosque and take title ("Vakuf") from the latter on payment of protection money (an annual tax), than to remain the owner of it himself; the mosque alone enjoys legal security in Turkey! Similar transfers often occurred among us in the middle ages, as is well known. In the time of the later Roman Empire, this purpose was one of the motives for transferring one's claims to powerful persons.[55]

In contrast with the *economic* value of legal security, which I shall not develop further in this place, is its *moral* value. I find this in the importance of legal security for the development of *character*. Among the characteristic phenomena of communities under a despotic government is the striking absence of characters. All the despotisms in the world put together have not produced as many characters in the course of the ages as the small city of Rome in its good days produced in the course of a century. Shall we seek for the reason of this in the national character? The national character itself is formed by the process of time; why is its development in Rome so completely different from that in Turkey? There is only one answer. Because the Roman people understood early how to gain possession of legal security. It must not be said that this is an argument in a circle; that the law is made the condition of the national character, and this again the condition of the law; for there is the same reciprocal influence here as in art (p. 283). The people make art, but art in turn makes the people; the people make the law, but the law in turn makes the people.

Without objective security of the law there is no subjective feeling of security, and without the latter there is no development of character. Character is the inner firmness and stability of personality; in order that the latter may develop, it must find favorable conditions outside. Where the national morality consists in

[55] Cod. II, 14. "Ne liceat potentioribus patrocinium ligitantibus præstare vel actiones in se transferre." In the middle ages cession to the clergy (I, 41, ch. 2, X de alien.). In Turkey more than three fourths of the entire landed estate has come in this way into the hands of the mosques.

accommodating and subordinating oneself to others, in a policy of cunning, craft, dissimulation and dog-like submissiveness, no characters can be formed. A soil of this kind produces only slaves and servants. Those of them who conduct themselves as masters are only servants in disguise, domineering and brutal toward their inferiors, cringing and cowardly toward their superiors. For the development of character man needs from the beginning the *feeling of security*. But this inner, subjective feeling of security presupposes an external objective security in society; and this man possesses through the law. Man on the law is as firm and unshaken in his confidence in it as the believer in his confidence in God. Or, more precisely, both of them put their trust not merely in something outside of them, but rather they feel God and the law within them as the firm ground of their existence, and as a living part of themselves; which therefore no power on earth can deprive them of, but can only destroy in and with them. This is in both of them the source of their power. The anxiety of the ego in the world, which is the natural feeling of the animated atom thrown entirely upon itself, is removed with trust in the higher power which supports it. It feels the power within itself and itself in the power. In place of anxiety and fear develops a firm, immovable sense of security. An immovable sense of security; this is, in my opinion, the correct expression for the state of mind which law and religion produce in man when they correspond to the ideas we form of them. The law gives him the feeling of security in his relation to *man*, religion in his relation to *God*.

The security which these two grant is at the same time dependence. There is no contradiction in this, for security is not independence — there is no such for man — but *legal* dependence. But dependence is the reverse side, security the obverse. Therefore I cannot accept the well-known definition of Schleiermacher, who defines religion as the *feeling of dependence* upon God, for it makes the reverse side the face. It may be suitable for that stage in the development of the religious sense which corresponds to the stage of despotism in the history of law — here the feeling of dependence in reality correctly designates the relation — but it does not hold for the final conclusion of the development. This final conclusion consists, in religion as well as in law, in the fact that the feeling of security overcomes the feeling of dependence. In this sense, therefore, *i. e.*, from the psychological standpoint, law may be defined as the *feeling of security in the State;* and religion, as the *feeling of security in God.*

To the sense of right as the inner guarantee of the secured existence of the law I opposed above the *administration of justice* as the *outer* guarantee. The peculiar character of the administration of justice in contradistinction to the other tasks and branches of the State's activities, is based upon two factors; the *inner* peculiarity of the *purpose*, and the *outer* peculiarity of the *means* and *forms* by which it is carried out. In respect to the former, the distinction of the administration of justice from the other branches of the State's activities consists in the fact that its intention is *exclusively to realize the law*, — its motto is *the law and nothing but the law.* The administrative authorities of the State, too, to be sure, are in duty bound to apply the law as far as it extends, but with them there is a second factor associated with the law, *viz.*, its *adaptability to the end.* In contradistinction to these, the authorities who are entrusted with the administration of the law in the narrow sense, *i. e.*, the *judicial* authorities, have their eye exclusively upon the law. The judge must in a certain sense be nothing else than the law become alive in his person and endowed with speech. If justice could descend from heaven and take a pencil in its hand to write down the law with such definiteness, precision and detail that its application should become a work of mechanical routine, nothing more perfect could be conceived for the administration of justice; and the kingdom of justice would be complete upon earth. For absolute equality and the strict dependence of the judicial sentence upon it are so far from being incompatible with the idea of justice that on the contrary they form its highest aim. The idea of adaptability to an end, on the other hand, is so opposed to this constraint by a norm determined in detail in advance, that complete freedom from constraint of any norm would be more advantageous than absolute constraint. To transfer the idea of constraint in the administration of justice to the other branches of the activity of the State would bring the whole State into a condition of torpor and rigidity.

Upon this contrast of the two ideas, of the *constrained* character of *justice* and the *freedom* of *adaptability to an end*, is based the inner distinction between the administration of justice, and the executive function of the government; and language expresses this properly.[56]

[56] In the expression "*Rechtspflege*" (administration of justice), "*Recht*" (justice) is emphasized as its subject, and "*Pflege*" (administration), *i. e.*, the zealous care and effort applied to the law, as its task. In "*Justiz*" (administration of the law) is emphasized "justitia," justice, *i. e.*, what is in accordance with law, as its highest aim. In "*judex*" is emphasized "jus dicere," and in "*Richter*" (judge), direction in a straight line in accordance with the prescribed rule of conduct. On the other hand, "*Regierung*" (government) contains the idea of mastery ("regere," "rex"), and "*Verwaltung*" (administration) that of force which rules ("waltet") freely (from "valdan," "waltan," to be strong, to compel, related to "valere"). An administrator ("Verwalter") is he who has to observe the interest of his principal. The methods he is to follow are not prescribed for him,

To the internal difference, or difference in purpose, between the administration of justice and the executive function of government corresponds the difference in external organization.

Among all civilized peoples there appears at a certain stage in the development of the law the separation of the administration of justice from the other branches of political activity; the *judge* is a figure which meets us everywhere. This does not exclude the external combination of the judicial and administrative functions in one and the same person. The important thing is only that the two spheres should be internally distinct, *i. e.*, that the principles indicated for the one are different from those indicated for the other. But experience teaches that the internal distinctness of the two spheres is essentially furthered and secured if external separation according to persons, separation of the judicial from the executive, is added to internal. This is so because it exceeds the power of man so to develop in his mind and to master two entirely different modes of conceiving and of acting as to be able, according to the difference of the subject, to apply now the one, now the other, without the one influencing the other. The separation of the administration of justice from the executive function must be an external one according to persons and offices if it is to be quite sure of its purpose.

The reason for this requirement is not merely the principle of division of labor, *i. e.*, the consideration that the law, on account of its extent and difficulty, requires a special person. The principle of the division of labor holds also of the executive function. The public works

but they consist in the interest, utility and welfare of his superior. It is left to his own intelligence to do the right thing in a given case. The Roman antithesis is expressed in the terms "jus" ("jurisdictio") and "imperium."

require a different person from the mint; forestry requires a different person from mining; and the State appoints different officials for all these different purposes. The separation of the judicial from the executive function was already carried out historically at a time when the law had not yet by any means attained so rich and fine a development as is supposed in the assumption. Compare, for example, Rome and Germany, where the "judex" and the "Schöffe" (lay judge) long preceded the higher stage of the development of the law; and in our institution of the jury at the present day, the requirement of a special knowledge of the law is entirely ignored.

The separation of the judicial from the executive function cannot therefore be referred to the principle of the division of labor; and there must be another reason. It lies in the peculiarity above mentioned of the problem of the law in contradistinction to all the other problems of the activity of the State. The separation of the judicial as a separate branch of State activity means the retirement of the law into itself for the purpose of solving its problems with security and completeness.

The mere fact of the external separation of the judicial function from the executive, quite apart from the institutions and guarantees to be named forthwith which accompany the same, is of great value for that purpose. By separating the judicial function, the State authority recognizes in principle that the law is a distinct problem, and that the considerations determining its solution are different from all those other problems which the State reserves for itself. In handing over the administration of justice to the judge they actually declare before all the people that they wish to renounce that privilege. The establishment of the judicial office signifies *self-limitation in principle* on the part of the State authorities in reference to that portion of the law which is handed over to the administration of the judge. It means empowering the judge to find the law independently of them and in accordance altogether with his own convictions, and the assurance of the binding force of the sentence handed down by him. They may lay the boundaries as narrow or as wide as they please; within these boundaries they have given the judge independence. Disregard of this fact will bring them in open contradiction with themselves, and will stamp their proceeding as a breach of the law, as a murder of justice. The State authorities who lay a hand upon that order of justice which they themselves have created pronounce their own condemnation.

According to what has just been said, therefore, the purely external separation of the judicial from the executive function denotes a highly important development along the path of the law. It represents, if I may be allowed a juristic comparison, the emancipation of the administration of justice from the State authorities by means of division of labor. Justice changes its abode, and the mere removal has the consequence that if the State authorities desire to lay violent hands on it, they must first cross the street; whereas, as long as it lived under the same roof with them, they could have done the thing within the four walls without being noticed.

Now let us examine more closely justice's household, and the arrangements which it contains. It is composed of four constituent parts:

1. *Material law*, which is handed over to the
2. *Judge* for his *exclusive* application. It is applied to
3. Two disputing *parties*, and
4. In the form of a fixed and prescribed mode of *procedure* (*law-suit.*)

Of these four elements the first contains nothing which is peculiar to the administration of justice; it is common to it and the executive power. The difference consists only in this, that the judge is expected to be guided *exclusively* by the law (p. 289), and this requirement makes it necessary that the law should be fixed with the greatest possible completeness and precision. The effort to bind the judge to the law as much as possible is responsible for an arrangement which is repeatedly met with in the history of law in very different stages of its development. It consists in the requirement of express reference to the law, whether on the part of the party who desires to set the activity of the judge in motion (Roman procedure of "legis actio,"[57] bill of indictment of modern criminal procedure), or on the part of the judge in handing down the sentence (modern criminal procedure). We might designate it as the system of *procedural legalism*. This prescription raises the conformity to material law of judicial procedure to a procedural requirement of the act in question; the procedural act is not possible unless it can show its legitimacy in material law. Being calculated to exclude judicial arbitrariness and to keep constantly before the judge's mind the fact that his power extends only as far as the law permits, this arrangement purchases this advantage at the cost of making the development of the law beyond the prescribed frame in practice difficult in a high degree, and handing it over exclusively to the legislature — a consequence which may seem desirable for criminal law as a guarantee of legal security, but which contains a decided evil for civil law. For the latter, the obligation of the judge to assign reasons for his decision contains a much more useful form of the same idea. It forces him to justify his judgment objectively without restricting him to the immediate content of the law.

[57] [The procedure by which, by the solemn act of the parties themselves, a legal issue was made in a legal controversy at Roman law.]

Another form of the law, which follows the same purpose as the above, except that it does it in a still less appropriate way, is the *casuistical.* This, instead of giving the judge general principles and leaving their correct application in a particular case to his own insight, gives him detailed regulations for every case, juristic recipes for the decision of all possible law-suits, which are intended to free him from all further searching. The impossibility of seeing beforehand the infinite variety and manifold formation of cases, stamps this attempt of absolutely fixing the judicial decision as a wrong one from the start. The idea in the mind of the author is to make the application of the law a purely mechanical thing, in which judicial thinking should be made superflous by the law. We are reminded of the duck constructed by Vaucanson, which carried out the process of digestion mechanically; the case is thrown into the judging machine in front, and it comes out again as a judgment behind. Experience has judged here also — the brain of the judge cannot be replaced by the legislator. The result which he obtains through attempts of this kind consists in reality only in stupefying the judge.

I now turn to the three other requirements of the administration of justice. These are peculiar to it. The form in which the law is applied in the administration of justice is based upon the fact that it takes place between *two conflicting parties*, by following a prescribed procedure (*law-suit*), through the *judge.* The point about which the whole administration of justice turns is the *law-suit.*

A dispute presupposes two disputing members, the *parties.* In a civil action, they are the plaintiff and the defendant, in a criminal action, the State authorities and the defendant The conflict must be settled by a third party, who has no personal interest in the decision.

This is the task of the *judge;* and the position which the State assigns to him must be such as to enable him to fulfil this task. To assign the judge the role of one of the parties (of the State which prosecutes the criminal) in addition to his role as judge, as was the case in early criminal procedure, was a form of the relation which hindered in the highest degree the requirement of impartiality in the judge; to be a party and to be impartial is an impossible combination.

The relation of the parties to the judge is that of legal *subordination;* their relation to each other is one of *legal equality.* The State, too, when it appears as a party in a civil or criminal case, subordinates itself legally to the judge; it stands on the same line with a private person, and becomes a party like any other. In those relations where this seems to it inappropriate, it must by law not assign the decision to the judge, but reserve it to itself. If it has once done the former, it must take the consequences also, and go to law like every other party, *i. e.*, it must subordinate itself entirely to the judge and the rules of the case.

The relation of the parties in the case to each other is that of legal equality. The weapons with which they fight each other must be apportioned equally, light and shade must be equally distributed. It is the first of all requirements which the organization of procedural law must realize, that of *procedural justice*, which here again coincides with equality (p. 275). All the other requirements are secondary in comparison with this, and have *adaptability to an end* as their object.

Parties, judges, law-suits, form accordingly the three peculiar criteria of the administration of justice. It follows from this that martial law or lynch law does not belong to the administration of justice. The State authorities are not in this case *seeking* justice from a judge who is placed above them; they *declare it themselves.* The court-martial which they order represents themselves; it has only the name of court, in reality it functions like an administrative authority. How far the State must extend the scope of the administration of justice in the true sense of the word is a question of policy. Up to recently the latter was confined to the administration of *civil* and *criminal* law. We knew only the *civil* and *criminal judge,* the *civil* and *criminal process.* But the progress in public law which our modern period has made, gave a wider extension also to the administration of justice (court for State controversies, administrative justice), and will do so in all probability more and more in the course of time.

Now, no matter how precisely the law may be laid down which is to be applied materially and procedurally, the entire success of the administration of justice depends ultimately upon two requisite conditions in the person of the judge; the securing of which must therefore form the chief aim of legislation. One is *intellectual* in its nature; the necessary knowledge must be his and the requisite readiness in its application; in short theoretical and practical *mastery* of the law. The arrangements of the present day which are intended to secure this are well known; the study of the law, the State examinations and probational service. The second is *moral* in its nature, and a matter of character; he must have the necessary firmness of will and moral courage to maintain the law without being led astray by considerations of any kind, by hate or friendship, sympathy or fear. It is the quality of justice in the subjective sense, "constans ac perpetua voluntas suum cuique tribuendi" (1. 1. 10. pr.). The true judge knows no respect of person; the parties who appear before him are for him not these definite individuals, but abstract persons in the mask of plaintiff and defendant; he only sees the mask, not the individual behind it. Abstraction from all concrete accessories, elevation of the concrete case to the height of the abstract situation as decided in the law, treatment of the case in the manner of an example in arithmetic where it is immaterial what it is that is numbered, whether it be ounces or pounds, dollars or cents, — this is what characterizes the true judge.

Knowledge may be bought, character cannot. There is no arrangement which can secure against partiality in a judge.

But in this direction also a great deal can be done. Legislation may follow one of two ways in this matter. It can either try to prevent partiality in the germ by removing as far as possible the occasions which might induce it (*prophylactic* method), or it can combat it directly, either by counteracting it psychologically or by trying at least to make it as harmless as possible in its consequences (*repressive* method).

The psychological counterpoise which presents itself first to the law, for counteracting the temptation of the judge to partiality, is the moral one of the oath, the well-known *judge's oath* which we meet among all civilized peoples, and from which our present "Geschworene" and "jury" has its name. But the effectiveness of this means depends upon the conscientiousness of the individual; if he has no conscience it fails of its purpose. For such there is the fear of the disadvantageous consequences of violation of duty which the law threatens (disciplinary investigation, civil liability, criminal punishment). But this means too has only a limited effectiveness, it strikes only the gross violations of duty, which are plainly seen to be such on the surface; partiality escapes it under the guise of free subjective conviction.

On the other hand, legislation has no dearth of means for making the *consequences* of partiality harmless up to a certain degree, partly by the constitution of the court, partly by the procedure. The evil consequences of partiality may be avoided by the former method through the appointment of a bench-court. Where the majority of the judges of a country are animated by the spirit of loyalty and conscientiousness, the method of appointing a bench-court gives a guarantee, according to the law of large numbers, that the conscientious judge will dominate in them, and co-operation with him will put a certain limitation upon the less conscientious also. With a single judge, on the contrary, there is room for chance; here the judge of no conscience stands by himself; the equalizing and restraining influence of his colleague is absent, and at most there still remains his regard for the higher court. But for this very reason the latter is of two-fold value as against the single judge. With adequately filled bench-courts appellate courts are scarcely necessary, but in the case of a single judge an appeal should never be denied. The standard of the amount of the object in dispute, according to which the permission of appeal to a higher court is regularly measured, is scarcely to be justified. The interest of justice is measured not merely according to the value of the *object*, but also according to the *ideal value* of the law, and as I feel I would rather submit the most important matter to the single decision of a bench-court than the most insignificant to the decision of a single judge.

In addition to the repressive method just discussed, there is open to legislation the above-mentioned prophylactic, which is calculated to remove as far as possible the occasions and inducements to partiality on the part of the judge. It is clear that this is possible in a limited measure only. The sword of justice presupposes in the person who is called upon to wield it the moral courage to strike the guilty one with it and take upon himself his ill-will, hatred and enmity. Say what you will, these possible injurious consequences cannot be taken away from the judge; and in this sense we can say that the just judge must "carry his own skin to market."

But legislation can and must see to it that the risk which the judge has to stake for justice shall not be higher than is absolutely necessary; and that he should not be required to jeopardize his existence. The annals of the administration of justice exhibit splendid and elevating examples of the fearlessness, steadfastness and moral heroism of judges, but society has the most vital interest in not straining its demands on the moral strength of the judge too far. The judicial office must not be founded on the presupposition of heroism and martyrdom, but on a moderate proportion of human strength. The father must be spared the torture of condemning his own children to death as did Brutus of old. The judge should not be expected to sit in judgment over his wife and child, and if he desires it, the law, as is actually the case, should forbid it. No one should judge in a matter affecting himself; and even when an enemy or a friend or a near relative stands as a party before him, the judge himself as well as the party should be given the privilege of proposing the withdrawal of the judge from the case. The law must not cease for a moment its endeavors to keep away from the judge all palpable temptations and allurements; not only for his own sake, but also in the interest of society.

In this direction the establishment of bench-courts, — and we come to the second invaluable point of superiority of these over the single judge, — is of quite extraordinary value.

The sentence of the single judge is *his own*. *He* must answer for it, and take upon himself the hatred, ill-will and persecution of the person injured by it. In a bench-court of justice the part of the particular judge in the verdict cannot be known; and if the legal obligation of official secrecy in reference to the vote is observed, the public knows nothing about it. No one can hold a particular member responsible for the verdict with certainty. And this uncertainty, this veil which the "court of justice" throws over the part of the individual, does the same service for weakness as the secret ballot in elections.[58] For this very reason legislation should make it a most stringent obligation to preserve official secrecy in the internal proceedings of a judicial college, and visit every breach of this secrecy with a heavy penalty. Official secrecy is one of the most effective guarantees of judicial independence.

Among all the powers and influences which may become dangerous to the impartiality of the judge, the influence of the State authorities which gave him his office takes by far the first place in the case of the professional judge, with whom I am primarily concerned. The office to which he is called constitutes as a rule the economic basis of his whole existence. If they can take it away from him at will, they are in a position, when they desire a definite judicial decision in their interest, to put before him the alternative of submitting to their wish or losing his position and his income.

[58] In Rome they adopted in later times this form of voting ("per tabellas") not only in elections but also in popular courts and jury courts ("quaestiones perpetuae"). Where the strength is wanting not to allow oneself to be influenced, it is already a gain when weakness is given the possibility, by means of secrecy, of free self-determination. It is deplorable that we should have to count with weakness, but it is after all better to obtain a tolerable result by doing this, than a bad one by counting on a power that does not exist.

The judge's independence of the mere pleasure of the State authorities, the security of his position by law, and the use of the same strictly in accordance with the directions laid down in the law, are therefore the indispensable guarantee of legal security, and constitute an infallible sign whether the State authorities take the recognized principle of the independence of justice seriously or not. To the impossibility of removing a judge our time has frequently added the impossibility of transferring the judge against his will; and it cannot be denied that the latter forms a valuable complement to the former.

But the protection against the loss of his position alone is not sufficient to give the judge independence unless the office itself makes him economically independent. Adequate pay of the judicial office according to the point of view which we established above (p. 152) for salary, is a requirement of the first rank for a healthy formation of the administration of justice. Economy in the management of the State is nowhere applied with greater injury than here. And it is a shameful proof of the imperfect political insight of many popular representatives in Germany that instead of taking the initiative, in the interest of society, to raise the salaries — most glaringly incommensurate with the higher cost of living — of judicial officers to the proper measure, they have even in a number of instances opposed in an irresponsible manner the proposals of the governments for this purpose. The experience of other countries could have taught them that the people must pay two-fold and three-fold, in the form of bribe, what the State economizes in the salaries of its officials.

The three means just mentioned, namely, security of position, secrecy in voting, and adequate salary, are sufficient to enable the judge to state his convictions freely in regard to a private person as well as the authorities of the State. A judge so placed is *inviolable.* But he is not yet for this reason *inaccessible.* The way of intimidation alone is closed to the tempter, but he can steal upon him by another way also; and this secret path can be used by the State as well as the private person. And in the case of the former it is particularly dangerous. Not merely because the means which the State commands (preferment, honors) are far superior to those of the private person, but for another reason also. The mere attempt to bribe the judge on the part of a private person carries the stamp of illegality on its face. The mere offer denotes the tempter, and reveals him in his true colors. The State, on the other hand, does not need to make an offer. It does not have to name the venal judge a price for his compliance. The possession of the price in its hands performs the same service — servility and ambition divine its thoughts from a distance and meet it half way.

There is no means of protection against *this* danger. You cannot take away from the State by law the power freely to dispose of those means. This could be done only by applying the principle of length of service to preferment, bestowal of rank and decorations. Nor can you blindfold justice so tight as to prevent it from casting ogling glances at the external reward beyond. But where the judiciary of a country is inspired on the whole by the spirit of loyalty to duty and conscientiousness, — and we shall see later to what extent this spirit is developed and strengthened by the vocation itself — there the danger arising from the servility and lack of character of a small fraction of the judiciary is really not very great. The danger would be great only if the the State authorities had it in their power to pick out the judges in a particular case or to compose the court for a given action. Under these conditions it would really not be difficult for them to bring together the useful instruments; and arbitrary officials have always made use of such means to carry out their aims. The Star Chamber of Henry VII and the High Commission of Elizabeth in England, the "Central Commission of Investigation" appointed by the earlier German confederacy in Mayence (1819) "for the purpose of further investigating the revolutionary activities and demagogic associations discovered in several States of the confederacy," and the Central Commission of Investigation in Frankfort (1833) devoted to the same purpose, have shown by a warning and memorable example what the nations may expect when despotism and absolutist tyranny select their own judges. But they owe it to these very experiences that the more recent constitutions have forbidden on principle all such regulations. This is the basis of the eminently political side of the doctrine of the *judiciary* and the *province* of courts, which the jurist loses sight of only too easily when he treats them in a purely dogmatic way.

But the arrangement has its weak side. The latter is found in the State authorities appointing the judges to the courts. The State authorities cannot, it is true, select their own *court*, but they appoint the *judges* who *form the court*. Their legal constraint as far as the *court* is concerned may therefore be paralyzed by their administrative freedom in reference to the choice of *persons*. The State authorities transfer the inconvenient persons to another court and put others more compliant in their places. Then they have the court as they wish it.

There is no security in my opinion against this danger. The State authorities offer the inconvenient judge a better place and he goes. The regulation that a judge cannot be transferred *against his will* offers no adequate protection against this. He simply makes room for his successor for whom the place was intended. But the State authorities will not allow any encroachment of their right to fill judicial positions according to their judgment. And all the means that might be invented to prevent the possibility of applying this right dishonestly in the manner indicated are seen in advance to be impracticable. There is nothing left, therefore, except to recognize that the possibility of the government exercising an influence on the administration of justice cannot be removed by law, and protection against this danger should be looked for simply in public opinion and the feeling of justice and honor of the government itself. For the government to fill the judicial positions in a court of justice with a special purpose in view is a step so striking and so evident in its motive that they must expect to see the people judge it as on the same line with open violation of justice. Whether the gain is worth the cost, that is the question. We need not go too far into the past to find support for our statement.

I have spoken so far exclusively of the *professional judge, i.e.*, the permanent, learned, and salaried judge. And the result of my discussion consists in the conclusion that it is not possible to make the administration of justice completely independent of the State authorities in this form of the judicial office. On the other hand there is *one* form of court which really solves this problem completely, and that is the *jury*. The juryman has nothing either to fear or to hope from the government. His appearance, *i.e.*, the choice of a particular juryman, is too sudden and incalculable, his function too brief to make an attempt at subornation on the part of the government practicable. Time and place put insurmountable difficulties in the way. If the ideal of the judge depended merely upon his independence of the government, there would be no more perfect institution than the jury. But dependence upon the government is not the only dependence which we have to fear in the judge. Whether he allows himself to be guided by his political and religious prejudices, by a side glance at public opinion and the press, by the blame or praise of his friends, by the authority of one of his fellow jurymen, or whether his judgment is influenced by regard for the government, what difference does it make? We cannot speak of real independence either in the one case or in the other. In all these cases the judge is not what he should be.

The only consideration, then, for deciding in favor of the one or the other institution is, which of the two promises the relatively higher measure of independence and the greater security for carrying out the law. And here, I think, the decision should not be doubtful. Obedience to the law is the first virtue of the judge; but the obedience of the judge, like that of the soldier, must first be learned. As military discipline becomes by long service not merely a habit, but second nature, to the extent that an old soldier feels antipathy to insubordination and disorder, so it is with the judge's obedience to the law. It is the beautiful fruit of all continued exercise of a given virtue that habit not merely facilitates it, but makes it a necessity, so that a person cannot leave it without losing in his own esteem. This is true in a higher degree when the exercise of this virtue constitutes the vocation and the duty of an entire class. Here there is added besides, the habit of the class and the power of custom developed therefrom, *i.e.*, the special ethics and honor of the class. And the disposition resulting therefrom becomes so powerful and compelling within the class itself that no member can ignore it without suffering considerable injury. The fulfilment of the duty incumbent upon the class becomes *a matter of honor*, *i. e*, a condition of the respect of others and of self-respect. It is only the class that develops the qualities of its profession to such an extent that the novice who enters it is seized by the class spirit and the feeling of class honor, and is guided in the right path even before he has gained the conviction of their necessity through individual experience. It is the treasure of peculiar experiences and views which accumulates gradually, and in which every new member participates without his knowledge and desire, guarding and preserving it in turn, and handing it on after him. It is the unwritten law of the class developed in the form of the class spirit.

The two factors just developed, *viz.*, the *constant* practice of a virtue elevated to a duty and a life-work, and the supporting, educating and compelling influence which the tradition of the *class* exerts upon it, these two determine the superiority of the professional judge to the occasional, as is the juryman. The advantage which the former has in comparision is not merely the *technical* advantage of the specialist over the amateur in greater knowledge, readiness and *cultivation of judgment*, but it is also *moral*, namely the habit of subordination to the law, the exercise of the *will* in a definite direction. As the soldier has to learn subordination in the strict school of military discipline, so must the judge learn obedience to the law in the practice of the administration of justice. *Practice in judicial decision is the school of justice.* That which makes the judge must be learned, namely, strict obedience to the law, closing one's eyes to all respect of persons, equal measure for the vulgar and the respectable, the rascal and the man of honor, the rich usurer and the poor widow; closing the ear to complaints of the poor and miserable, and the lamentations of their dependents, from whom the judge's decision will take away a husband and father. It is not the *bad* man in him he must suppress, but the *good;* and this is the hardest test which the service of justice imposes, similar to that demanded of the soldier who must shoot his comrade. For it is not the base motive that entices one in this case from the law but the noble, — humanity, sympathy, mercy. Now let us suppose — to fill our measure to the brim — a case in which the law which the judge must carry out is in diametrical opposition to his own feeling of justice. Imagine a case in which the law recognizes capital punishment, and the judge is doubtful in his own mind whether the act should be punished at all, and you will form an idea of what it means to pay obedience to the law. Can we expect that a novice should be equal to this task, who takes his seat as a juryman today to leave it forever the next day? You might just as well expect the same discipline from a national guardsman as from the professional soldier. As the latter is different from the former, so is the professional judge different from the juryman. The former is the professional soldier in the service of justice, with whom the exercise of justice has become a habit and second nature, and who must pledge his honor for it. The latter is the militiaman, to whom his uniform and arms are something strange, and who, when he must play the soldier for once, feels himself not the soldier, but the citizen. He may wear everything which denotes the soldier outwardly, but he misses that which makes the soldier inwardly: the full sense of discipline and subordination.

It is for experience to decide whether the judgment which I have thus expressed of the juryman is too harsh. Experience shows us cases everywhere in which the facts of the crime were as clear as daylight, and yet the jury acquitted the accused. It is an open contempt for the law, which they presumed to disobey because it did not agree with their opinion.

But if the jury is to have the power to measure the guilt of the accused not according to the law, but according to their subjective feeling, as actually happened once in Rome in the popular court for criminal law, let this power be given them constitutionally. But as long as this has not been done, as long as it is not the business of the jury to sit in judgment over the law instead of over the accused, every such act is arbitrary and an open revolt against law and order. Whether it be the State or the jury that tramples the law under foot, whether it is done to punish the innocent or to acquit the guilty, it is all one; the law is disregarded. And it is not merely a particular law that is disregarded. It is possible indeed that it really challenged opposition, though even this palliation in many cases does not apply. But in this particular law the respect and majesty of law in general is injured; its power is put in question, and the belief in its inviolability shattered. The security of the law, which rests upon the certainty that the law will be applied uniformly in all cases, ceases. In place of the objective law, the same for all, we have the changeable, incalculable, subjective feeling of the jury, arbitrariness and chance. Here the accused is acquitted; there, for the like offence, he is condemned. The one goes free, the other goes to prison or mounts the scaffold.

And who will assure us that a court which places itself above the law to acquit the guilty will not some other time do the same to condemn the innocent? Once the firm path of the law is abandoned, the way opens to the right as well as to the left, and no one can tell in advance in what direction the stream which has once broken through its dam will take its course. It is only a question of what mood will get the upper hand in the masses in a time of excitement. Today the Royalists condemn the Republicans, tomorrow the Republicans the Royalists. Today the Conservatives condemn the Liberals, tomorrow the Liberals will condemn the Conservatives. The correction of the law by the jury is a two-edged sword ,which may in certain circumstances strike in quite a different direction from that intended and expected by many of its supporters.

To sum up my judgment of the institution of the jury, I can only say that apart from the single factor of its independence of the government, the jury in all other respects combines in itself those qualities which a judge should *not* have. Without the knowledge of the law which *study* alone can give; without the sense of legality which the *class* alone can inculcate; without the feeling of responsibility which the *office* alone can develop; without the independence of judgment which *practice* alone can form, — without all these qualities the men from the "people" take their places in the box, perhaps already prejudiced by the judgment which has been formed on the case in the public mind or by the press. They are easily led and determined by the art of the defender, who knows how to hit the point where he has to apply his lever, namely their heart, their humanity, their prejudices, their interests, their political tendency. They are accessible to the influence of authority in voting, and swayed by the confidence with which a view is presented to them, though it be different from that in favor of which they would have otherwise decided. For they console themselves with the thought that the others must know better, and throw the burden of responsibility from themselves upon the shoulders of those others. "Good people but poor musicians," they are mere militia of the administration of justice. One real soldier is worth more than a dozen of militia.

And is all this to be outweighed by the *one* factor of independence of the government? We ask ourselves in astonishment, how could an institution so wholly imperfect gain such successes, and find an open door everywhere? It is clear that powerful causes must have assisted in the process. And it is actually so. The institution of the jury freed our administration of justice from a two-fold pressure which weighed heavily upon it hitherto; that of absolutism and of the mediæval theory of evidence — a service in both cases of inestimable worth. In both directions it was necessary to break completely with the past; and there was no means more appropriate for the purpose than the introduction of the institution above named. The juryman who is quite independent of the government took the place of the dependent judge for that branch of the administration of justice in which the influence of the governmental authorities was most to be feared, namely, the criminal law. In this way absolutism lost its most effective means of suppressing all endeavors directed against it. And the feeling of the security of law and the possibility of assured legal progress took the place of the earlier feeling of the insecurity of law.

This gave us Archimedes' point for lifting the hitherto existing world out of its hinges. From this fixed point of vantage has proceeded, according to my opinion, all that stamps our present legal status internally as well as externally. *Internally*, the strengthening of the national feeling for right, and the removal of that dull submissiveness with which in the last century the people bore the most brutal acts of mean, arbitrary despots;

the general diffusion of the knowledge of the sacredness and inviolability of the law, as the palladium of civil society, as the power before which the bearer of the highest governmental authority must bow, as well as the most insignificant subject. To this feeling for right we owe that jealous watching over the law, our hard-won treasure, and the determination and courage to maintain the same, and on the part of the government the corresponding fear of violating it. *Externally*, the realization of the idea that the administration of justice is independent of the arbitrary control of the government, through the constitutional security of the judicial office (irremovability of the judge, prohibition of cabinet justice). Trial by jury formed the watchword of the reform of our law. In the eyes of the people it was a question directed to the governments, "Shall it be justice or despotism?" And it exerted its wholesome effects even before it came, by the mere fact of its being in sight, by the fact that it existed in other places. The legal institutions of one nation reacted from a distance upon the whole civilized world.

Trial by jury therefore marks the transition from absolutism to government by law, and this service we shall never forget. With all the defects that cling to it, it was not paid for too dearly. But the temporary justification of an institution is one thing, the permanent is another. The former I willingly grant for the jury, the latter I contest. And I am convinced that a time will come when, in safe possession of the security of the law, we will say to the jurymen, "The Moor has done his duty, the Moor can go." For he is a Moor and will remain one, and all the art of his supporters will not be able to wash him white. To be sure, much soap will be expended uselessly before people will be generally convinced of the fact.

The second service, too, which the institution of the jury has done us, *viz.*, the removal of the mediæval theory of evidence, is a highly valuable one, but, like the first, of a temporary nature. One might suppose that this service can be contested on the ground that there was no real need for this institution; that the theory of evidence might have been removed by law for the professional judge. This would be unjust according to my opinion. It is of no use to pour new wine into old bottles. The break with the old theory of evidence could be accomplished much more easily and safely by means of the lay judge than by means of the professional judge for whom its application had become a second nature. Not merely the *theory*, but the *habit* also had to be removed. But in this matter, too, there is no reason why the Moor should be retained after he has done his duty.

The disapproving judgment which I have just now passed upon the institution of the jury is not based on the fact that the juryman is as a rule a layman. The decisive point for me is not the contrast of layman and jurist, but that of the sporadic judge and the permanent. Against the layman as a *constant* judge placed by the side of the jurist, *i. e.*, the *lay judge*, I have nothing to object. I believe, on the contrary, that this form of taking a man from the people to assist in the administration of justice has its future. But the vitality of the institution of lay judges is conditioned, according to my opinion, by two requirements for its organization. One is that the service of the lay judge should be long enough to educate him in the exercise of the judicial function. The second condition is that provision should be made by law for maintaining a fixed body amid the change of the particular members, which should be in a position to preserve the tradition, and to hand down to the newly entering members their developed sense of legality. In short, the institution should be so organized that it be assured of the two decisive advantages of the permanent judicial office, *viz.*, a long schooling in the administration of justice, and the moral disposition of the individual and the class discipline controlling him, which are developed therefrom. The institution of lay judges would, in these circumstances, give us a solution of the problem which we sought for in vain in the salaried professional judge (p. 303); namely, it would present us with a permanent judge who could be completely independent of the government. Experience must show whether the essential condition of the institution, *viz.*, the necessary number of intelligent laymen who are in a position to devote themselves for a length of time without pay to the service of justice, will be created everywhere.

3. *The Limits of the Subordination of the Government to the Law.* By the law the government ties its own hands. How far should the government do this? Absolutely? In this case every man would have to obey the law only. The government would have no right to command or forbid any thing which was not provided for in the law. The law of the State would thus be placed on the same line as the law of nature. As in nature so in the State, the law would be the only power which moves every thing. Chance and arbitrariness would be completely suppressed on principle, and the machinery of the State would go like clock-work, which carries out all the prescribed motions with unfailing certainty, regularity and uniformity.

This would be the just State, as it seems, as perfect as one can think it. Only one quality would be missing—*vitality*. Such a State would not be able to exist a month. In order to be able to do so, it would have to be what it is not, clock-work. Exclusive domination of the law is synonymous with the resignation, on the part of society, of the free use of its hands. Society would give herself up with bound hands to rigid necessity, standing helpless in the presence of all circumstances and requirements of life which were not provided for in the law, or for which the latter was found to be inadequate. We derive from this the maxim that the State must not limit its own power of spontaneous self-activity by law any more than is absolutely necessary — rather too little in this direction than too much. It is a wrong belief that the interest of the security of right and of political freedom requires the greatest possible limitation of the government by the law. This is based upon the strange notion that force is an evil which must be combated to the utmost. But in reality it is a good, in which, however, as in every good, it is necessary, in order to make possible its wholesome use, to take the possibility of its abuse into the bargain.[59] Fettering force is not the only means of preventing that danger. There is another means which does the same service: personal responsibility. This was the method of the ancient Romans. They had no scruples in granting their magistrates such a fullness of power as, to us, savors of monarchy; but they demanded of them a strict account when they laid down their office.[60]

But however wide the scope which the law allows to freedom, there will always be the possibility of unusual cases in which the government finds itself placed before the alternative of sacrificing either the law or the

[59] I have in mind the happy saying of *Cicero*, "De Legib." III, ch. 10, concerning the tribunate, "Fateor in ipsa ista potestate inesse quiddam mali, sed bonum quod est quaesitum in ea, sine isto malo non haberemus."

[60] See my "Geist des römischen Rechts," II, § 35.

welfare of society. What shall be the choice? A well-known saying advises, "fiat justitia, pereat mundus." This sounds as if the world existed for the sake of justice, whereas in reality justice exists for the sake of the world. If the two stood in a relation of opposition to each other the maxim would have to read, "pereat justitia, vivat mundus." In reality, however, this is not the case, for the two as a rule go hand in hand. The motto should read, "vivat justitia, ut floreat mundus."

But it is quite a different question whether the government must respect the existing law absolutely and without any exception. And I do not hesitate at all to answer this question most decidedly in the negative.

Let us take a concrete instance. A fortress is being besieged, and it appears that in order to withstand the siege it is necessary to demolish some buildings in private possession. Now let us suppose that the constitution of the land had declared private property absolutely inviolable, without taking into consideration such cases of necessity as the one in question, and that the owners of the buildings refuse to give their consent to have them demolished. Must the commander of the fortress, in order by all means not to encroach upon private property, sacrifice the fortress and with it perhaps the last bulwark upon which the preservation of the whole State depends? A commander who did this would lose his head. So the breaking through of a dam, or a fire, or similar cases of necessity present a common danger, which can be warded off only by encroaching upon private property. Shall the authorities respect property and allow the devastating element to take its course?

Natural feeling suggests the decision at once to every one, but it is our problem to justify it scientifically. The justification lies in the point of view that the law is not an end in itself, but only a means to an end. The end of the State as well as of the law is the establishment and security of the conditions of social life (see below, § 12). Law exists for the sake of society, not society for the sake of law. Hence, it follows that when in exceptional cases, as in those above mentioned, the relations are such that the government finds itself facing the alternatives of sacrificing either the law or society, it is not merely empowered, but in duty bound, to sacrifice law and save society. For higher than the law which it violates stands the consideration for the preservation of society, in the service of which all laws must stand, the "lex summa," as Cicero ("De Legibus" III, 3) calls it in his well-known saying, "Salus populi summa lex esto." A private person may, in such a case, where there is a conflict between saving his own life and encroaching upon the right of others, sacrifice the former, although the law does not demand it of him (right of inevitable necessity). He sacrifices himself only. But if the government did the same thing, it would commit a mortal sin. For it must carry out the law not for its own sake but for the sake of society, and as the sailor throws the cargo overboard when it is a question of saving the ship and the crew, so the government may and must deal with the law if this is the only way to preserve society from a great danger. These are the "saving deeds," as our language fittingly calls them; a designation which embraces their whole theory, their justification as well as their requisite conditions. It is true that conscienceless statesmen have played wantonly with them; that the welfare of the State often served only as a pretext or a cover for arbitrary acts of despotism; but in principle the authority of the government to do these acts can no more be disputed than in the above case the right of the sailor to throw the cargo overboard. It is the *right of inevitable necessity* accompanying the *state of necessity* which the government thus exercises, and which can no more be denied to it than to the private person. The government not only *may* apply it, but it *must*. But the two are conditioned by each other; it *may* where it *must*.

At the same time, however, the open violation of the laws is a deplorable proceeding which legislation must spare the government as far as possible. It can be done by bringing the right of inevitable necessity itself under the form of law, as is done more or less in all modern laws and State constitutions. The regulations having this object in view may be designated as the *safety valves of the law*. They open an outlet to necessity and thereby prevent a violent explosion.[61]

[61] A detailed discussion of them is unnecessary, it is sufficient simply to enumerate them. They are the following: Encroachments of the State force upon private property — and first of all upon *possession* by administrative measures without previous legal procedure (*condition of necessity*, for example, in case of danger from fire or flood, war, etc.). Deprivation of *ownership* by course of *law*, *i. e.*, *expropriation* — whether in the form of an individual statute (p. 257), *i. e.*, the statute of expropriation, or by carrying out through judicial or administrative authorities the norms laid down in advance for the given case. Temporary suspension of certain statutory regulations (for example, the protest of promissory notes in France during the last war) or of normal legal aid ("justitium" in Rome), proclamation of a state of war or of martial law (in Rome the naming of a "dictator"; "Senatus consultum: videant consules, ne quid detrimenti capiat res publica"). Removal of subsisting rights by legislation (for example of serfdom, of the rights of banishment and coercion; "novae tabulae" in Rome, etc.). Encroachments upon such rights by a statute with retrospective force. All these measures come under one and the same point of view, and it shows a defect in the power of abstraction when one grants the admissibility on principle of some of them and denies it to others, as has often been the case in legal literature as well as in legislation. Note in reference to the question of the regulation of the retrospective force of a statute, even in the case of a man so radical otherwise as *F. Lassalle*, "System der erworbenen Rechte," I, pp. 3–11.

The question whether the requisite conditions are present for such encroachments is one concerning the politics of the particular case, and need not be discussed here. That the government must reimburse in these cases the private person affected by these encroachments is a requirement that follows from the nature of the social relation. The social relation is based upon the principle of equality in the sense developed above (p. 277), and it is in accordance with this principle that that which is for the good of all must also be borne by all.

The *right of pardon* also comes under the category of disregard of the law by the government. Formally considered, it appears as an interference with the order of law. The punishment of the criminal, which is threatened by the law and which has already been recognized against him, is afterwards remitted. The law is therefore in reality not carried out. The right of pardon seems therefore incompatible with the idea of the administration of justice. What becomes of the law when it is applied in one case and not in the other? What becomes of equality before the law when the recognized penalty is carried out in the case of one criminal and not in the case of another? It is pure lawlessness that sits in the place of law in the right of pardon, the recognition in principle of arbitrariness in the administration of the criminal law.

What answer have we to this? It *may* be arbitrariness that sits in the place of law, but it *need* not — and it *must* not be. The place must not be given to arbitrariness but to *justice;* to justice, which finds that its spirit was not properly understood in a particular case by the law, and must therefore be given the opportunity of rectifying its error and thereby saving an innocent man from suffering. In this sense we may define pardon as the correction in a particular case of the law which has been recognized to be imperfect; in short, as the *self-correction of justice.*

But the imperfection of the criminal law may be seen not only where it is the task of the right of pardon to obviate it, but also in the opposite direction. It is possible that the comprehensive catalogue of crimes which legislation has drawn up on the basis of long experiences appears defective in a particular case. Refined wickedness may invent new crimes which are not provided for by law, and for the punishment of which the existing law may offer a handle but no penalty commensurate with the seriousness of the offence.[62] What shall be done in this case? Shall justice declare itself powerless against the fiend who threatens society in a manner surpassing in danger all the crimes of the law which are provided with penalties, and who shows an abyss of depravity which leaves that of the ordinary robber and murderer far behind? Shall justice declare itself powerless before such a fiend, because the written law does not give it the possibility of inflicting upon him the penalty he deserves? The answer of the jurist is, Yes. His motto is the well-known saying, "nulla poena sine lege." The unsophisticated sense of right of the people demands punishment here also, and I agree with them completely. That saying just quoted, which assumes the character of an absolute postulate of justice, has really only a limited justification. It is meant as a guarantee against arbitrariness, and this task it fulfils. But the highest aim of law is not to keep away arbitrariness but to realize justice; and in so far as that principle stands in the way of this it is unjustified. The problem is to combine

[62] I name as an example the well-known case, *Thomas* in Bremerhaven: A chest provided with an explosive apparatus was placed on board for the purpose of destroying the ship selected for its transport, with a view to collecting the high insurance money.

the two purposes; and it is a question of finding a form which will afford a guarantee that the release of the judge from the positive law will be to the advantage of justice alone and not also of arbitrariness. For this purpose there is need of establishing a highest court of justice *above* the law, which will, by the manner in which it is constituted, exclude in advance all apprehension that it might become some day an instrument in the hands of an arbitrary government.

The idea which I have just expressed is already realized in fact. In Scotland a court of justice of this kind exists. But even if it did not exist anywhere, for me it is not a question of what *is*, but of what *should* be; of what the purpose of law and the idea of justice require. If it is true that in criminal as well as in civil law the law alone must rule, then there must be no pardon. If the latter is admitted, as is the case among all civilized peoples, then the principle of the *exclusive* domination of the law in criminal administration is thereby given up. The principle of right acknowledges thereby that it cannot get along with the positive law alone, that it must have the higher justice which stands above the law, in order that it may harmonize in a particular case the penalty with the requirements of the sense of right. If this holds in one direction, why not in the other? Either the law alone absolutely in both directions, or justice above the law in both directions. The highest court of justice recommended by me for unusual cases, such as legislation has not taken into consideration, is nothing but the logic of the right of pardon followed up in the opposite direction. The two are different in direction only, not in principle. A further step would consist in assigning to this highest court standing above the law the exercise of the right of pardon also in the name of the sovereign, or the proposal thereof to the latter. It would thereby receive the exalted mission of mediating between the formal justice of written law and the material justice standing above it;[63] and there would thus also be created an organ for the development of the criminal law in the way most appropriate for it, *viz.*, by means of adjudications. Perhaps, too, in that case the jury would be less frequently misled to acquit a criminal against the plain facts. In addition to the two formulæ, "guilty" and "not guilty," they would have to be allowed a third form of judgment, *viz.*, reference to the highest court, the "court of justice" ("Gerechtigkeitshof"), as I should like to call it. Similarly in cases like the one mentioned above (Thomas), the public prosecutor should be given the right to propose a penalty not provided for by law.

In the form just outlined, the higher judge, placed superior to the one who adjudicates strictly according to the written law, removes the imperfections of the law in the spirit of the legislator, by deciding the particular case as the legislator would have decided it when he issued the law. But this form of the matter must not be confused with the absolutely free and unrestrained use of the penal power which was applied by the Roman people in the "comitia tributa," and which I do not by any means intend to advocate. To be sure, it offered the advantage of the unlimited possibility of individualization, both in reference to the question what shall be considered a crime, and the degree of punishment. But this advantage was completely neutralized by the fact that it was not a judicial authority, but the sovereign people, accessible to all kinds of influences, that exercised this power of punishment freely without being bound by the restraint of

[63] "Inter æquitatem jusque interpositam interpretationem," as *Constantine* expresses himself in Cod. 1. 14. 1.

any law. The guarantees which are found in the separation of the judicial office from the other functions of the government (p. 291) are here entirely wanting. I am not defending individualization of criminal administration in general (this is found also in the despot, who pays attention to no law), but individualization by a *judicial* authority. The idea of individualizing the administration of justice in this latter form has been realized in the later civil procedure ("Formularprozess," formulary procedure); not indeed in the person of the ordinary judge, who could naturally not be entrusted with this power, but in the person of the praetor who, by his position and the advice of the jurists who assisted him ("consilium"), offered a guarantee for its proper use. In his quality of chief of the entire administration of the civil law was actually included that of legislator. It was his task and his duty to keep the law up to date; and as he did so by laying down new legal principles in his edicts, he also considered himself justified and called upon to exclude the severities of the old law in its application to a particular case. He rejected charges which the old civil law recognized; he allowed pleas which were not provided for in the written law; and he restored lost rights ("restitutio in integrum"): in short, he exercised in the particular case what amounted to a criticism of the existing law. He was the living organ of the law, as the Roman jurists call him ("viva vox juris civilis"), the personification of the idea of justice; not the justice of the judge who is bound to the law, but of the legislator who stands above the law, who always excludes it when it seems to him opposed to justice. The praetor accustomed the Romans to the idea of an individualizing justice that frees itself from the existing law; and they had so little fault to find with it that the institution was not merely enabled to maintain itself for centuries, but was even extended in the time of the emperors. Not merely did the emperors assume it for themselves ("constitutiones personales"), but they also granted to some specially trustworthy jurists, by means of the "jus respondendi," the power of laying down the law in a particular case ("jura condere").[64]

Such an institution is foreign to our present administration of the civil law. It has maintained itself with us only in the right of pardon. In the administration of the civil law we require the inviolable application of the law; and we take the severities and the unfairnesses into the bargain. The security of the formal justice of the judge stands higher with us than the advantages of an uncertain material justice, behind which arbitrariness could conceal itself only too easily.

I have now concluded my discussion of the *form* of law. We have seen how

1. *Force* rises from an individual command to an abstract command, *viz.*, the *norm*, and how then

2. The *unilateral norm* rises to the *bilaterally* binding norm, *viz.*, *law*, and how

3. The law produces from itself the *mechanism* for its realization (administration of justice).

Combining these three factors, the picture which we have gained so far of the law presents itself as the *political mechanism* for realizing the *coercive norms*

[64] "Auctoritas conscribendarum interpretandarumque legum," Cod. 1. 17. 1 § 4; "legislatores" Cod. *ibid.* 2. § 20; "Juris conditores," Cod. 1. 14. 12; "Quibus permissum est jura condere," *Gaius*, I, 6. It is to this that the "inter æquitatem jusque interposita interpretatio" of Cod. 1. 14. 1 (p. 322, note) refers, by which *Constantine* removed the regulation. The essence of it can be stated in one word; legislative force for a single case (which is pending in court); individualizing justice in contradistinction to abstract justice by statute.

recognized by the *State* as binding *absolutely* (*i. e.*, upon itself also).

From the form of the law we now proceed to its content; or, since the content is determined solely by the object, to its *purpose*.

§ 12. *The Purpose of the Law,—The Conditions of Social Life.* The two elements of right in the objective sense (law) that have been developed so far, *viz.*, norm and coercion, are purely *formal* elements which tell us nothing about the *content* of law. By means of them we know only that society compels its members to certain things, but we know not why and for what purpose. It is the external *form* of law, remaining always alike and capable of receiving the most varied content. It is through the content that we learn the purpose which law serves in society, and this forms the problem of the following exposition.

An insoluble problem, I hear one exclaim, for this content is ever changing, it is one thing here and another thing there, a chaos in unceasing flux, without stability, without rule. What is forbidden here is allowed there, what is prescribed here is prohibited there. Belief and superstition, barbarism and culture, vengeance and love, cruelty and humanity — what else shall I name?—all these have found a willing reception in the law. Unresistingly it seems to yield to all influences which are powerful enough to make it serviceable to them, without having a fixed support of its own. Contradiction, external change, seems to constitute the essential content of the law.

The result would be truly hopeless if the problem of the law were to realize *truth absolute.* Under this supposition we could not help admitting that the law is condemned to eternal error. Every successive period, as it changes the law, would break its staff over the period preceding it, which believed it had found absolute truth in its legal principles, and would then again in its turn be accused of error by the period succeeding it. Truth would always be a few steps in advance of the law without ever being overtaken, like a butterfly chased by a little boy — no sooner does he steal up close to it than it flies away again.

Science too is condemned to everlasting search. But its searching is not merely searching, it is constant finding. What science has actually found remains forever. And its search is absolutely free. In the domain of science there is no authority which lends to error the force of truth, as is the case in law. The principles of science can always be attacked; those of law have positive validity. Even he who recognizes their errors must submit to them.

He who brings such charges against the law has himself to blame, for he applies an improper standard to the law, that of *truth*. Truth is the aim of *knowledge*, not of *action*. Truth is always one, and every deviation from it is error; the opposition of truth and error is absolute. But for action or, which is the same thing, for the will, there is no absolute standard in the sense that only one will-content is true and every other false. The standard is relative. The content of the will may be different in one condition from what it is in another, and yet be right ("richtig"), *i.e.*, appropriate to the purpose, in both.

The rightness ("Richtigkeit") of a content of the will is determined by the *purpose*. Language characterizes an act as either "correct" ("richtig") or "incorrect" ("unrichtig") in accordance with the element of "direction" ("Richtung") to a purpose which is involved in every act of the will, *i.e.*, the aim of the will. *Correctness* is the standard of *practice*, *i.e.*, of conduct;

truth is the standard of *theory, i. e.,* of knowledge. Correctness denotes the agreement of the *will* with that which *should* be; truth, the agreement of the *idea* with that which *is.* When a physician prescribes a wrong medicine we do not say that he chose an untrue medicine but an improper ("unrichtig") one. Only where the finding of the truth is thought of as a *practical* problem, that is as something requiring investigation, struggle, taking pains, in short, exertion of the *will*, do we apply the expression "correct" ("richtig") also to the problem which is concerned solely with truth. We say of the pupil that he calculated his example correctly, of the physician that he diagnosed the condition of the patient correctly. We are not considering here the truth as such, but the subject who *seeks* it, and has made its discovery his *aim.* From the subjective standpoint we designate the attainment of the end as *correct.*

The expression "correct" ("richtig") contains the idea of direction, *i. e.*, of the way one has to follow in order to reach the end, *viz.*, to attain one's aim. It is the same idea that language employs so fruitfully in law as we have seen above (p. 261) ("Richter" [judge], "Richtsteig" [foot-path], "Weg Rechtens" [way of law, legal proceedings], "recht" [right]—"rëht," *i. e.*, straight, "regere," "rex," "regula," "rectum," "regieren," "dirigere," "directum," "diritto," "derecho," "droit"). All these expressions are not derived from the peculiar essence of law as such, but from that which the law, as prescribing human conduct, has in common with all conduct, *viz.*, the maintenance of the straight, right, correct way, the direction to an aim and a purpose.

This explains why we use the expression "right" ("recht") in a non-juristic sense also for correct, proper. So we say of the physician that he found the *right* means, *i. e.*, that which answered the purpose. Nay, here, too, (as in the word "correct" ["richtig"]) we even go a step further. We use the expression "right" for truth also, in so far as it stands in relation with purpose. We say of the pupil that he did his problem "right," and of a person who makes a statement or passes a judgment we say that he is "right." We call a person "*recht*haberisch" (positive, dogmatic), who defends his views obstinately. In all these cases it is a question of truth, to be sure, but of truth from the point of view of a practical purpose (seeking, finding, asserting, defending, denying).

I return now to the statement I made above. The standard of law is not the absolute one of truth, but the relative one of purpose. Hence it follows that the content of law not only *may* but *must* be infinitely various. As the physician does not prescribe the same medicine to all sick people, but fits his prescription to the condition of the patient, so the law cannot always make the same regulations, it must likewise adapt them to the conditions of the people, to their degree of civilization, to the needs of the time. Or, rather, this is no mere "must," but a historical fact which happens always and everywhere of necessity. The idea that law must always be the same at bottom is no whit better than that medical treatment should be the same for all patients. A universal law for all nations and times stands on the same line with a universal remedy for all sick people. It is the long sought for philosopher's stone, for which in reality not philosophers but only the fools can afford to search.

This view, although false in its innermost essence, and in irreconcilable contradiction with history, because it transfers to the will what is applicable only to knowledge, has nevertheless a certain semblance of truth in it. Certain legal principles are found among all peoples;

murder and robbery are everywhere forbidden; State and property, family and contract are met everywhere.[65] Consequently, in these cases, one may urge, we actually have absolute truth; these are, you will say, evidently absolute "*legal truths*," over which history has no power. You might as well call the fundamental arrangements of human civilization, *viz.*, houses, streets, clothing, use of fire and light, truths. They are possessions of experience having reference to the assured attainment of certain human purposes. Securing the public streets against robbers is just as much a purpose as securing them against floods by means of dams. The thing done for a purpose does not lose its purposive character because this quality of it is placed beyond all doubt, and is therefore in this sense true.

Now a science which, like the science of law, has the purposive as its object, may indeed separate all those institutions which have stood the test of history in this way from the others which can boast only a limited (temporal or spatial) usefulness, and combine them in a separate class, as the Romans did with "jus gentium" and "naturalis ratio" in contradistinction to "jus civile" and "civilis ratio"; but it must not forget that here too it has to do not with the true but with the useful. How little this has been observed, I shall have occasion to show in the second part of this work. The "legal," which is regarded in the science of law as the properly true because it always remains in the law, and which is contrasted with the "useful" ("zweckmässig") as the

[65] The concept of the Roman "jus gentium." "Quod vero naturalis ratio inter omnes homines constituit, id apud omnes peræque custoditur vocaturque jus gentium, quasi quo jure omnes gentes utuntur," D. 1. 1. 9. "Ex hoc jure gentium introducta bella, discretæ gentes, regna condita, dominia distincta, agris termini positi, ædificia collocata, commercium, emptiones venditiones, locationes conductiones, obligationes institutæ," 5 *ibid.*

temporary and evanescent, will be found there to be a species of the latter. It will appear as the part which is precipitated and condensed in a fixed form in contrast to that which is still fluid and movable. It is the useful which has stood the test of many thousands of years; the lowest stratum lying deep down at the bottom, which bears all the rest, and is therefore fully secure in its position. But the process of formation of this deepest layer was no different from that of the more recent. It is nothing else than the useful, stored up, tested by experience and placed beyond all doubt.

Everything found on the ground of the law was called into life by a purpose, and exists to realize some purpose. The entire law is simply one creation of purpose, except that most of the particular creative acts reach back into such a distant past that humanity has lost remembrance of them. It is a matter of science, in the history of the formation of law as well as in the formation of the earth's crust, to reconstruct the actual processes, and the means are found in the idea of purpose. Nowhere is purpose so certain of discovery as in the domain of law for him who is not afraid to investigate and reflect. To look for it is the highest problem of jurisprudence, whether in the dogma of law or its history.

Now what is the purpose of law? To the question, what is the purpose of animal activity, I gave the answer above (p. 5), the realization of the conditions of his existence. I now make use of that thought when I define law in reference to its content as the form of the *security of the conditions of social life*, procured by the power of the State.

The justification of this definition requires an understanding of the concept "conditions of life," here laid down as a basis. It is a relative concept and is determined by the requirements of life. What are the requirements of life? If life means mere physical existence, the concept is limited to the bare necessities of life, food, drink, clothing, shelter. Even here it retains its relative character, for it is determined quite differently in accordance with the individual needs. One needs more than, and different things from, another.

But life means more than physical existence. Even the poorest and the lowest demands more of life than its mere preservation. He wants well-being, not merely existence, and no matter how differently he may think of it — for this larger life begins with one person where it ceases with another — the idea of it which he carries in his mind, his ideal picture of existence constitutes for him the standard by which he measures the value of his actual life; and the realization of this standard forms the aim of his whole life, and works the lever of his will.

The subjective requirements to which life is bound in this wider sense I call *conditions of life.* I understand by this term, therefore, not merely the conditions of physical existence, but all those goods and pleasures which in the judgment of the subject give life its true value. Honor is not a condition of physical life, and yet what is life for a man of honor without it? Where the two come in conflict he sacrifices his life to save his honor, as the best proof that life without honor is worthless for him. Freedom and nationality are not conditions of physical existence, but no freedom-loving people ever hesitated to go to death for them. The suicide lays hands on himself when life has lost its value for him, although perhaps he is not at all in want of its superficial requirements. In short, the goods and enjoyments by which a man feels his life conditioned are not merely sensuous and material, but also immaterial and ideal. They embrace everything that forms the aim of human striving and struggling: honor, love, activity, education, religion, art, science. The question of the conditions of life of the individual as well as of society is a question of the national and individual education.

In laying down *this* concept of the conditions of life at the basis of my above definition of law, I intend in the following to prove two things: first, that it is a *correct* concept, and secondly, that it is scientifically *valuable* and *fruitful*.

The *correctness* of the concept will be proved by the fact that all legal principles, no matter of what kind and where found, can be reduced to it. Its *value* will be shown by the circumstance that our insight into the law is advanced by it. A point of view which is correct and nothing more is only a vessel, into which you put an object to take it out again. The object itself remains as it was, without its knowledge being advanced thereby. A point of view is of scientific value only when it proves to be productive, *i. e.*, when it advances the knowledge of the object, when it discloses sides of it which were formerly overlooked. Let us try whether our point of view will stand the test in both directions.

I expect some objections to its correctness. If the law has as its object the conditions of social life, how can it contradict itself to such an extent as to forbid in one place what it allows or commands in another? Which suggests that a point capable of such various treatment cannot belong to the conditions of social life, and is simply incidental, to be used as society's pleasure dictates.

The objection overlooks the relativity of purpose. As the physician does not contradict himself when he prescribes today what he forbade yesterday, in accordance with a change in the condition of the patient, so neither does the legislator. Conditions change in society as well as in the individual; what may be dispensed with here is necessary there; what is useful in one place is injurious in another.

In order to make clear the extraordinary contrast in the attitude of legislation to one and the same question, resulting from the relativity above mentioned, I shall select the two following examples. The first concerns the question of instruction. Our present State has made elementary instruction obligatory. Formerly it was left to the pleasure and inclination of the individual, except that the State took care of institutions in which any one could acquire an elementary education. In a still earlier period not even this was done. In some of the slave States of North America, before the Civil War, it was forbidden on pain of death to teach negroes to read and write. Here we have an attitude of the State to one and the same question varying in four different ways; securing the purpose in form of compulsion; furthering the same by political means, but without compulsion; complete indifference of the State, and lastly, prohibition to pursue the same by certain classes of society on pain of death. If we apply our idea of conditions of life to this matter, we shall find that the last form of this subject, from the standpoint of the American slave States, signifies that the slave State is incompatible with the education of the slaves. If the slave can read and write, he will cease to be a working animal, he will become a human being and claim his human rights, and thereby threaten the social order built upon the institution of slavery. Where life depends upon darkness, the introduction of light is a capital crime. In antiquity this danger was not feared because the belief in the lawfulness of slavery was not yet shattered. The first form of the subject, indifference of the State to instruction, signified from the standpoint of that time that school education does not belong to the conditions of social life; the second form, support by the State, means that it is desirable; the third, compulsory education, that it is indispensable. Which of these conceptions is the true one? All four were true, each one in its time and place.

The second example concerns the attitude of legislation to religion. When Christianity arose, the heathen State raged against it with fire and sword. Why? Because it believed that it could not co-exist with it. It persecuted it because it saw in the latter a danger to one of its conditions of life, *viz.*, the State religion. A few centuries later the same State, which formerly prohibited the Christian confession on pain of death, imposed it by force with the most cruel means. The view that it could not co-exist *with* it was now transformed into the view that it could not exist *without* it. Formerly it was, "Woe to the Christians," now it was, "Woe to the heretics." The prisons and the funeral piles remained; only the victims changed who were thrown in. A thousand years later the government arrived at the view, as a result of severe and bloody battles, that the existence of society is not merely compatible with freedom of belief, but is impossible without it. Which of these conceptions was the true one? Again all three, each one for its time.

The second objection which I must expect is this. Far from being true that law always *serves* the conditions of social life, the opposite is the fact; namely, that it is frequently in diametrical *opposition* to the true interests of society.

I admit this perfectly. But if I am allowed once more to use the comparison of the physician, I answer that the same thing often applies *objectively* to his prescriptions also, and yet this does not overthrow the fact that *subjectively* their purpose is to advance life. The physician may make a mistake in the choice of his means. So may the legislator. He may be influenced by prejudices of all kinds, but this circumstance does not remove the fact that he believes he is securing or advancing the existence of society thereby. In Rome to draw away the seed of another's land to one's own field by means of incantations ("segetem pellicere"), and to lay a charm upon another's fruit ("fruges excantare") was forbidden in the XII Tables on pain of death; just like robbing a field by night and removing the boundary. Why? The Roman peasant believed he could not maintain himself against these imagined or real dangers to the security of his property. Security of real property and agriculture was considered by him as a condition of social life. Therefore a capital penalty was demanded for every one who laid hands on it.

It was the same case in the middle ages with witches and sorcerers. All society trembled before the devil, who was in a compact with them; they seemed more dangerous and uncanny than robbers and murderers. For the Church there was, in addition to the idea of their common danger, the religious motive that the kingdom of Heaven must be protected against the works of the devil. Society, as well as the Church, was firmly convinced that witches and sorcerers threatened it in the foundations of its existence. We may find fault with them for having been able to give themselves up to such a belief, but the matter is not changed thereby. The motive which guided them *subjectively* was the security of the conditions of social life, and the point of view suggested by me is meant in this subjective sense only. It is not meant to signify that a given thing *is* an objective condition of life, but that it is *regarded* subjectively as such.

But even in this subjective sense it does not seem to apply to society absolutely. Experience shows that the government does not by any means always serve the interests of the whole population, but frequently only those of a single powerful class. And consequently legislation also does not make the law to correspond uniformly to the interests of society, but, above all, to those of a privileged class. The concept of the conditions of social life seems in this case, where the interests of a single class are put in place of the interest of society, to disappear entirely. I shall lay this objection aside for the present to answer it later (§ 14).

The last objection which I think I must fear is the following. The definition which has been laid down for the law as a whole must apply to every constituent part of it, to every statute, to every ordinance. A stamp act, a law concerning the tax on brandy, regulations concerning the declarations of duty, concerning the measures of controlling the tax in distilleries, breweries, etc., concerning the stamping and naming of new coins — all these must be conditions of social life.

This objection is just as if one intended to refute the statement of the necessity of nourishment for the preservation of human life by proving that the *special form* in which nourishment is taken by a particular individual is not at all required for that purpose. The answer to this must be, the fact is necessary, the manner is free. That a particular individual should take this particular food and this particular drink, in this particular quantity, at this particular time, is a matter of individual choice; but that he should take food and drink generally is a peremptory demand of nature. That the State should just select a tax on stamps and brandy and the monopoly of tobacco and salt, to procure the necessary revenue, is a matter of free choice, but that it should procure these means generally is an absolute requirement of its existence, and consequently a condition of social life. If it has once decided on a definite form of taxes then all the measures it takes to secure their payment or to facilitate their collection are only the necessary consequences of such choice once made. Whoever desires the purpose must also desire the proper means. I can think of no legal ordinance, no matter how detailed and petty, in which I would not undertake to show its connection with my point of view. Coins, measure, weight, construction and maintenance of public roads, cleaning the sewers, keeping fire buckets, taxes of all kinds, reporting servants and strangers in hotels to the police, and even the most annoying police regulations of former times, as for example, the viséing of passports — all these are reduced, according to their purpose, to the security of the conditions of social life, no matter how faulty the choice of the means might be.

If we consider all the requirements upon which the existence of society depends, they can be divided, in reference to the attitude of the law toward them, into three classes, which I shall designate as the *extra-legal*, the *mixed-legal* and the *purely legal*.

The first division belongs to nature, whether she offers them to man freely and without trouble, or whether he has to win them from her by means of toil. The law has no share in them. The law has power only over man, not over nature. They are excluded therefore from the following discussion, as extra-legal conditions of life.

The second division belongs exclusively to man, and for him also there is the difference between those needs which are offered freely and those which must be gained by force. The individual acts voluntarily in the service of society where his interest coincides with that of the latter, and this is the case on the whole in four fundamental conditions of social life, *viz.*, *preservation of life*, *reproduction of the same*, *labor*, and *trade*. For there are three powerful motives at work in man for these purposes, *viz.*, the instinct of self-preservation, the sexual impulse and the instinct of acquisition. Society need feel no anxiety in reference to these, and may find consolation in the words of Schiller (in his "Die Weltweisen"):

> "Until one day philosophy
> The structure of the world will hold
> It is held now in motion
> By hunger and by Love."

The instinct of self-preservation, the sexual instinct and the instinct of acquisition are the three powerful allies of society which enable it to dispense with force in reference to the services which they render it.

Exceptionally, however, these three instincts may refuse their service. In regard to the first, this is the case in the suicide; in regard to the second in the celibate; in regard to the third in the beggar and the vagabond. Suicides, celibates, beggars, offend against the principles of human society no less than murderers, robbers, thieves. To be convinced of it one need only refer their attitude toward society to the Kantian generalization of the maxim of individual conduct. If their conduct became universal, it would be all over with society.

This is true first in reference to *preservation* of individual life, secured by the instinct of self-preservation. If it were thinkable that the pessimistic view of life of a recent philosopher,[66] "that from the standpoint of the ego or the individual, the negation of the will or resignation of the world and renunciation of life is the only rational

[66] *E. von Hartmann*, "Philosophie des Unbewussten," (Berlin 1869), pp. 613, 626.

procedure"—could become general; if we could imagine that the "longing for absolute painlessness, for nothingness—Nirvana,"—should descend from the rigid, icy region of a philosopher despairing of the solution of the world-problem, into the valleys and the plains, where fresh life is pulsating, and where the masses, even though unceasingly *struggling* with life, do yet take *joy* in it,—if it were thinkable that a time would come, "when not this or that particular individual, as before, but *humanity* would long for nothingness, for annihilation," this would constitute a danger to society equalled by none of all those others which it has met with in its course. For the present, society is fortunately still in a position to be able to leave the care for the preservation of life to the instinct of self-preservation. The danger with which suicide threatens its existence is so vanishingly small that it need feel no apprehension on this score.

The case is somewhat different with *reproduction* of life, secured by the sexual instinct. The sexual instinct, to which nature has handed over the care of this matter, is not sufficient to secure it by itself. Man can deceive nature in reference to this matter. He can limit the number of births, the mother can destroy the germ of life, kill the new-born babe, the parents can expose it or castrate it. Here there is a danger threatening the State, which it is obliged to meet, and the penal regulations against abortion, child murder, exposure and mutilation of children, which are found in the criminal laws of all civilized nations, show that the State is well aware of the danger which threatens it. It is not merely regard for the child, whose prospects for life are thus taken away, that has dictated this measure. This is the religious standpoint, which I do not deny, but which it is not at all necessary to introduce in order to justify the regulations. The wholly profane standpoint of the conditions of social life is quite sufficient to explain them. Society cannot exist if the new generation is threatened.

Our modern law is content with negative regulations against *endangering* the new generation. But examples are not wanting in which legislation has tried to further it positively. This was the object of the stringent "Lex Julia" and "Papia Poppæa" of Augustus, which was called forth by the decrease of the free population during the Civil Wars and the corruption of morals that became prevalent in Rome. This law endeavored to tax celibacy and childlessness by incapacitating the celibate and the childless, wholly or partially, from testamentary inheritance, and by otherwise reducing them to an inferior position in favor of married persons blessed with children.[67] And Louis XIV went so far in the interest of more rapidly increasing the population in Canada that he even compelled single persons to marry by force.[68]

From the same Rome which in the time of Augustus carried on a campaign against celibacy and childlessness, went forth in later times the command of the Church, which forbade its servants to marry. I do not mean

[67] The comparison which *Tacitus*, "Germania," ch. 19, institutes between Roman and German custom will serve to explain the measure of Augustus: "Numerum liberorum finire aut quemquam ex agnatis necare flagitium habetur, plusque ibi boni mores valent quam alibi bonæ leges."

[68] According to *Parkman*, "France and England in North America," he laid down the marriageable age for the male sex at 18 to 19, for the female at 14 to 15. Every father, who did not marry his children at the respective ages of 20 or 16 years at the latest, was punished. When the ships came with female volunteers from France, all young men had to provide themselves with wives within fourteen days. Whoever evaded this duty was deprived of the few joys and advantages of Canadian life. He was not allowed to hunt, to fish, to go in the woods, to trade with the Indians, nay, they went so far as to provide him with degrading marks.

to ignore in this matter the weight of the ecclesiastical policy, which caused the Church to introduce celibacy. And I am also fully sensible of the ethical point of view that renunciation stands higher than indulgence. But it is one thing when a person, for reasons which we cannot help acknowledging or perhaps even admiring, voluntarily renounces marriage, and it is another thing when his continence is forced by *law*. I leave the question unanswered whether it can be practically carried out as is conceived, and how dearly the individual must pay for it. I am not the spokesman of the Catholic priest, demanding for him in his name the right of a human being, but I place myself solely upon the standpoint of society. And from this point of view the judgment cannot, in my opinion, be otherwise than that celibacy is in its principle an anti-social institution. It may in its limitation to a particular class of persons be practically tolerable for society, but we need only think it as general to be convinced that society is incompatible with it. In Russia there is a sect of Old Russians who try to secure sexual continence not merely morally by means of vows, but mechanically by means of castration. They deserve the credit of consistency, from which the Roman Catholic Church shrank; but the Russian government deserves the praise of not having been deterred from persecuting them with all the means at its disposal despite the shield of religious conviction with which the sect covers itself.

The third of the fundamental conditions above mentioned is *labor*. The hours of society would be numbered if all workmen (taking the expression in the widest sense, in which it embraces all persons active for the purposes of society) should conclude one day to put their hands in their pockets. Provision is made here too that this should not occur. The doing of work needs no more securing by legal prescription than self-preservation and reproduction; it is guaranteed by the needs of the individual and his instinct of acquisition. But in a limited way the government may have occasion to interfere in this matter; permanently against begging and vagabondage, temporarily against the conspired suspension of work on the part of whole classes of laborers for the purpose of compelling higher wages (strikes). From the abstract standpoint of personal individual freedom interference would not be justified in any of the three cases. That it does take place as a matter of fact shows that this point of view cannot practically be carried out. The appeal of the individual to his freedom is met by the command of social self-preservation.

The same thing applies to business exchange as to work. It constitutes a condition of social life, but society has no need of commanding it by law. His own interest is sufficient to determine the farmer to bring his corn and cattle to market, and the merchant to sell his wares. But the possibility of taking advantage of necessity for the purpose of raising prices offers to legislation an opportunity of interference here also. I have already expressed myself before (p. 103) concerning the necessity and justification thereof. The most dangerous case of this kind in former times was usurious trade in corn, which legislation prohibited with heavy punishment. Telegraphs and railways have made it possible to strike out this species of offence from the criminal law books. This shows clearly that the leading motive of the law book is not the unethical character of the subjective purpose, but the objective danger to the community arising from the act.

The four fundamental requirements of the existence of society just considered, *viz.*, self-preservation, reproduction, work and trade, I designate as *mixed-legal* conditions, because their security does not depend upon the law in the first instance, but upon nature, upon the power of the three natural impulses above named. The law only comes to assist them in exceptional cases when they fail. In contradistinction to these are the *purely legal.* These are those for the security of which society is beholden exclusively to the law. We need only think of the requirements of these two classes in the form of a command, to be convinced of the fundamental distinction of the two. Legislation has no need of issuing such legal prescriptions as, eat and drink, save your life from danger, reproduce your species, work, sell, but we meet everywhere with the commands, "Thou shalt not kill, thou shalt not steal, thou shalt pay thy debts, thou shalt be obedient to the government, pay taxes to the State, perform military service," etc. To be sure, in these commands also the State does not prescribe any thing that is not demanded by the true interest of its members. We have only to think of them as absent to become aware of this fact. No one would be sure of his life or property without them, it would be the war of all against all. But even if we thought of society as devoid of all moral principles, if we thought of it as composed of nothing but egoists of the purest water, or of criminals as in a convict colony, or of robbers as in a robber band, egoism would immediately raise its voice, and demand for the relation of the comrades among themselves the inviolable observance of almost the same principles as the State prescribes in the form of law. And it would punish their violation no less, or rather far more harshly and cruelly than does the State through the criminal law.[69] As a matter of

[69] An interesting proof of this is furnished in the cases of secret criminal justice administered by comrades among the military and on warships. When the entire crew has to suffer for the offence of a

experience, *popular justice* is always more cruel than *State justice.* The former, when it seizes a person stealing sheep, simply strings him up, the latter merely throws him into prison for a short time. The organization of the criminal law by the State constitutes no less a benefit for the criminal than for society. Our present administration of the criminal law does rather too much for him in this matter than too little. But the indulgence which it shows the criminal is bought at the expense of the State.

How does it happen then that egoism trangresses the law which serves its own purposes? The egoist would not do it, if he expected that it would be done by every body, but he counts upon its not happening. In other words, he wants the law in so far as it limits others in *his* interest, he does not want it in so far as it limits *him* in the interest of *others.* He wants the advantageous consequences but not the disadvantageous ones.

It is the opposition of *social* egoism to *individual.* The former determines him to *desire* the law, and when the State has not the power to carry it out he even *enforces* it himself (lynch law), the latter determines him to *transgress* it. The law has social egoism as its ally, individual egoism as its opponent. The former pursues the *common interest,* the latter, the *individual interest.* If the two interests were mutually exclusive, so that every one had the choice of desiring either the interests of society or his own, his choice would not be doubtful.

single person, who will not give himself up, they administer justice to him, in case of repetition of the offence, on their own account. And they do it so effectively that there is no fear of a relapse. In barracks it is usually done in a dark room, on warships the execution takes place during the noonday meal of the officers, over the cannon in steerage. It always happens so that the subordinate officers are on the quarter deck, and from the steerage there rises up to them only the joyful and clear singing of the crew.

But the realization of the law by the State, *i. e.*, the legal order, enables him to desire both. When he transgresses the law he desires *his own* interest, otherwise he desires the law *in addition*.

If all legal measures have as their purpose securing the conditions of social life, then society is the *subject* of this purpose. A strange subject, it will be objected, a mere abstraction. The real subject is man, the individual; every legal measure is ultimately for his benefit. Perfectly correct. All legal measures, whether they belong to private law, criminal law, or public law, have man as their purpose.[70] But social life, in joining mankind into higher groups through the community of permanent purposes, extends thereby the forms of human existence. To man as a single being considered by himself (individual), it adds the social being,—man as a member of a higher unit. When we elevate the latter (State, Church, associations) instead of the former as subjects of the laws relating to them (juristic persons), we do not lose sight of the fact that they only intercept the advantageous effects of these laws to hand them over to the *natural* person, man. The mechanism by which the purpose of the law is realized for man is various, *immediate* and *mediate;* and the jurist in the latter case cannot dispense with the concept of a higher legal subject, standing above the particular individual. How far he can proceed in the application of this concept is a question of technical jurisprudence which does not interest us here.[71] For the sociologist this does not come into consideration. Having allowed the jurist the free use

[70] A Roman jurist carries over the idea of purpose in the active sense to nature. Nature made everything for the sake of man, "Omnes fructus natura hominum causa comparavit," D. 22. 1. 28 § 1.

[71] I treated the question in my "Geist des römischen Rechts," III, 1, p. 356 ff. (4th ed.).

of his concept of the "subject of the *law*," he may and must claim in his turn the right to use the concept of the "subject of the *purpose* of the law," as *his own* problem demands.[72]

In this social-political sense I have designated society as the subject of the purpose of the law, and stated the problem of the latter to be the security of the conditions of social life. But we may again distinguish within society in this widest sense special subjects. These are first, the four named above, *viz.*, the individual, the State, the Church, associations. All of these are at the same time *juristic subjects* in the sense of the jurist,— bearers of rights, persons. But they do not exhaust the content of the law. There still remains a surplus of legal measures which does not relate to any of these four legal subjects. If we raise the question of the subject of these extra laws, as we *must* in all laws, nothing remains but to name the indeterminate multitude, the masses, society in the narrower sense. We shall use the term *social* in the sequel for these laws and institutions.

The whole law refers to these five subjects as its purpose. They are the personal *centres* of the *purpose* of the whole law, around which all its regulations and principles are grouped. In the relations, purposes, and problems of these five subjects the whole life of society is represented. It is the *schema* of the purpose of the law which is valid for all times.[73]

[72] In reference to the ethical element I shall do this later (Vol. II); here I confine myself to law.

[73] The Roman classification above mentioned of "jus privatum" and "jus publicum," in D. 1. 1. 1 § 2, which is based upon the difference of the subject for whose purpose the law in question is made, embraces under the last category ("quod ad statum rei Romanæ spectat") State and Church ("in sacris, sacerdotibus magistratibus consistit"). The systematic status of associations ("collegia," "corpora," D. 47. 22) is not precisely stated. To what extent the

I shall endeavor in the sequel to illustrate and to test by means of three fundamental concepts the classification of the whole law as I drew it up by reference to the subject of its purpose. I believe, however, that I can leave the Church and the associations out of consideration, because what I am going to say about the State or the individual can without difficulty be applied to them, where there is at all an occasion to do so. I will therefore limit my schema to the three categories, Individual, State, Society.

1. *The Legal Relations of Things.*[74] In reference to the economic functions of things as they are determined by human need, the *Roman* law distinguishes two forms, which we may designate as ***primary*** and ***secondary*** functions. The normal form of the first is property, of the second the "jus in re."

But in one direction the first relation goes beyond the form of property, namely in reference to "res publicæ." The primary subject of these is doubtless not the State, the city or the community as a juristic person, but the indefinite multitude of individuals who make use of them, *viz.*, the masses, the people. The subject in this case is one to which the concept of property as the Roman jurists conceive it, namely as the exclusive right of a *definite* (physical or juristic) person, does not apply. They bring it instead under the category of public use ("usus publicus"). It is not merely an actual function, but is protected by law (by "actiones populares"). It

Romans were familiar with the concept of society as here laid down will be shown later.

[74] I had worked over completely the following part for the second edition, but the new exposition assumed such proportions that I thought it proper to publish it independently in another place. The following presentation contains a short extract from it in which I limit myself to suggestions.

is a peculiar *legal function of the thing.* I call it *public right.*[75]

According to our division in three subjects, we have three forms of the functions of a thing as determined by human need.

(a) Individual property (subject: physical person).

(b) State property (subject: the State, the Church or corporation, respectively).

(c) Public right (subject: society in the narrower sense).[76]

In the non-juristic sense in which the term property is so frequently used in life, and in which it is applied also by political economists, public right might be called *social* or *popular property.* The same relation is found also in the Church and in associations in reference to those things which are assigned to the general use of its members ("usus publicus"), such as the use of the church building, of the union local, of the periodicals kept there, etc., in contrast to their property ("bona," "patrimonium universitatis").

All the three forms named have as their object the security of the conditions of social life in the wider sense. None of them can be dispensed with. Not *individual property* — for we have shown above (p. 47, *et seq.*) how physical self-assertion produces economic, in other

[75] Proved and expounded in detail in my "Geist des römischen Rechts," III, 1, p. 360 (4th ed.).

[76] The Romans place the above distinction in the *thing,* and distinguish (a) "Res singulorum," "propriæ," "familiares," "res, quæ in bonis alicujus sunt," "res sua," "suum," "privatum," etc. The expression "res privatæ," which has become very common today, is found only in *Gaius* so far as I know in 1. 8. 1. pr. (b) "Pecunia," "patrimonium populi," "res fisci," "fiscales." (c) "Res publicæ," "res, quæ in usu publico habentur," "publicis usibus in perpetuum relictæ," "publico usui destinatæ," "communia civitatum," "res universitatis."

words, private property, as a necessary consequence. Not *State property* — for the State must always have a supply of economic means ready to use for its purposes, and this is exactly what constitutes the function of property. Nor can *public right* be dispensed with — for without the community of public roads, places, rivers, human intercourse is unthinkable. The exclusive institution of private property would make all spatial communication impossible.

The security of the last function is today taken care of by the police. The Romans were intelligent enough to allow the public itself the right to represent its interests by giving every one the power to complain ("actio popularis")against the person who encroaches upon the use of the "res publicæ" by means of some illegal measures.[77]

The destination of a thing for the use of an indefinite number of persons (social property in the above sense), which is the characteristic mark of "res publicæ," is found also in *foundations for the public welfare.* The juristic form which is applied to them, and the practical necessity of which I do not intend to dispute, I mean the personification of the foundation ("universitas bonorum"), must not deceive us here either concerning the true relation. The property of the merely imaginary juristic person is an empty phrase. It is not for the benefit of the latter, but of the individuals who, according to the terms of the foundation, are to enjoy its advantages (beneficiaries). Such property is nothing but an apparatus constructed for the purpose of realizing this object in a juristically convenient manner, without any practical reality for its subject. The latter is merely the *bearer of rights* in the interest of others, not the *subject of the purpose.* The subjects of the purpose are

[77] Quite appropriately the Byzantines designated the right lying at the basis of this *popular action* as *popular right* (δίκαιον δημοτικόν).

the beneficiaries, and Roman law recognized this by giving them the right of "actio popularis" as in "res publicæ."[78] Putting the juristic form altogether aside and applying exclusively my idea of the subject of the purpose, I arrive at the result that foundations for the public welfare must be placed on the same line as "res publicæ" in reference to the economic function for which they are intended.

To be sure, their resemblance to the latter is not true in the sense that their use is absolutely free to every one, as in "res publicæ." There are some in which this is the case, for example, picture galleries established in the form of a foundation, which any one who desires to do so may visit, just as he can make use of the public roads and springs. But there are also those in which certain conditions must be fulfilled in order to participate in them, which do not depend upon the beneficiary himself, for example admission to a home for widows, or the award of a scholarship. But this difference must not hinder us, after we have once applied the idea of the subject of the purpose, from recognizing society in the above sense as the subject in these also. The interest which the foundations have for society will justify me in pointing out their essential elements.

By "foundations" language understands the devotion of things or capital in favor of *indefinite* persons, but for a *permanent* and not a temporary purpose. The element of *indeterminateness* of the beneficiary distinguishes the foundation from a liberal assignment of property to a

[78] Cod. 1. 3. 46 § 6. . . . "cogere pium opus aut piam liberalitatem omnimodo impleri et cuicumque civium idem etiam facere licentia erit; cum sit enim *communis* pietatis ratio (a purpose for the public welfare), *communes* et *populares* debet etiam affectiones constitui harum rerum executionis, habituro *unoquoque* licentiam ex nostra hac lege movere ex lege condictitia et postulare relicta impleri."

determinate person ("inter vivos," gift; by testament, institution of an heir, legacy). The element of *permanence* of the purpose, or rather of continuity, the recurrence of the appropriation from the income of the foundation's capital, distinguishes the foundation from single gifts to a number of indeterminate persons, which are at once consumed; public *alms* ("Spenden"), as they may fittingly be called.[79] In both of these elements benevolence rises from the sphere of individual generosity, inspired by *personal* relations or qualities (friendship, poverty, p. 78 f.), to that of abstract generosity. It is not a definite single person to whom generosity applies itself but a *class*, wide or narrow (the poor, the local poor, the local poor of a particular confession; widows, widows in general, widows of servants of the State, of servants of the State of a particular class; students, students of the State university, students of a particular subject). We may call them acts of *social liberality* in contradistinction to those of *individual*.

In reference to the purpose the foundations extend much farther than alms. The latter is limited to giving support to those who need it. It is public *charity*, and its acceptance, like that of ordinary charity, is a confession of need on the part of the recipient, and hence has something embarrassing and humiliating

[79] From mediæval Latin "spendere" (expendere — to spend, "expensa," "spensa," "spesa" — expense, costs, to which is related our German "Speise" [food], "spîse," "spîsa"). In Rome such alms ("largitiones") to the people (grain, meat, wine, oil, etc.) were very frequent, as is well known. Concerning their social significance, see my "Geist des römischen Rechts," II, 1, pp. 249–253. Modern forms of the same thing are the distribution of soup, wood for fuel, etc., in times of necessity by special associations (in former times this was done by the monasteries, the removal of which produces a sensible loss in the care of the poor). To the same category belongs also the Roman Law concept of "jactus missilium."

about it (p. 79). But the purpose of foundations extends as far as the need of human life. It embraces in addition to physical needs (nourishment, clothing, shelter, medical care,—poor establishments, homes for widows, orphan asylums, hospitals)[80] also spiritual (affording the means for artistic or scientific education or enjoyment,—libraries, art institutions, scholarships).

In reference to the juristic form the jurist distinguishes foundations that have a personality of their own ("universitates bonorum") from those without such. The latter embrace those foundations in which the money set aside for the purpose is given to an already existing personality (State, community, church, university, etc.) by imposing upon it the permanent application of the money in accordance with the terms of the foundation, as is for example the regular form today in scholarships for students. The first may be called *independent* foundations, the latter, *dependent*. In both cases the capital of the foundation exists as the property of a person. In the former the person is the foundation itself, in the latter it is the trustee.[81] To the foundations of the latter sort belong also, according to the juristic conception, those which consist in the construction of

[80] The "piae causae," "pia corpora" of later Roman law. The earliest is the "tabula alimentaria" of Trajan, the greater number date from Christian times. Examples in Cod. 1. 2. 19, "xenodochium," "orphanotrophium," "ptochotrophium," "gerontocomium," "brephotrophium." The Greek names indicate their late origin. They contain a new proof of what was above mentioned (p. 214): the influence of Christianity in promoting the benevolent feelings.

[81] For the non-juristic reader I observe that a trustee ("Fiduziar") is one to whom a right is given not that he may have himself the benefit thereof, but that he may exercise it in behalf of another. He is the possessor of the right not for his own interest, but solely as trustee ("*Rechtsträger*" [bearer of a right], see my "Geist des römischen Rechts," III, 1, p. 217 ff., 3d ed.).

"res publicæ." In the present time they are rare, in Rome they were very frequent, for example the construction of public springs, theatres, erection of statues, etc. Mohammedan law has even formed a special concept for this.[82]

If finally I speak of the *form* of the establishment of foundations, I do so merely in order to make clear a concept of the Roman law referring to foundations; I refer to the "pollicitatio" (p. 215). The jurist as a rule emphasizes in it only the formal juristic element of the binding force of a unilateral promise, whereas he leaves out of consideration the social significance of "pollicitatio." It consists in the fact that "pollicitatio" is the form of *foundation "inter vivos."* It is the counterpart of *testamentary* foundation. The two together are combined in the idea of *social liberality.*[83] Whereas the ancient Roman law had not yet risen (p. 208) to the independent juristic recognition of liberality to an *individual "inter vivos"* (gift), it recognized early *social* liberality among living persons as an independent concept. And it even disregarded in this matter the technical objection which the theory of contract opposed to "pollicitatio" in the requirement of mutual consensus. The Roman does not sacrifice himself for the individual, but he does so for the community. And the Roman law corresponds to this feeling in refusing its form to the former and putting it at the disposition of the latter.

[82] "Wäkf'om" — dedication or devotion to the common welfare or for purposes pleasing to God. A second species of "wäkf" is the one for children ("wäkf ewlod"). We should call it family settlement. Mohammedan law emphasizes expressly the permanence and ethical character of the purpose. It forbids, for example, devotion for the welfare of unbelievers. See *von Tornauw,* "Das Moslemitische Recht" (Leipzig, 1855), pp. 155–159.

[83] "Liberalitates in civitates collatae," D. 50. 12. 3 § 1. "Donationes, quæ in rem publicam fiunt," *ibid.* 1 § 1.

The Roman law never developed an independent form for the *testamentary* foundation (the establishment of a foundation as the only content of a will and testament). This purpose could be attained only in an indirect way by the institution of an heir who would make the foundation a real fact. As the lax custom of drawing up wills in later Christian times brought to light testamentary dispositions directed immediately to this end (for example the institution of "captivi," "pauperes," etc., as heirs), there was still need of a circuitous course adopted by Justinian (substitution of the Church and the community as the heir entrusted with the execution of the disposition) to invalidate the objections which were opposed to their legal possibility. After our modern theory had risen, as a result of many struggles, to the recognition of the permissibility of a direct testamentary establishment of a foundation, the legal concept of social liberality, which in Roman law received in "pollicitatio" its first partial recognition, reached its final form. And theory must take account of this fact by enunciating the principle that the subject in liberality may be not only a person in the legal sense ("persona certa," physical, juristic), but also society ("persona incerta"). The goods which are given to it in this way — no matter what form technical jurisprudence may appply to them— must be marked from the political-economic point of view as *social* wealth or property.

In reference to the secondary functions of things, we have again our three different subjects in *servitude*, namely,

(a) For the individual, personal and land servitude.

(b) For the State, State servitude.[84]

[84] According to Roman law the usual personal servitude is possible for juristic persons, hence also for the State — scarcely a happy idea, and surely not worthy of being retained in modern legislation. Its

(c) For society, public use of private lands, protected by law.[85]

2. *Obligation.* I assume the concept as known and confine myself merely to pointing out the different forms which it assumes according to our three subjects.

The subject may be (a) The Individual. In this case the relation belongs to private law. The means of making it valid is to prosecute the claim by way of a civil process. The specifically juristic expression for this is *obligation.* For the two following classes, for political and social obligatory relation, this expression is not used; it is one entirely peculiar to private obligation.

(b) The State. The State too can conclude ordinary contracts of private law. In this case the principles of private law are valid for the State also, actively as well as passively. The State (the treasury) may sue and be sued. It is different, on the other hand, when the legal bond has its ground in the peculiar purposes and problems of the State, as for example, the payment of taxes and duties (active), and of salaries (passive). Here the legal bond belongs to public law, and it is made valid not by means of civil action, but in forms especially provided for it.

unnatural character is shown among other things in the fact that it was not possible to admit here the feature which goes hand in hand with personal servitude, namely, its duration till the death of the person, but they were compelled to restrict it by positive prescription to a maximum (100 years), D. 7. 1. 56.

[85] The legal ground may be twofold, statute and permission of the owner. The former, for example, in a towing path, D. 1. 8. 5; 41. 1. 30 § 1; the latter in public passages through courts and landed estates, 9. 3. 1 § 2, " . . . locus privatus, per quem vulgo iter fit." 9. 2. 31. The counterpart of the private thing in public use is the public thing in private use, "tabernæ publicæ, quarum usus ad privatos pertinet," D. 18. 1. 32.

As the term "Obligation" is applied specifically to private law, so the term "Pflicht"[86] (duty) and the adjective "pflichtig" (bound to render a certain performance, liable) pertain to public law.[87] To be sure we apply the expression "Pflicht" (duty) also to the relations of private law, but the manner in which it is done proves the correctness of the definition here given, and shows at the same time the fine power of distinction residing in language. We speak of duties of guardians, parents, children, husband and wife, but not of duties of the buyer, the seller, the lessor, the lessee. In so far

[86] Old High German "fliht," Middle High German "phliht" from "pflegen" — to care for, manage, administer, hence "Pfleger" (= guardian, especially "Güterpfleger" [trustee]), "Pflegekind" (foster-child), "Pflegeeltern" (foster-parents).

[87] "Staatsbürgerpflicht" (duty of a citizen), duties of jurymen, judges, officials, "steuerpflichtig" (bound to pay taxes [person], dutiable [article]), "wehrpflichtig" (liable or bound to serve in the army), "pflichtig" (bound, liable), etc. All these expressions are found in our new German imperial codes. I compared the latter for the terminology observed in them and have arrived at the following result. In the codes concerned with public law (Constitution of the German Empire, Judiciary Act, Code of Criminal Procedure) are found the terms "Pflichten" (duties), "pflichtig" (bound), "verpflichten" (to bind), "Verpflichtung" (legal bond), "verpflichtet" (bound). On the other hand, "Verbindlichkeit" (obligatory relation), is so far as I remember not found. In the statutes dealing with private law (general German Bills of Exchange Code and the German Commercial Code) are found "Verbindlichkeit" (obligatory relation), "Wechselverbindlichkeit" (obligation arising out of commercial paper), "verpflichtet" (legally bound), "Pflicht" (legal duty), for example, "Haftungspflicht" (liability), duty of timely presentation, duties of trade brokers, of the board of directors of a joint-stock company, etc. For the *contractual* basis of the obligatory relation both use regularly the word "Verbindlichkeit" [obligatory relation] (to enter, undertake), but also "Verpflichtung" [legal bond] (to enter, undertake). "Verpflichtung" is therefore the general expression, "Verbindlichkeit" the special expression restricted solely to private law. The application of the expression "Pflicht" (duty) is governed by the point of view presented in the text later.

as, in certain relations of private law, as for example in those above mentioned of guardians, parents, etc., the law prescribes for the person, in the interest of society, a fixed form of obligatory relation which cannot be changed by the autonomy of the party (that part of private law which the Romans designate as "jus publicum quod pactis privatorum mutari non potest"), we speak of *duties* also in these relations. And this without considering the circumstance whether one has entered into the relation of his own free will like the husband, or by compulsion as the guardian, since it is indifferent as far as the obligatory status is concerned. But the case is different where the person himself determines the character and measure of his legal bond, as in contracts. In this case we say indeed that the person binds himself ("sich 'verpflichte'"); that he takes a legal bond upon himself ("Verpflichtungen übernehme"); but we do not call the latter "duties" ("Pflichten"). But in so far as the State's legal constraint is added to the free will of the individual establishing the obligation, this merges into duty ("Pflicht"). The seller, unlike the guardian, does not take a duty but an obligatory relation upon himself, to do a certain thing. But after he has established it, it changes into a duty before the tribunal of the judge if he refuses to carry it out. The latter would have to say to him, if he wanted to express himself correctly, "Since you have put yourself under *an obligatory relation* ("Verbindlichkeit"), since you have undertaken a *legal bond* ("Verpflichtung"), you have the *duty* ("Pflicht") to carry it out." The same difference is expressed by the Romans in the terms "obligatio" and "oportet." "Obligatio" like all verbals in "io" denotes primarily an *act*, the act of binding oneself on the part of the debtors ("Schuldner") ("ligare" toward another — "ob-ligare"). It denotes in the second place the *condition* established by the act ("obligatum esse," *being bound, obliged*). To this state of being bound which the party has taken upon itself,[88] the law attaches as its consequence the "oportet," the command to carry it out. It is the same difference between the private and public side of the relation that is expressed in the terms "Verpflichtung" (legal bond) and "Verbindlichkeit" (obligatory relation) on the one hand, and "Pflicht" (duty) on the other. Those two expressions and "obligatio" refer to the party, "Pflicht" (duty) and "oportet" refer to the judge. When the party makes use of the latter expression, he does so with an eye to the judge.

(c) Society. The law imposes a number of legal bonds upon us which have as their subject ("Destinatär") neither a definite individual, nor the State (municipality, Church), but the whole people, society. They are such as have for their purpose the good of the community, — public safety; as for example, the obligation of maintaining in repair the roads in front of our lands, the dikes, etc. Nowadays their enforcement is left as a rule to the police. Among the Romans, the point of view that this matter concerns the interests of the people ("populus") and constitutes a social duty found its legal expression in the "actio popularis," to which every citizen was entitled as a representative of the people.[89] In view of

[88] An "obligatio *lege* introducta" (D. 13. 2. 1) is a product of later times, which would have seemed as contradictory to an ancient Roman as the so-called "pignus legale." Both concepts, that of obligation as well as that of pledge, presuppose in the original conception an act of will of the subject. Upon this primitive national conception was based the necessity of the many "cautiones" of Roman procedure. Plaintiff, defendant, representative, had to bind themselves by their own deed. With us the law imposes upon them the legal bond in question — "*Verbindlichkeit*" (private obligatory relation) has become "*Pflicht*" (legal duty).

[89] D. 47. 23. 1, actually designates the "jus populi" as its basis. Example, the "actio de posito et suspenso" against the person who

the changed form of this matter at the present time, we might designate this third class as *police obligations* in contradistinction to *private* and *public*.

In addition to the expressions for obligation which we have met so far, the German language possesses a few other terms, which refer to a special form of the relation. They are the following: —

Compulsion. The expression denotes the obligation of a person not so much to do a thing himself, as to *have it done*. Compulsory vaccination obliges us to vaccinate our children; compulsory education, to educate them; compulsory testimony, to be heard as witnesses. The application of compulsory methods for the purpose of carrying out these obligations comes under the category of *execution*, not under that of *punishment*. The "penalties" threatened in case of insubordination are nothing else than means of pressure to break down resistance.[90]

Burden. The original meaning of the expression seems to have been an obligation imposed upon a person not directly, but through the medium of real estate, a form of taxing a person, which constitutes a peculiarity of the old German law as against the Roman. The subject in whose benefit the burden is imposed might be an *individual* (perpetual charge, charge on realty), the *State* (Church, municipality; State and communal

endangers the public passage by placing obstacles or suspending objects from his house.

[90] The Roman concept of "multa" in contradistinction to "poena." The example of the Romans, who fixed a maximum for "multa," on the attainment of which no further coercive measures were applied, has been imitated in the Law of Civil Procedure of the German Empire, § 355, in compulsory testimony. The disadvantages which it entails upon the refractory witness have not the significance of a punishment, but of means of pressure for the purpose of carrying out a public law obligation.

charges, tithes), *society* (service-burden of repairing dikes, of road-repair, and of the building of churches). Some of these burdens were later transferred from the real estate to the person (for example, quartering charges, communal charges), and the name burden should then have been replaced by another. But, as often happens, the existing name was retained although it was no longer suitable. The expression was extended even to the recently proposed legal obligation of municipalities to support the schools, and it was called school charge, although it would be more correct to speak of school duty ("Pflicht").

Debt. In modern legal phraseology we understand by this term a private obligation referring to money (debts = money debts). *Payment* ("Zahlung") corresponds to it as its fulfilment (counting ["zählen"] of the money; so "numerare" from "numerus"). Consequently the expression debtor and its correlative creditor would have to be limited to this connotation. But juristic terminology did not bind itself to this, and uses both expressions of the persons having respectively the right and the duty in general, as the Romans did in the use of their "creditor" and "debitor"; which were also originally confined to money debts.

Service. We speak of "Dienstleistungen" (deeds of service) when it is a question of particular temporary acts. We speak of "Dienst" (service) and "Dienstverhältniss" (relation of service) when the entire service power is engaged (attendants, domestic servants, footmen, service-hire, State and Church service, military service). "Burden" ("Last") rests on the thing, "service" ("Dienst") on the person.

3. *Crime.* Crime (including also offences and misdemeanors punished by fine or imprisonment)[91] has been

[91] Etymologically "Ver-*brechen*" (crime) is characterized as the *breaking* ("Brechen") of order, "Ver-*gehen*" (offence) as *going* beyond

defined as an act involving a public penalty, or one that is in violation of the criminal law. The definition is correct, it contains the external criterion by which crime may be recognized, but it is purely formal. It enables us to classify human acts in accordance with a definite positive law as being crimes or not, without giving us information concerning the important question what crime is and why the law attaches a penalty to it. In short it gives us the external *mark*, but not the internal *essence* of crime.

Other definitions have tried to remedy this defect, but, according to my opinion, with little success. One regards the essence of crime as being the violation of subjective *rights* (of the individual or State). But crimes against morality, perjury, blasphemy, etc., do not violate any subjective right. Another definition regards crime as the violation of the *freedom* secured by the State. But freedom is not violated by the crimes mentioned. Still another regards crime as the violation of the legal order. But the legal order embraces also private law, and private law is not protected by penalty; and not every act contrary to law is a crime. The same objection applies to the definition of crime as the revolt of the individual will against the *general*. For in so far as this general will has assumed a legal form (and beyond this there can be no question of its *legally* binding force) it coincides with the legal order. This definition contains exactly the same idea as the one before, except that it is not so good because less definite. If we apply it as it reads, then deviation from the prevalent fashion or the domestic mode of living is also a crime, and if we

("Hinaus-*gehen*"), "Über-*tretung*" (misdemeanor) as *stepping* beyond ("Hinaus-*treten*") the path of right. Similarly the Roman "*delictum*" from "de-*linquere*," "*linquere*," leaving the way prescribed by law.

supply the missing element "legal," then all violations of private law must also be characterized as a revolt against the general will. The latter commands the debtor to pay his debt. If he does not do so, he revolts against it.

The purpose of the criminal law is no different from that of any law, *viz.*, the security of the conditions of social life. But the manner in which it pursues this purpose is peculiar. It makes use of ***punishment.*** Why? Is it because all disregard of law is a revolt against the authority of the State and therefore deserves punishment? In that case every violation of law should be punished; the refusal of the seller to fulfil his contract, of the debtor to pay his debt, and innumerable other cases; and then there would be only one kind of punishment, *viz.*, for disregard of the law, and only one kind of crime, *viz.*, the insubordination of the subject to the commands or prohibitions of the government.

Wherein lies the reason of the fact that whereas the law punishes certain acts which are in opposition to it, it leaves others unpunished? In the one case as well as in the other we are dealing with disregard of the law, and hence, if the latter is the sum of the conditions of social life, we are dealing with an attack upon these conditions. Society can no more exist if contracts of sale are not carried out, and loans are not repaid, than if one man kills or robs the other. Why punishment in the one case and not in the other?

Self-preservation also, and reproduction and work are conditions of social life. Why does not society secure these by law? The answer is, because it has no need of doing so (p. 338). The same consideration which causes society to take refuge in the law at all, namely the recognition that it needs it, guides it also in reference to the criminal law. Where the other means are sufficient for the realization of the law, the application of punishment would be an irresponsible measure, because society itself would be the sufferer by it (p. 280). The question for what cases legislation shall fix a penalty is purely a question of social politics. I do not mean the social politics which directs its attention merely to the external goods, but politics in the full sense of the word, which is synonymous with the practical estimation and security of all conditions, including the moral, of the prosperity of society. The Roman law thought it necessary, for good reasons, to set a limit in their own interest and in the interest of the children upon the liberality of man and wife toward each other. It forbids for this reason gifts between man and wife. But it assigns no penalty to the transgression of this prescription. Why not? Because the nullity of the gift is quite sufficient for the purpose, and punishment would be useless. The same thing applies to the case of the seller refusing to carry out the contract of sale, or the debtor refusing to repay the loan. Enforcement of the contract is quite sufficient, and there is no need of punishment. There as here the disregard of the law, the revolt of the particular will against the general, ends with the *powerlessness* of the individual will; it can go no further than the mere *attempt*. The anticipation of this result is sufficient as a rule to stifle the attempt itself in the germ. To *one* case of attempted resistance there are millions of cases of unresisting submission to the law. Resistance is to be feared as a rule in well ordered conditions of the law only where either the fact or its legal judgment can be an object of dispute.

But suppose these conditions changed, and the civil law assumed dimensions in certain directions, for example in reference to the reliability of weights or the genuineness of goods, dimensions which bring the national honesty and solidity into discredit abroad, and as a consequence diminish the export trade, what would the legislator have to do in such a case? Would he have to put his hands in his pockets for the academical reason that it is a violation of the civil law and not of the criminal law? The difference between the two and their limits he determines himself. He does not have to take his concepts of civil and criminal law from theory, but theory must shape itself according to his views. The criminal law begins where punishment is required by the interest of society. And when loyalty and honesty in business cannot be kept straight without it, the law must make use of punishment.

This is the condition in which we find ourselves today in Germany. Too long has our legislation looked on idly while irresponsibility, dishonesty, deception, have raised their heads ever more insolently in contract relations, and have brought about a state of affairs which makes an honest man almost disgusted with life. The idea of the "genuine" has almost disappeared in Germany in the case of most articles, not merely in articles of food. Almost anything we take into our hands is spurious, counterfeit, falsified. Germany once had a large export trade in linen. Now the German linen industry in foreign markets has been crowded out almost everywhere, and rightly so. The thousands of dollars which dishonest weavers or manufacturers gained by the mixture of cotton have lost the German nation millions, quite apart from the injury done to our good name abroad. If these falsifiers had been threatened in good time with the penalty of imprisonment, we should be better off. Our forefathers in the free imperial cities, simple artisans and tradesmen, without any knowledge of the difference between civil and criminal offences against the law, showed in this respect a much truer insight of what was necessary than we with all our education in theory. They did not hesitate to inflict punishment upon breach of contract, and under certain conditions very heavy punishments; as for example exile and exposure on the pillory;[92] and they cared for solid work, good means of nourishment and honesty in trade and intercourse by means of all kinds of institutions. We shall probably have to have many bitter experiences yet before we can become as intelligent as they were, and free ourselves from the academic prejudice that the sphere of contracts is a privileged wrestling ground for civil injustice, which is regarded in principle as inaccessible to punishment.

Once more, then, the question of the legislative use of punishment is purely a question of social politics in the above sense. It is comprehended in the maxim:—use punishment wherever society cannot get along without it. As this is a matter of historical experience, of the conditions of life and morals of the various peoples and times, the sphere of punishment in contradistinction to that of the civil law or, which is the same thing, the sphere of crime in the widest sense, is a historically changing one, just as the sphere of law in relation to morality. There was a time in Rome when certain contract relations, as for example "fiducia" and "mandatum," were entirely devoid of *legal* protection, and depended solely upon the protection of *custom* ("infamia"). Then came the protection of the *civil* law ("actio fiduciae," "mandati"), and finally the protection of the *criminal* law ("crimen stellionatus").

But no matter how variable the extent of crime may be, the concept is always the same. It always represents

[92] Rich material in *Wilhelm Sickel*, "Die Bestrafung des Vertragsbruchs und analoger Rechtsverletzungen in Deutschland" (Halle, 1876).

to us, on the part of the criminal, an attack on the conditions of social life; on the part of society it represents its conviction, expressed in the form of law, that it can ward it off only by means of punishment. *Crime is that which endangers the conditions of social life, and of which legislation is convinced that it can be removed only by punishment.*

The standard by which the legislator measures this character of crime is not the *concrete* danger of the *particular* act, but the *abstract* danger of the whole *category* of acts. The punishment of a particular act is only the necessary consequence of the threat of punishment once it is made, for without it the latter would be ineffective. Whether the particular act endangers society or not is quite indifferent, and there is no error more serious in criminal law than to substitute the standpoint of the *execution* of punishment for that of the *threat* thereof.

Violation of the civil law is also in opposition to the conditions of social life, but it is an attempt of the powerless against the powerful, which glides off without producing any effect. The means of the civil law (legal action and nullity) are quite adequate for society to defend itself against the attack. The complete failure of the latter makes punishment superfluous.

The criminal law shows us everywhere a gradation of punishment according to the nature of the crime. It will be granted that a definition of crime which gives the key for the explanation of this fact, and at the same time supplies the standard for the gravity of the penalty, is to be preferred to every other that cannot do this. I believe I can claim this for my definition. The standpoint of endangering the conditions of social life embraces two elements that are capable of gradation, and should therefore be considered in the legislative estimation of punishment. They are, the *conditions of life*—not all are equally important, some are more essential than others: and the *danger* accruing to them — not every injury to the conditions endangers society equally.

The higher a good stands, the more thought we take to make it secure. Society does the same thing with its conditions of life (I shall call them social goods) in so far as the legal protection is concerned which it summons for their security. The higher the good, the higher the punishment. *The list of penalties gives the standard of values for social goods.* What price is for business, that punishment is for criminal law. If you put the social goods on one side and the penalties on the other, you have the scale of social values. And if you do this for the various peoples and times, you will find that the same fluctuations in value which commerce shows in *economic* goods as indicated by the price, are also seen in the criminal law in reference to the *social* goods as indicated by the penalty. Life, honor, religion, morality, military discipline, etc., did not always have the same rate of exchange.[93] Some things stand low with us which

[93] Exemplified in my "Kampf ums Recht," (7th ed.), p. 32. I print the passage here, "Theocracy stamps blasphemy and idolatry as capital crimes, whereas it sees in the removal of boundary marks only a simple offence (Mosaic law). An agricultural State on the other hand will conversely inflict the entire weight of its punishment upon the latter, whereas it lets the blasphemer go with a very mild punishment (old Roman law). A commercial State will give the first place to the counterfeiting of coins and forgery in general; a military State will give it to insubordination, malfeasance in office, etc.; an absolute State, to *lèse-majesté*; a republic to ambition for royal power, and all of them will exhibit a severity in this place which forms a strong contrast to the manner in which they prosecute other crimes. In short, the reaction of the sense of right of States and individuals is most violent where they feel themselves immediately threatened in their peculiar conditions of life.

were high in former times, and conversely. The judgment of society concerning the greater or lesser importance of certain conditions of life varies. This point of view of the valuation of injured goods in the criminal law meets us in all its simplicity in the regulations of the old German laws concerning bodily injury and homicide. All parts of the body had their precise values. Nose, ears, teeth, eyes, foot, hand, finger, everything had its definite price; "price currents of the criminal law," as they have been called.[94] Similarly the life of a nobleman, of a freeman, of a slave. It was the valuation of man from the standpoint of the criminal law. The valuation of society in the same way is the criminal law. What is the value of human life, honor, freedom, property, marriage, morality, security of the State, military discipline, etc.? Open the book of the criminal law and you will find it.

In commerce, the system of money, *i. e.*, the differences in value of gold, silver, copper and nickel, and the divisibility of the metals, makes possible the fixation of minimal differences in value. The criminal law solves the same problem likewise partly by the *variation* of the penalties (penalties affecting life, honor, freedom, money), partly by their *divisibility* (penalties affecting freedom and money, permanent or temporary withdrawal of civil rights — *honor* cannot be taken away temporarily). Between the lowest penalty affecting money or freedom and the death penalty there is a wide field, wide enough to make possible the finest nuances and particularizations in the criminal law.

In addition to the *objective* element of the threatened *good* on the part of society, there is the *subjective* element, on the part of the criminal, arising from his disposition and the manner in which the crime was carried out,

[94] *Wilda*, "Strafrecht der Germanen," (Halle, 1842), p. 729.

which constitutes him a *danger* to society. Not every criminal who commits the same crime endangers society in the same degree. Society has more to fear from the relapsing or habitual criminal than from the novice in crime; it has more to fear from a conspiracy or band than from a single individual. Cunning threatens greater dangers than passion; design than negligence.

I now turn to the classification of crimes according to the nature of the subject against whom they are directed.[95]

[95] *Hugo Meyer* also, "Lehrbuch des Deutschen Strafrechts," (2d ed., 1877), § 84, to which my attention was not called until after the appearance of the first edition of my work, arrives at a threefold classification of crimes, which coincides with mine in *content*. The first two classes are the same as mine, crimes against the individual and against the State. The third he characterizes as crimes against *general legally protected interests*, by which he understands those which I designate as crimes against society. The author thus gives up the basis of classification from which he derived the first two members, *viz.*, the person against whom the crime is directed, and substitutes another, that of the legally protected interest. His classification, therefore, lacks the unity of the "fundamentum dividendi," not to speak of the fact that no crime can be committed against a good, the crime is always directed against the bearer of the good. The injury or the endangering of the good is forbidden only in the interest of the bearer and not in that of the good itself. If we have to bring in the objective standpoint of the good, then the two first categories also must be determined in accordance with it as the injury of the interests of the individual and of the State. The important element of the classification set up by me, *viz.*, the idea of the *subject*, which is laid at its basis, was not seen by Meyer despite the similarity of the three categories in content. And I attribute so much importance to my presentation of this idea because the application of the idea of the subject in the classification of crimes is only a special case of this point of view which I set up and carried through to the widest extent, not merely in the world of law but in the entire ethical world-order (II, pp. 133–154). My classification has no value for me as such, but only because it confirms the correctness and realizability of the quite general idea discovered by me in another way. Let him who adopts it in criminal law see how he can do without it in other applications.

There will be no danger of misunderstanding if for the sake of brevity I shall speak of the subject in crime also, though it would be more correct to say, the subject for whose sake the crime is *forbidden*.

The subject in crime may be

(a) The Individual. Crimes against an individual have long been comprehended by criminologists in a unitary concept and designated by the name of *private crimes*. I distinguish three classes, according as they threaten the conditions of the subject's *physical*, *economic*, or *ideal* life.

The *physical* conditions of life are threatened in their *totality* (life) by murder and homicide, and by the exposure of helpless persons (for abortion and the duel see below); *partially* by bodily injury (mutilation of the body, injury to health and to the intellectual powers).

The *economic* conditions, *i. e.*, property, are threatened by robbery, theft, embezzlement, damage, removal of boundary marks, extortion, criminal self-seeking, deception, treachery.

By *ideal* conditions of life I mean all those goods which are not outwardly visible, but exist only in idea, and without the security of which in accordance with the notions of society, a satisfying and ethical life is not possible. These are, *freedom* (crimes against it are kidnapping, seduction, rape, taking away the use of one's personal freedom, illegal imprisonment, constraint, breach of domestic peace), *honor* (insult, false accusation, violating another's secrets, soliciting for sexual intercourse), *family* (adultery, bigamy, crimes against personal status, in particular the substitution of children).

(b) The State. The crimes directed against it are not limited to the *State crimes* of criminalistic theory, but extend as far as the conditions of political life which may be threatened by them. The expression public crimes is not appropriate according to my opinion, because like the Latin "publicus" ("publica utilitas," "publice interest"), it is also used in application to society (crimes against public safety, see below). To differentiate these crimes from the social, I use the expression *political*.

Political crime is characterized as an attack on the conditions of political life. Can the latter be classified? If this were possible, we should at the same time obtain a classification of the crimes directed against them.

The simplest method would seem to be to carry over the classification made above in the individual; which, as we shall see later, is applicable also to society. The only objection is that the State has no physical existence in the true sense of the word. Physically considered it is nothing more than the sum of all the members of the State. But the State, too, *exists*, and we can place the indispensable conditions of its existence on the same line with those of the individual, except that in the former also as well as in the latter we separate the economic conditions from the physical; although the physical life is just as impossible in the State without the economic means for its preservation, as in the individual.

Indispensable in this sense, *i. e.*, postulated with absolute necessity in the concept of the State, hence, metaphorically speaking, a *physical* condition of the life of the State, an element constituting its essence — is the possession of a *territory*. Next comes the possession of the highest *power;* hence the organization of the forces of the State (government), the system of officials, including the sovereign as the highest officer of the State, determined by birth, and the army. All acts which have as their purpose to remove or to threaten this *power* of the State which is posited in its *existence*, I would class among those that endanger the physical conditions of the life of the State; hence treason to the country, high treason, revolt, riot, hostile acts to friendly States. Then come the peculiar offences of the officials, upon whose dutiful conduct the whole system of the State power depends; and of the soldiers, of whose dutifulness in the service (evasion of service, desertion) and obedience (insubordination, mutiny) the same holds true.

The *economic* conditions of the life of the State are threatened by refusal of taxes, defrauding the government, embezzlement of public moneys.

I called freedom, honor and family the *ideal* conditions of the life of the individual. We can speak of a crime against honor in the State also (insult to the sovereign, to the honor of the office). By crimes against the *freedom* of the State I understand those which hinder its *voluntary action*, *i. e.*, the functions of its organs or citizens which are necessary for its purpose; hence resistance to the authorities, refusal to serve on the jury and the witness stand, crimes in reference to the exercise of the rights of citizens.

I must not conceal the fact that in this attempt to carry over to the State the division of physical, economic and ideal conditions of life which are applicable to the individual and society, I have the feeling that this is possible only in a forced manner. I shall be the first to feel gratified if this classification be replaced by another which shall answer better to the peculiarities of the State.

The subject in crime may be finally

(c) Society. I designate these crimes as *social*. They are those by which neither the individual nor the State is threatened, but the masses, society (acts dangerous to the *community*).

The *physical* conditions of the life of society, *i. e.*, the *external security of its existence*, are threatened by arson, the causing of an inundation, destruction of dikes, dams, railroads, and also by breach of the peace of the land. It is not this or that person whom the perpetrator has in mind; or, even when such is the case, it is not a particular person who suffers from the deed, but an indeterminate number of people, the masses.

The *economic* conditions of the life of society, *i. e.*, the *security of commerce*, are threatened by false coinage and the counterfeiting of documents. It is a complete mistake, in my opinion, to place the first of the two among political crimes, for the State is in nowise injured thereby, not even as the proprietor of the prerogative of coinage. For what injury can false coins do to the *State?* The privilege of coining money has nothing to do with the essence of the State, *i. e.*, with its power. Instead of the State the banks could issue coins as they, in fact, issue banknotes, the counterfeiting of which must be, and is, punished in the interest of the public quite as much as the paper money or the coins issued by the State. Society alone is injured by false coins or money, not the particular person who happened to have gotten it, for counterfeit money passes from hand to hand. Business in general suffers, and the feeling of security disappears. The same is true of false documents. Business can not go on if every coin and every document must first be tested for its genuineness.

The *ideal* conditions of the life of society are threatened in their ethical and religious foundations by perjury, for example, and offences against morality and religion. Is it possible to commit a crime against religion and morality? Only in the same sense as against property and honor, *i. e.*, the crime is not committed against these concepts. This would be as absurd as a crime against the air, by infecting it, or the water, by poisoning it. The crime is committed always against a *person*. In crimes against honor and property the injured person is the individual, in the crimes above named it is society. It is not God, as was formerly assumed in reference to religious offences and perjury, for God cannot be injured. And the circumstance that crime denotes a falling away from God, *i. e.*, a sin, is true of all crimes, not of particular ones only. Nor is it the State, for its power is not threatened by them.

To the category of social crimes in the wider sense belong also most offences against the police. The police are in a very proper sense the representatives of the interests of society, using the term in the more limited meaning as defined here.

I have omitted so far two crimes of a dubious nature, and I want to say a few words about them.

First, *the duel*. We may see in the duel an interference with the judicial sovereignty, inasmuch as the duellists fight their differences out alone instead of allowing the courts to decide them. If they did it with sticks or a squirt or by means of a contest in running instead of deadly weapons, no one would see in it anything criminal. The deciding elements are the *deadly* weapons and the reciprocal *danger to life* caused by them. For this reason the duel does not belong to political crimes, but to private (reciprocal danger to life).

Secondly, *abortion*. Who is the subject here? The future child? It does not yet exist as a person. It is at the time, as the Roman law properly says, a part of the mother. The subject in abortion is therefore not the child, but society. Its criminality consists in the fact that it endangers the coming generation, which belongs to the conditions of the life of society (p. 339).

I will not deny that some of the crimes I classified above may also be brought under a different category. I arranged them according to the point of view that seemed proper to me.

The classification of crime according to the subject in whose behalf it is forbidden, which I attempted in the above discussion, does not claim to exercise a determining influence upon the systematic treatment of criminal law. I made it with the sole purpose of showing that my idea of the subject is applicable also to crime, and this, I hope, I have succeeded in doing. The criminalist may reject this classification as not available for his purposes, just as the civilian will and must reject my conception of foundations. There are various points of view from which a subject may be considered, and every one of them is justified if it furthers the matter in any way. I think I may claim this for mine.

My discussions of the subject in law are now finished. Whether they will gain assent in all details I am not much concerned. But I do lay great stress upon introducing the fundamental idea that the highest principle of classification in law from the philosophical point of view is the subject for whose sake the law is made; and that in addition to the individual and the State (Church, associations) society also, in the narrower sense, must be recognized as such a subject. The less the jurist will be reconciled to this third subject, which can not be classed in his category of *legal subjects*, the more I think it imperative to strengthen the above proof of its justification by giving it a historical safe-conduct on its way, issued by no less a person than the model nation of the law, the Romans. They apprehended the concept of society in the above sense and gave it expression in their government with a clearness, keenness and consistency belonging to a theoretical problem, as if it had been a question of an abstract and systematically correct formulation of a concept not in any way restricted by practical considerations. Witness the offices of *censor* and *aedile*.

The subject to which the censors and aediles had to

turn their attention and their care was society in the sense we defined it above. It was the business of the *censors* to determine what was the condition of Roman society at the time, and what means it was in a position to place at the disposal of the powers of the State. They had to keep the government informed of the number and increase of population, of the number of men under arms and their equipment, of the amount of capital, etc., in short their problem was, in a word, the *statistics of the national forces*, in the interests of the government administration. Out of this statistical function developed in a natural progress the censorious function. If the wealth of any one retrograded since the holding of the last census, it was the most natural thing for the censor to inquire after the reasons; and if the man was not able to give a just account of himself, to deliver him a lecture and remind him of his duties to society. In case of repetition of the offence, the admonition changed into a reprimand and a public censure ("nota censoria"). Bad management, careless cultivation of the field, was a censorial offence, for the well-being of society could proceed only if every man did his duty and obligation as a proprietor. The same applied to celibacy and childlessness; for society had need of the new generation. For this reason a person who had had no children with his wife regarded himself, in consequence of the censor's admonition, as required to separate from her and marry another. Here we have two of our "mixed-legal" conditions of social life, *viz.*, work and reproduction (p. 338), as the object of the censor's care. But they were not protected in the form of law. The requirements which the censor made were not *legal* in their nature. He could not employ the penalties of the law (fine, imprisonment, death) against disobedience;[96] the

[96] See my "Geist des römischen Rechts," II, 1, p. 54 ff. (3d ed.). *Cicero*, "Pro Cluentio," ch. 42. "Majores nostri (animadversionem

only pressure he could bring to bear was the moral one of ethical disapproval, by which *society* emphasized its ethical demands (Ch. IX), and which he, as the representative of public opinion, employed. The censor was the legal personification of public opinion, of the ethical judgment of the people. His power extended farther than public opinion only in this, namely that whereas the latter could realize the idea of exclusion from the community of one's fellowmen only in a social way, he was able to give this idea a legal form by depriving an unworthy person of positions of political honor, which indeed are dependent upon the respect of one's fellowmen (exclusion from the senate, from the order of knights, from the "tribus"). The point of view which guided the censor in his ethical regimen was not regard for the individual as with the pastor, and the father confessor, but for society. Morality interested him only on the side of its *practical* value to *society*, *i.e.*, as an indispensable condition for the progress of society; for the conservation and increase of the national power. It was the thought, in short, that national *morality* is national *power*.

The office of the *aediles* also turned exclusively about society. They had nothing to do with the State as such. The interests which they had to guard were solely those of the people, of the masses.

They were the following, 1. Care for the *physical* conditions of the life of the people; *viz.*, maintenance, grain, water, baths, cook-shops, security of public thoroughfares, repairs of houses and of public roads, etc.

2. The *economical* conditions: trade, market police, genuine coinage, measures, weights, usury in money and grain, transgressions of the social-political regulations of

et auctoritatem censoriam) nunquam neque *judicium* nominaverunt neque perinde ut *rem judicatam* observaverunt."

the "Lex Licinia" concerning the use of the "ager publicus," etc.

3. The *Ideal* conditions: morality (prosecution of offences against chastity, ancient press police, *i.e.*, the destruction of immoral or dangerous books), public decorum (offensive appearance in public, disrespect to the sovereign people),[97] economy and sobriety (limitation of luxury even at funerals, management of the sumptuary laws, confiscation of dainties exhibited in public), pleasures of the people (popular festivals, games).

The province of the aediles[98] as shown in this by no means exhaustive sketch presents them as the protectors of Roman society in the narrower sense, as police administrators of the public safety and welfare. The requisite external power of enforcement they enjoyed was the natural consequence of the task assigned to them. Without going further into the matter, which would be out of place here, it may suffice to remark that the three fundamental forms of the existence of *society* shown above in connection with the fundamental concepts of law (p. 347 ff., under c), *viz.*, social *property*, social *obligations*, and protection against *crimes* dangerous to the community, were placed in Rome essentially under the care of the aediles. In certain cases they actually interfered, for example in obstructions of the public thoroughfare, by in person removing the obstruction;[99] in others

[97] The well-known case of Claudia (*Gellius* 10, 6). It is not without importance in the discussion of principles because an authority like *Th. Mommsen*, "Röm. Staatsrecht," II, p. 461, wanted to bring it under the concept of "a crime directed immediately against the State," in which case the entire conception above given of the province of the aediles would be changed.

[98] See the complete presentation in *Th. Mommsen*, "Staatsrecht," pp. 461–491.

[99] D 43. 8. 2–24; 43. 10. 2. The well-known case of 18. 6. 12 and 13, "Lectos emptos, cum in via publica positi essent, aedilis concidit."

they gave an order to the private person to undertake the necessary measures, and the order was followed by the infliction of a "multa"[100] in case of disobedience. In other cases still they issued edicts of their own,[101] and finally in all grave offences they came before the "comitia tributa" themselves with a motion for a fine. This fine had not the significance of a *criminal charge*, as was the case in the "comitia centuriata," but was a proposition of "compositio," *i.e.*, of redeeming the guilty from punishment by means of money.

The moneys which they realized in this way were not delivered to the State treasury ("aerarium"), and were not collected by the fiscal officials of the State, the quaestors, as was the case with the property of those who committed an offence against the *State*, but, in accordance with the social character of their office, the aediles themselves collected them and used them in the interests of *society*, by providing therewith the expenses of the public games, roads, buildings, monuments, etc. The crime committed against society was to be made good to society.

Thus the standpoint of society is seen to accompany us throughout the aedile ministration. I have not found a single point in which it is wanting.[102] The other

[100] D. 43. 10. 1 § 1 ". . . . multent eos, quousque firmos fecerint (parietes)." *Ibid.* § 3, "construat vias publicas unusquisque secundum propriam domum."

[101] "Actiones aediliciæ," to which belongs also the criminal action in 21. 1. 40–42.

[102] *Mommsen*, "Staatsrecht," p. 463, misses in the criminal function of the ædiles the connection with their province in other matters, especially in the case of "by far the greatest number of crimes." He thinks therefore that it must be conceived as "a province quite distinct from the rest of their official activity." I for my part know of no case in which the point of view established by me of social crimes (p. 372) dangerous to the general welfare, does not hold good.

magistrates, with the exception of the censors, have nothing to do with society. If we want to characterize briefly the legal tasks of all the Roman magistrates in accordance with our point of view of the subject in whose behalf they exercised their functions, we may say that the subject of the *consuls* is the *State* on its *political* and *military* side; of the *quaestors* likewise the State, but on its *economic* side; of the *tribunes*, the *plebs;* of the *praetors*, the *individual*, so far as it concerns the protection of his private legal claims (to which according to the Roman conception belong also delictual actions and "actiones populares"); of the *censors* and the *aediles*, *society*. If the officials are not equal to their tasks, then the State suffers in the consuls; the treasury ("aerarium") in the quaestors; the plebeians in the tribunes; the individual in the praetors, and society in the censors and aediles.

I have now reached the end; not merely the end of my discussions of the subject in the purpose of the law, but the end of my whole development of the concept of law. We began with the formal element, *i.e.*, the external form of the law. To this we added later the content or,—since the entire content of the law is determined by the purpose,—the purposing element. We have thus been led to the exhaustive definition of law with which we now close our whole investigation.

Law is the sum of the conditions of social life in the widest sense of the term, as secured by the power of the State through the means of external compulsion.

We now leave the standpoint of society, which we have held and had to hold till now in order to present the content or teleological element of the law, and turn our attention to the individual. Society is nothing more than the sum of the individuals; and even though, in order to present the significance of law as a part of the whole order of human things, we may look away from the individual and substitute the community for it, still it is after all the individual upon whom the law exerts its activity; it is for his benefit, and it is upon him that its limitations are laid. Is the individual reimbursed for the limitations to which he submits in the interest of society, by the advantages which the latter offers him? The following exposition shall give the answer to this question. Its purpose is to settle accounts between the individual and society in reference to the regulations of the law, by placing credit and debit in parallel columns.

We shall begin with the price which the individual must pay in order to partake of the advantages of the law. I call it the *pressure of the law upon the individual.*

§ 13. *The Pressure of the Law upon the Individual.* The progress in the development of the State and the law is a continuous increase in the demands which both make of the individual. Society becomes ever more covetous and pretentious. Every satisfied desire bears the germ of a new one. But every new purpose which is added on the list of social purposes to those already existing magnifies, with the measure of labor power and money which it requires, the contribution demanded of the individual. And as this contribution, whether it consists in personal service or in money, must be secured by force, there is also increased the strain put upon the social apparatus of force for the purposes of society. This is most plainly evident and most deeply felt in the budget. The enormous increase which it has experienced in our century, and which, as far as can be foreseen, will keep on growing, has its ground and justification (in so far as it is not merely a consequence of the increase in the price of goods and labor power), in the recognition that our present society can no longer be satisfied with the aims and problems which were sufficient for the past;

that it needs more and has more to do than its predecessor. Every new step in its course brings new social problems. But every important problem is indicated in the State budget in millions.

However high or however low we may estimate the duty of the individual to contribute to the charges of the State, every one must say to himself, I, too, for my part contribute to the purposes of society; and were the contribution ever so small, I participate by means of it in all the expenses of the State. There is no expense for which the contribution, perhaps only the millionth part of a penny, could not be calculated precisely. This assertion is just as certain as the one we made above (p. 171), that in the price of a cup of coffee which a person drinks, or of a cigar which he smokes, he must pay all the costs needed in its production. The administrators of the public revenue have solved the problem of making all persons and things tributary to the purposes of society. They stretch out their hands everywhere, and as there is scarcely a person who does not have to pay his contribution in form of an income tax, an industrial tax or a head tax, so there is scarcely a thing from which, before it comes into the hands of the consumer, the State or the municipality has not deducted its share in advance.

But what have taxes to do with law, you will ask? Very much. The obligation to pay taxes is synonymous with the duty of the citizen to assist as far as he can in the pursuit and the furtherance of all the purposes of society for which the taxes are used. In place of every item in the budget of expenditure we may put down the rule of law: "You are legally bound to contribute to this." The expense budget of the State or the municipality resolves itself into as many *legal rules* as it has *items*. Every one says to you, contribute to this item. It is your duty to support the army and the fleet, to build streets, to provide for schools and universities, etc. With every new purpose which arises in the system of the administrative authorities you get a new obligation, and the expense budget of the State or of the political and ecclesiastical community tells you for what purposes society makes these claims upon you.

In taxes you see what society costs you in cash money. But there are besides the personal services which it requires of you, *viz.*, the duty (in Germany) of military service, which costs you a few years of your life, and if there is a war, may cost you your life or your limbs; service on the jury and other services besides. Then there are the police and criminal laws, which prescribe to you the paths to which you must hold in order not to come in conflict with the authorities of the State.

Now, you will say, I have finally done with society. What remains now belongs to me alone. Society can not interfere in the sphere of my private rights; here her empire ends and mine begins. Here is the point where I can say to her, so far and no further.

If we might expect to see this demand realized in any law in the world, it would have to be the old Roman law, for there never was any other law that conceived the principle of individual independence so clearly and consciously, and carried it out so energetically and in so extensive a manner as the Roman.[103] Let us hear what is its attitude to that demand.

"You have "patria potestas" over your children, a power such as no other people knows," says the old Roman law to the father, "but you must not," it adds forthwith, "sell your children as slaves. They remain free citizens even if you should make the attempt to sell

[103] See my "Geist des römischen Rechts," II, pp. 133–218.

them, and I place a limit even upon your right to sell them into servitude ("mancipium"). If you transgress this limit, you lose your right of power over them by reason of your abuse of it, for your children are not only for you, they are also for themselves and for the community, which cannot use citizens who have been accustomed to slavish obedience.

"Your property belongs to you, do with it as you like while you live. Your egoism is my guarantee that you will guard and take care of it. But if you are frivolous enough to squander it, I will place you under the care of a guardian as a spendthrift ("cura prodigi"); for your property is not only for you, but also for those who belong to you.[104] After your death it falls to them. If you want to exclude them, lay your reasons before the people, and they will decide whether they are valid or not.[105] You must do the same thing if you want to put yourself under the paternal power of another, for the people lose an independent citizen thereby, and they have to see whether it is agreeable to their interests."

Our present law has increased considerably these legal limitations upon the individual in the interest of society.

Let us take as an example the relations of parents to their children. Even before the child is born, society stretches forth its hand for it, protecting and desiring it. "The child which you bear in your body," the law says to the mother, "belongs not to you alone, but also to society. Woe to you if you interfere with its rights" (abortion, exposure). When the child is born, the law imposes as a permanent duty the obligation to support

[104] D. 28. 2. 11. ". . . quiet iam vivo patre *quodammodo domini* existimantur."

[105] "Testamentum in comitiis calatis." Concerning the guarantee which this form gave to children to their right of succession, see my "Geist des R. R." III, 1, p. 147 (4th ed.).

it; as a temporary duty, compulsory report of its birth (until recently also compulsory baptism); then a little later compulsory vaccination, and when the child is grown up, compulsory education. The law sets limits to the abuse of the right of chastisement; similarly to the right of exploiting the child by putting it in factories (maximum number of hours of labor, age). The judge gives his consent to the marriage which is arbitrarily refused by the parent, and in cases of necessity he even forces the parents to provide the daughter with a dowry.

In spite of these limitations, the right of parents over their children is still more extensive today than, it seems to me, is consonant with the nature of the relation and the degree of civilization of our present society. It is perhaps the sorest spot of our entire private law today, and I am firmly convinced that in the distant future there will be a change here, and the moral neglect of children in houses which are breeding places of vice and crime will be prevented by putting them into public homes. Of what avail is it to fight vice and crime if we leave their breeding places open? Resistance and struggle against the two must pursue them into the home; and I doubt not that this conviction will one day gain ground and will overcome the false timidity which still keeps us back today from interfering in the home and the rights of parents. To be sure, a mighty transformation must take place in legal opinion before this can happen, and it will require perhaps thousands of years. In reality the change would not be greater than that from the power of the Roman parent to the limitations above mentioned which our law imposes upon him, and which would have scarcely appeared in a different light to an ancient Roman than those I anticipate for the future.

If the idea that a right exists exclusively for the person entitled is to be verified in any institution of private law, it could only be *property*, and this is as a matter of fact the prevailing conception. Jurists and laymen agree in the view that the essence of property consists in the unlimited control of the owner, and that every restriction is essentially an encroachment upon it, which is incompatible with the idea of the institution. How is this? My view is that this conception is fundamentally wrong. The relation of property to society is subject to the same conditions as that of the family. The only reason that the demands of society are not so evident in property is the circumstance that the proprietor's own interest determines him as a rule to use his property in such a way as will further the interest of society along with his own. The same thing is true here as in our mixed-legal conditions of social life (p. 337), *i. e.*, there is no need of law because his own advantage and pleasure lead a person in the right path without any other stimulus. But suppose there were large tracts of arable land lying uncultivated, and weeds grew where corn might grow, or that whole stretches of land were withdrawn from cultivation and given over to hunting, should society look quietly on? In later Roman imperial times it often happened that on account of the enormous burden of land tax, owners allowed their lands to lie desolate. If the land existed only for the owner, the Roman government would have had to endure this quietly as a consequence of the concept of property. But the land exists also for society, that it may bear fruit, and therefore they did not endure it; but they offered the estate to one who was willing to cultivate it and make it useful for society.[106] A garden on the street is an impropriety in a large city, for the site is intended for a house

[106] Cod. 11. 58. 8. The rest does not belong here. The title contains besides a series of other ordinances calculated to secure the cultivation of estates. It signifies a complete misunderstanding of

and not for a garden. Appreciating this point of view many systems of law offer the owner the alternative of building up the ground himself or of selling it for a fair price to one who volunteers to do it. Another example is found in the law of mining in connection with the freedom of prospecting. Society has an interest in bringing the treasures of the ground to the surface. If the owner neglects to do this, the law gives the right to anyone else who is ready to do so to "burrow" and to "search."[107]

The limitations mentioned so far refer altogether to immovable property. In respect to movable property, the law did not consider it necessary to secure legally its use in the interest of society. The prohibition of cruelty to animals is no objection to our view, for its ground is not the consideration that the animal is used in a manner opposed to the *economic* interest of society (for in that case the uneconomic use of other things would have to be forbidden also), but the *ethical* point of view (see Vol. II). The only danger to society that might arise from misuse of property in movable things would be their destruction, which would mean their effective loss to society, but it is secured against this danger by the inter-

the meaning of that constitution to try to explain it on the basis of the idea of "derelictio" (abandonment). The motive was the public interest, "ad *privatum* pariter *publicumque compendium* excolere." It is from a similar consideration that a tumble-down house, which on the refusal of one of the joint owners was repaired on his own account by the other, is made over to him, D. 17. 2. 52 § 10. *Suetonius*, "Vespas." ch. 8, tells of a temporary measure of the same tendency, "Deformis urbs veteribus incendiis ac ruinis erat, vacuas areas occupare et ædificare, *si possessores cessarent, cuicumque* permisit." The lax landowner was in ancient times reminded of his duties to society by the censor. *Gell.* 4, 12.

[107] This is already the case in Roman law. See Cod. 11. 6, "De Metallariis." In 1 of the same place the same point of view is emphasized as in Cod. 8 of the preceding note, "*sibi et rei publicae* commoda compararet."

est of the owner himself. That the owner squanders his fortune is (apart from the loss to his next of kin, p. 384) indifferent to *society*, it only passes into other hands, but its constituent parts are preserved for society. The contrary is possible only in testamentary disposition. It is conceivable that a miser, who grudges everybody everything after his death just as he did in life, might direct in his will that his documents and valuables should be put in his grave or be destroyed. From the standpoint of the individualistic conception of property such a disposition would have to be carried out, but natural feeling will tell everyone that this cannot be allowed, and so the Roman law decides, too.[108] Not because there is no room in a will for anything except the institution of heirs and legacies (for the testator can make any kind of regulations besides that he pleases), but solely and simply because such a disposition would oppose the social destination of property. Goods belong to man and not to the worms. The necessity of bequeathing is based upon the same principle. The law knows no form of excluding an heir. The property which a man loses by death must fall to man again.[109]

[108] D. 11. 7. 14 § 5. "Non autem oportet ornamenta cum corporibus condi nec quid aliud hujusmodi, quod homines simpliciores faciunt."

[109] The Romans emphasize this idea by saying that the inheritance belongs to the *present generation*. The testator must choose his heir among those who are living at the time, he cannot skip over his generation and assign his property to a succeeding one. For the same reason the addition of a "dies ex quo" in the institution of an heir is not valid; the testator can neither deprive the present of its right, nor can he restrict it. The only privilege he has is to *choose* his heir among the individuals already living (or conceived) at the time of his death. To be sure he can, by the addition of conditions, effect a delay in the accession to the inheritance, but — and here the above idea comes out again — even before the condition comes in force, the inheritance is assigned to the person entitled provisionally ("Bonorum possessio secundum tabulas"). The dead cannot restrict the living.

It is therefore not true that property involves in its "idea" the absolute power of disposition. Property in such a form society cannot tolerate and never has tolerated. The "idea" of property cannot contain anything which is in contradiction with the "idea" of society.[110] This standpoint is a last remnant of that unhealthy conception of the Law of Nature which isolated the individual as a being all apart. It needs no proof to show where it would lead to if an owner could retire to his property as to an inaccessible fortress. The resistance of a single person would prevent the construction of a public road or a railway; the laying out of fortifications — works upon which may depend the well-being of thousands, the prosperity of an entire province, perhaps the safety of the State. If he said, "The house, the land, the cattle, the horses are mine," society would have to look on helplessly upon the ravages of fire, water, disease; and in case of war, men would have to pull the cannons if there were no horses to be bought. The principle of the inviolability of property means the delivery of society into the hands of ignorance, obstinacy and spite; into the hands of the meanest and most frivolous egoism of the individual— "Let everything go to ruin, as long as I have my house,

[110] I am glad to have found now the above view, which I had already expressed in my "Geist des R. R." I, p. 7, in the brief formula, "There is no property which is independent of consideration for society" (with which compare the discussions in Vol. II), expressed by *Adolf Wagner*, in his "Allgemeine oder theoretische Volkswirtsschaftslehre," Part I (Leipzig and Heidelberg, 1876), p. 499 *et seq.* in an exposition which in my opinion leaves nothing to be desired; and I gladly make use of this opportunity to express to this writer my fullest and warmest agreement. I know of no work in which the fundamental conception of the social function of law has been developed so carefully, uniformly and convincingly as in his; with what success the future will show.

my land, and my cattle." But will you really have it, you short-sighted fool? The dangers that threaten everybody threaten you also. The flood, the fire, the epidemic, the enemy, will overtake you also; in the general ruin you will also be buried. The interests of society are really your own; and if the latter interferes with your property and puts restrictions upon you, it is done for your sake as much as for the sake of society (see below).

The limitations of property just touched upon reduce themselves to the so-called social right of inevitable necessity of which we spoke above (p. 317). The jurist knows that there are many others besides, which have as their purpose not the interest of society, but of a single person. Does it contradict the idea of property to demand sacrifices from the owner in favor of other persons who do not concern him? The answer to this question will remove the last remnant of the problematical in the theory of property, which our investigation so far has left.

An avalanche has covered the way to my land, or the river has flooded it. The only access still remaining leads through the land of my neighbor. What shall happen now? The Roman law obliges him to give me a way in return for compensation (way of necessity).

A person used another man's stones in building the foundation of his house, thinking they were his own. After the building is finished, the owner appears and claims his stones. How shall the judge decide? If we are to carry out the idea of property to its last consequences, the entire structure would have to be destroyed to get out the stones, or the defendant would have to come to terms with the plaintiff, and in view of the critical situation in which he is placed, would be forced to pay him perhaps a thousand times the value of the stones. According to the Roman law the judge awards the plaintiff double the value of the stones ("act. de tigno juncto"). Even if the defendant stole the stones, the judge does not decide to take them out, but imposes a higher amount.

In both cases it is not a question merely of the interest of a single party, but also of that of society. If the owner cannot get access to his estate, he cannot cultivate it and it will not bear him any more fruit. The damage will affect not only him but society as a whole, for the sum total of national production is thereby diminished. If the house is torn down to take out the stones, a valuable product of labor is completely destroyed to no purpose, and the man himself perhaps will go to ruin along with the house. If property exists solely for the owner, the loss which society must suffer in both cases can be no reason for limiting it. But if it exists also for society, the law must try to reconcile the interests of the two. This is done in all such cases by means of expropriation or by putting an injunction upon the exercise of one's rights.

The meaning of expropriation is completely misunderstood in my opinion by those who see in it an *interference* with the rights of property, an *abnormality* which is in opposition to the "idea" of property. It can appear in this light only to him who views property solely from the standpoint of the individual (*individualistic theory of property*).

But this standpoint is no less false for property than for contract.[111] The only correct one is the social (*social theory of property*). From this standpoint expropriation far from appearing as an abnormality, or as offending against the idea of property, is on the contrary peremptorily demanded by the latter. Expropriation solves the problem of harmonizing the interests of society with

[111] See the arguments on the binding force of contracts, p. 201.

those of the owner. Only by means of it is property made a practicable and feasible institution. Without it property would become the curse of society, and that too not only in the case of general necessity, but also in that of the individual. The former is met by the expropriation of *public* rights, the latter by the expropriation of *private* rights.

The last concept is virtually unknown to modern theory, although it is expressed distinctly enough in Roman law. From the application which the Romans made of it, it is clear that they were fully aware of the dangers which a regardless realization of the abstract, formalistic concept of property (absolute mastery of the thing) contains. In reference to the legal protection of property the Romans combine two methods: *actual realization* of property, and *money payment*. Roman procedure grants the judge the power to *decide* for the actual restitution of the thing without giving him the authority of *enforcing* it ("arbitrium de re restituenda"). In case of disobedience of the order, the judge is merely directed in his final sentence ("sententia") to condemn the defendant in money, which is practically equivalent to expropriation. In this regulation the Roman law gave the realization of property an elasticity which excluded entirely the dangers accompanying the attempt to follow out rigidly the consequences of property and realize them absolutely — the *dangers of property* as I might call them. And it enabled the judge at the same time, in estimating the amount to be paid, to do complete justice to the party expropriated, by paying due regard to his position (function of money as equivalent), as well as to the possible unreasoning resistance of the opponent (penal function of money). I see in this arrangement one of the most ingenious ideas of Roman procedure.

Of what practical value the possibility of this money payment was and to what horrible result an action "rei vindicatio" must lead which would make it its task to realize absolutely the individualistic theory of property, the reader may be convinced by the following case.

In building a house the boundary was exceeded a few inches. After the house is built, his neighbor, who with malicious purpose perhaps looked on quietly while the house was building, brings a possessory action ("act. negatoria") against him. How shall the judge decide? According to the textbooks of our modern Roman law he would have to decide to have the wall set back, *i. e.*, to destroy the entire house. According to my opinion the outcome in this case was that the judge condemned the defendant to pay the value of the strip of land, *i. e.*, the latter was *expropriated* by him. In this way the house was saved and the opponent received compensation for the lost strip of land. If the latter wanted to prevent this he had to move as long as it was still time, *i. e.*, he had to raise a protest when the building operations began ("operis novi nuntiatio"), and in that case the latter had an injunction put upon them. This is surely the most intelligent solution of the problem.[112]

But it is solved at the expense of the *law*, the legal rigorist will tell me, and purely in favor of *expediency*. In this objection is expressed the fundamental difference which exists between the prevailing conception of law and my own, and which I shall not be able to settle scientifically until the second part. According to my

[112] I stand quite alone in the opinion ("Jahrbücher," VI, p. 99) that this is valid also for our modern law. Whether my opponents made clear to themselves the above consequence, and whether they would be sufficiently masters of themselves to apply their theory in practice as judges, I should like to be allowed to doubt. In any case the confidence of the people in jurisprudence would likely be considerably shattered by such a judgment.

theory, utility forms the sole concern of the law. What is opposed to this as legality ("ratio juris") is simply the deepest and firmest stratum of the expedient, deposited in the law (p. 330).

As a second instance of the application of the idea of expropriation in private law I name "adjudicatio" in procedure in partition. The authority given by the praetor to the judge to adjudicate ("adjudicato") was synonymous with the right to expropriate, and the point of view by which the judge had to be guided in this is expressly designated by the jurists as *utility*.[113]

But the case of expropriation is not the only one in which the above point of view is proved, *viz.*, that the rigid consequences of individualistic property must yield to the social interest. Other instances are found in "usucapio" and "accessio." In the former the Roman jurists themselves emphasize the point of view of the public interest as the deciding one. The interest of the owner, they say, must yield in this case to that of society.[114] By "accessio," they understand the case of an adherence of another's thing to one's own. I planted another's tree in my land. The owner demands it back. Must I pull it out again? The answer of Roman law is, as long as it has not yet taken root, yes; after it has taken root, no. Why is this? The reason with which the jurist satisfies himself, *viz.*, that in the latter case the

[113] So, for example, for the "act. finium regundorum," I, 4. 17. § 6, . . . "*commodius*," D. 10. 1. 2 § 1; for the "act. familiæ erciscundæ" 10. 2. 3, . . . "*incommoda*"; for the "act. communi dividundo" 10. 3. 6 § 10, 7 § 1, 19 § 1, *ibid.* 21, "quod omnibus *utilissimum*." Cod. *ibid.* 3. 37. 1 . . . "*commode.*" A modern example, unknown to the Romans, of private law expropriation is found in parcelling out a farm for the rotation of crops.

[114] D. See 41. 3. 1, where the two are placed in opposition to each other, "bono *publico* usucapio introducta est, cum sufficeret *dominis*," etc.

tree has become a constituent part of the land, has disappeared as an independent thing, and therefore its ownership is extinguished,—is not appropriate, for there is no doubt that the tree may nevertheless be separated from the land. And if it were the task of the law to carry out the idea of property to its fullest consequences, then, if the owner desired it, its separation would have to be carried out even if the tree died as a result — "fiat justitia, pereat arbor." But the tree is saved for the same reason that the house is saved into which another's material has been built, and for the same reason that the possessor of an object belonging to another and claimed by its true owner must not destroy the expenditures made in it, if he has no advantage therefrom, or if the former is disposed to compensate him for the advantage he may have. The reason is because the economic result for the one party would be altogether out of proportion to that of the other. The tree, the house, the tapestried wall, the constructed hearth, is preserved, and the other party is paid off with money. The law stands in the way of property, which, to maintain itself, would destroy the object,—either by prohibiting its exercise, or by taking away its ownership and awarding it to the opponent, *i.e.*, by expropriating it.

This is Roman property in its true form, and every one is now in a position to form an idea concerning it and to judge whether it gives any support to the current conception, which has found its scientific expression and sanction in the usual definition of the jurist, that property is the *complete* legal mastery of a thing. I was not concerned in rectifying an erroneous conception about a *Roman* institution, but in withdrawing from the individualistic conception of law the support which it is supposed to have in this institution.

The content of the entire discussion from page 383 on

may be condensed in one word, *viz.*, in the idea of the *social* character of private rights. All rights of private law, even though primarily having the individual as their purpose, are influenced and bound by regard for society. There is not a single right in which the subject can say, this I have exclusively for myself, I am lord and master over it, the consequences of the concept of right demand that society shall not limit me. One need not be a prophet to recognize that this social conception of private law will continually gain ground over the individualistic. There will come a time when property will bear another form than it does at present; when society will no more recognize the alleged right of the individual to gather together as much as possible of the goods of this world, and combine in his hand a landed possession upon which hundreds and thousands of independent farmers might live, than it recognizes the right of life and death of the ancient Roman father over his children, or the feudal right, the highway robbery of the knight, and the law of salvage of the middle ages. Private property and the right of inheritance will always remain, and the socialistic and communistic ideas directed to its removal I regard as vain folly. But we must have little confidence in the skill of our financial artists if we think they can not succeed, through increased taxes,—income, inheritance, sumptuary and other taxes,—in exerting a pressure upon private property which will prevent an excess of its accumulation at single points and which, by diverting the surplus into the State treasury, will make it possible to lighten the pressure upon the other parts of the social body. This will bring about a distribution of the goods of this world more in accord with the interests of society, *i.e.*, *more just* (p. 274 ff.) than has been and must be effected under the influence of a theory of property which, if it is to be called by its right name, is the ***insatiability and voraciousness of egoism.*** The name which it applies to itself is "sacredness of property," and the very men to whom nothing else is sacred, the miserable egoist, whose life has not a single act of self-denial to show, the crass materialist, who respects only what he can grasp with his hands, the pessimist, who in the feeling of his own nothingness, carries his worthlessness over into the world, —all these are at one on the sacredness of property; for property they invoke an idea which otherwise they know not; which they mock and in reality trample under foot.

But egoism has always known how to unite God and holiness to its purposes. When the law governing salvage was still in force, there was a passage in the prayer of the Church which read, "God bless our strand," and the Italian bandit recites an Ave Maria before he goes out to rob.

I have drawn up the account of the individual, as I have promised. It says, you have nothing for yourself alone, everywhere society or, as the representative of its interests, the law, stands by your side. Everywhere society is your partner, desiring a share in all that you have; in yourself, in your labor power, in your body, in your children, in your fortune. Law is the realized partnership of the individual and society. Wherever you are, you are surrounded by the law, society's invisible, omnipresent representative, as by the atmospheric air, and you can no more find a spot in society where the law does not follow you, than you can find a spot on the earth where there is no air. It is habit alone which brings it about that in most cases you do not feel at all the pressure which it exerts upon you. As a matter of habit you move, without being conscious of it, in the paths which the law marks out for you, and it is only where error, haste, or passion carries you away that you become aware, in the resistance which the law offers to you, of the limits within which it restrains you. Conscious reflection is necessary to become aware of all the limitations with which law in a civilized people has surrounded individual freedom.

And must we still be continually prepared for new restrictions? Must the claims of society, as is alleged, keep on increasing (p. 381)? Is there not a point where the individual may exclaim, "Enough of pressure, now, I am weary of being the beast of burden of society. There must be a limit between me and it, beyond which it must not interfere in my affairs: a sphere of freedom which belongs to me exclusively, and which society must respect"?

Here I touch upon a question of the highest fundamental importance, the question of the limits of the State and the law over against the sphere of individual freedom. I touch upon it not because I believe I can solve it, but simply because the sequence in my development of the concept of law puts it in my way and I cannot avoid it.

For me it denotes the closing point of this development, the "so far and no further." The formula in which I comprehended above (p. 51) the relation of the individual to society, *viz.*, "every one exists for himself,—every one exists for the world,—the world exists for every one," does not afford us the least answer to this question. For the latter is not concerned with the *that*, it wants to know *how far* the individual exists for society; but the above formula gives not the slightest information on this matter. Shall we ever succeed in determining clearly this "how far"? I doubt it. According to my opinion the matter will always be fluid. As society progresses, and purposes and requirements, ever newly produced, attach themselves to it irresistibly, the idea of the debt which the individual owes society will keep pace with it. Standing upon a relatively very low stage in comparison with the immeasurable future which lies before us, we cannot at all see the end.

These doubts of mine concerning the solubility of the problem, far from being shaken by the attempts which have been undertaken so far to solve it, have on the contrary been confirmed by them. I know only of two such attempts. They bear the names of two of the most important thinkers of our century, Wilhelm von Humboldt and John Stuart Mill, both, as I think, equally influenced by the fundamental error of the (individualistic) doctrine of the Law of Nature in vogue in the last century, that the State and society can be built up from the standpoint of the individual. In the theory of the Law of Nature the individual is the cardinal point of the whole law and the State. According to it the individual exists for himself alone, an atom without any other purpose in life than that of maintaining itself alongside of the innumerable other atoms. To be able to do this it gets along with them according to the Kantian formula of the compatibility of one's own freedom with that of others. The State and the law merely have the task of realizing this formula, *i.e.*, of preventing the encroachment of the freedom of one upon the sphere of the freedom of the other, — a dividing off of the spheres of freedom in the manner of cages in a menagerie; that the wild beasts may not tear each other to pieces. With this purely negative relation all that is necessary is attained; apart from this these individuals have nothing to do with each other. The State and the law have solved their problem completely with the cordon of safety which they drew about them.

It is the system of individualism in law, which we

have already met above (p. 201) in connection with the question of the binding force of contracts; the construction of the moral world from the standpoint of the individual regarded as an isolated being and referring the whole purpose of his existence to himself; the idea that every one exists for himself and nobody exists for the other.

From the standpoint of this conception, Wilhelm von Humboldt[115] demands of the State that it "shall not interfere in the private affairs of the citizens any further than to prevent the injury of the rights of one by the other" (p. 16). It must not limit their rights any further "than is necessary in order to secure them against themselves and external enemies" (p. 39). Everything else is an evil, hence, in particular, "its efforts to raise the positive well-being of the nation, its whole care for the population of the land, the support of the inhabitants, partly in a direct way by means of institutions for the poor, partly in an indirect way by furthering agriculture, industry and commerce; its financial and coining operations, prohibitions of import and export, all arrangements for guarding against or restoring injuries of nature, in short every institution of the State which has as its purpose to conserve or further the physical welfare of the nation. All these arrangements have injurious consequences and are incompatible with true politics, which proceeds from the highest but always human points of view" (p. 18). Nor should the State concern itself about marriage, but leave it simply to the free choice of the individuals and the autonomic regulation by contract (p. 29). Even public acts of immorality

[115] In his work, "Ideen zu einem Versuch, die Grenzen der Wirksamkeit des Staates zu bestimmen" (Breslau, 1851), which was written in the preceding century, but was not published until after his death.

must not be forbidden, for "nobody's rights are in themselves injured by them, and the other person is free to oppose his own strength of will and reasons to the evil impression" (p. 108). The State must "absolutely refrain from endeavoring to influence directly or indirectly the morals or character of the nation. All special charge of education, religious institutions, sumptuary laws, etc., lies absolutely outside the limits of its activity" (p. 110). Every one must guard against deceit himself (p. 111). If he consents, all crime against him is excluded, and even "the murder of another with his consent must remain unpunished, unless the too likely possibility of dangerous abuse should make a criminal law necessary in this latter case" (p. 139).

Thus all restrictions which the historical State put about individual freedom are torn down, with the only exception of those which are inevitably demanded for the security of mutual rights. The only thing the individual cannot attain with his own powers is the security of his rights (p. 45), and for this, and only for this is there need of union in the State. The latter is "only a *subordinate* means, to which the *true end, man,* must not be sacrificed" (p. 104).

"Man, *i. e.*, the individual, as the true end"—in these few words the whole view is characterized. The thought that man exists also for others, that society which has made him a real man also has a claim upon him and can demand of him that he should help to further its purposes as it has helped further his,—this thought which the most superficial observation of life brings before one constantly and in actual realization, is altogether foreign to the entire book.

But in justice to the great thinker, whom we have thus seen gliding down the steep path of an aprioristic construction of the State and the law widely diverging from historical reality, we must add that the aim which he has before his mind is, despite all the devastations which he must carry out on the way thither, after all an ideal one. It is not low, insipid egoism which he intends to establish thereby, but freedom as a means of the highest and harmonious development of all the powers of man. "That upon which the whole greatness of man finally rests, and which the individual man must always struggle to 'attain, . . . is *individuality of power and education*. This individuality is brought about by freedom of action and the diversity of the agent; and it in turn produces them" (p. 11). "The highest ideal of the existence of human beings together is in my mind that in which every one develops only from himself and for the sake of himself" (p. 13). "True reason can wish man no other condition than that in which not merely every one enjoys the most unrestrained freedom to develop himself from himself through his individuality, but where physical nature also receives no other form from human hands than that which every individual involuntarily and by himself gives it in accordance with his needs and inclination, limited only by the boundaries of his power and his right" (p. 15).

Upon such freedom all his hopes are based. The men who are educated in its school will do of their own accord all that ordinarily the State forces them to do. They will unite of their own free will to ward off great catastrophes, famine, flood, etc. (p. 44). They will, of their own free will, further the purposes of the State, "for they will find all the motives thereto in the idea of the use which the regulations of the State will afford them in attaining their individual aims" (p. 76). "The State can even abstain from positive regulations of educating the nation for war. Training of the citizens in the use of arms is the only thing that is absolutely necessary, but patriotism will imbue them with such virtue as will not merely bring out in them the bravery, readiness and subordination of the soldier, but will inspire them with the spirit of true warriors; or rather of noble citizens who are always ready to fight for their fatherland" (p. 53). Such is the conception of the citizen he was able to form.

We must not forget that it was not the mature statesman Wilhelm von Humboldt who wrote this, but the young man, not yet thirty years old, with the warm pulsation of enthusiasm for all that was noble and beautiful, and a complete faith in the spring of national freedom which seemed to have dawned with the French Revolution. The mature man Humboldt kept the work from publication. No one was in a better position than he to observe the enormous gulf which separated the dream of his youth from reality.

The case is quite different with the attempt which John Stuart Mill undertook in his work on Liberty [116] to assign the law its limits. For this is the effort of a ripe mind, and between him and Humboldt lies a period long and fruitful in political experiences. An entire revolution in political science lay between: from the political and legal individualism of the Law of Nature to the enlightened understanding of the real historical State and law as revealed to history and science in recent

[116] (H. M. Caldwell Co., New York, s. a.). The author directs his attacks not only against law, but also against custom and public opinion; and anyone who knows what unjustifiable pressure the latter exerts in the land of the author in many things which are of a purely external and conventional nature (II, p. 375), and have not the least to do with ethics, will not only fully comprehend the resistance which he thereto opposes, but will recognize this as highly meritorious in him. For our consideration, exclusively concerned with law, *this* side of his polemic against the existing order does not come in question at all.

times. The authority which the name of Mill rightly enjoys makes it doubly necessary to characterize in its true form the erroneous doctrine which, clothed with it, attempts to question our entire social order. And I beg the reader to permit me for this reason to treat this matter with a degree of detail which I should decidedly not have allowed myself in the case of a less important opponent.[117]

The formula which Mill sets up for the attitude of the law toward the individual is essentially the same as that of Humboldt. It is as follows: "The sole end for which mankind are warranted, individually or collectively, in interfering with the liberty of action of any of their number, is self-protection . . . The only purpose for which power can be rightfully exercised over any member of a civilized community, against his will, is to prevent harm to others. His own good, either physical or moral, is not a sufficient warrant. . . . The only part of the conduct of any one, for which he is amenable to society, is that which concerns others. In the part which merely concerns himself, his independence is, of right, absolute" (p. 21).

The formula maintains that there are two ways of exercising individual freedom. One is where the effects are confined exclusively to the agent, the other is where they extend also to others—I use instead of this my own expression, society. If the latter are injurious in their nature, the legislator is authorized to prohibit such use of liberty. In the first case he is not.

But all acts of sufficient meaning to make it worth our while raising this question at all extend in their effects

[117] In England also *Mill* met with decided opposition. See especially the work of *James Fitzjames Stephen*, "The Watchwords Liberty, Equality, Fraternity."

to others. Always are others affected,[118] and this is the only reason why society takes any notice of the acts. I know of no example of a legal rule which has as its purpose to force an individual against his own will in his *own* interest for his good. Where it appears to do so, it is always in the interest of society. Securing the good of the individual is not an end in itself, it is only a means to the end of securing the good of society. Society is not concerned in preventing the primary injurious effect upon the subject, but in preventing the secondary effect upon itself. If we grant it the absolute power, as Mill does, to resort to self-protection through the law in case of such injury, then it is all over with individual freedom. Armed with this formula I promise so to compress and tight-lace it that it will not have the power to move. If the father squanders his money, do not the children suffer? And when the children become a charge upon the poor-box, does not society suffer? Surely it does. Hence I forbid prodigality. But not this alone, I forbid also stock-jobbing, all daring speculations, every extravagant expenditure; in short, I bring the entire control of a man's property under police superintendence. If the parents affect the children by their bad example, do not the latter suffer? If the husband becomes a drunkard, and ill-treats his wife and children and refuses to work; if the wife becomes dissolute and neglects the home, do not the husband and children suffer? Certainly. This circumstance is sufficient to open to the police an entrance into the interior of the

[118] *Mill* himself recognizes this fact in one place in his book (p. 133 f.), "No person is an entirely isolated being; it is impossible for a person to do anything seriously or permanently hurtful to himself, without mischief reaching at least to his near connections, and often far beyond them." But he neglects to draw therefrom the conclusion to his theory.

house, and to place the moral life as well as the economic under surveillance.

But if a man is quite alone in the world, without wife or child, has he not then at least the right to ruin himself? Has he the right to sell himself as a slave? Mill himself forbids it. Why? "By selling himself for a slave, he abdicates his liberty; he foregoes any future use of it beyond that single act. He therefore defeats, in his own case, the very purpose which is the justification of allowing him to dispose of himself" (p. 171). Freedom is therefore dependent upon the *permission* of society. But in that case the latter is also authorized not merely to forbid complete renunciation thereof, but also to lay down its partial measure and aim, and this authority society has indeed always claimed. But not for the sake of the logic of the concept of freedom, — the law of logical contradiction, as Mill says, because "the principle of freedom cannot require that he should be free not to be free. It is not freedom, to be allowed to alienate his freedom" (p. 172), but for the practical reason, namely, because society has come to recognize that slavery is incompatible with it. The standpoint of the logic of the concept, which Mill brings to bear to avoid the last consequence of individual freedom, *viz.*, selling oneself as a slave, takes us much further than he can venture to admit according to his theory. For what is true of the whole must also be true of a part. But every contract contains a partial renunciation of freedom. And what is true of freedom must also be true of life, which is the condition of it. Can we not maintain in respect to life the same thing that Mill says of freedom? "The *idea* of life implies that one *has* it. It is not life if one renounces it."

The law punishes duelling and homicide committed with the consent of the subject. According to Mill's theory there should be no punishment since the persons involved give their consent.

Has legislation a right to fix the maximum hours of labor? Has it the right, according to the theory of freedom, to prevent the laborer if he wishes to shorten his life by excessive labor? Mill also agrees with this legal measure, the introduction of which will always redound to the credit of the enlightened and practical sense of his countrymen. He approves of the provisions for the protection of the health of the workmen and for their safety in dangerous works. But the reason he assigns,—"the principle of individual liberty is not involved here" (p. 159),—is again of such a nature that his whole theory can be lifted by it out of its hinges. For if the prohibition to work as much and as little as I please does not constitute an interference with my personal freedom, where does such interference begin? It is a peculiar picture of freedom that is composed of the particular examples which Mill cites. "The laws which, in many countries on the Continent, forbid marriage unless the parties can show that they have the means of supporting a family do not exceed the legitimate powers of the State . . . they are not objectionable as violations of liberty" (p. 181). "If either a public officer or any one else saw a person attempting to cross a bridge which had been ascertained to be unsafe, and there were no time to warn him of his danger, they might seize him and turn him back, without any real infringement of his liberty; for liberty consists in doing what one desires, and he does not desire to fall into the river" (p. 160). I ask, does the frivolous person, the lover of pleasure, desire to ruin himself? He only wishes to enjoy his life, hence he can also be prevented without an infringement of his liberty. And suppose the man on the bridge really *wants* to take his own life, can he still be seized without an infringement of his liberty? A man who is penetrated by the respect for freedom would first have to ascertain his real purpose before restraining him. "If, either from idleness or from any other avoidable cause, a man fails to perform his legal duties to others, as for instance to support his children [I add another example, payment of debts and public duties], it is no tyranny to force him to fulfil that obligation, by compulsory labor, if no other means are available" (p. 163). So the lazy should be put in institutions of compulsory labor! And this too on the platform of liberty! "Drunkenness," says Mill (p. 163), "in ordinary cases, is not a fit subject for legislative interference; but I should deem it perfectly legitimate that a person who had once been convicted of any act of violence to others under the influence of drink, should be placed under a *special* legal restriction, *personal to himself;* that if he were afterwards found drunk, he should be liable to a penalty, and that if when in that state he committed another offence, the punishment to which he would be liable for that other offence should be increased in severity." A young man breaks a window in a state of intoxication. Henceforth, according to Mill, a special law, issued personally for him, dogs his footsteps, follows him as long as he lives, and stands as a spectre behind his chair at every joyful feast.

And now again we see his strange sensitiveness to liberty in reference to Free Trade. "The restrictions of the sale of poisons and the prohibition of the importation of opium into China are infringements on the liberty of the buyer, because they make it impossible or difficult to obtain a particular commodity" (p. 159). So the Chinese government has not the right to prohibit the opium trade? It must stand idly by with folded arms and look on while the nation is ruining itself physically and morally, simply out of academic respect for liberty, in order not to violate the inherent right of every Chinaman to buy whatever he pleases? Will Mill censure the English government for prohibiting the importation of cattle from a country where there is an epidemic on cattle, in order to prevent contagion of the cattle at home? And the Emperor of China should not be allowed to do in the interest of man what England does in that of cattle?

The fine shipwreck which two thinkers like Humboldt and Mill have suffered in the above question is not due to their own fault, but to the insolubility of the problem. If one steers his ship upon a rock to force a passage through it, he must not be surprised if his ship is shattered. We keep back our ship because we have no hope of the possibility of a passage. Will a fortunate pilot find some day the means of passing through? I do not believe it. Legislation will, in the future as in the past, measure restrictions of personal liberty not according to an abstract academic formula, but according to practical need.

Having shown how society *restricts* the individual in his liberty by means of the law, let us now show what it *offers* him in return.

§ 14. *The Benefit of the State.* I do not say the benefit of the *law*, but of the *State*. The *demands* which the State makes upon the individual we could designate as the demands of the *law*, because they bear the form of law, but we cannot do this in reference to the *benefits* of the State, for they do not coincide with those of the law, they extend far beyond it.

He who wishes to settle his account with the State must be careful to keep the following two questions distinct from each other. One is, do I get a corresponding equivalent for my contribution; is the service I do the State paid for in that which I receive from it? The other is, do not others get more than their due in proportion to me; does the distribution of the advantages of political community to all the members correspond to the principles of justice?

He who answers the first question in the negative, either condemns the State *as such*, and must, if he desires to be consistent, retire from political community to a desert island or the primeval forest; or his charge is directed only against this *particular* State, and in that case, if he does not want to submit without resistance, he must either endeavor to bring about a change of the existing political and legal institutions with the help of those who think like him and the means at his command, or look for another State instead of the one in which he is. The last two alternatives are true also if he answers the first question in the affirmative and the second in the negative. If he is not alone in this judgment, if it is the feeling of the entire social class to which he belongs, such a State of real or supposed social injustice leads either to *emigration en masse* like the attempts at secession of the plebeians in ancient Rome, or to the so-called *class struggle*, like the struggles of the plebeians against the patricians in Rome, the rise of the peasants at the time of the Reformation, the labor movement of the present day, the strikes of certain classes of labor, etc., etc.

The following investigation has to do exclusively with the first question, which alone permits of abstract treatment; whereas the second can be answered only in reference to given historical conditions. Only so much must be quite generally admitted for the second question also, *viz.*, that there have not been wanting examples in history of the kind of social injustice which favors one class of the population at the expense of the other. And this leads me again to an objection which I already raised above (p. 336) against my definition of law as the sum of the conditions of social life secured by compulsion, but left unanswered in that place to be disposed of in the present connection. How is this fact, this exploitation of the law in the interest of a particular class, compatible with the assertion that the law has as its purpose the conditions of life of *society*, *i.e.*, of every body?

Let us suppose a strong man combining with a weak one. If we remove in thought all considerations which may restrain his egoism, he will arrange the social compact in such a way that he will himself get the lion's share (the so-called "societas leonina"). If we apply this to civil society, it means that its order will always correspond to the relative power of the several strata or classes of which it is composed. When the victor admits the vanquished nation into his State, he will not give them an equal station with himself, but will reduce them to a state of dependence. In the same way the more powerful class within the same uniformly growing up people will give expression to its predominant power in the regulations of the law. Unequal rights appear here as the *modus vivendi* between the stronger and the weaker, as the presupposition upon which the peaceful living together of the two is dependent. And it is the weak one who has the most vital interest not to shake it, as long as nothing has changed in the relative powers of the two parties. The law which the stronger dictates to him, be it ever so hard, constitutes, however paradoxical it may seem, after all relatively a benefit in comparison with the condition which would be awaiting him if it were wanting—the benefit, namely, of *relative* pressure as opposed to *absolute*. The measureless self-will of the powerful is still always possible, yet only at the price of violation of the law, and we have shown above (p. 264) how important this moral element is even in comparison with physical force.

Although it is true (p. 276 f.) that justice is the vital principle of society and hence the highest purpose which it has to realize, still it would be mistaken to refuse to recognize that there may be situations in the life of nations when social injustice may have a temporary and relative justification and necessity, like so many other institutions which have no permanent justification, as for example, slavery. Better slavery than slaughter of the enemy; better a society established on the basis of inequality of rights than bare force and lawlessness. In such a society too the law fulfils the function I assigned it, *viz.*, to secure the conditions of social life, except that the latter are not everywhere the same, as was shown above (p. 332).

I shall now return to the *first* question mentioned above, though I do so not without some hesitation. There are questions which one has to propose in the systematic connection of the development of an idea, but which one is almost ashamed to answer, because the thing is self-evident. The above question is of this kind. A few words may suffice.

What does the State give me? If we confine ourselves to the *immediate* services of the State, and leave altogether out of consideration its indirect significance for the development of social life, we shall have to distinguish, I think, three kinds.

The *first* thing the State gives me is protection against injury from without. In the present time the security of this good takes up, as is well known, by far the greatest part of the national strength, personal as well as economic. In comparison with the amount which the individual contributes for this purpose by means of military service and that portion of the taxes which forms his share of the military budget, all other services he has to perform are scarcely appreciable. Of all goods which a nation possesses none is paid for so dearly as the independence of the State on an external power, and the permanence of nationality secured thereby. No nation that feels itself such has ever found the price too high. In case of necessity it has freely offered infinitely greater sacrifices than the State demanded from it.

The *second* good is protection within the State, namely, law. There is no good which costs the individual so little, after it has been once acquired, in comparison with its incalculable value, as the security of rights. Our ancestors paid the dear purchase price in the form of hard-fought, bloody battles, the descendants have to bear only the relatively small costs of maintenance.

The lowest standard by which we may measure the value of this good is the economic, the money value which legal security has for property. How high this is in money is shown by comparing the value of real estate in the Christian States of Europe with that in Turkey. If legal conditions in Turkey could attain to our standard, the value of real estate would at once increase twofold and more. And even within the European civilized States, the fall in the price of land during great political upheavals shows what share the security of rights has in the sum total of the national value of property. What is lost at such times is to be placed to the account of the law.

And yet, how insignificant is the legal security of property in comparison with that of the person. To waste words on this point would mean to forget for what readers this work of mine is intended. I shall only allow myself to recall two remarks made above. One concerns (p. 287) the emphasis of the ethical significance of legal security for the development of character, the other (p. 343) the proof of the value of criminal law for the offender.

The *third* good which the State gives to its members consists in all those public arrangements and plans which it brings to life in the interest of society. There seems to be a certain amount of opposition in reference to these. What benefit does the peasant derive from universities, libraries, museums? And yet he must contribute his share, be it ever so small (p. 381). But if he charges these institutions to the scholar, the latter charges him with those devoted to *his* interests, and for which the scholar must pay his contribution. And then, how insignificant are these contributions, and how valuable they prove ultimately for the whole of society, and hence also for him! The agricultural chemistry of Liebig has done the most valuable services to agriculture. It originated in the laboratory of the University of Giessen supported at the expense of the State. In the observatory of the University of Goettingen, Gauss and Weber made the first experiments with the electromagnetic telegraph. The economic value of the telegraph, as developed today for trade and commerce, mocks all computation. Have these two institutions paid for themselves?

But enough! It needs not science to enlighten the thinking person of the measure in which he finds his benefit in the State; it is sufficient to open one's eyes to become aware of it. But it is demanding too much of the unthinking masses to expect them to do this. If you hear their complaints about the burdens and restrictions which the State imposes, you might believe that it is more a plague than a benefit. The advantages which it affords they take as a matter of course, — that is what the State is for! — or rather they are not conscious of benefits at all. The State is like the stomach, one speaks of it only to complain against it; it is felt only when it becomes a matter of discomfort. Every thing is nowadays brought near to the understanding of the people, — nature, history, art, technics; there is scarcely a subject about which the layman cannot inform himself from popular treatises. The State alone and the law, which touch him so nearly, form the exception, and yet it is only fair that not only the educated man but also the man of the people should have the opportunity to find out what they do for him and why they can not be essentially different from what they are. I thought formerly of filling this want by a legal catechism for the people intended for the citizen and the farmer. My aim was to reconcile the unbiased judgment with the legal arrangements at which it takes offence in so many ways; to make an apology for the law and the State before the forum of the simple and healthy common sense of man, after the model of Justus Moser. I am convinced that the task is beyond my powers. I hope some one else will take it up. He who will carry it out right will earn great credit from society, but he must think like a philosopher and speak like a peasant. It would be a worthy theme for the establishment of a prize. A hundred thousand marks would not be too high a premium; they would be repaid a hundred and a thousand fold. The work would be translated into all languages and would bring the world more blessing than entire libraries.

§ 15. *Solidarity of the Interests of Society and the Individual.* We have so far let the individual settle his accounts with society as if the two were strangers to each other, each going his own way and intent only upon his own advantage. But this conception does not correspond to the nature of their mutual relation, for the State is the individual himself — the dictum of

Louis XIV, "L'état c'est moi" is true of every member of a State — to settle his accounts with it is exactly the same thing as when the husbandman settles his account with his field: how much it cost him to cultivate it and how much it brings him in. To be sure, there is one difference, the field belongs to him alone, the State he has in common with all other citizens. And it is because of this difference that his imagination puts him into seeming opposition with the State instead of showing him that relation of unity and mutuality which in reality subsists between them. If the State were myself, the individual will reply, it would not have to compel me to do all that it requires of me, for I care for myself for the sake of my own interest, and do not have to be compelled.

When the child is forced by the teacher to learn, is it done for the sake of the child or the teacher? And yet the child must be compelled. Why? Because he is still a child. If he were grown up, he would do from his own impulse what he requires compulsion to do now. So the State compels you to do that which, if you had the true insight, you would do of your own accord. Imagine the State as non-existent, or in a condition of powerlessness at the time of a revolution, and you will realize what the State and the law mean for you. The times of upheaval, revolution, anarchy, are the school hours of history, in which she gives the nations a lesson on State and law. A year, perhaps a month, teaches the citizen more about the significance of law and State than his whole experience hitherto. The State and the law which he formerly reviled, he *now* invokes when he is in trouble. And the same man who laughed at us when we said to him, "*In the law you protect and assert yourself*, defend the law, for it is the condition of your being," — has suddenly understood us.

Upon the presence or absence of this insight is based the political maturity and immaturity of nations. The politically immature nation is the child, which thinks that it must learn for the sake of the teacher. The politically mature is the adult, who knows that he must learn for his own sake. The former regards the State as its opponent, the latter as its friend, confederate, protector; there the State meets with resistance, here it finds support; there the people help the criminal against the police, here they help the police against the criminal. What is meant by political education of a nation? Does it mean that the common man can talk politics? That shoemakers, tailors and glove-makers can lecture the skilled statesman? In my opinion political education of a nation means nothing else than the correct understanding of their own interests. But there are two kinds of interests, the proximate, which can be seized with the hands, so to speak, and the remote, which only the practised eye can see. And so there are two kinds of politics, a far-sighted and a near-sighted. The former alone deserves the name politics in the true sense of the word. True politics defined in a word is *far-sightedness*—the eye of the far-sighted, which extends far beyond the narrow circle of immediate interests, to which the glance of the short-sighted is confined. In this sense we can speak also of the politics of business life. It is that of the penetrating business man. The bad business man has sense only for the advantage near by, like the bad chess player who is happy when he takes off a pawn, and loses the game thereby. The good business man sacrifices his pawn and wins the game. To express ourselves in more abstract terms,—the characteristics of bad business politics consists in its attention to the particular act and the passing moment, of good business politics in its attention to the whole and the future.

This is also true of social politics in its application to State, law and society. Linguistically politics is characterized as the sight of the πολιτικός, *i. e.*, of the man whose wit has been sharpened by life in a community (πόλις), in comparison with the peasant whose horizon is limited by his vocation to himself and the narrow circle of his immediate interests. The former knows that his own success is conditioned by the success of the whole and that he advances his own interests along with the general; the latter believes he can exist by himself. The demands which the community makes upon him are regarded by him as sacrifices which he must offer to the purposes of others. The former considers the community as his own affair, the latter as that of others.

This is the light in which the ancient Roman regarded the State. What belongs to the State belongs also to him. They are the "res publicæ," which he has in common with all others, in contradistinction to the "res privatæ," which he has for himself alone. The officials of the State are *his* officials. For his private affairs he chooses a representative, for his public affairs, the official. Of both he requires an account of their management of the business entrusted to them. The law is his own work. As he disposes of his private interests through the "lex privata," so he disposes of his public interests through the "lex publica." Both stand upon the same line in his mind; the one represents an agreement with an individual, the other, with the community.[119] For this reason he regards himself also as the guardian of the law; and as he enters the lists in behalf of his private interests by means of the "actio privata," so he defends the common interests by means of the "actio popularis"

[119] "*Communis* reipublicæ *sponsio*," as *Papinian* expresses himself in 1. 3. 1 — a tradition from the time of the Republic, which had for his time only the significance of a historical reminiscence.

(p. 349). The solidarity, or rather the identity, of the interests of the community and of the individual could not have been more clearly expressed than is done in the Roman law by means of the last named action. The plaintiff guards his own interest at the same time with the interest of the nation.

If we compare with this picture which ancient Rome presents to our mind, and to which our own national past offers a refreshing counterpart in the history of the Hanse towns, the dreary conception of the State which modern absolutism and the police State has produced among the nations of modern Europe, the complete estrangement, nay, opposition in the relations of the individual to the State, we are astonished at the almost incredible difference which one and the same relation can exhibit. We shall have to suffer from its effects for a long time to come. The theory of private law has not yet overcome these effects by any means. A remnant of them has been preserved to this day, according to my opinion, in the theory of juristic persons. The Roman knew that just as the State is nothing else than its citizens, so the "gens," the "municipium," the "colonia" are nothing else than the "gentiles," "municipes," "coloni." Our modern science has placed the juristic person in place of the particular members for which alone the former exists (the beneficiaries as I call them), or the subjects for the sake of whom the juristic person is constituted, as if this imaginary person, which cannot enjoy or feel anything, existed for itself.[120] If what I said above is true, that the State is I, I make the same assertion about the juristic person.

But if that statement is true, why should it be necessary to exert force against me? Is not my interest alone

[120] See, against this formalistic conception, my "Geist des R. R.," IV, pp. 216–220, 311–344.

ordinarily sufficient to guide me in the right path? Why compulsion, if society requires nothing of me except what my own interest involves?

For two reasons. The first reason is, *deficient knowledge.* Not every one has the insight to know that the common interest is at the same time his own. To perceive an advantage which concerns himself exclusively, the eye of the most near-sighted is sufficient, it is the politics of narrow egoism. Thinking of himself only, he sacrifices others to save himself; determined by the moment alone, he waits until the danger which he could and should have met in the proper time when it started, knocks at his door and seizes him by the throat.

Law may be defined as the union of the intelligent and far-sighted against the near-sighted.[121] The former must force the latter to that which their own interest prompts. Not for their own sake, to make them happy against their will, but in the interest of the whole. Law is the indispensable weapon of intelligence in its struggle with stupidity.

But supposing even that the understanding of the solidarity of the common interest with one's own were fully alive in every individual, and the consequences involved in the former were objectively so free from doubt that no difference of opinion could at all arise regarding them, this would not yet in any way make the law superfluous. And here we touch on the second reason which makes social coercion necessary. The imperfect knowledge of the individual is not the only reason that makes law necessary; the second reason is the bad or weak will, which sacrifices the more remote common interest for the sake of his own more proximate interest. This leads me again to a point which I had frequent occasion to

[121] So *Papinian* in his definition of law in 1. 3. 1, "Lex est commune præceptum, *virorum prudentium* consultum."

touch upon in various connections (pp. 163, 220, 344), *viz.*, the difference between the *particular* and the *common* interest which is in the essence of the social relation. It is found again in civil society,[122] and therein lies the *weakness* as well as the *strength* of law. *Weakness*, in so far as the particular interest (I understand by this every motive in which the agent has himself only in mind, not merely, therefore, interest in the ordinary sense, *i. e.*, desire for gain, but also hatred, desire of revenge, etc.) tempts the individual to assert his own ego at the expense of society. *Strength*, inasmuch as the common interest combines all other individuals in a defensive union against him, and opposes to the interest which he has in *injustice* the interest which they have in *justice;* to the power which he commands for the purpose of *attack*, the power which they command for the purpose of *defence* (p. 219).

When we said that the person who violates the law desires *himself* at the expense of society, it did not mean that he desires *himself only*, but as was brought out above (p. 344), he desires *himself* and *society;* and just herein lies the morally objectionable character of violation of law. It is not simple egoism which wants to

[122] This opposition Rousseau also emphasizes in his "Contrat Social," I, ch. 7, to which my attention was called after the passages of my book quoted before had already been printed. "En effet," he says, "chaque individu peut, comme homme, avoir une volonté particulière contraire ou dissemblable à la volonté générale qu'il a comme citoyen; son intérêt particulier peut lui parler tout autrement que l'intérêt commun; son existence absolue, et naturellement indépendante, peut lui faire envisager ce qu'il doit à la cause commune comme une contribution gratuite, dont la perte sera moins nuisible aux autres, que le paiement n'en est onéreux pour lui; et regardant la personne morale qui constitue l'état comme un être de raison, parce que ce n'est pas un homme, il jouirait des droits du citoyen sans vouloir remplir les devoirs du sujet; injustice dont le progrès causerait la ruine du corps politique."

exist for itself only and not for others; it is egoism raised to the highest power, which profits by the advantages and blessings of society for *itself*, but refuses the moderate price which the latter demands in turn. If all acted like the egoist, his account would not square, nay, he would come to be convinced that his own interest peremptorily demands co-operation for the common purpose. His thought therefore is not, "The common purposes are indifferent to me," but, "I leave their realization, with which I can no more dispense than any one else, to others, and pursue my own interests only. Let *them* bother with it, I for my part care only for myself." If he were given the alternative, "either your own ego or society," his choice would not be doubtful.

But modern society does not present this alternative before him, it does not deprive him of the blessings of the law because he himself disregards it. It is only in the lowest stages of the development of law that we meet with the opposite mode of treatment in case of a heavy offence (expulsion of the offender from society: Roman "societas," German outlawry and proscription,—a remnant of these regulations of primitive times in later Rome is voluntary exile in case of imminent condemnation). In scientific discussions this alternative is made use of by the individualistic theory of law and the Law of Nature, to base upon it the criminal law of society.[123] The deduction is as follows: If you free yourself

[123] So by *J. G. Fichte* in his "Grundlage des Naturrechts nach Prinzipien der Wissenschaftslehre" (Jena and Leipzig, 1796). "The least injury to property destroys the entire property contract, and it justifies the offended in taking away everything from the offender if he can" (Vol. II, p. 7). He who violates the civil contract in any respect, whether deliberately or thoughtlessly where the contract counted on his thoughtfulness, loses thereby, strictly speaking, all his rights as a citizen and as a man and becomes an outlaw completely" (p. 95). In place of outlawry comes the "expiation con-

from us, we free ourselves from you. You have lost the protection of the law because you have disregarded it; you are deprived of all right, hence any punishment we inflict upon you is justified. The consequence of this would be that the smallest opposition to the police, nay, even a violation of the civil law, might be punished with death or confiscation of one's whole property. That society does not do this is merely a kindness on its part.

The result with which the discussion closes is *the social indispensability of coercion.*

But however indispensable it may be, it is also at the same time *insufficient.* If it should attain its purpose completely, there would have to be no crimes. This gives us the point of transition to the next chapter. What keeps a man from committing an injustice where he knows that he will not be found out and need not therefore fear compulsion? The answer to this will be found in the next chapter. The two egoistic levers of which society makes use to make the individual serviceable to its purposes, are not the only ones. There is still another, which appeals not to the lower egoism, but to something higher in man — *morality.*

tract" (p. 98), the thief must make amends, or if too poor, by labor. So long as he has not done it, "he ceases to be a citizen, as is the case in all penalties" (p. 112). "With exclusion is connected *ipso facto* confiscation of the entire property" (p. 130). I know of no work in all literature in which the folly of consistency in following up an erroneous fundamental idea rises to such dizzy heights as in this one.

APPENDICES

APPENDIX I

RUDOLF VON IHERING[1]

BY ADOLPH MERKEL[2]

The man and his works! How much alike! He who would describe the work must characterize the man; and to explain the personality is to interpret the accomplishment. Ihering's literary effort represents the progressive unfoldment of his nature in the domain of theoretical pursuits.

Ihering's personality was of a kind so original and energetic that in whatever field of endeavor he entered, he immediately made a distinct impression on its thought and reached its central position, with a sympathetic, and if need be, antagonistic understanding. Rare warmth of disposition, sociability, a candid and upright nature, unenvious recognition of the merits of others, a quick sympathy for the misfortune of strangers, and especially a lively interest in the welfare of his friends, gained for Ihering many attachments. A man of great conversational talent, eloquent, rich in humor, buoyant of spirit, with a talent for initiative in a hundred different directions, of an impulsive nature, impartial in the estimate of his own work, sensitive to opposition, and unreserved in the expression of his convictions, he achieved enemies. One is struck by the combination in Ihering of a prudence of life and a certain naïveness of

[1] [The text translated is a reprint from *Ihering's* "Jahrbücher für Dogmatik des heutigen Römischer und Deutschen Privatrechts," Bd. xxxii, N. F. xx (Jena, Gustav Fischer, 1893).

It was translated by *Albert Kocourek*, Lecturer on Jurisprudence in Northwestern University, and member of the Editorial Committee.]

[2] [Late Professor of Law at the University of Strassburg. To Professor *Merkel* the first edition was dedicated by the author.]

expression of thought, and the conjunction of a matter-of-fact judgment upon men and things, with an imaginative and enthusiastic tendency of mind, concerning the practical and practicable. He possessed a joyous nature such as is not found often among those of conspicuous learning. While his life is closed, yet as a sanguine spirit he richly experienced the alternation of heaven-high exultation and the depths of despair, though with far more joy than unhappiness in his career. Happiness poured from a hundred springs, and yet did not suffice.

He was a modern through and through, with the most finished sense of the realities of life, but wanting in contemplative inclinations, and an enemy of the twilight and the Romantic in poetry and action. A mighty passion for intellectual domination of the objects within the province of his thought surged within him. This found expression in a two-fold aspect: on one hand, in a struggle for unconditional precision of ideas, and the greatest completeness of what is utilizable, clear, and essential; and on the other hand, in a rapid elevation of thought to a far-reaching outlook. No matter, though, to what height he arose, the concrete actualities of earth were always clearly within his range of vision. He might be likened to the eagle which, perched upon the cliff, surveys at a glance, all that crawls or moves below. Moreover, the view from aloft did not lessen his sympathies. The things that engaged him were not apprehended alone by the intellect, but were grappled by all the faculties of his mind. His whole personality moved as a unit, and he identified himself with his problems.

All these characteristics are mirrored in the literary style of his scientific works, and give them their attraction and meaning. Ihering's effectiveness, in large measure, is the product of his style. The same fact has contributed chiefly to his fame beyond the borders of Germany, and gained him an enthusiastic following in foreign countries. It is interesting in this connection to compare him with Savigny. From the standpoint of literary expression no other German jurist can be considered in the class of these two men. Both had the gift of crystal clearness of statement, but in other respects what a difference! Savigny's writing has the quality of aristocratic coldness and repose, balance of coloring, aloofness, and personal withdrawal behind the shadows of his work. His canvas seemed to lie far from his soul. As Ihering has remarked, the subject does not express itself with Savigny through the material, but the matter itself takes hold of the form of thought.

Ihering's style, on the contrary, possesses a lively coloring, is frequently oratorical and exuberant; the author does not conceal himself with his thoughts; he projects himself in living form in every line; and he seeks not only to clarify his subject, but also to carry his reader with him by storm. He coins apt phrases and winged words to serve as carriers for his ideas. His exposition is marked by profusion and breadth; he would illuminate his thesis to the point of triviality and leave nothing in doubt. A major device which he employs is to resort to things plain to the senses. Ihering was a master in combining the abstract and the self-evident. His so-called "natural historical method" is founded throughout on this plan of combining diverse ideas; although, perhaps, Ihering may at times have considered this method as having another and higher function. By all means, this combination of general and special ideas accounts for the abundance of his striking and frequently witty comparisons. In this regard, and in yet another, Ihering suggests a German philosopher who in the basic trends of his system is farthest removed from him — Schopenhauer, who in the sphere of philosophy, in the same way that Ihering in the domain of jurisprudence, is distinctive for his clearness of literary expression, wealth of sprightly comparisons, and constant association of the abstract with the concrete in thought. There is also to be remarked a common tendency in both to battle against the dominion of idea as opposed to reality.

It hardly needs to be said, in speaking of these qualities of Ihering's writing that they are based on eminent scholarship. If Ihering as a "Docent" did not attain the position of a Vangerow, the chief reason lay in that his temperament prevented a superior, magisterial bearing necessary for great success, and made laborious for him a satisfactory treatment of student-like miscellanies for the purpose of a balanced, comprehensive, reliable, and understandable notebook of the materials in hand. This temperamental defect naturally did not apply to the practical courses where Ihering was in his proper element. To the present writer, the lectures of Ihering were far more interesting than those of Vangerow. After I had heard Ihering, Vangerow's discourse was a closed book.

Ihering was an inspired jurist in his reading of the "Corpus Juris." He was fascinated by the juristic world into which he entered, a world of intellectual materials, in which "the motive power of ideas" appeared to be a reality, and he was attracted by the mental powers and independence of the rulers and masters of this world. Jurisprudence appeared to him a science in which, notwithstanding its practical purpose, speculative talent had free scope, and in which this talent best served its practical objects, in that it was subject to its own laws. In the third volume of the "Geist," and in the treatise with which he introduced the

"Jahrbücher," he exhaustively characterized and glorified the speculative problems here set forth. The operative sphere for this speculative mission is that which Ihering calls the higher or productive jurisprudence as opposed to the lower or merely receptive jurisprudence. Within its domain the juristic skill of the Roman jurist is to be emulated. However much the position of practical and professional jurists in the development of law differs from that of Labeo and Julian, yet Ihering appears to have made possible, in large degree, the prosecution of a productive effort in jurisprudence, even to the present day. The content of ideas which the positive law involves goes beyond it to make all necessities conformable to the conditions of the present time. The point is that the positive law is to be more completely developed and extended, but not in slavish dependence on the Roman jurists at the point where their labors ended.

Construction was for Ihering the chief form of this productive labor, and the "Jahrbücher" were especially designed for this purpose. For him, a revival of constructive jurisprudence together with a restoration of the sources of the law led the way to a new epoch in the science of law, advanced by Savigny's treatise on possession.

Ihering's positive contributions from the standpoint of constructive jurisprudence are in the main unassailable. But it is clear that the elaboration of his ideas brought out his fiercely contested and much derided logical cult. He was the unmistakable high-priest of this doctrine. His exposition is biased, and the conditions under which the constructive operation promises real results and the limits which mark out an unprofitable Scholasticism are not made clear — at least not in the treatment of the "Jahrbücher."

However, if we examine the long series of dogmatic labors which followed Ihering's statement of his program, we shall fail to encounter any over-valuation of the logical element, or any over-extension of its limits. Surveying the range of these efforts, no difference is to be encountered in them as between the youth and maturity of Ihering, apart from more general points of view. From the beginning he possessed a lively sense of the nature of the relations of life and their commerce, and the way in which legal rules operate on them. Even there, where his investigations did not directly serve practical trends, as perhaps in the treatment of the reflex action of laws, and in his discussion of the passive effect of laws, one does not find a mere juggling of concepts. He found occasion here to deal with a group of phenomena of legal life which, while interesting enough, had previously escaped attention. His purpose was to show their practical bearings, to unify them under a single point of observation, and to disclose in them at the same time the terminal point of civil protection of private legal interests (not however "conceptionally necessary" interests but actual interests conforming to relative ends). This exposition was designed to combine a series of related (although in previous juristic thought, wholly unconnected) phenomena and to reduce their distinctive qualities to a common and simple characteristic; that is to say, the state of perpetual legal constraint of persons and things alongside of a temporary absence of a person entitled. As to the rest, so far as the present writer can see, the conceptual process never extends in the dogmatic labors of Ihering, beyond the point where an obvious, practical interest may be found. In fact, the objective factor is, after a fashion, directively present even in Ihering's earlier works (for example, that concerning the limits of ownership of land), which, in his later works, is established as the leading principle of juristic thought. Not infrequently practical cases were encountered which appeared to offer a conflict between the traditionally accepted view and the necessities of legal life, which gave occasion to these labors. Thus his exposition of the doctrine of "caveat emptor." Participation in decisions, in the rendering of opinions, in the discussion of cases in juristic associations, and his practical experience, influenced to a very large extent the trend of his dogmatic studies, and exerted at the same time a profound and even revolutionary power over his more general, scientific views. Among these influences, mention must not be omitted of the happily composed legal instances to which Ihering gave a general value. Especially characteristic is his "Law in Daily Life"[3] which brought to juristic notice the trivialities of the day with their manifold complications.

Ihering with a preference for theories yields not to conceptual but to casuistic proof. The results achieved by casuistic reasoning concerning the interests involved in a legal proposition furnish the chief measure of legal judgment, even as against the "lex lata"; for he will not admit its conflict with purpose without cogent ground. He therefore delights to start with these interests, and examines to find whether the protective mantle of the law is adequate to safeguard them. If defects appear in the armor of legal protection, according to the prevailing theories, then these theories for him are not to be trusted. He thinks that prejudices have intervened between law and necessity, and that this evil is attributable not to the Roman jurist but to the narrow point of view of the modern jurist. He therefore searches through the intellectual domain of Roman jurisprudence for the materials to supply the deficiencies of modern

[3] ["Jurisprudenz des Täglichen Lebens," translated, with notes, from the 8th (9th and 10th) edition of the German under the text title, by *Henry Goudy*, Oxford, 1904.]

law, and to combat the hindering obstacles of traditional dogmatic thinking. As a rule he finds what he is looking for. Many of the legal propositions of the Roman jurists, however, attain only a fragmentary expression, or are stated only within the limits of the legal transactions, and in response to the practical occasions of the day, and are not founded on any system of legal thought. Ihering here exerts his whole energy to make way for a more universal application of Roman legal principles conformable to the necessities of the present time. Examples in his labors of this effort of reconcilement are his studies of "culpa in contrahendo," the extension of the law of obligations to things of special value ("affektionsinteresse"), and civil protection against injuries to reputation. In all these discussions, it would be of no little interest to compare Ihering's method with that of Windscheid, but that must be left to others.

The dogmatist Ihering does not change character even in his contributions to the doctrine of possession. The only difference is that in these writings there is also found the characteristic method expressing his scientific views which first attained an unlimited validity for him in his sharp controversial attitude against Savigny and others. The method of operation assimilates the corresponding theory with Ihering, and dogmatic inquiry becomes a process of demonstration for the theory.

Whether the views of the author as to what is expedient and his notion of legal justice did not unduly influence, in these labors, the interpretative function, is a question which Romanists may decide. But possible defects of this kind do not detract from the stirring interest of his works or their legitimate influence on legal thought. Nor can it be denied that these writings actually contain something of the productive jurisprudence postulated by Ihering, and also serve practical interests.

Yet, as to productive jurisprudence, much remains to be said, if this were the place to say it. It may, however, be stated with due reserve, that this jurisprudence has brought to light a certain amount of difficulty in dealing with the legal life of the present day,[4] and that this awkwardness, as it seems to the present writer, is coextensive with a defect in its method.

Ihering's original overvaluation of the logical element in jurisprudence later harmonized with his desire of freedom from the spiritual letter of the law, in which attitude the purely positive standpoint had its influence. This highly characteristic position, however, found expression in another and more important manner. Two ways lead to this end — to freedom from the burdensome difficulty of the material content of law, or rather, to intellectual domination of this content. These were the dogmatic and the genetic methods: logical treatment and concentration on one hand; and, on the other, exposition of the intellectual process by which the positive law arises, is maintained, and develops, and in which likewise the test of its interpretation is to be found. Without doubt the latter method is the more difficult and important, and Ihering applied himself to it in its connection with Roman law in his earlier years with

[4] The unwilling attitude which our jurists schooled in the Civil law have always maintained with reference to an extension of liability for injuries to third persons in the domain of culpable acts, in the face of obvious necessities and a present legal sense of the desirability of such extension, is an example of this. We have not made a possession of the legal generalizations of the Roman system, which, with respect to civil liability, has, like our criminal law, scarcely (and illogically) made application of the legal consequences of intentional and negligent legal injuries. Productive jurisprudence in *Ihering's* view of its meanings coincides with the mission of a positivistic legal philosophy in that its content of ideas as to legal principles is to be reduced to the simplest possible term with the most complete range of application.

incomparable ability. Ihering's desire to master the law in the sense noted, corresponded to our national desire for legal independence growing out of the fact of reception of Roman law. This law had made itself a part of the intellectual organism of the German people; it was an authoritative and invisible force, and an unassailable factor of our practical philosophy. But this philosophy was, and is, a foreign element in national life, so long and to the extent that it is not critically examined as to its sources and made conformable to the conditions of our own economic, political, and cultural life. Ihering was an instrument of the existing national impulse for independence, and his greatest work, the "Geist des Römischen Rechts" was destined to serve this tendency. Its purpose was a full understanding of Roman law and the history of its development; in order to derive from it its standards of legal measurement, and to create the possibility of future national legislation, by a method of selection and exclusion, revision and adjustment, the connection of the new with the old, and the forging of a conformable law agreeable to the requirements of the present day and our national genius. "Through Roman law and beyond Roman law" was the motto for this side of his activity. That such was the task which he set for himself, and that he achieved actual results in this direction — upon this chiefly rests his title to fame.

Savigny laid down the program of an evolutionary history of law. But the historical labors of his school (apart from Puchta's "Institutes") did not yield results showing an appreciably intimate relation to this platform. Without dwelling on their antiquarian character, these labors were principally directed to the service of legal dogmatic, and not to the explanation of the psychic side of law, and its development in connection with cultural life. Ihering undertook the work which the Historical

School only proposed; but what he brought forth quickly showed him numerous contradictions of its thesis.

The historical view of law found its origin in the age of Romanticism, and took form in the war against the ideas of revolutionary times. This relation was outgrown with Ihering, and the Romantic vestment was cast aside. This explains his anomalous position with reference to universalism in law. The contrast of the revolutionary period against cosmopolitanism led the Historical School to an exclusive accentuation of the national element in the law. Law, for this school, is an integral part of a specific national culture, as was the case among the Greeks and in ancient Rome (unlike modern peoples) where custom and law had a distinct national character. Ihering sought in his "Spirit" and elsewhere to show how, in what form, and by what means the Roman law developed out of national character in the period of classical jurisprudence, beyond the range of mere national disposition, and became a cultural element fit to have a universal position in the modern world among other national elements of like character. Were it otherwise, then with the re-invigoration of our national life, our purpose could be only to eliminate this foreign law, root and branch, as speedily as possible; an object which was farthest from the thought of the Historical School. In other respects touching the national origin of law, the Historical School contented itself with attributing it to a "Volksgeist" or the consciousness of the people. Ihering, on the contrary, sought to discover the intellectual forces which constituted this "Volksgeist," and to explain in detail their part in the development of law. He further opposed the notion of this school of an unconscious creation and growth of law arising out of the mysterious bosom of the spirit of the people. His contention is (and his view is correct), that in the formation of distinctive legal institutions, there is operative, from the very beginning, a conscious activity of will; and there is present a reflective participation of the understanding. His history of ancient Roman law aims to furnish the proof of this position; and in this connection he arrives at a different estimate of legislative effort from the Historical School. With Leist and others, he asserts the eminent importance of legislation in the self-assertion of law, against the narrowness of view of this school in its emphasis upon customary law. This Roman history affords him tangible proofs for his standpoint. Altogether, the evolutionary concept has a different complexion with Ihering than with Savigny. This central thought of modern science has a conservative reception with Savigny and those of his school. They make prominent always the stability of history, and the dependence on one hand of the present on the past, and on the other, of individuals on objective forces. Ihering, however, in harmony with general, modern science, gives this idea a progressive coloring. Yet, as already indicated, he represents the opposition against the intellectual self-independence of positive law.

Ihering's exposition of the self-assertiveness of Roman law in relation to other cultural elements, that is to say, the distinctive forms in which it distinguishes itself from them and develops and manifests itself as a special domain, is a lasting contribution. The same may be said of his explanation of the working methods of Roman jurisprudence, and the ethical and intellectual qualities which show themselves in these methods and predestined the Roman people for this system. Ihering is right in accepting that the prodigious marvel of Roman jurisprudence is not to be explained by mere reference to a logical virtuosity of its jurists; and that there are to be considered pre-eminently, as conditions of this labor, the singular practical tendencies and talents of the Roman mind, and definite underlying qualities of character, rather than bare logical skill. Pertinent in this connection is what Ihering says concerning the disciplined egoism of the Romans, their impulse toward power and freedom, and the importance of these factors for the self-independence of their law. Indeed, the specific function of law lies in the delimitation of the sphere of might and freedom. The working-out of this function in its distinctive qualities is essentially favored by the energy of colliding interests whose proper spheres of power are to be marked out against each other. Among a people with an overbalanced spirit of passivity or altruism, the development of the characteristic quality of law, as it was in Rome, would be unthinkable; the generative force of law would be lacking.

Ihering had the intention from the beginning of contributing a "natural science of law" through an exposition of the evolutionary course of Roman law; in other words, to present a philosophy of law. His assumption of a coincidence of mission of legal philosophy and history was well founded. Condensed evolutionary history is philosophy. The mind which should be able to make a complete survey of the evolutionary history of mankind, and render a unified, concentrated, and precise statement of this history, would belong to the greatest of philosophers. What such a mind could teach us, would, in any given age, exceed the whole of general knowledge.

Ihering's work, however, affords a contribution in this direction, and future legal philosophy will have to draw on him. His discussion of his subject repeatedly lays off almost entirely its historical garments. Particular parts of his work will admit of simple incorporation in a system of legal philosophy. Thus, the excursus in the last volume of his "Geist," concerning the notion of rights.

Complete harmony between these writings and a philosophy of law, of course, is not to be expected. Ihering's views on philosophy of law underwent numerous changes. Apart from this fact, there is apparent, in many of his elaborations, a certain amount of incongruity due to the animated manner in which he seized the matters in hand in an effort to bring out a brilliant illumination of a point under consideration. Judgments, which in themselves are compatible, thereby end sometimes in contradictory explanations. Ihering's strength did not lie in a calm understanding and contemplation of the results of his labor, permitting a harmonious, proportionate, and complete view of things. Accordingly, the revision of the first edition of the "Geist" here and there mitigated these incongruities (as in the valuation of the logical element in law), but did not conceal them. It may be said in general, that as to all the chief problems of general jurisprudence, Ihering's work will admit of pointing out such defects; for example, his notion of rights.

In the second volume of the "Geist," in his consideration of ancient Roman law, and under its influence, Ihering states that legal relations are in their essence relations of dominion or power; that the view that power and dominion are the sole starting points of the whole of private law is the correct one; and that the essence of jurisprudence lies in this, that it abstracts everything which does not react upon these two elements. In the fourth volume of the "Geist," on the contrary, rights are defined as interests protected by the State; the standpoint of power substitutes for conformable purpose; and the will theory is expressly overthrown. In two different volumes of the same work, different aspects of rights are treated in a superior manner, but in neither case is the fundamental notion thoroughly examined. It is clear that the point of view of power does not provide a satisfactory basis for the apportionment and delimitation of rights; that it cannot give the reason for their extension or restriction and an exhaustive explanation of their change; and that it cannot therefore be the "εἷς καὶ πᾶν" of jurisprudence. On the other hand, it is also certain that interests cannot be the substance of rights, if these rights are derived from the law. The law does not provide men with interests, but endows them with certain powers applicable to these interests. This would seem to be the correct notion, giving the proper position to both the idea of interest and of power, without running into difficulty. But Ihering's solicitude in making logically accurate definitions was always less than his effort to bring out fully the elements of legal relations.[5]

This duality of viewpoint in Ihering is also maintained in his position toward law. In his "Kampf ums Recht" the power idea has a new and vigorous representation while the "Zweck im Recht" turns entirely on the idea of purpose.

The personality of Ihering speaks out most distinctly in these two works. In the "Kampf" we see his force of character, his militant side, his strong sense of legality, and the whole dynamic energy of the man; in the "Zweck" his earlier intellectual side is portrayed. One like Ihering does not rest until his theoretical views attain the full expression of his distinctive character. The significance of his theories depends on the human side most prominently asserting itself, and their immediate operation depends on the relation which the personal element bears to opposing principles and problems for

[5] Cf. in this connection, *Ihering's* "Scherz und Ernst," p. 360.

the time being affecting it. How this comes about in Ihering's final theories will be shown.

In the "Kampf ums Recht," as already suggested, Ihering expressed in a manner fitting his personality the element of force in law. In an admirable work of earlier origin, "Das Schuldmoment im Römischen Privatrecht," he already touched on the questions raised in the "Kampf," but he glossed them as a historian. He sketched the progressive separation of the penal element from the domain of the civil administration of justice, and he correctly saw in this a species of the process of differentiation which underlay Roman law and which exhibited an essential aspect of its onward development. He soon observed, however, that with the retreat of penal law, certain related phenomena appeared, which have multiplied and extended in the modern world, and show a debilitated energy of legal will in the defence of law and rights. He was conscious of the contradiction which this evolutionary process offered against his whole intellectual attitude. This contradiction is brought out in his "Kampf ums Recht" in sharply vehement language, and the immense success of this writing proved that he did not stand alone in his views. It evoked a widely disseminated influence, which became apparent in a variety of endeavors, and particularly in the field of criminal law. Our modern legal life gives evidence of much sickly and pale cast of thought, against which the influence of this work reacts. Our law had lost some of its courage, and this was especially true of private law. Since the social question has come to the fore, doubt has arisen as to the universal justice of the law, and this question, taken in connection with the inspired social movement of the age, will prevent a reversion of legal attitude in the sense intended by Ihering in his "Kampf" notwithstanding its wide influence.

That essay, for the rest, has to do with the validation of rights and represents the thesis, that an energetic defence against wrong is a duty. This part of the work might be called a homily on the Kantian text, "Do not let your rights be trodden under foot without resentment." But this sermon contains a legal philosophical core, and in its essence is unassailable.[6]

Ihering based his theory of duty in the maintenance of one's rights, firstly, on the connection between rights and personality; and secondly, on the solidarity of law and rights. The relation of rights to personality is admirably stated. In truth, our rights involve a parcel of our social worth, our honor. Whoever violates our rights, attacks our worth, our honor.

If rights had not been accepted as isolated interests, as appears in the fourth volume of the "Geist," Ihering would not have hit upon personality, and it would not have been possible for him to take the position that the assertion of a right is moral self-assertion. Ihering's theory regarding the struggle for rights has been assailed frequently, but if certain exaggerations in the form of statement are laid aside, there is only one standpoint from which it may be attacked consistently. This is the Christian point of view, in so far as it requires that when our coat is taken away we shall also surrender to the taker our cloak. Ihering's ethics, an ethics of assertion of life and will, does not harmonize with this demand; but it does express the spirit which has created the law, and lives in it. The energy with which rights

[6] The present writer has already developed the legal philosophical ideas of this work, in part, in various works. But although *Ihering* may have been familiar with the latest of these writings, it is certain that they did not have the slightest influence on him. Ihering had to find his way always by his own efforts. He therefore consistently carried behind his own flag his own equipment; the same, unfortunately, cannot be said of all authors.

maintain themselves against wrongs belongs to the same system of assertiveness in life as that by which law defends itself against wrong. The same human interests are involved in both cases. This brings us to the second proposition: the solidarity of law and rights.

That this solidarity ever could have been misunderstood is curious. Nevertheless, a right detached from law, through which it gains expression, and derives its life and being, is unthinkable. The idea that there may be a penal violation of a right which does not come in contact with law is absurd, and an essential distinction between pure (penal) civil wrongs and criminal wrongs is therefore impossible. For this reason the functions of civil protection in a certain degree coincide with those of criminal protection, as Ihering correctly understood.

What this same work says regarding the force element in law and the struggle in which the law is formed, changed, and asserted, is beyond attack.

Of greater importance in relation to Ihering's final system of thought than the "Kampf ums Recht," is his "Zweck im Recht." This work grew out of the labor on the "Geist" and is its culminating point. Here, the child slew its mother. In his development of the theory of rights, the thought of the dependence of legal rules on social purposes seized him with such power, and brought about such a change in his general views, that it now appeared to him to be the chief problem of his life to give this idea adequate treatment in an independent work. He thought that he had found the principle from which all legal establishments take their origin, and by reference to which they may be understood. He found the position of that natural science of law, which, from the beginning, had been in his mind as the object of his labors. Instantly, there arose a program of treatment, and it extended to colossal proportions. Extending beyond the limits of a mere legal philosophy, it widened out as a project of a phenomenology of the whole ethical and social world. This work was to demonstrate this entire domain as the creation of human purpose, and this creation itself, and its products, were to be set before the eyes of the reader in the unified system of social life.

Ihering distinguishes the objects resting on egoistic self-assertion (that is to say physical, economic, and legal objects) of the individual from those based on social self-assertion. The latter correspond to ethical objects of individual self-assertion. This logical classification is adopted by Ihering as the plan of a doctrine of evolution. He seeks to show how "one object is connected with another, the higher to the lower; and not simply connected, but the one derived from the other as a consequence of itself by the force of necessity." In the beginning, there is egoism. This is "the mother, from which everything issues, fructified by the force" of historically determined conditions. Serving itself, individual egoism transforms into social ends, and produces the material for the legal structure. This is the organization of social power controlled by the State for these objects, that is to say, for security of the social conditions of life. The ethical spirit, which is characterized by the identity of individual ends with objects of the community, makes its entrance then into this legal structure for the purpose of setting up therein its dominion. That which is conformable to law, and what is ethical, therefore, are not contrary to what conforms to purpose. They simply designate "the deepest and most permanent stratum of a matured expediency of ends in the social organization." Furthermore, they are not an original endowment, not a "lex innata," but the product of an adjustment to definite social conditions. There is therefore no absolute ethics, any more than a system of absolute ends. Every evolutionary stage of society has its own objects, and accordingly its own fortune, and its own standards of ethics; and on each page turned over by the history of humanity, there appears always the word "verte." The ends achieved admit of new purposes; the ethics attained changes to a new ethical creed.

The ethical and legal philosophy of Ihering with which we have to deal is that of social utilitarianism. This utilitarianism does not imply scepticism, or a destructive attitude toward the ethical law. The theoretical utilitarian is a practical idealist, and Ihering intends that his elucidation of ethical sources shall not diminish the power of ethics but elevate it.

This work did not gain the reception which Ihering had hoped; especially not among professional specialists who failed to see in it either a juristic or a philosophical contribution. This attitude of the specialists, led by Windscheid, caused Ihering to give up the further development of this program, and to apply himself to labors of more direct interest to jurists.

It would be a mistake, however, to suppose that the "Zweck im Recht" was without influence in the juristic world. Its relation to the general content of modern thinking is too great to admit that belief. Unfortunately, this is true not only of its merits, but also of its defects. The influence of the demerits of the work is easily recognized in present-day juristic literature. Modern naturalism has also made its entrance in this field and found a support in the "Zweck im Recht." This work has lent to naturalism the purpose idea, but employed in such a manner as to utilize not the strength of Ihering's thesis but its weakness.[7]

[7] The present writer's "Festschrift" for *Ihering* entitled "Vergeltungsidee und Zweckgedanke" deals with this point.

The hostile judgment of the juristic critic was not deeply thought out. There was neither a recognition of the importance of this work of Ihering's, nor was an accurate account given of its deficiencies. Thus one reviewer could only see in this labor "a loose construction of a clever idea" (*Nation*), while, on the contrary, it exhibits a wonderful unity and cohesion in its arrangement of thought. Again, the question has been put, "Where and when will all the things come to pass that Ihering writes about?" and the answer is given, that they have an existence only in Ihering's mind (Dahn). It might be replied, from Ihering's point of view, that these things have happened everywhere that law and ethics have been developed. His work was intended as a compendium of the history of evolution, a summary, giving the typical examples of its complete statement. Such a program does not admit of essential criticism. National dissimilarity in laws does not alter the proposition, since this diversity does not exclude a common element. Certain identical functions are universally essential to law, because in these functions similar necessities and similar mental powers are brought to expression. These agencies have everywhere been determinative in the creation of the legal world, and it is Ihering's purpose to make conspicuous their creative reality. Another question is presented, whether his delineation is universally applicable, and, in general, whether this work is suited to provide an insight into this creative history. More favorable judgment has been rendered here on the philosophical side than on the juristic. The elegant and distinguished philosopher, Eucken, has aptly remarked that the important problem essayed by Ihering entered a new phase in this work.[8] According to him, a new series of ideas is constructed, new groups of facts are

[8] *Allgemeine Zeitung*, 1883, Nos. 362–3.

brought forward, and the questions involved receive a new and more sharply defined form. He promotes a recognition of the importance of the essential value of the work and praises its execution.

Comparing Ihering's performance with other utilitarian systems, we find as its chief characteristic the accentuation of the notion of society and social purpose, in agreement with certain fundamental trends of modern science, and the energetic reduction of legal and ethical problems to this basis. This social utilitarianism is far superior to the purely individualistic utilitarianism of Bentham who was not able to explain ethical motives as against egoistic impulses, or ethical norms as such. Again, Ihering's central thought of social utilitarianism had never before the "Zweck" received such a powerful statement, and at the same time, such a comprehensive representation founded on the materials adduced. Ihering's work has been contrasted with Spencer's and rated above it. Whether the "Data of Ethics" was prior to Ihering's work I do not know, but the dominant thought of social utilitarianism was not treated by Spencer with the definition and clearness of Ihering's work. There is apparent in Spencer's system a certain amount of indetermination, and, as a result, a defect of treatment such as cannot be charged against Ihering: in this, that the opposition between moral conduct of individuals (or to use the language of Ihering, their ethical self-assertion) and their egoistic conduct is not fully appraised. In other respects both writers exhibit a frequent harmony of view.[9]

At this day, this social utilitarianism has become a mighty force in the domain of science, to which every

[9] *Cf.* "Data of Ethics," Secs. 4–6, 63. There is a difference between them, of course, with reference to the question of the proper scope of State activity.

discussion turns, which would be more than a mere working-over of details. It derived from Ihering a support not to be despised. That Ihering was a man with only an imperfect philosophical training does not alter the fact that it was a man of such sense of reality who has given us an inspired account of this system as the product of his experiences and labors.

A general estimate of Ihering's philosophical position would be out of place here, but some additional observations are necessary with respect to special phases of his system in order that my valuation of his performances may not be without critical value. Anyway, my object is not to praise, but to characterize.

A thought touches the relation of individual personality to society in Ihering's system. According to him, human beings enter the world and begin their lives as pure egoists. From this foundation he derives a legally organized society which generates an ethical personality. Ethical personality is a later birth which takes possession of the legal system as a completed construction. The world of law cannot, however, be conceived without ethical support, and it has nowhere been found without the co-operation of ethical forces. We thrive here in a circle. Ihering, the historian, has more correctly apprehended the matter than Ihering, the dogmatist. In this connection, as well as in many others, it is possible to oppose his "Zweck" with his "Geist" (I, 118 seq., 263 seq.; II, 61–4th edition). Social impulses are not the products, but the conditions of society; they are not implanted in individuals in a disciplinary world of legality from without, but have developed in the individual parallel with social organization, due to the reciprocal influence between the individual and his surroundings.[10] Ihering

[10] This point was developed in detail in my "Vergeltunsidee und Zweckgedanke."

also does not make any explanation of the initiative of individuals in the domain of ethics. And yet the inquiry of the ancient systems of ethics returns. A new ethos has not been brought into the world within our reckoning of time by society and its organs, but by a Christ.

Another thought relates to the position of the purpose idea in Ihering. His notion in general is that of conscious purposes, and the social objects to which he attaches the law are regarded as the associated ends of individuals. It frequently appears that the ideas of purpose entertained at the beginning evolve, and at the end do not reach adequate expression, or perhaps are not realized at all. They set in motion forces which, under the interplay of new agencies, bring about results which may be far from the original purpose. Again, institutions generated by definite ideas of purpose may in the course of time alter, and later be maintained by an entirely different connection of thought than that which favored their existence. Naturally, all this was not unknown to Ihering; but the method by which purpose officiates in his view as an explanatory principle, conceals the evolutionary historical meaning of the matter and is a source of a great deal of misunderstanding.[11] Further a variety of institutions find their justification in the forum of history — and one thinks here of slavery — not in the purpose which evoked them, but in their importance for an advancing development of cultural life. Ihering here resorts to "objective purpose." This objective purpose raises a number of questions which do not find an exhaustive answer, and which in serious application would lead to modifications of his system.[12]

[11] See *Wundt*, "Ethik," pp. 98, 103, 131.

[12] An approach toward certain systems combated by *Ihering* would be unavoidable. The concept of society (the sum of individuals) would be different. Teleological speculation, to which the

Further comment in this direction may be omitted, to give way only to the most fundamental philosophical and juristic objections urged against Ihering's theory of purpose. These objections may be found in theories which regard the development of law and morals with Leibnitz as the "progressive disclosure and clarification of what from the beginning has lain dormant as an eternal law in the unconscious mentality of individuals"; an emergence, as it were, of a finished, harmonious, and valid system of concepts and principles in the consciousness of the race. In the domain of legal science, criticism is based on various forms of our juristic Scholasticism. The *a priori* method of philosophy, and Scholasticism in legal science, are internally related, and may be contested from the same point of view. Indeed, our Scholasticism, juristic logicality, or "jurisprudence of concepts," has its own sources. These sources are found in the technical problems of jurisprudence as Ihering has ably described them, and again in the inclinations of a concept-building reason which overvalues its progeny, its concepts, and regards them as entities of independent worth having their own existence and a predestined fruitfulness. It is therefore an ineradicable accompaniment of our dogmatic system; it is like a smoke which rises above and conceals its fire. If one would seek, however, for a philosophical foundation of this jurisprudence of concepts, resort would be had to theories such as indicated; for it assumes a stationary, *a priori*, and incontestable world of ideas, in which the governing

idea of objective purpose belongs, irresistibly compels the impression that it is not the nature of individuals with which it deals, but the race; that is to say, society in an entirely different sense than that which regards it as the totality of its parts for the time being. This alteration in the notion of society, however, would involve an advance towards idealism.

plumb-line for the regulation of a real world is to be found. Only on this premise can this world have any meaning for the logicians where at one time the protection of definite interests is inconceivable, and at another their injury is conceptually necessary; again, where at one time they deduce distinctions and limitations from ideas, and at another turn when they seek concepts which properly belong to definite words and names. This philosophy and this Scholasticism are scientifically shattered by the evidence that law in its essence, and not by way of exception, here or there, but always and everywhere, has an alogical nature. Ihering produced this proof in his "Zweck" by making prominent the reality factors in law. Yet, his proof requires an addition. This is furnished by a consideration of the compromise character of law, and the dependence of this compromise on changing forces which mock at any derivation credited to concepts, and do not admit of adequate expression in a system of concepts.[13]

Ihering's opposition to the concept system grew on him, and in the latter part of his life he attacked this cultus with all the vehemence of his nature. In his "Scherz und Ernst" he covered it with the biting acid of derision. Ihering erroneously supposes it peculiar to this system

[13] The "Zweck im Recht" does not deal with the compromise character of law. *Ihering* proceeds generally on the basis of a harmony of the normal interests of individuals which, as assumed, does not exist. According to him, the coincident purposes of individuals create social purpose which generates law. The postulate of a quiescent, logically unified system of concepts which constantly and symmetrically embraces the world of practical interests, would be consistent with this interpretation. In the "Kampf ums Recht," on the contrary, *Ihering* develops a position which shows the compromise nature of law. See my "Recht und Macht" in *Schmoller's* "Jahrbuch für Gesetzgebung, Verwaltung, und Volkswirtschaft," v. 1 seq.; *v. Holtzendorff's* "Enzyklopädie der Rechtswissenschaft," 5th ed., p. 16 seq.; and cf. my "Juristische Enzyklopädie," Sec. 40.

to deal with Romanistic literature, while in fact it makes its home in all departments of legal science. The formal trend in law — and it is here in question, — flourishes as well in criminal law and public law as among the Romanists. Ihering, therefore, is wrong in attributing it to Savigny and Puchta. They seem to him to be the leaders of the Muses who direct the dance from the heights. He is not disinclined to relegate them and the majority of their followers to a conceptual heaven, or rather, a conceptual pit.

Laying aside the extravagances of the work last mentioned, the later works of Ihering, as against his earlier labors, exhibit in a form more and more sharply defined that which will be permanent in him; namely, the realistic aspect of legal thinking applied to the ends of practical life and governed by the forces which set these objects in motion and create the institutions of society.

If a further comparison with Savigny may be permitted, I would say that Savigny's historical position was a more favorable one than Ihering's. Savigny's labors are the central point of a new experience in the world of Romanism in the first half of his century, and had an application in all directions; while the same fortunate situation did not befall the investigations of Ihering. Again, Ihering's work has a universal relation to the great problem of the mental sciences — mankind, an understanding of its conditions, and the laws of its own conduct. The value of his work in dealing with this problem is for the future to determine.

APPENDIX II

FINALITY IN THE LAW [1]

By L. Tanon [2]

Sec. 1. *Ihering's law as a means to an end.* The celebrated jurist and historian, Ihering, deserves a special place with reference to the Historical School. He not only renewed the attack on the views of Savigny and his leading disciples, amplifying criticism of this school with the rich colors of his imagination and style; but he constructed upon ideas of his own, and after a different interpretation of the evolution and facts of history, a complete system of Philosophy of Law. In this system, he sets up, over against the too idealistic concept of unconscious development of the juridical order proceeding from the hidden forces residing in the character of the people, a theory not less exclusive,— absolute finality, and a development of law always conscious of objective ends which it is called upon to realize.[3]

[1] The text translated is pp. 44–81 of "L'Évolution du Droit et la Conscience Sociale" (part second), third revised and enlarged edition, in "Bibliothèque de Philosophie Contemporaine," Paris (Félix Alcan, 1911).

The translation is by *Albert Kocourek*, Lecturer on Jurisprudence in Northwestern University, and member of the Editorial Committee.

[2] President of the Court of Cassation of France.

[3] *Ihering* is especially known in France on account of his "Geist des Römischen Rechts auf den verschiedenen Stufen seiner Entwickelung," translated into French as, "L'Esprit du droit romain," 2d ed., Paris, 1880; his "Kampf ums Recht," translated as "Le Combat pour le Droit," Paris, 1875; and his miscellaneous writings published by his faithful and learned translator, M. *de Meulenaere*, under the title, "Etudes Complémentaires de L'Esprit du Droit Romain." See particularly, in the last work," Du Rôle de la Volonté

Ihering asserts at the beginning of this work the principle of finality, which he applies, in this volume, to the law, and in the second volume,[4] to morals. This inversion of the natural order of treatment, in a system which assigns one and the same principle to morals and law, has introduced some confusion in his book, numerous repetitions, and certain contradictions. This results from the method adopted by the author in composing this work, and in pursuing his subject progressively in the course of publication.

The object is the governing principle of the law; there is no rule of law which does not owe its origin to a practical motive, to an end. A double law governs the sensible world: the law of causality for inanimate beings;

dans la Possession," A. Maresq, 1896. The first volume of *Ihering's* "Der Zweck im Recht," Leipzig, 1877–1883, 2 vols., (2d ed., 1884–1886), has been translated under the misleading title, "L'Évolution dans le Droit," A. Maresq, 1901. This work at once became famous. It was briefly reviewed by M. *Durkheim* (*Revue Philosophique*, 2 sem., 1897), and afterwards by M. *Aguilèra* in his book, "L'Idée du Droit en Allemagne depuis Kant jusqu'à nos Jours," Paris (F. Alcan), 1893, p. 220 seq. It has also been the subject of an interesting analysis by M. *Bouglé* in a study on "Les Sciences Sociales en Allemagne," Paris (F. Alcan), 1896. See, among the critical studies of this work in Germany, the book of *Felix Dahn*, "Die Vernunft im Recht, Grundlagen der Rechtsphilosophie," Berlin, 1879, which contains, as the title indicates, the personal view of the author on the Philosophy of Law. [See also the able account of Professor *Munroe Smith* of Columbia University in *Political Science Quarterly*, xii, 21, — *Tr.*]. M. *de Meulenaere* has also translated one of *Ihering's* posthumous works, "Vorgeschichte der Indoeuropäer," under the title, "Les Indo-Européens avant L'Histoire," Paris, 1895. He also translated another posthumous work which is only the beginning of a "Histoire de L'Évolution du Droit Romain" ("Entwickelungsgeschichte des Römischen Rechts—Einleitung und Verfassung des Römischen Hauses," Leipzig, 1894), which *Ihering* had engaged to write for a project of Binding's, and of which he composed only the introduction and some chapters relative to the Roman household.

[4] [Not translated in this series.]

the law of finality for animate creatures. Nothing happens in the world without a cause. An impulse of will without cause is as inconceivable as a movement of matter without cause. The only difference is, that cause is mechanical in the material world, while in will it is psychological. For the will, the cause is final — it is the end.

The most general end of law is a guaranty of the conditions of social life by the coercive power of the State. These conditions may be divided into three classes: extra-juridical, mixed, and juridical. Extra-juridical conditions are those which impose on man the natural surroundings in which he lives; the law has no power over these conditions; it operates only on man and his efforts. Mixed conditions concern the maintenance and conservation of society, and its normal development, by the organization of labor, commerce, and industry; the law ought only exceptionally to come to the assistance of the natural activities which minister to these various objects. Juridical conditions are those whose guaranty society assigns exclusively to the law.

When it is said that the law guarantees the conditions of social life, it is not by that to be understood that it ought to regulate them so as to apply to all of them without distinction the sanctions which it provides. The law relates only to juridical conditions. This concept of purpose in the law and its adaptation to the conditions of life, taken in its wide generality, leaves little open for criticism, and is perhaps accepted by all those who seek to establish the juridical order on a positive basis. But it has received in the second volume of this work (devoted more especially to morals), and in later writings of the author, enlargements which demand extended reservations. These reservations principally apply to the philosophical generalizations of the author touching the generative forces of morals and law, and regarding external causality. In this external causality Ihering, at the last, thinks that he has found a complete explanation of the creative impulses of law and morals, and from it he derives the evolution of the whole of social life. It seems that the bearings of Ihering's doctrine were not always well understood by him, and one is able to point out in the elaboration which he makes in the progress of his work a considerable number of variations. The position of the author, manifestly, has had a course of development, and has been subject to modification and transformation since his "Spirit of Roman Law," and up to the time of his last work. The progressive advance of his thought may already be noted in the two volumes of which the present work is a part, published six years apart, and, later, in a more marked fashion in the writings which followed. Whilst he distinguishes clearly in the first volume (the present work) between material and ideal conditions of life, and appears to recognize in human nature a duality consisting of egoistic instincts and moral and disinterested motives, yet in the second volume he lays stress throughout upon the egoistic forces, from which he derives all others. In his later writings he emphasizes sovereign action in evolution, the material conditions of life, and external causality from which, in the last analysis, he deduces all the elements of social life.

M. Neukamp in his "Introduction à L'Histoire de L'Évolution du Droit," thinks that in this connection he has discovered an inconsistency in the last work of Ihering on the evolution of Roman law. He observes that in different passages of this work, the author seems now to admit a double causality, internal and external, and then to hold to external causality alone. In a beginning passage, Ihering recognizes two kinds of efficient causes in the creation of law: first, internal impulses, the character of the people, their habits of feeling and thinking, their degree of culture in a given age; and second, external impulses proceeding from the economic, political, and social conditions of the same people in the same age. In other places, on the contrary, he asserts that the object of the science of law is to replace, everywhere, the point of view of internal spontaneity by external causality; and, as the special purpose of his book, he destroys the prevalent theory in the history of law, according to which, evolution moves from within outwardly, by substituting the contrary idea of an external force of the world exercised on the law.

This contradiction is not simply apparent. Ihering fully recognizes in history the existence of two kinds of phenomena, internal and external, which appear to exercise, concurrently, an influence upon the law, in the course of its evolution. But, for him, that is only a matter of appearance; it is not the substance of the thing. Internal phenomena, such as the character of the people, their habits of thinking and feeling, which he still regarded in his "Spirit of Roman Law" as established facts, as an ultimate principle of explanation, resolve themselves purely and simply by a final analysis, into external phenomena from which they spring. A part of his other book, the "Indo-Européens avant L'Histoire," wherein he discusses the Aryans, their migration, and the Babylonian civilization, is devoted to the illustration of this thesis. We are not able here to enter on a detailed examination of the effort to reconstruct an ante-historical past, or the bold hypotheses upon which he relies. In that book one may read the ingenious and brilliant disclosures in which the author has ferreted out the entire Babylonian civilization from a habitat, the soil, the proximity of the sea, and the manufacture of brick and the building of ships.

That work shows the same ultra-positivistic tendencies of Ihering which one remarks in the second volume of the present work, with its determination of motives of human conduct, and the final unity to which he restores them all. He finds this unity in mere egoism. One may believe, if he restricts himself to the present volume, that Ihering admits, alongside of egoism, another sentiment equally natural and coexistent with it — the feeling of disinterestedness, detachment from the self, or under its most usual modern name, altruism. But we see, in the second volume, that there this is not Ihering's real thought. Egoism is proclaimed as the sole primitive and natural sentiment, and it is from this feeling that social life has derived all the others, different in appearance, but yet rigorously connected. Hard and bare in the man of nature, transformed in civilized man, purified and especially elevated in the social body, it remains always egoism, fundamental, and primitive.

Ihering develops this idea in all its forms and with a character more and more absolute in his later writings. Nature has implanted egoism in the heart of man; history alone has drawn from him the moral sense and the feeling of justice. The egoist is the product of nature; the man of morals is the product of society. Morals is only egoism in its highest form; it is a repetition of the same thought raised to a higher degree of development. According to a formula which he delights to repeat, it is not the sentiment of justice which has created the law, but the law has created the feeling of justice. The law, like everything in the moral world, is a pure creation of man "in which nature has not had the smallest part."

Merkel, in apt terms, pointed out Ihering's error on this point, in his philosophical introduction to the science of law in Holtzendorff's "Enzyklopädie." An improved utilitarianism such as he finds in Ihering, John Stuart

Mill, Leslie Stephen, and others, does not grant the value to man which belongs to him; and denies to him any part in the origin of the moral sentiments which are found in him in all stages of his development. We have within us instincts and inclinations which find their root in the nature of man and the peculiar organization of the individual. The mind of a child is not a blank page upon which any content may be inscribed, and to which nothing is added. Man is a product of society only in the sense that an oak is the product of the soil where it takes root, and which, coming from an oak, is only able to grow into an oak. There are ethical forces which are coexistent with egoistic inclinations, in human nature; and both develop in varying degrees under the influence of social conditions. Goodness of heart is not a consequence of social influence in any different sense than hardness of heart. The notion that man comes into the world an absolute egoist, and that society causes to spring up, as by enchantment, from his egoism, all the moral forces of which he has need to attain his social ends, is as arbitrary as that which makes of the individual, marching in the ranks of society, an automaton susceptible of being changed in any degree whatsoever at the will of social interests.

To show the untenable character of such beliefs, it suffices to consider maternal love, which on one hand is an essential element of ethical humanity, and which there discovers itself as one of the forces of nature; and which, on the other hand, equally shows that it is in a high degree a power in the animal kingdom. The instincts corresponding to our moral feelings are, in general, represented in various ways in the animal world, where, nevertheless, they cannot be regarded as an artificial product of education, or explained finally by the experience of the individual with reference to his well-being. Now, it is impossible to accept without proof the assertion of a dogmatism which closes its eyes to the facts, that the organization of human nature in this regard is less favorable than that of animals, and that what in the one arises by natural inclination develops in the other only artificially. Man is sociable by nature; he is not such solely by virtue of social institutions. His experiences rest, from the beginning of life, at once upon egoistic instincts, and upon different forces which contribute to the formation of a definite, ethical ideal, and which are not solely the echo of a social imperative.

In the third edition, recently pubished, of the same "Enzyklopädie," the new editor, Kohler, estimates Ihering's concepts on this position, in the same way. They are, says he, contradicted by the elementary facts of history. We find altruistic sentiments in man, no matter how far we go back into the past. The love of children and hospitality are more ancient than the institution of property. The author likewise affirms that social instincts, doubtless more elementary, have nevertheless a large part in the origin of societies, and that it is only later that the egoism of the individual takes on its full extension. Ihering's interpretation of the historical facts regarding moral institutions is a perversion of the truth.[5]

Ribot, in his very acute work, "Psychologie des Sentiments," in like manner rejects the theory which makes altruism a simple product of a transformed egoism. He shows that the altruistic instinct is itself natural and primitive; that it is the same of moral feeling which is derived from it; that this sentiment

[5] *R. von Holtzendorff*, "Enzyklopädie der Rechtswissenschaft"; *Merkel*, 5th ed., p. 87; and *Kohler*, 6th ed., 1902, p. 13. See, on utilitarian morals, *Guyau*, "La Moral Anglaise Contemporaine"; and *Fouillée*, "L' Idée Moderne du Droit"; also the important work of *Wundt*, "Ethics," 3d ed., 1903, vol. I, p. 484, and vol. II, p. 9 seq.

does not in its origin spring from an idea, from a judgment; that basically it belongs not to the intellectual but the motor order, movement or arrest of movement, instinctive tendency to act or not to act. It is, in this sense, innate; and, in a word, is not fashioned according to an assumed, invariable archetype, illuminating everything and always from which the moral ideas, themselves innate and completely formed, arise; but is of the same nature as hunger and thirst and other fundamental feelings. M. Ribot, like Merkel, gives as the strongest proof of the innateness of altruistic feelings, the affection, the attachment which is found also in the animal world, and which cannot be attributed to calculation and interested prevision, and which appears to establish the original character of these forces without question.[6]

Ihering, again, at another point of view pushes his theory to extreme consequences in his perversion of absolute finality, which, for him, shows in all the periods of social life, even the most primitive, a conscious process in morals and law. He is in disagreement here with adversaries, also, of the Historical School, who generally recognize the unconscious growth of law in its earliest customary period. The same is true with reference to the philosophers most occupied with the methods of positive science.

M. Ribot, whose work we have cited, remarks that it is necessary to distinguish two distinct periods in moral development. The first is instinctive, spontaneous, and unconscious; it is determined by the conditions of existence of the group expressed by customs, and a diversity of beliefs and acts, moral, immoral, amorous, trifling. The second period is conscious and reflective

[6] *Ribot*, "La Psychologie des Sentiments," pp. 234, 286, Paris, (F. Alcan.)

in the multiple aspects as well as the superior forms of social life, and expresses itself in institutions, written laws, civil and religious codes, and chiefly in the abstract speculations of moralists and philosophers. The learned builders of moral systems have usually disdained the first period; but this is a mistake, because it is the source.[7]

Conscious finality, whatever may be its proper scope, and although its importance increases progressively with the periods of advancing civilization, is not sufficient to give a complete explanation of social life, and of all the rules of morals and law. This criticism of Ihering on two points, of which the first is of great importance for morals, but of much less interest for the law, ought not to obstruct our appreciation of all the value of this work in which this great jurist points out, better than had ever before been done, the true objective purpose of the law. Kohler, in this connection, does not render to Ihering the justice which is due. He does not properly limit his criticism to his theory of moral sentiments. He estimates with great severity, and, in our view, with much injustice, this whole effort, which Ihering valued well above his "Esprit du Droit Romain," and which constituted in Ihering's opinion the ultimate expression of his scientific elaboration of the law.[8] Kohler does not recognize any other philosophy of law

[7] Eod. op. p. 284.

[8] *Cf.* in the preface of the translation of M. *de Meulenaere*, extracts from letters written by *Ihering* April 3, 1883, "This work, and not the 'Esprit du Droit Romain,' sums up the results of my entire scientific labor. This will not be understood until this work is completed; [the preface to the first edition of the second volume is dated, Aug. 22, 1883]. In my judgment the 'Esprit du Droit Romain' is only a preparatory work; but it was necessary to write the 'Esprit' to be able to engage in this study, the elaboration of which achieves my highest scientific aspiration."

than that of Hegel, and condemns any system unprovided with a metaphysical basis.[9] We cannot undertake here a discussion of the philosophy of Hegel, which is on the whole justly abandoned, even in Germany, by contemporary thought.[10] Kohler's reproach of Ihering, that he has not fortified his system with metaphysics, proceeds upon a view which we are not able to share, as to the value of a transcendental principle of law in the domain of science. No doubt it is allowable to moralists and philosopher-jurists who desire to introduce a certain unity into their concepts of the world and of life, to connect their theories with some elevated metaphysical principle. But, at that moment, they leave the highway of observation and science; and they are not able to find in such a principle any tangible help in working out the concrete rules of morals and law.

Sec. 2. *Finalistic and utilitarian theories and their opposition.* If, besides following Ihering on this point, the current utilitarian theories exaggerate the rôle of conscious finality in primitive periods of the development of morals and law, a new school, by a contrary theory, is straining itself in these latter years to banish this notion entirely from these two domains. The utilitarian and teleological systems have not been combated long except in the name of idealism. Their supporters were regarded as the representatives of science against

[9] *Kohler*, loc. cit.: "When one descends from the elevation of the philosophy of Hegel to the system of a Krause, an Ahrens, or a Röder, it is like passing from a magnificent palace to the small cottage of a commoner; and when one arrives at Ihering, the impression is that of descending to a room filled with poor people. Ihering's whole work is built upon the sand, it has no philosophical foundation and its metaphysics is much like that of a Frisian shepherd. The picture is not overdrawn; it is diminished rather, and outlined."

[10] [This statement will require re-writing in the next edition of this work. — *Tr.*]

philosophical speculation, of the facts given by experience against abstract reason.

Latterly a new school has risen in opposition, under the name of science itself. The desire to exclude finality from sociology, morals, and law appears under a scientific impulse. But the discussions which have been raised on this subject exhibit a certain amount of confusion. After having with reason rejected finality in the natural sciences, and justly criticised the abuse which has been made of teleological explanations of natural phenomena, nevertheless finality should not be excluded from its proper sphere, where it manifests itself by irresistible evidence — that of voluntary and conscious human acts. Yet this is what some writers, and even including sociologists and moralists, appear to do. These writers desire to proscribe finality in all departments of science. They attack all the finalist concepts with such vigor that one would say that they desire to exclude even voluntary and conscious human action as indifferent, idle, and lacking all value.

There is here an equivocation which it is necessary to dissipate. It arises from a distinction, correct in the main, which these authors make between science and art, but which must not be unduly extended when treating the moral and political sciences. Science, it is said, is knowledge of what is; art is knowledge of what ought to be. The science of morals investigates the reality of morals and customs in the present and in the past. This reality ought itself to be studied in constructing abstractions of any finality. This entirely scientific inquiry has for its object the discovery of the laws which govern the social world. It will be a long and difficult study. It will give, nevertheless, when it shall be fully developed, some laws which will permit the anticipation of social phenomena: it will in a certain measure provide man with the most suitable means of securely realizing his ends; and, therefore, will substitute for an empirical method a rational art based on the simple facts of experience. But these results, however imperfect they may be, will not be attained except in a very remote future which we are not yet able to foretell.[11]

This distinction is applied to the law. The science of law is knowledge of what is, or has been, in other words the whole of juridical reality, made up of customary law and legislation, of the present and in the past. Legislation, which is improperly called a science, is only an art. Only the discovery of the laws of the social world will provide the means to pursue and attain its true objects and will give it the fixed bases which it now lacks.

These writers, however, do not explain what should be the method of proceeding in the discovery of these supposed laws, so necessary to know, and yet so remote and difficult of establishment. They appear to be almost wholly indifferent to the matter. Life will develop its course empirically, and we may say as it is able. The simple statement of this thesis discloses its extravagance. This assimilation between supposed social laws which are yet to be discovered, for the greater part, and of the rest of which none is admitted without dispute, and natural laws, is evidence of an exaggerated scientific

[11] See, especially, *Lévy-Brühl*, "La Morale et la Science des Mœurs," (F. Alcan, 1903). In this able essay which contains a learned and profound analysis of empirical moral reality, the author maintains that there can be no science of morals, but only a science of customs, and a rational moral art, which does not yet exist, and which this science alone will be able to discover, independently of all social purposes and ideas. This proposition has already, often and sufficiently, been refuted. See *Fouillée*, "Eléments Sociologiques de la Morale" (F. Alcan, 1903), p. 254 seq.; *Ch. Belot*, "Etudes de Morale Positive," p. 112 seq. (F. Alcan); and quite recently, *E. Faguet*, "La Démission de la Morale," Paris, 1910, p. 115 seq.

optimism which misconceives the nature of things, and confuses two distinct worlds — the sciences properly so called, and the political and moral sciences. We find here a legacy of the philosophy of Comte, which regarded knowledge of these laws as highly advanced upon the mere appearance of his philosophical system, and which believed that it saw in this system a valuable instrument ready to forecast the course of social phenomena. We know that this hope of Comte has been shattered.

Whatever social laws we may be able to discover will always be marked by a character of contingency much greater than in the case of other scientific laws, such as the laws of the natural sciences, regardless of the degree of our learning. This results from the infinite complexity of the elements which the investigator must take into account, and which he is only able to encompass in their entirety, under great difficulty, with any degree of assurance. It is not without a certain abuse of language, that learned sociologists speak so glibly of true sociological laws, with such imperfect means of their establishment; when in the sciences properly so called, we find that experimental laws better sustained carry certain hypothetical qualifications. But even though knowledge of what is shall be established in sociology, morals, and law, which is the most important object of scientific investigation, still it will be improper to maintain in these departments of learning, a separation so absolute between science and art.

A large part of social reality is composed of voluntary and conscious human acts, and it is not possible even in the bare study of this reality to exclude all consideration of finality. It is, no doubt, dangerous and erroneous to attribute to institutions the purposes which we conceive for them and the objects which they serve today, in discovering the causes of their original establishment. But it is not less useful and indispensable for our complete understanding of this reality to know, in addition to the actual objects of institutions, the motives which gave them birth.

To diminish the practical value of all finalistic concepts, it is objected that the object sought in individual or social acts is frequently imperfect, and that the choice and selection of the means of action are much more important for conduct than the end to be attained. Experience incontestably proves that an end pursued is often defective, and that acts carried out for a definite purpose and with a view of a certain effect, may produce an entirely different, and even contrary, result. But though, by force of the complexity of our acts, and the reactions which they exercise the one upon the other, and also because of the infirmity of human foresight, our acts never attain the purposes at which they aim, it does not follow that better results would be accomplished by purposeless action. Otherwise, the most incoherent life would be the most reasonable. The best means for obtaining an individual or social existence with the greatest possible coherence, is to have a clear view of its ends. Change from an unconscious to a conscious stage in society is one of the certain characteristics of evolution and progress.

Another fact well recognized is opposed against finalism. It is that of institutions established for a certain purpose, serving afterwards other objects which are substituted for the first. This is what is called the heterogeneity or metamorphosis of ends. This substitution of objects proves nothing against finalism. It simply demonstrates the extreme plasticity of human institutions. It shows that man is always strongly influenced by tradition, and that he is thus brought to adapt his old institutions to new ends in place of inventing others. This phenomenon explains and justifies itself all the more by this, that such an adaptation which, perhaps, may not be more imperfect than a newly created institution, has nevertheless the advantage of disturbing in the least possible manner continuity with the past, and renders unnecessary a general readjustment of settled conditions, which the invention of a new institution requires. It has been observed that frequently the best method of introducing and perpetuating a reform is to adapt it, as far as possible, to the conditions already established, by allowing to remain all that may be preserved of the older situation. Old institutions, therefore, may be maintained alongside of new purposes, but on condition that they adapt themselves in a more or less complete fashion to these objects. If this adaptation is impossible, or if its ends have failed, then the institution falls; it becomes a mere survival, and finally disappears.

Another objection from a more general and fundamental standpoint has been leveled against finalism, especially in recent years. It is asserted, that in reality, ends do not determine even our conscious and voluntary acts; that the end projected is only a sort of epiphenomenon which is not able to exert the slightest influence on the natural course of things.[12] No doubt it is true that the immediate objects of our acts are not their primary causes, and that these acts are determined by a complex series of phenomena of which a large part escapes our observation, and the succession of which is lost to our view. But, even though these objects, proceeding through an infinite series of antecedent

[12] See *Le Dantec* ("Le Conflit," Paris, 1901; and "Les Influences Ancestrales," Paris, 1905) who drives this theory to extreme consequences.

phenomena, generators of a given act, lose themselves in an hypothetical, universal, mechanical process of which our understanding doubtless only attains an imperfect notion, their consideration is not in less degree of capital importance for practical matters, since they are incontestably the most proximate conditions of our acts. To say that these pretended epiphenomena, because they accompany necessarily conscious and voluntary acts, do not have any influence upon the course of things, and that everything would happen in the same manner as if they did not exist, appears to us as nonsense, even from the standpoint of universal determinism.

Finality cannot be ignored in the study of social phenomena. These phenomena may always be studied under the two different aspects of finality and causality. These two principles are not mutually exclusive—one presupposes the other. Application of finality is not possible except on condition of the validity and simultaneous application of causality.[13] Yet Ihering's confusion must be avoided, of classifying physical cause and purpose, which he calls the psychological cause, as of the same order. Representation of purpose does not necessitate action in the same way that a natural cause requires a certain effect. The act may not be performed; it may perhaps be stayed. If executed, the act may not accomplish the object projected, or it may result in a different end. Finally, many different acts may be imagined which are effective to realize the same end. If these contingencies make the teleological method less secure than the causal approach, yet they do not deprive it of its utility. The nature of the phenomena to be studied and the sciences or arts under investigation will determine the employment of the one or the other of these methods, according as their application will be

[13] *Wundt*, "Logik"; "der Zweck," p. 642 seq.

more or less difficult, or more or less effective, for solving the practical problems of social life.

Finality manifests itself especially and with irresistible force in the law. There is no law, important or unimportant, whether it concerns the fundamental organization of the State, the interests of the general community, or dispositions supporting the most trifling advantages, which has not been inspired by a purpose, or which is not justified by an end. Any judgment which may be supported regarding it, its expediency, its validity, or its character as harmful or inopportune, is, above all, a teleological judgment. That which is discussed in the deliberations preceding its promulgation, is the effect which it will produce.

It is not otherwise in the political sphere. All parties invoke public welfare as the most general object of their activity. This, at any rate, is the mark with which they cover and conceal even their most self-interested intentions. All political régimes, whether monarchical, oligarchical, or democratic, and all systems of government, may invoke other principles, but they lay stress in the highest degree, for justification of their acts, upon their objects and the benefits which they diffuse among individuals and the community. Political eloquence itself is more and more throwing over abstract principles, fine language, and verbal idols. It still employs these devices, no doubt, like a military standard, to lead the multitude and to arouse popular passion. In reality, however, it is ends and concrete objects which are the material of discussion and of which account is taken for the purpose of obtaining enlightened judgment upon all those things which should be the subject of thoughtful deliberation.

Sec. 3. *Latent Finality.* The several systems which appear to base law upon religious, mataphysical, or ideological and *a priori* foundations do not, however exclude all finality. Finality is not entirely inconsistent with theological principles. As it is impossible to connect all rules of law with commandments claiming an origin in divine authority, consideration may be taken, without contradiction of the theories of these systems, of concrete ends of life, for the purpose of establishing the varied and complex residuum of juridical prescriptions. Purpose here is not simply secondary; it is necessary always that these prescriptions should be in accord with revealed truth, or what is regarded as such. In a word, the law, in this regard, is dependent on theology. This dependence may be much or little, according to the theological views of the writer in question; it exists none the less of necessity, and it is precisely on this point that the essential character is seen which distinguishes these systems from all others.

Finality is capable of harmonizing, and quite easily too, with the social contract theories. The theories of Hobbes and Rousseau show this in a somewhat inexact and incomplete fashion. It is frequently said that in the system of Hobbes, the just and the unjust are arbitrarily determined by the absolute sovereign. This statement is true only with reference to the relation of the sovereign and his subjects. But in the view of Hobbes, the just in itself, as it is understood by the philosopher, and even by the sovereign lawgiver himself, is that which conforms to the general good, and injustice is the contrary. The exposition of the general will of the people ("volonté générale") by Rousseau, gives rise to similar confusion. Finality is not excluded; it is simply presented in an indirect form. General will, in this theory, has the same significance as that which Hobbes attributes to the absolute sovereign: his commands are infallible and must be obeyed. But the general will is always good and always right, because it is not able to desire other than the common welfare. This necessary conformity of general will with what Rousseau calls "common welfare" best explains and reconciles the obscure passage, standing in apparent contradiction, in which he defines general will.

The purely rationalistic systems, which appear to exclude all finality with the greatest rigor, are not able to any extent to render account either of the content of law or of its true origin. When, by rare chance, the writers of these systems lower their abstract speculations to the level of practical concerns, they are not able to explain even the most elementary juridical rules except by unfounded hypotheses, or forced deductions, entirely arbitrary, and under a logical appearance; and when they give good explanations, it is by a process of unconscious teleological reasoning, more or less artfully disguised. The proof of this is often found in Kant in the application of his standpoint to the simplest juridical rules; as, for example, the rule against breach of a bailment relation. This subject has had renewed investigation and been largely developed in its connection with morals by Sidgwick ("Method of Ethics"), in his critical inquiry into the different forms of intuitional morals.

Latent finality, either more or less openly displayed, is implicated in all the theories which propose any other basis whatever for the juridical order; and they are not able, in their practical applications, to escape the objective consideration of purpose. Admissions of this finality are frequently found among those authors themselves who have recently combated most vigorously in morals all finalist concepts in the name of science. It is thus, that Lévy-Brühl speaks ("Science des Mœurs," p. 17) concerning the reasonable application of existing things for *the essential welfare of all;* of turning social conditions to the best account *for the best and happiest life* (p. 165); and yet more decisively in an article in the *Revue Philosophique, of the exception made* "of ends which are universal and instinctive, so much so, that without them, there could be no question either of moral reality, of a science of this reality, or of applications of this science." He speaks, lastly, *of the object conceived for reconciling* "the coexistence of individuals and societies, in order that each may live, and live in the largest sense." [14] But everything accords with these universal ends, so indispensable, it is said, to the science of morals, which necessarily decomposes them into a series of particular ends consistent with the same object.

The historical realism of Marx and his school, which is today energetically battered in the breach, is itself completely colored with finality. It would make a new society, of which it predicts the coming, from the necessary evolution of the economic order, and due alone to the irresistible operation of natural forces. It has long since been shown that this theory does not, in reality, exclude the idea of finality; and that it is thoroughly penetrated by teleological notions in its postulate of a new society, and yet more, in the measures pointed out to hasten its approach. Appeal to a conflict of classes does not have any meaning, if human purposes have no influence upon evolution. Stammler, in a notable work dealing with economics and law, was one of the first to perceive this fact.[15] This author has clearly shown, as Croce has called to mind, how finality is always

[14] *Revue Philosophique,* July, 1906, p. 14.

[15] *R. Stammler,* "Wirtschaft und Recht nach der Materialistischen Geschichtsauffassung." Leipzig, 1896.

assumed by historical materialism in all its affirmations of a practical nature.[16]

Stammler does not limit his investigation, however, to discovery of the relations of political economy and law. He has sketched in this first study, and elaborated in a second work dealing with the theory of justice, a system of philosophy of law which, emanating from a jurist so esteemed and so learned in all the departments of social science, cannot be here passed in silence.[17]

While Stammler, in his much more profound study of finality, in agreement with Ihering, recognizes that juridical regulation of social life necessarily implies the idea of purposes to be realized and that the law is always the means to an end, yet he develops a system which differs entirely from that of Ihering. He states from the first the general principle of finality in the law. He asserts that all juridical rules tend by their very nature to stimulate a certain conduct on the part of those subject to them; that the idea of purpose is necessarily given in such rules; and that with the law, entrance is made into the domain of teleology, its validity being determined by the ends which the law seeks to realize. He puts aside, however, concrete purpose in law, conditioned historically or variant according to time and place, and seeks a rule of validity for law, independent of all contingency. To establish this rule, he invokes the notion of a community of men of good will, the members of which shall be free from all subjective feelings and all interested motives, and in which each may pursue all the legitimate ends of all others. It is in

[16] *Benedetto Croce*, "Le Matérialisme Historique," translated by A. Bonnet, Paris, 1900.

[17] "Die Lehre von dem richtigen Rechte," Berlin, 1902. [See, also, *Stammler's* latest effort, "Theorie der Rechtswissenschaft, Halle, 1911. — *Translator*.]

conformity of the creative will of the law with that of this ideal community, that he discovers the formal law of all juridical purpose, and the governing standard by which its validity is determined.

It is not necessary to demonstrate that this community of men of good will is entirely imaginary; that the notion of an impersonal purpose, stripped of all subjective and concrete desire, is a contradiction in terms; and that an object cannot be established in pure abstraction, nor separated from a subject, be it what it may. If the thought be extended to include a subject, that subject cannot be a community, whether large or small, a party, a nation, or a State; and, finally, this imaginary community is as much inconceivable from a logical standpoint, as unreal in experience (as Stammler himself has admitted).[18]

Stammler, in his second work, derives, and exerts himself to apply, four leading rules from the principle which he had stated as the object of his earlier book. But it has been justly observed that the results at which he thus arrives are hardly appreciable; and that they are besides, an application in appearance only of this method and could be attained more directly and more securely by other lines of reasoning.[19] Stammler's principle is manifestly inspired by Kant's law of good will; again, so far as it requires that each one may make his own the legitimate ends of others, it is the altruism of Comte, or rather the egoistic altruism of Spencer. It exhibits a tendency of thought and a direction of motive very desirable from the viewpoint of the legislator; but it is not a principle from which the concrete rules of law may be deduced. While appreciating at its true value the

[18] *G. Simmel*, in "Schmoller's Jahrbuch," 1897, p. 578.

[19] *M. E. Mayer*, in "Kritische Vierteljahrschrift für Gesetzgebung und Rechtswissenschaft," 1906, p. 178 seq.

entire critical part of Stammler's earlier work, notably that which deals with natural law, finality, and historical materialism, Simmel says, with some severity, that it proves again that in works of this class the instability of the foundation does not detract from the solidity of the superstructure.[20]

[20] *G. Simmel*, loc. cit., p. 578.

INDEX

[The numbers refer to the pages.]

[The numbers refer to the pages.]

[The numbers refer to the pages.]

[The numbers refer to the pages.]

[The numbers refer to the pages.]

Published by

Facsimile Publisher
Ashok Vihar, Delhi-110052 (India)
Website: www.facsimilepublisher.com

Distributed by

Gyan Books Pvt. Ltd.
5, Ansari Road, Daryaganj, New Delhi-110002 (India)
E-mail: books@gyanbooks.com, Website: www.gyanbooks.com

2 222000 014087